TAINTED DEMOCRACY

ZSUZSANNA SZELÉNYI

Tainted Democracy

Viktor Orbán and the Subversion of Hungary

HURST & COMPANY, LONDON

First published in the United Kingdom in 2022 by
C. Hurst & Co. (Publishers) Ltd.,
New Wing, Somerset House, Strand, London, WC2R 1LA

This paperback edition first published in 2026 by C. Hurst & Co. (Publishers) Ltd.

Copyright © Zsuzsanna Szelényi, 2026

All rights reserved.

The right of Zsuzsanna Szelényi to be identified as the author of this publication is asserted by her in accordance with the Copyright, Designs and Patents Act, 1988.

Translated into English by Richard Robinson.

Distributed in the United States, Canada and Latin America by Oxford University Press, 546 Fifth Avenue, New York, NY 10036, United States of America.

A Cataloguing-in-Publication data record for this book is available from the British Library.

ISBN: 9781805265931

EU GPSR Authorised Representative
Easy Access System Europe Oü, 16879218
Address: Mustamäe tee 50, 10621, Tallinn, Estonia
Contact Details: gpsr.requests@easproject.com, +358 40 500 3575

www.hurstpublishers.com

To Annamari, Tomi and Bori,
who were still kids when all this started

CONTENTS

List of Abbreviations	ix
Acknowledgements	xi
Preface	xv
Introduction: Viktor Orbán's Revolution at the Polls	1

PART I
POLITICAL LANDSCAPES

1. Without Orbán, There's Nothing: How Fidesz Became Hungary's Ruling Party — 25
2. 'My Worldview Is Hungarian': The Ideology of Orbánism — 61
3. 'Alone We Would Fail, but Together We Will Win!' Orbán's Political Opposition — 97

PART II
ESTABLISHING CONTROL

4. The Illusion of Democracy: Overhauling Parliament and the Judiciary — 127

5. 'Neither the IMF Nor the EU Is My Boss':   157
Unorthodox Economic Policy
6. 'I Don't Deal with Business Matters': Corruption,   193
Scandals and Cronyism
7. Press-Ganged into Service: The Assault on the   229
Free Press
8. From Communication to Propaganda: The Making   265
of the Perfect Campaign
9. A Passive People?: Intimidating and   283
Depoliticizing Society

PART III
HUNGARY IN EUROPE AND THE WORLD

10. Who Controls the Past Controls the Future: 305
Historical Revisionism and Collective Memory
11. A Political Tap Dance: Viktor Orbán at Large   323
Afterword   357
Epilogue: Turning the Tide?   361

Notes   371
Index   439

LIST OF ABBREVIATIONS

CDU	Christian Democratic Union
CEMP	Central European Media and Publishing
CEU	Central European University
CÖF	Forum of Civil Unity
CSU	Christian Socialist Union
DK	Democratic Coalition
Együtt-PM	Together Party
EPP	European People's Party
Fidesz	Federation of Young Democrats
Fidesz-MPP	Fidesz-Hungarian People's Party
GVH	Hungarian Competition Authority
HÖOK	National Union of Students in Hungary
HUF	Hungarian forint
IIB	International Investment Bank
KDNP	Christian Democratic People's Party
KESMA	Central European Press and Media Foundation
LMP	Politics Can Be Different (Green Party)
MCC	Mathias Corvinus Collegium

LIST OF ABBREVIATIONS

MDF	Hungarian Democratic Forum
MEP	Member of the European Parliament
MFB	Hungarian Development Bank
MKB	Hungarian Credit Bank
MNB	Hungarian National Bank
MSZMP	Hungarian Socialist Workers' Party
MSZP	Hungarian Socialist Party
MTI	Hungarian News Agency
MTVA	Media Services Support and Asset Management Fund
MVM	Hungarian Electricity
NAV	National Tax and Custom Administration
NCA	National Civil Fund
NEA	National Cooperation Fund
NKM	National Utility
NMHH	National Media and Infocommunications Authority
NOE	National Association for Large Families
OLAF	European Anti-Fraud Office
OSCE	Oganization for Security and Cooperation in Europe
PISA	Programme for International Student Assessment
PM	Dialogue for Hungary
SAO	State Audit Office
SZFE	University of Theatre and Film Arts
SZDSZ	Alliance of Free Democrats

ACKNOWLEDGEMENTS

Many wonderful people helped me to reach this point and write this book.

First and foremost, thanks are owed to Katrin Kinzelbach, Charles Kovacs, Ivan Krastev, Joshua Muravchik and Ákos Róna-Tas, who encouraged me to write *Tainted Democracy*, reiterating that Hungary's story should be told by the Hungarians who lived through it.

I would also like to thank Amanda Coakley, Judy Dempsey, Mónika Hajdú, Cas Mudde, Nick Thorpe and Rosie Whitehouse for giving me invaluable practical advice on how to plan a book. Without them, I could not have started writing.

I am deeply grateful to Gordon Bajnai, Rosa Balfour, István Hegedűs, Tim Judah, Stefan Lehne, Natalie Nougayrède, Doug Saunders and Ivan Vejvoda for their friendship and for the many discussions that helped me to formulate my ideas by identifying what the right questions were to ask.

I am immensely thankful for the many Hungarian friends—Petra Bárd, Bea Bodrogi, Gergely Brückner, Zsolt Enyedi, Botond Feledy, András Jakab, Krisztina Kovács, Eszter Kováts, Róbert László, László Lőrincz, József Péter Martin, Zoltán Miklósi, Márta Pardavi, Gergely Romsics, Gábor Szelényi, Gábor Attila Tóth, Ágnes Urbán and Ákos Valentinyi—whose comments

ACKNOWLEDGEMENTS

helped me to find the most important stories to tell and kept the book factually accurate. Some friends wished not to be listed here, which is a shameful indictment of the regime in which we live. But I am very grateful to them, and I hope they know it.

I owe the deepest gratitude to my great friends, György Kerényi and Éva Vajda, who accompanied me during the entire book-writing process, commenting on content and format and sharing a wealth of tips on how to make the story better. Their unwavering enthusiasm helped me to overcome the ups and downs during the long process of writing my first book.

I am deeply indebted to Richard Robinson for the careful translation. I am also very thankful to the wonderful team at Hurst Publishers: Michael Dwyer for trusting me to write this book; Alice Clarke for her excellent editorial suggestions, for showing me when less is more and for shepherding the entire process all the way to print; Russell Martin for carefully copy-editing the manuscript, Daisy Leitch for managing the production process and Raminta Uselytė, Kathleen May and Rubi Kumari for the publicity support and marketing efforts.

I can't express how grateful I am for my parents, Katalin Péterfia and Pál Szelényi, and grandparents Karola Patek, Erzsébet Lovász, Zoltán Péterfia and Pál Szelényi, whose life was a never-ending pursuit of freedom, and an inspiration for me to act. In this activity, my husband Ferenc Karvalits has been my life-long companion and a constant source of support. He always encouraged my political and professional ambitions; he discussed and constantly probed my political insights and stood by me in my successes and failures. I am so very thankful to you.

Finally, special thanks to the ERSTE Stiftung for offering me the Europe's Future Fellowship at the Institut für die Wissenschaften vom Menschen in Vienna and the Robert Bosch Academy, who granted me the Richard von Weizsäcker Fellowship in Berlin. Time spent amongst fellows in Vienna and

ACKNOWLEDGEMENTS

Berlin provided me with a rich intellectual environment and a safe haven from turbulent Hungarian public life, and made the writing of this book possible.

Zsuzsanna Szelényi
Budapest, July 2022

PREFACE

I will always remember the thrill I felt when I read in the newspaper that a group of Hungarian university students and young intellectuals had established an 'illegal organization' on 8 April 1988, and that the 'competent police authorities' had warned them to cease their activities. A couple of days later I joined the founders of this group, the Federation of Young Democrats (Fidesz), a courageous, energetic and politically conscious crowd, who brought a spark of excitement to sleepy late-communist Hungary, where, although everyone was aware of the hypocrisy of the system, open anti-regime political activity was not permitted.

I quickly became integrated into Fidesz, and within six months I was elected as a member of the board. I stood next to Viktor Orbán, one of Fidesz's leading personalities, in 1989 as he delivered his historic speech at the reburial of the 1956 martyr Imre Nagy. We were fighting for liberal democratic principles and openly opposed the Soviet regime that had suppressed our country for decades. We were committed to overcoming our country's century-old internal divides, and to building a strong European democracy. We entered the National Assembly together in 1990 after the first free elections. It was a rewarding experience to represent Fidesz in Hungary and the world.

PREFACE

Viktor Orbán was an important actor in this unique party from the very beginning. After 1993, however, when he was elected party chairman, his influence morphed into dominance. Ever since, he has been crowding out his critics and steering his party into fighting an endless political war. Twenty years after we entered Parliament together, Orbán was at the helm of the strongest party in Hungary. Following a landslide victory in 2010, he was ready to force Hungary into an anti-democratic experiment. By then, however, Fidesz bore hardly any resemblance to the fascinating group that I had once represented with great pride, and which I left disappointed in 1994.

From 2010 onwards, Orbán's name became synonymous with the Hungarian state and his grip over the country verged on the autocratic. Twelve years after he took power it was highly doubtful whether another political force could replace him in a peaceful, democratic way.

* * *

But back in spring 1988 I had good reasons for joining the Federation of Young Democrats—Fidesz—right away.

I grew up in the 1970s and 1980s as a happy child in the period of what is known as 'goulash communism'. Under party leader János Kádár the country was modernizing the economy and provided a reasonable standard of living for Hungarians. As a result, a new Eastern European middle-class model took shape, which was able to give people a sense of well-being—something unattainable in most socialist countries.

Kádár was unique in the Eastern bloc in that he managed to conjure up the impression that there was no need for resistance because the regime took care of its citizens. This paternalism became the defining mentality of Kádár's 'goulash communism' and a pivotal way for communists to ensure that after the 1956 uprising Hungarians would never revolt again. But this system of 'socialism with a human face' was no more Western than the harsher communist dictatorships. There may not have been open violence, and the means of oppression may have been milder, yet it was just as totalitarian a system as the others in the Soviet bloc.[1] The only sphere in which you could exercise a bit of independence was within the limited area of family life, and I grew up in a politically aware family.

My grandparents, all of them teachers, made every effort to live a creative and active intellectual life while they established families in the 1930s. One of my grandfathers joined the Hungarian 'népi (folk)-traditionalist' democratic movement, which stood against the power embodied by the neo-conservative, old, aristocratic elites and condemned the fascistization of both the extreme right groups and the communists. These traditionalist intellectuals represented a kind of 'third way', hoping that if the peasant class were lifted out of provincial backwardness and poverty, then a more democratic society would emerge. They avidly discussed the issue of the unity of the nation divided by the Treaty of Trianon,[2] but also recognized the right of ethnic groups to self-determination.

The other important democratic current in the 1930s was represented by the urban bourgeois intellectuals, who wanted to overcome the alarming social inequalities through an egalitarian democracy founded on classical Western liberal traditions and the rights of the individual. They challenged the traditionalists, who were sceptical of the prospects for Western-style development and the modernization of the country. They were concerned that the traditionalists' ethnic-based concept of the nation often went hand in hand with anti-Semitism. Although they created a significant body of literary and political work in their journals, neither of these democratic intellectual groups exerted a strong influence on society between the two world wars. The ruling elite of Admiral Miklós Horthy, Hungary's conservative leader,

PREFACE

was driven by revisionism and ultimately dragged Hungary into the Second World War on the side of Nazi Germany.

My parents survived the Second World War as children. Democracy made a brief appearance in their lives after the war years, but by 1948 the communist takeover was complete, and Hungary was neither independent nor free any longer. My parents met in the 1950s in the youth movement of the Lutheran Church, which provided them with an intellectual haven: faith and an anti-regime identity at a time when oppressive power used force to bend people into submission.

The greatest, life-changing experience of my parents was the anti-Stalinist revolution in 1956, when Hungarians all over the country revolted and took up arms against the Soviet-backed communist party and for freedom from Soviet oppression. As university students in the southern Hungarian city of Pécs, my parents participated in revolutionary activities along with their family members. One of my grandmothers, a language teacher, served as translator into Russian for the city's revolutionary council. After the revolution was crushed, they suffered reprisals ranging from being barred from university to being imprisoned. At the time of the Kádárist consolidation, like most Hungarian families they attained a state of relative well-being. Freedom, however, was something they could not hope for.

My parents never joined the communist party, so they were denied their political rights. But at home as children we learned our family's stories about the war years and 1956, and the anti-communist tradition gave us a framework through which to perceive reality.

As far as their means allowed, our parents gave me and my siblings a middle-class liberal upbringing: we learned languages, played musical instruments, and went on many trips. Each summer, we filled the Škoda with luggage, and set off on a two-week camping holiday. We travelled through Central and Eastern

PREFACE

Europe from the Baltic Sea to the Black Sea in the Soviet bloc. When in 1983 Hungarians were finally allowed to travel to the West—though only every three years and with limited currency—our family was among the first to set off on a tour of Austria, where we encountered another world, compared with which Hungary was drab and poor.

In my university years in Budapest, in the mid-1980s, I threw myself into the cultural life of the metropolis. At university the friends I made had very different family stories, for example young Jewish people whose grandparents were Holocaust survivors and who saw the end of the war and the communist takeover with relief. I learned of the complexity of Hungarian history and society through these friends. The underground concerts, book readings and university clubs that I attended in growing numbers were an eye-opener to me: voicing political criticism was possible after all. First, I met with members of the dissident democratic opposition, who published books and journals banned by the regime. They told me of the gulags, a more nuanced story of the 1956 revolution, and the Polish Solidarity movement. I admired their courage and intellectual rigour, and this deeply influenced my democratic ideals. It was these friends who took me to the first meeting of Fidesz on 10 April 1988.

* * *

After leaving Fidesz in 1994 I quit professional politics in Hungary and joined the Council of Europe. At this international organization, I had a chance to work on democratic development in the Balkans, Russia and countries as far as the Caucasus. I witnessed many efforts by people to build independent nations and sustainable democracies after decades of dictatorship. I witnessed the revival of nationalism and the Balkan wars in the 1990s, and learned that revisionist elites are prepared to use murky ideologies and violence to gain power. I noticed the

PREFACE

emergence of democratic fatigue in Eastern Europe and observed the rebirth of the far right in the countries of the West around the millennium. I learned that democratic development is not linear and could not be taken granted. As a Hungarian, however, I always felt that I was on stable ground and confident about the country's future.

Against this backdrop, it was more than dispiriting to see the weakening democratic commitment of my own country in the 2000s. I had already left the party a long time before Fidesz achieved its historic victory and constitutional majority in 2010, and Orbán embarked on his aggressive political experiment in Hungary.

When I observed Orbán's pugnacious, hard-line politics and his fan dance towards Eastern powers such as Vladimir Putin's Russia, it was time for me to give up my international career and return to Hungarian politics. I joined committed democrats and liberals in 2012 to organize a new centrist party, Együtt (Together). Soon afterwards I was elected as a member of Parliament again, now in opposition to the party I had once represented. My second period spent in Hungarian politics as well as my country's struggle with Orbán's power in these years has motivated me to report on what I have witnessed and learned of my country.

This book tells the inside story of the early days of Fidesz as the communist reign was coming to an end. It recounts how Orbán's party won a landslide victory in 2010 and how he used this unique power to pioneer the 'illiberal state', now serving as a model for Europe's would-be autocrats. The book provides a detailed 'twenty-first-century autocratic playbook', charting the key elements of the new politics of intolerance. The twelve chapters explain why Orbán's tactics have been so successful and show how Hungarians have dealt with this particular challenge. The book is broken into three parts. The first shows how Orbán turned the country's political landscape upside down. The second part shows how Orbán established control in the country

PREFACE

in various ways. Finally the third part reveals how Hungary is navigating between past and future and in the world at large.

My book also examines the unique position of Orbán's peers, who entered adulthood together during the regime change. In the free and democratic Hungary after the end of the communist regime, the sky was the limit for us. Today my historically fortunate generation is the leading elite in Hungary but we seem to have let the opportunity to build a flourishing democracy slip through our fingers. Despite having studied and understood Hungary's difficult political history over the 150 years leading up to the regime change, my generation of politicians have still managed to lose their way.

For those of us who remember the courage and astuteness Orbán displayed in his early days, his complete political volte-face is baffling. Nevertheless, over twelve years he has been perfecting the art of masking an authoritarian regime as an ideological movement. Orbán's radical turn took place step by step over time and efforts to counter his aggressive push also took time to emerge both in Hungary and Europe.

By the 2020s, a consensus of opinion had formed that behind the global populist challenge lies an autocratic threat. Polarizing and intolerant narratives are present in the West, and populist parties have been elected to government. Autocrats have stabilized their power in several significant countries, thus jeopardizing the democratic international order. Finally, Vladimir Putin's war in Ukraine, which began in February 2022, demonstrated the ultimate threat that autocracies pose to the world.

Hungary's story shows how easy it is to undermine democracy if leaders abandon basic norms. No society in the world can confidently say it is immune to autocracy. As a Hungarian, I felt compelled to speak up for democracy beyond my country's borders and encourage democrats all over the world to resist illiberalism and work for a democratic revival.

INTRODUCTION
VIKTOR ORBÁN'S REVOLUTION AT THE POLLS

Tense and expectant, we sat in front of the TV. Slowly the election results from the single-member constituencies rolled in. This election was simply never going to have a positive outcome. Hungarian public life had been a scene of chaos for years. The left-wing government had lost its legitimacy; the liberal party was in the throes of disintegration; and a new extreme right-wing party was gathering traction. In opposition, Fidesz had been engaged in constant, radical street-level mobilization for years. But there was no doubt that Fidesz would win a majority.

On the evening of the 2010 general election, I had some friends over for an election night party. We had been founding members and friends of the Fidesz movement and had all lived through the 1989 change of regime. A few of us had gone into active politics, while others worked as experts in the field of economics or as communications consultants alongside the party. But, by the end of the 1990s, everyone in that group had left front-line politics. Some had joined public opinion pollsters, think tanks and newspapers. Others found attractive challenges in the liberalizing financial world, and some dived into academia. At the time of our meeting, in 2010, we comprised a group of successful folk who, together, had set out on their professional careers with the world as their oyster.

In 2010 the results started coming in at around 10 pm. An enormous lead was immediately apparent, and it became clear that Fidesz would be forming the country's new government. In view of the highly disproportionate election system,[1] the 52% victory on the party lists effectively meant that Fidesz had won a two-thirds majority of seats in Parliament, giving it full power to rewrite the constitution. We all knew Viktor Orbán well and, on seeing the results, pondered what he would use this newfound power to do. The more optimistic in the group believed that although Orbán was audacious, he would genuinely seek to address our country's problems. Perhaps now he would make the reforms that leaders of previous decades had failed to carry out: developing the economy's competitiveness, consolidating the pension system, and safeguarding our health service. In all likelihood, he would want to build a successful country. However, many of us were sceptical. Orbán was clever, but he was also ambitious and hungry for power. After all, it was because of this characteristic that, over time, we distanced ourselves from Fidesz.

Orbán's victorious tones could be heard from the television set. He was holding forth in his familiar, slightly strident voice, with a clerical intonation:

> Today a revolution has happened at the polls. [...] The Hungarians have given their verdict on an era. On this day in Hungary, a historical lesson has been fulfilled, the lesson of the change of regime, which goes like this: a regime cannot be changed. A regime can only be overthrown and toppled, overthrown, and a new one founded in its stead.[2]

Had we heard right? We couldn't believe our ears. Was Orbán speaking of a revolutionary situation? Did we really hear him question the previous twenty years and the achievements of those

INTRODUCTION

that had laid our democratic foundations? This sounded very worrying. Orbán continued: 'From this day, the political and economic system of Hungary is called the system of national cooperation. [...] The system of national cooperation founded today will operate according to new rules ...'

A declaration of change was understandable after such a decisive victory. Yet it was cause for disquiet that Orbán spoke of revolution and the introduction of new rules. The word revolution, even when used symbolically, is foreign to the essence of parliamentary democracy. Before 2010, during the socialist–liberal coalition government, Orbán had asserted that the change of regime of 1990 was not complete, and that he considered it his own mission to bring it to completion. Yet it was difficult to imagine that Orbán would be able to change the basis of the existing status quo. In the 2000s, although Hungarian politics went through a serious crisis, the country was also a member of the European Union and deeply integrated into the system of global markets. But this victory speech made it obvious that Orbán was preparing for radical transformation, that he was willing to engage in a purge, and that political conflicts would not soften just because the campaign was over. 'We shall start to clear away the ruins of the era we have left behind, and to assume responsibility'.

Exactly how this would proceed was impossible to imagine on election night. Many might still have been hoping that Orbán would set about building a new system with the attitude of an enlightened absolutist ruler. That evening we did not remember his statement made just a year earlier: 'To win just once, but decisively, that's the way'.[3]

Before we start to study Orbán's 'revolution at the polls', it is perhaps best to first examine how he won in 2010, and how he came to wield unprecedented powers in Hungary.

TAINTED DEMOCRACY

The Path to a Constitutional Supermajority

Unlike almost all the other countries in the region, Hungary did not experience a change of regime in the revolutionary autumn of 1989, but earlier, in a gradual process. Careful economic liberalization was started by the Hungarian Socialist Workers' Party (MSZMP), the ruling communist party itself, as a kind of experiment in the communist bloc. Modest opposition groups had been forming against the communist state since the end of the 1970s, mainly among 'modernist' intellectuals, dissidents and 'traditionalist' writers. Within the MSZMP, a group mainly made up of economists was trying to get liberal social reforms passed. By the end of the 1980s many intellectual groups had formed in universities, research institutes and cultural institutions, and they demanded democratic reforms. In the spring of 1988 the major opposition groups initiated political public debates, and that is when Fidesz was formed too, consisting of young university students and intellectuals.

Initially the communist regime tried to silence the opposition, but pressure steadily grew on the state party, and in 1989 it was forced to legalize the presence of alternative parties and open up politics to the public. In the spring of 1989 the opposition organizations, including Fidesz, formed an 'Opposition Round Table' and managed to have the martyred leaders of the 1956 revolution reburied in a large commemorative ceremony in June. In the summer, national negotiations were held between the Opposition Round Table and the Hungarian Socialist Workers' Party, about the conditions for multi-party free elections. In line with this, the constitution was fundamentally amended and on 23 October 1989 Hungary was proclaimed a republic (as opposed to the former 'people's republic').

Simultaneously, the Hungarian communist leadership was in negotiations with President Gorbachev about the withdrawal of

INTRODUCTION

Soviet troops, as the Soviet Union could not afford any longer to maintain its troops abroad. As part of the reforms commenced by the communist government at this time, the Cold War border with Austria was opened in August 1989, thus enabling tens of thousands of holidaymakers from East Germany to reach West Germany via Hungary. With this act, Hungary actively contributed to the fall of the Berlin Wall on 3 October 1989. What finally clinched the change of regime was the hosting of free and fair elections in April 1990.

That in Hungary, as in Poland, the fall of communist rule came through negotiation carried great significance. As one of the leaders of Fidesz, I myself took part in this marvellous revolutionary period when, without a gun being fired, we created the foundations for the new, democratic Hungary and our passage to the free world.

Free Elections in Hungary

In the first elections in April 1990, the successor to the communist party, the Hungarian Socialist Party (MSZP) lost, gaining a mere 10% of the votes. A whole generation of leading communist politicians disappeared from politics. MSZP was ideologically insipid, and its politicians were reformist technocrats.

The elections were won by the Hungarian Democratic Forum (MDF), which formed a government out of three right-wing parties. The task of the first years after the regime change was to create the institutions of democratic politics and a market economy, and to ensure the country could ride out the enormous economic crisis that ensued with the collapse of the communist planned economy. This right-wing government, which came together on an ideological basis, struggled with this gargantuan task. To cover the difficulties, government parties often filled the political air with symbolic debates, triggering harsh criticism from the liberal Alliance of Free Democrats (SZDSZ) and Fidesz and from the socialist opposition. From the very beginning, a deep ideological mistrust in the democratic political elite took root.

József Antall's governing party soon lost its popularity under the social and economic burden of the transition. In the first years following the regime change, many Hungarians lost their regular income. They resented the material differences caused by rapid privatization. In this social and political uncertainty, the technocrats of the post-communist MSZP were able to return to power in 1994 and build a coalition government with the liberal SZDSZ. Under the MSZP–SZDSZ coalition, democratic institutions became stabilized and a vigorous economic adjustment programme helped to balance public finances.

Hungarian Politics Become Polarized

Fidesz was formed as a liberal party of young people and entered Parliament with twenty-two representatives in 1990. Viktor Orbán was elected as the party's first president in 1993, and when the right-wing governing parties fell visibly into decline, he saw an opportunity in the political vacuum that opened up. Believing that Fidesz had better prospects as a moderate right-wing party, he changed the party's position from liberal centrist to conservative right-wing, making noticeable overtures to the deeply anti-communist and traditionalist voters. This move meant giving up Fidesz's original identity and prompted considerable resistance among members. In 1993–4, many politicians like me left the party.

In 1998 Fidesz, now as a right-wing party, won the elections and, together with the MDF and the Smallholders Party, it was able to defeat the socialist–liberal coalition, which had become unpopular after introducing austerity measures. Orbán's coalition government inherited an economically stabilized country. Owing to the political stability and sound economy despite changing

INTRODUCTION

governments, more foreign direct investment flowed into the country than in previous years. There was a broad desire for Western-style consolidation in both the political elite and the public at large. Hungary joined NATO and prepared for accession to the European Union. At the turn of the millennium, Hungarian politics was enjoying its golden age, and the country was undeniably a success story in the region for its transition to a democracy and market economy.

And yet in 2002 Fidesz narrowly lost the elections. The MSZP and SZDSZ came back to power. Orbán blamed his party's defeat on the concentration of media and financial resources in the hands of his opponents. An acquaintance of mine, who was a close colleague of Orbán for decades, once said: 'Orbán changed noticeably after 2002. Up until then he was a democrat, but afterwards it became important to him to have as many resources as possible'. Together with his confidants, Orbán set about creating servile media and building assets to finance the party. Simultaneously, he adopted divisive, markedly nationalist rhetoric. 'The nation cannot be in the opposition!' he announced at the great assembly held after the elections.[4] Fidesz was moving towards populist politics.

In 2004, socialist Ferenc Gyurcsány became prime minister, following the resignation of Péter Medgyessy. His bitter rivalry with Orbán further polarized Hungarian politics. The small centrist parties—the liberal SZDSZ and the moderate conservative MDF, which continued the tradition of Antall—found themselves talking into thin air. The former was slowly mopped up by the Socialist Party, the latter by Fidesz, and Hungarian politics became characterized by fierce competition between the two large parties. At the same time, Fidesz's defeat in 2002 enabled a new party, Jobbik, to appear on the right edge of the political map. It gained popularity mainly through anti-Roma campaigning.

TAINTED DEMOCRACY

The 2006 general election campaign was unusually acrimonious, and resulted in a very narrow (1.5%) victory for the MSZP ahead of Fidesz.[5]

The Weakening of the Democratic State

> Obviously we lied our way through the last one and a half to two years. It was perfectly clear that what we were saying wasn't true. [...] Whatever could be done in secret in the preceding months to ensure that documents about what we planned to do wouldn't come to light in the last weeks of the election campaign, we did it. [...] There's not much choice. The reason is this: because we fucked up. Not a little: a lot. [...] We lied, morning, noon, and night.[6]

These words of socialist prime minister Ferenc Gyurcsány became public two weeks before the municipal elections of autumn 2006, and had the effect of a bombshell. The speech from which these excerpts were leaked had in fact been given at a private party meeting held half a year beforehand, just after Gyurcsány was sworn in as prime minister for the second time after his coalition won the parliamentary elections in April that year. After the election victory, he needed his party's support for a new package of austerity reforms. In the speech, he indicated that true information on the state of the country's economy had not been made public during the campaign, but that, after winning, corrective measures were unavoidable. Whether his considerations were necessary or rational counted for very little when these words came to public knowledge in September, in the heat of the municipal election campaign. Prime Minister Gyurcsány's personal brand collapsed, his credibility was obliterated in one fell swoop, and he provided a golden opportunity for Fidesz in opposition to mount an all-out attack on him and his government.

The year 2006 proved to be a watershed in Hungarian politics. The profane speech acted like tinder in an already highly combustible political atmosphere, and ignited a political quarrel

INTRODUCTION

that would erode the institutional framework for democratic politics in Hungary. People took to the streets demanding Gyurcsány's resignation. Extreme right groups stormed the state television building. I remember watching in amazement as the attack was shown that evening on television. Central Budapest immediately became a battleground. People were aggressive, throwing stones and setting cars alight. The TV news transmitted events live from the windows of the TV station building, and from the corridors inside. Then the broadcast broke off, without any further information. The attackers had occupied the television building but left a few hours later. Never in my lifetime had there been comparable street violence in Hungary.

The municipal elections took place in this chaotic time, and Fidesz won a landslide victory in the towns. The demonstrations demanding the prime minister's resignation showed no sign of abating. Fidesz convened its own mass demonstrations, including one on 23 October, the anniversary of the 1956 revolution. But organizational errors meant that extremist groups mingled with peaceful demonstrators, and when the police fired rubber bullets to disperse the rioters, law-abiding marchers were injured too. In response to the police violence, Fidesz stepped up its campaign for the government to stand down.

One morning, the party's parliamentary group, led by Viktor Orbán, dismantled the security cordons around Parliament, to allow the demonstrators to get closer to the building. Fidesz viewed this deed as civil disobedience. In my view, however, the leaders of a major party represented in Parliament, through a physical act, enabled demonstrators to attack the Parliament building, a democratic institution.

There were several interpretations of these critical autumn events. In the right-wing view, this was a collision between the elemental power of a 'spontaneous democratic protest' following the shameful revelations about Ferenc Gyurcsány, who had lied his way to power, and the 'dictatorial violence' deployed against it, leading to a 'bloody drama'. In the left-wing reading, the frustrated Viktor Orbán, who had suffered another defeat in the parliamentary elections, through an act of betrayal by someone on the left (who leaked the speech), secured a deadly political weapon against his opponent.[7]

Fidesz may not have organized the anti-government demonstrations, but it certainly supported and exploited them. Between 2006 and 2010 Fidesz took politics on to the streets, and its representatives in Parliament regularly obstructed parliamentary proceedings. Elected officials themselves called into question respect for democratic institutions, and thus with Hungarian representative democracy still young, the rot set in. The socialist–liberal government was constantly forced onto the defensive by the Fidesz-led opposition. Growing mistrust in institutions and the crumbling moral foundation of the political system made it impossible to implement economic reforms. The socialist-led government tried to prop up support by raising pensions, salaries and social handouts. Public debt increased again.

Hungary's economy was already struggling when the 2008 financial crisis hit. The Hungarian forint dropped dramatically in a matter of days. Hungarian public and household debt rocketed. As a result of the double crisis, the socialist–liberal coalition government broke up, and finally the prime minister resigned. A technocratic government, led by non-party member Gordon Bajnai, took over and focused on negotiating a financial rescue package with the International Monetary Fund and the European Union. Bajnai stabilized the country's economic situation, but debt continued to rise. The crisis government's achievements could not save the socialist leadership of the country, which had been treading water for years. The political and economic crisis that took shape by 2010 opened the way to a victory for Fidesz.

INTRODUCTION

In his campaign, Viktor Orbán promised to end the political uncertainty—even though he had played a significant role in its creation.

An All-Out Attack

The very day it formed in May 2010, the newly elected Parliament voted on a political resolution in which Fidesz confirmed what Orbán had said on the election night, that in the April elections 'Hungarians decided to form a new system, the System of National Cooperation'.[8] This act bore some resemblance to the day in 1990, when after forty-five years of communism, the first freely elected Parliament started its session with a symbolic resolution on the 1956 revolution. Fidesz was attempting to magnify the importance of the 2010 election to one of monumental historical weight. The ruling party also ordered that the resolution on the System of National Cooperation should be hung in all easily visible public places in state institutions. This pointed to the arrogance of the Orbán government, and presented a threat to the democratic principle of the separation of powers.

The National Assembly immediately started churning out legislation, giving effect to Viktor Orbán's sporting metaphor: to incapacitate the opponent with an all-out, across-the-board attack. One of the government's first proposals was to change the status of the Constitutional Court. The number of Constitutional Court judges was raised from eleven to fifteen. The new law dictated that Parliament no longer needed to reach a consensus to appoint new judges. Within a year, seven new Fidesz-loyal judges were elected to the Constitutional Court, and the scope of the body's powers was trimmed and its fundamental political neutrality was called into question.

In the first months of the new government, Fidesz nominated Pál Schmitt, previously the party's member in the European

Parliament, to be the new president of the republic. In his parliamentary hearing, Schmitt admitted, 'I will not be an obstacle to the government's drive to legislate; rather, I will be a motor. I do not wish to be a counterweight; rather I shall strive for balance'.[9] Shortly afterwards Péter Polt, a former Fidesz politician, was appointed chief prosecutor, a role he had previously held under the first Orbán government. His mandate was quickly lengthened from six years to nine, and replacing him would require a supermajority vote in Parliament. A new standing order of the house made it possible to enact legislation more quickly and without necessary consultations.

In the first six months of the Fidesz-led government, dozens of laws were passed that presented serious constitutional concerns. It was clear why the ruling party had moved so quickly to remould the Constitutional Court. Now made up of Fidesz supporters and stripped of much of its power, the court rarely objected to these new statutes. Similarly, in the first six months of Pál Schmitt's tenure as president, he signed into law around a hundred acts and never questioned any law's constitutionality.

The European Commission initiated a series of infringement procedures against the Hungarian government, for instance regarding the media regulations and the forced retirement of judges at the age of sixty-two. These cases were brought to the Court of Justice of the European Union, where the Hungarian government lost them. But these procedures failed to place an effective check on the Orbán government's drive for power. By the time judges forced into retirement had secured a legal victory against the government, most of them had long since been replaced in the courts.

Half a year after the elections, Fidesz started drafting a new constitution, known as the Fundamental Law. Within weeks, it was adopted by Parliament. Most of the text was written in secret, outside Parliament and in restricted Fidesz circles. In protest,

INTRODUCTION

opposition parties withdrew from the parliamentary committee set up to draft the constitution. The National Assembly debated the text for only nine days, but even before it was voted on, basic amendments were made to it. Although it was passed by a democratically elected majority, the way in which it was drafted makes the Fundamental Law controversial. It clearly was not the result of consensus sought in society, nor did it express the popular will.

Most of the Fundamental Law followed the text of the previous constitution, while incorporating many contentious new elements. One controversial element is that the new preamble to the law sets out a collectivist, nationalist worldview, no longer basing its system of fundamental rights on the individual. Political analyst Péter Tölgyessy, one of the leaders of the constitution-making process in the 1989 negotiations, wrote that with Orbán's Fundamental Law 'we left the world that made the West successful'.[10]

The Fundamental Law specified dozens of so-called cardinal laws,[11] which, like the constitution, also require the vote of two thirds of parliamentarians to be modified. This means effective governing becomes possible only when a government has a supermajority. The leaders of various state institutions saw their mandates extended to nine and even twelve years, and in this way the positions of Orbán's loyalists were secured for long terms. All these problems, and the fact that the opposition rejected the Fundamental Law, pointed to a future crisis in Hungarian constitutional law and represented a serious erosion of democracy.

When the Fundamental Law came into force, Viktor Orbán opened a grand historical exhibition in the Hungarian National Gallery. In his speech, the prime minister repeated that a 'two-thirds parliamentary revolution' had led to the Fundamental Law, which created a 'granite-solid foundation' for the future of the country. He declared that the values of the Fundamental

Law, Christianity and the sovereignty of the state represented a thread so strong for Hungarians that ten centuries could not erode it.[12]

Critics emphasized that the way the text was drafted, as well as the content itself, was in conflict with some of the basic features of democratic constitutionalism.[13] Others stated that the problem was not necessarily the making of the Fundamental Law as such, but that its individual elements—written rules and actual democratic practices and narratives—lacked unison and cohesion. Narratives broadly comprise everything from the raison d'être and goal of institutions, to their symbolism, the public discourse surrounding them, and social attitudes towards them. The lack of these informal institutional elements meant that the Fundamental Law threatened to render institutions less stable and less capable of inducing compliance with the law and that it would fail to deliver prosperity to the country.[14]

It soon became apparent that the Fundamental Law was merely the beginning of a process aimed at increasing the governing party's constitutional room for manoeuvre, and giving it a free hand in as many issues as possible. The renaming of the constitution as the Fundamental Law and the months-long ceremonies around its inception served to maintain the feeling of catharsis after Fidesz's election victory, and to convince people that a new historical era had begun. Tens of thousands of copies of the Fundamental Law were printed with a Hungarian folk design, like a small Bible, and sent by name to every eighteen-year-old finishing school.

The internal contradictions soon showed. After six months, Fidesz started to amend the Fundamental Law and Viktor Orbán's deluxe edition of the 'granite-solid' constitution was superseded in just one year. Twelve years later it had been amended ten times.

INTRODUCTION

Respect for Hungary!

The morning of 15 March 2011 was unusually warm; other years had seen snow fall on this day. In the spring sunshine, crowds walked to the National Museum to hear Orbán's ceremonial speech on the anniversary of the 1848 bourgeois revolution. Just like the revolutionaries in 1848, the prime minister stopped at the top of the steps leading up to the museum and began his speech. 'It was here we Hungarians swore an oath that "we would no longer be slaves"', he quoted from a poem by Sándor Petőfi, heroic poet of the 1848 revolution. 'We rose up against the entire Habsburg Empire, we dismantled a system thought to be immovable. [...] So it has always been, in 1956, in 1990, and in 2010',[15] said Orbán, drawing a parallel between his own 'revolution at the polls', the bourgeois revolution of 1848, and the anti-communist revolution in 1956. To an outside observer it might sound strange to hear talk of oppression in Hungary in 2011, but Orbán's believers understood the leader's train of thought, and he explained where things had gone wrong since 1989:

> We wanted to believe that by sending the Soviet troops home, with democratic elections and liberalizing the economy we would arrive in the other Hungary [...] which is strong and successful. [...] We soon had to acknowledge that we had not arrived after all. [...] Then came the years of wandering. [...] We do not find it in the model of either Brussels or other capital cities.

Then he added: 'It's an old truth that a nation can be conquered in two ways: by the sword and by debt'. Finally, to give sufficient weight to his words, he proudly announced: 'In 1848 we would not be dictated to by Vienna, and in 1956 we would not be dictated to from Moscow. And now, we will not be dictated to from Brussels, or from anywhere'.

At the end of Orbán's speech, cheers resounded and there was a long round of applause. The believers had not walked to the museum in vain. The story they heard spoke to their hearts. It mattered not that the European Union was a community of free countries, which the Hungarians, Orbán's believers among them, had waited for years to join, and did so by referendum. This speech was so heartfelt that perhaps it would have moved the other crowd of thousands, if they had heard it—the crowd gathered a few hundred metres away on Szabad sajtó út (literally, Free Press Road) by the foot of the Elizabeth Bridge, which spans the Danube. This was where I came to listen to the dozen or so speakers, well-known artists and previously unknown civil activists, who passed around the microphone, as they protested against the newly passed media law and the government's appropriation of the national public service television, radio and news agency. On this stage, just as in front of the National Museum, someone recited a March 1848 poem by Petőfi the revolutionary: 'Though ships bob on the surface / And oceans run beneath us / It is the water that rules'.[16]

Although seventeen years have passed since I left Fidesz and Hungarian politics, this was the day I first realized that what was happening in my country was unacceptable. It was time for me to return to Hungarian politics.

The Populist Fairy Tale

In the wake of the 2008 financial crash, everyone knew someone who was in financial difficulty. Orbán's new government could justify overstepping its constitutional scope by citing the extraordinary situation created by the crisis. But it was necessary to construct a narrative that would prove workable in the long term, when the extraordinary situation had passed.

In his 15 March speech at the National Museum, Orbán constructed a populist fairy tale. The most wonderful thing

INTRODUCTION

about the tale is that it creates a reality in which anything can happen, everything turns out well in the end, and the truth is victorious.[17] In populist storytelling, the people are the victim. The hero, a simple scion of the people, represents all that is good and pure. The enemy is a dangerous foreigner. Both the people and the enemy are homogeneous groups, who are irreconcilably at loggerheads with one another.[18]

The 'revolution at the polls', which Orbán used to interpret his 2010 political victory, opened the door to the populist tale. This extraordinary victory entitled him to transgress boundaries, undo the status quo, establish new rules, and take revenge. Based on the logic of the folk tale, the people's sense of justice demanded that accounts should be settled in order for the bright future, the golden age, to come at last.

In his March 2011 speech, Viktor Orbán presented the enemy as multinationals torturing Hungarians, foreign-owned banks extracting high interest rates, and the IMF and the European Union, because the loan package that had helped the Hungarian economy back onto its feet in 2009 called for severe austerity measures. But he was prepared to do battle with them, in the name of the people. He levied a large special tax on banks and other multinationals, and proclaimed a struggle to drive out the IMF.

Orbán's fight against the 'evil ones' did not stop here. The foundations of the populist fairy tale had been laid so well that Orbán's fight continued steadily for the next twelve years.

We Shall Not Be a Colony!

All the same, 2011 was a challenging year for Viktor Orbán. People took to the streets of Budapest to protest against the avalanche of laws as the government overstepped its democratic mandate, and against the open rejection of European values. The European Commission and the Venice Commission, the Council of Europe's advisory body on constitutional matters, began to scrutinize the Fundamental Law. While the government's own legal experts were at work on closing the European Union's legal procedures against them as quickly as possible and minimizing their losses, a year later Orbán's communications team opened a new chapter in the populist fairy tale. Once more, the leader chose 15 March to introduce his story. He reminded crowds of his earlier speech: 'The Hungarian submerged in debt, whose own home is just a dream, is he free?' Then he pointed to a new enemy: the European Union. Taking on the role of the people, he declared:

> Among other things, freedom means that we decide on the laws for our own lives ourselves, we decide ourselves what is important, and what isn't. With a Hungarian eye, Hungarian thinking, and following the beating of the Hungarian heart. That is why we write our constitution ourselves; we do not need any donkey-leaders.[19]

A careful listener may have remembered that the Fundamental Law was made without any concern for social consensus, amid enormous opposition from experts and politicians, and unprompted by the Hungarian populace. But this did not matter in the alternative reality of the fairy tale—a tale in which everything is possible, even for Orbán to compare the European Union with the communist occupiers of Hungary: 'We know all too well the nature of the uninvited helping comrades, and we recognize them even when instead of uniforms with epaulettes, they don well-tailored suits'.

The day commemorating the freedom struggle created an opportunity for Orbán to expound the most important foundation of his regime, the principle of sovereignty. 'In the rumbling coming from the international financial system [...] we must ask and we must answer the greatest of questions: do

INTRODUCTION

we accept exploitation lasting up to the grave?' he asked, then answered his own question: 'We shall not be a colony!' After saying these words, the audience started chanting: 'We will defend, we will defend [Hungary]!'

Using his populist fairy tale, Orbán demonized those political players who he believed could curtail the sovereignty of the people—in reality, the ones that restricted his constitutional power. According to his story, the previous unfit governments were traitors, the 'leftish liberal elite', who opened the way for international capital, international institutions and the European Union, and who conspired to plunder the country of its resources and deprive it of its freedom to act.

With this misrepresentation, Fidesz raised the notion of national sovereignty to the central principle of government. Orbán's invocation of the notion of sovereignty came five years before the British clamour for Brexit, and openly questioned the dominant thinking in European politics, which for some time had seen national sovereignty as a debatable and dangerous concept. For decades the notion of sovereignty had fallen into disuse in the West, and it occurred only in the narratives of explicitly anti-Europe right-wing populist parties. By emphasizing sovereignty, Orbán's governing party joined this political camp, and clearly signalled that it was demanding greater room for manoeuvre both within Hungary and in the European Union. It justified this by pointing out that in the first decade of the new millennium, people's utopian faith in the power of globalization to curb human conflict had been shaken. The 2008 crisis made it clear that the era of conflict had not ended, and power and force would once more be important.[20]

By rekindling the illusion of a country under attack, Orbán assumed the task of defending the country and deploying force, as well as the right to do so.

TAINTED DEMOCRACY

Wall-to-Wall Fidesz[21]

Viktor Orbán's revolutionary drive did not slacken for one minute after 2010. My friends, who on the 2010 election night hoped that Orbán's political maturity or perhaps the system of checks and balances would protect the integrity of the democratic system, were proved mistaken. Fidesz dismantled the checks and balances in the first year after it came to power. By amending the constitution and personalizing politics, Hungary came to acquire a level of concentration of power never seen in European democracies.

Within one or two years, Orbán had placed his own friends in all the leading positions of the state. After twenty years, few of Fidesz's early team had stayed with Orbán, but they all held important positions in the Hungarian state. János Áder, president of the republic, László Kövér, speaker of Parliament, Tünde Handó, chair of the National Judiciary Office and wife of József Szájer, the leader of the Fidesz group in the European Parliament, and István Stumpf, constitutional judge, had all studied at Bibó College, an elite, specialist social sciences institution, alongside Orbán. Other Fidesz politicians who obtained crucial positions of authority include Péter Polt, chief prosecutor, György Matolcsy, president of the Hungarian National Bank, Annamária Szalai, president of the Media Council, András Tállai, president of the National Tax and Customs Administration, and László Domokos, president of the State Audit Office. Later, Polt's wife, Marianna Gabriella Palásthy, became vice-president of the Government Control Office (responsible for financial control). Confidants of the prime minister sat at the helm of the Election Commission, the Competition Authority, and Hungarian Radio and Television, or occupied senior roles in several hundred other television radio stations and media outlets.[22]

The friends at the helm of the institutions checking the government and guaranteeing the constitutionality of the state made it possible for Orbán's government to exert an unusually strong influence on Hungary's economy and build powerful control over the media. Business people personally close to Viktor Orbán and his family could gain ownership of strategically important, highly profitable companies, often excluding all competition. In just a few years, Lőrinc Mészáros, a gas fitter from Orbán's village, acquired assets of tremendous value, and became the richest man in Hungary. The Orbán family's assets, or at least those known to the public, became visible mainly through Viktor Orbán's father's and his children's business interests. Orbán's government had decisive influence over a considerable part of public property, education, the arts, churches and religious organizations, and sport too.[23] Subsequent chapters in this book will demonstrate how this system worked and how it continued to grow.

In Orbán's regime permanent battle has led to a hitherto unseen concentration of power, made acceptable by constantly renewed versions of the populist fairy tale and conspiracy theories. However, the end of the story, the golden age of contentment, in Orbán's words 'peace in modern times',[24] would never appease some in Hungary. For them, the situation was always getting more urgent.

Orbán's 'System of National Cooperation' cannot be understood purely at the institutional level. Through supreme authorization to a monopoly on legislation, it constantly changed its own environment, which brought instability for all other players. By the time someone had understood yesterday, they found themselves in a different institutional framework, with different political opportunities.[25] This is another reason Viktor Orbán's regime could not be called conservative. For Orbán's partners and rivals, every day brought something new. He was not the first populist politician to obtain power over the last few decades, but he was the first in Europe who built a regime different in nature from European democracy, one tailored to the twenty-first century.

PART I

POLITICAL LANDSCAPES

1

WITHOUT ORBÁN, THERE'S NOTHING
HOW FIDESZ BECAME HUNGARY'S RULING PARTY

Fidesz represents a political generation 'that sees the strengthening of the Hungarian nation as its own historical mission', wrote Gábor G. Fodor in his book *Az Orbán szabály* (The Orbán rule). According to the former leader of Fidesz's most important think tank, Orbán is the first man of this chosen generation, and pursuant to this mission he has two tasks: 'change, which necessarily entails conflict, ... and conserving and protecting the changes enacted against all those who are enemies of the changes, whose interests run counter to them'.[1] At the online book launch held in May 2021,[2] emblematic figures from Fidesz's intellectual circles lavished praise on the book.

According to András Lánczi, then rector of Budapest's Corvinus University, Orbán has exceptional abilities and 'gets to metaphysical depths in his management of every issue'. Zsolt Bayer, once one of Fidesz's founding members and today a leading radical journalist, added that Western civilization is headed for final destruction, and in this historical situation Viktor Orbán was the first to recognize that if we want to save Western culture, then we must do so on the basis of a national renaissance. Mária Schmidt, a key theoretician of Orbán's system, was of the opinion that the prime minister had practically transformed Hungary, and there was a good chance he would transform the whole of Europe: 'Nothing better could happen to Europe'. Finally, István Stumpf, a former Constitutional Court justice, concluded that it is impossible to understand the power that defines Orbán's enigmatic person.

Under Viktor Orbán's leadership, since 2010 Fidesz has become one with the government and even with the Hungarian state. The most important trait of this system is that it is ruled single-handedly.[3] Orbán keeps every personal and political decision of his party under total control and no state institution exists independently of him. In his party, however, he consolidated his position of total power and as the maker of unquestionable decisions much earlier.

There Was Once a Liberal Fidesz

A heated debate was under way as my friend, the dissident oppositionist Róza Hodosán, and I entered the crowded cellar of the Kisrabló restaurant in Budapest near the Technical University in early April 1988. About fifty or sixty young people, almost all men, were talking about how to respond to the paper *Magyar Hírlap*, which had accused their newly formed organization of being illegal and under the influence of imperialist agents. Some of the young men were lawyers, who argued that the matter could not be allowed to pass, because the organization had been formed within the framework provided by Hungarian law. Others were wary of police warnings and perhaps more serious consequences, and advised caution. The debate was passionate and spirited, yet everyone spoke in an orderly, intelligent manner. By the end of the debate, they decided that the newspaper should be asked to publish a correction, and if this did not happen, they would initiate legal proceedings against it. I was impressed by this political maturity, decisiveness and courage. I joined Fidesz that very same evening.

Fidesz, or the Federation of Young Democrats, had been founded one week earlier, on 30 March 1988, by thirty-seven young people, students and alumni of university specialist colleges. Already in the late years of Kádár-style socialism, some specialist colleges encouraged critical thinking about public life. Uniquely, these colleges were led by student councils, which in the 1980s operated as 'small circles of freedom'. In this exceptional circle a highly aware, informed group critical of the system came into being. Its members founded the first formally independent political organization, which looked on itself as an alternative to the Young Communist League.

The next few weeks and months completely upended my life. I went to the Bibó College in Budapest almost every day—it was the regular Fidesz meeting point, because several of the activists lived there. I soon became friends with them. My first memory of Viktor Orbán is of him weighing up what steps the regime might take during a legal action brought against *Magyar Hírlap*, and of their risk. He struck me as a clever, strategic thinker. Viktor Orbán and his two younger brothers came from a small village, where his parents worked themselves out of poverty into communist Hungary's 'middle class'.[4] His father was a traditional authoritarian at home and made great demands of his sons.[5] Once Orbán described his family background thus: 'Where I came from, in that milieu there wasn't any special cultural tradition. They were employees, nothing to do even with the peasant class. My father's family ... workers' culture, there wasn't anything ... not to mention civic, middle-class culture. I came from a cultureless place, from an eclectic milieu'.[6] As a youngster Orbán wanted to be a footballer. By his own admission, the first time he met boys different from himself was when he was at grammar school, as his fellow students came from more bourgeois, middle-class or even religious families.[7] At this time, he was active in the Young Communist League, basically to 'have a good time as a youngster', and he didn't become involved in politics until he was studying law at the Bibó College of ELTE University's Law School, where he met prominent figures from the dissident opposition. This was where he became politically aware.

When it was established, Fidesz immediately came under fire politically and several of the founders received police warnings. From the beginning, Fidesz's thinking was political, taking the hypocritical 'democratic' spirit of the communist constitution at face value, and exploiting every opportunity it afforded. The idea that someone would attack them on the basis of their own laws was new to the state-party. Neither police threats nor 'friendly interviews' in the communist party bureaus at universities or the communist party committees of provincial towns deterred Fidesz's members from political activity. Membership grew every day.

Fidesz was extremely open and welcoming as an organization. Anyone who joined was immediately involved and given a task. A couple of weeks after the founding, I spoke at an international press conference, where I gave an account of our growth in the provinces. Because the official Hungarian press carried no news about Fidesz, we tried to reach Hungarian listeners on Radio Free Europe, the Voice of America and other Western media.

In spite of pressure from the regime, the organization developed quickly. Work was started on writing a programme, an effort coordinated by László Kövér, a jurist and a senior founding member of Fidesz, who from the outset was one of Fidesz's theoreticians, and whose systematic way of thinking was an inspiration to me.

I'll never forget the speech I made at the first general assembly: the intellectual challenge was so great I could hardly speak for nerves. Moreover, of all the speakers, I was the only woman. After this, the 'lads' took me on in the central team, and soon I was sent to Cracow, to give a speech at an international meeting organized by Human Rights Watch. There I met dissident opposition leaders of other Eastern European countries and international human rights activists from the West. These experiences were enormously inspiring, and I learned a great deal.

In autumn 1988, we held Fidesz's first congress, where our programme was decided, and where we elected the executive board, of which I became a member.

In 1988 many other opposition groups became registered organizations. The Hungarian Democratic Forum (MDF) and the Network of Free Initiatives were founded by opposition thinkers from previous decades. The opposition organizations demanded multi-party elections, democracy and the rehabilitation of the 1956 revolution, things which in 1988 were still considered taboo. Many demonstrations were broken up by the police. Fidesz was constantly in action: we organized marches and sit-ins, and wrote and submitted manifestos. The rapid decay of the communist-socialist regime was all too apparent.

In September 1988, as a group of women we organized a women's demonstration against the construction of a hydroelectric power station in Nagymaros, on the banks of the Danube. This was unusual at the time, because until then only men had represented opposition politics.

The main difference between Fidesz and the other organizations was that it defined itself as a youth organization with an age limit of thirty-five. We built our identity on the fact that we young people born after 1956 had grown up in the era of 'goulash communism'. The regime had become milder, so we could express our message more determinedly and clearly, and it meant we set out with a clean slate.[8]

Another important aim for us was not to define ourselves as the successors of earlier conflicting political trends. Although Fidesz drew on the Hungarian progressive liberal tradition, we didn't want to become entangled in rekindling the divisions between the modernist-liberal and the 'traditionalist' (*népi*)-left intellectual camps of the interwar years. Like the Belgians with the Walloons and the Flemings, we strove to move beyond this inherited cultural conflict. This centrist 'Belgian ideology' enabled Fidesz to embrace the values of liberalism, the market economy, and the role of civil society in restricting the activity of the state.[9]

In 1989 we identified ourselves as a radical, liberal and alternative organization. We were convinced that we were most suited to represent the culture of freedom, and we set this out in our first programme statement: 'The trustee and final guarantor of democracy is not the power of the state, but a society with a culture of democratic politics'.[10]

The Marvellous Year of 1989

By the end of 1988 the deepening economic crisis of 'goulash communism', and the growing popularity of the opposition movements, prompted the Hungarian Socialist Workers' Party (MSZMP) to follow President Mikhail Gorbachev's glasnost policies. This decision was also influenced by the fact that in summer 1988 serious miners' strikes broke out in Poland, which forced the Polish communist party (PZPR) to enter into negotiations with the opposition trade union Solidarność (Solidarity). To avoid this situation, the MSZMP preferred to lead the changes itself. It allowed freedom of association and freedom of speech. Following the Polish model, the opposition organizations made a united effort to formulate their demands and present them to the one-party regime.

Bowing to political pressure, the government consented to the reburial of the heroes of 1956, an act which symbolized the rehabilitation of the revolution. The state-party and the opposition forged a compromise and planned the memorial event together. Shortly before the reburial, the idea arose that there should be a speech on behalf of Hungary's young people, which led to Fidesz as a youth organization being invited to do this. We in Fidesz immediately realized this represented an extraordinary opportunity. We planned the basic message of the speech and, after a short discussion, we selected Viktor Orbán to give the address, as he spoke well and his delivery had force.

On 16 June 1989, the building of the Műcsarnok Art Gallery on Heroes' Square was draped in an enormous black-and-white cloth, creating an extremely solemn atmosphere. People started arriving at the square from early morning. Together with thousands of others, my parents travelled to Budapest for this historic occasion. By 10 am 250,000 people had gathered in the square. As leaders of Fidesz we were given the role of guard of honour next to the black-draped coffins. We were fully aware that this day would go down in history. I was in the guard of honour just as Viktor Orbán stepped up to the microphone.

Orbán said that we young people respected the martyrs for being statesmen who, although they were communists, identified with the will of Hungarian society, and were able to overcome the communists' sacred taboos: unconditional servility to the Russian empire and the dictatorship of the party. He added that from their fate, we had learned that democracy and communism are incompatible. I listened to the speech with incredible pride, tingling with excitement. With the leaders of the state-party sitting in the first row, he continued: 'Unless we lose sight of the ideals of 1956, we can elect a government that begins immediate negotiations about starting the imminent removal of the Russian troops'. The speech was determined and radical throughout, but this statement was the point where it became truly cathartic. Although the withdrawal of Soviet troops was among the demands of the opposition, and at the time had already begun, nobody spoke of this. Orbán expressed Hungarians' decades-long desire. He had spoken the unspeakable, and had exposed the government, which wanted to manage the withdrawal unnoticed, allowing the Soviets to save face.

After the reburial, round table talks began in Hungary too between the state-party and the opposition parties, and in September 1989 an agreement was made which opened the way to organizing the first free elections.

Meanwhile, in autumn 1989 things were on the move all over Eastern Europe. On 9 November the Berlin Wall came down, and the Soviet empire crumbled before our very eyes.

In autumn 1989 Viktor Orbán won a scholarship from the Soros Foundation to study political philosophy at Oxford University, but in December he returned to Hungary to stand in the elections. Of all of us, Orbán was the most decisive in preparing for a role in politics. 'Then Viktor said something to the effect that a man should want to be the best at what he does. If he chose science, he should want to be the most outstanding scientist; if he chooses politics, he should become prime minister', recalled a friend of mine later.[11] At the dawn of the regime change, when most of us twenty-somethings were just starting to think of a role in politics, Orbán was already gearing up for the highest political position. Nonetheless, at that point there were still several leading personalities in Fidesz alongside Orbán.

In the first free election campaign in 1990 we tried to convey the positive feeling that many Hungarians shared at the time with a catchy rhyming slogan '*Hallgass a szívedre, szavazz a Fideszre*' (Listen to your heart, vote for Fidesz) and an eye-catching poster. During the campaign Fidesz became a genuine team, and we worked through this period in an astonishingly positive mood. When on 25 March 1990 we learned that we had won 9% of the votes and gained entry to the National Assembly, we were bursting with joy, and for weeks we were in a state of elation. All of us began a new life.

The Sky's the Limit

Twenty-two of us entered the National Assembly as members of Parliament. Since Fidesz's membership was small compared with that of other parties, our parliamentary group was also the party's main decision-making forum. After a long discussion we elected Orbán as leader of the group. By this time his name was the most familiar, and he had skills in organizing and especially in debating, which we would badly need in the political disputes in Parliament.

A good few of us went straight from university lecture halls to parliamentary benches. Being 'semi-intellectuals'[12] helped us to master the role of politician quickly. The group was assisted by excellent advisers, work was organized well and went smoothly, and our team was full of optimism and self-confidence. There was a great sense of unity, and, in spite of disagreements, on every major issue we were able, by consensus, to make a decision that everyone identified with.

Orbán's leading role became visible at the helm of the group in the management of day-to-day matters and in directing policy. He was a good strategist, a persuasive speaker, and basically a winning personality; perhaps his restlessness and impatience were a bit much for me, along with the constant football metaphors and gestures, which made this male-dominated group even more macho.[13]

In Parliament, Fidesz became highly critical of the government coalition led by the populist-conservative MDF. We criticized the government for its amateurish approach to policy, and for giving extremist nationalist figures a voice in the government party.

When taxi drivers created a blockade on Budapest's main streets and bridges after the government wrong-headedly raised the price of petrol in October 1990, Fidesz adopted a commonsense, rule-of-law approach. 'Everyone ought to know that if popular anger, fed by social dissatisfaction and revenge, were to sweep away the government and the Parliament, it would also sweep away democracy', said Orbán.[14] Little did we know that a decade and a half later it would be Orbán who would try to radicalize dissatisfied people in order to bring the government to its knees.

Fidesz's principles were clear and consistently liberal. We believed firmly in constitutional democracy and human rights, but we were reasonable in such matters as calling the previous regime to account and compensating for assets seized by the communists. The economic programme stated: 'At the centre of our thinking is the individual, the human with free will, not some community of people, some social group, class, or the entire so-called nation'.[15] This thinking was far indeed from the collectivist narrative that Fidesz adopted later.

In 1992 the party joined Liberal International. The leader of the organization, Otto Graf Lambsdorff, president of the Free Democratic Party in Germany, became Orbán's mentor, and drew him into the European liberal circuit.

With the orderly behaviour of the Fidesz parliamentary group, and its firm, commonsense and often cheeky contributions to parliamentary debate, the party's popularity continued to grow after the April elections. Half a year later, at the municipal elections in autumn 1990, several hundred of the party's candidates won seats. This success was tangible and inspiring.

The First Ruptures

It was a sunny Saturday afternoon in January, and we were coming to the end of our two-day parliamentary group meeting, which had been full of thorough analysis and lively discussion conducted in a cosy mansion in the city of Sopron, close to the border with Austria. Before the closing session, we took a photo of our twenty-two-member parliamentary group outside the building. Everyone was cheerful and smiling. During the first year in Parliament, we had become a cohesive, joyful political group. During the break, I distributed a paper I had written during a recent skiing holiday with my two friends and fellow Fidesz members István Hegedűs and Lajos Kósa to provide food for thought. The title of the two-pager, 'The club of clone-heads', indicated the semi-official nature of the piece. It dealt with the phenomenon of 'groupthink', something I had recently become acquainted with while preparing for my university thesis. Following the assessment inventory developed by political psychologist Irving Janis, we listed the eight symptoms he identified as key characteristics of 'groupthink'. Janis found that in cases where these phenomena existed in a decision-making body, the chances of flawed decisions were high. We were eager to analyse our group and collected examples from our own practice. Illusions of vulnerability, belief in our inherent morality, out-group stereotypes, collective rationalization, self-censorship, the illusion of unanimity, direct pressure of dissent, and self-appointed thought control were all typical in our group. We found the analysis thought-provoking, and hoped the parliamentary group would consider the note to guard ourselves against serious political mistakes in the future. Contrary to our expectations, the reaction was baffling: Orbán and Kövér, a strong Orbán ally, took the paper as a personal attack. They went on the offensive right away. An open quarrel started without any room for reasonable debate. Kövér, a self-appointed moral authority, who often presented himself as a guardian of Orbán, began shouting, questioning our loyalty, and stated that, as from that moment, he regarded us as his political adversaries. Everyone was bewildered. Nothing like this had happened since we started working together. The three of us realized that we had involuntarily and naively revealed something that should have remained unexpressed.

It became clear that Orbán and Kövér were systematically manipulating the parliamentary group in order for their viewpoints to be turned into action. Orbán tried to patch things up as far as possible, and at the end of the meeting he referred to our shared experiences, and the next day we carried on working together. Yet something had broken. Never again was there a group photo of Fidesz's first parliamentary group. None of this was visible from outside: the parliamentary group continued to appear unified. Fidesz's popularity climbed unchecked, and in December 1992 we were polling at over 30%.[16]

In the following year, behind the differences in personal and political style, divergent strategies started to become more conspicuous. According to one idea, the strategic goal was for Fidesz and the SZDSZ (the other liberal party) to gain enough strength in the centre of Hungarian politics to be able to form a government. Between the increasingly feeble right-wing government coalition, and the post-communist Socialist Party, the centrist parties could have formed a strong base. At a forum in 1992 Orbán said: 'The fate of this country [can be improved] by a civic liberal government that is undeterred from trimming back the state despite accumulated [social] tension, one that does not give in to the temptation of either right- or left-wing etatist economic policy'.[17]

However, very early on László Kövér expressed the view that the SZDSZ represented an existential threat to Fidesz, and that Fidesz's most important goal should be to distance itself from the other liberal party. 'The greatest political opponent is always the one who is closest to you', he said.[18] To rally Fidesz people behind this argument, Kövér drew a moral distinction between Fidesz 'from the provinces' and the SZDSZ, which he identified as consisting of Budapest intellectuals. As someone from a provincial town myself, I considered Kövér's distinction embarrassing and pointless.

Over time Orbán also came round to the idea of distancing Fidesz from the SZDSZ as much as possible. Supporters of a liberal centrist strategy became a minority group, and those who endorsed it (Gábor Fodor, Péter Molnár, István Hegedűs and me) were subjected to growing criticism. The mood in the parliamentary group became increasingly hostile.

The party decided in 1993 to finally elect a party leader. In spite of Orbán being the only candidate, the mood at the congress in February 1993 was extremely tense. This was because, despite strong protests, Orbán insisted that his divisive ally, László Kövér, become his successor as leader of the parliamentary group, and the new statutes of association that he submitted to the congress gave the party leader very strong powers.

Once elected as party leader, Orbán quickly centralized the use of financial resources, decision-making and the distribution of positions. Debates in the parliamentary group showed a harshness that would previously have been unthinkable. A bullying style became the norm, along with a policy of force. Humiliating and degrading language was used openly, especially towards Gábor Fodor, who was the key representative of the moderate-liberal group within the party. The relationship with the SZDSZ became a sore point. The level of mistrust was such that Orbán's people started compiling dossiers of information on members of the parliamentary group, in a clear effort to intimidate them. In this intra-party dispute I too was in the moderate-liberal camp, and this increased level of mistrust hurt me greatly as well.

The differences in strategy behind the personal rivalry became apparent to the general public when Orbán announced a change of direction in 1993 and defined the party as a 'national liberal' party, which was new to all of us.[19] By that time the governing conservative coalition had become incredibly unpopular, and with the death of Prime Minister József Antall it was thrown into confusion. It was difficult to understand why Orbán, instead of agitating against the unpopular conservative governing parties, unexpectedly set upon the Socialist Party. This strategy, which placed Fidesz alongside the failed right-wing parties, was utterly counterproductive, and was at odds with the fact that Fidesz had made a cooperation agreement with SZDSZ before the elections in 1994. While Fidesz was shifting to the right, some leaders in the SZDSZ were cooperating with the technocratic Socialist Party, because they feared the far right would gain ground. The increasing polarization between conservative and left-liberal forces led to bitter and intense arguments within Fidesz. The party's popularity began to wane.

In this toxic environment, in May 1993 a financial scandal broke out around Fidesz, called the 'headquarters corruption scandal' (see Chapter 6). It transpired that Orbán had made secret deals with MDF politicians without the knowledge of the Fidesz leadership, and the party had invested hundreds of millions of forints of party money in businesses of Orbán's childhood friend and financial adviser Lajos Simicska. At this point the reason for Orbán's increasing power within the party became clear to us: for the party leader it was crucial that the leading positions in the party be held only by people loyal to him. Nobody could be allowed to obstruct the intermingling of party funds and political power.

In order to counterbalance Orbán's growing dominance, Gábor Fodor made a last-ditch effort to secure the chairmanship of the National Council, the second most important position in the party, but Orbán did not accept this and, in a carefully orchestrated session, his candidate defeated Fodor. A few weeks later, only half a year before the next general elections, Fodor left the party and soon joined the liberal SZDSZ. The centrist-liberal group that I represented within Fidesz remained in a political vacuum. These turbulent events contributed to a crisis in the party and put Fidesz on a slippery downhill slope. But no one could stop Orbán running his harsh anti-communist campaign, which was a significant shift compared with the party's earlier politics.

Fidesz, a party that in 1990 had entered Hungarian politics by virtue of its 'innocence' and that three years later was preparing to be in government, with over 30% of the popular vote, performed terribly in the 1994 elections, and gained only 7% of the popular vote. Orbán theatrically resigned from the position of party chairman, but after the departure of Fodor there was nobody who could have been a genuine alternative to him. Entrusting them to his close ally Simicska's care, Orbán retained the assets acquired from incoming funds to the party, which entrenched his supporters at the helm. After Orbán was re-elected as party leader in June 1994, I too left Fidesz, together with my colleague István Hegedűs. We felt that it was no longer the party for us, as it drifted to the right, was led in an autocratic style, used questionable methods to secure political success, and was prepared to be in league with anyone. Fidesz was such an important experience in my life that coming to terms with the personal and professional losses that leaving the party involved for me took two years.

A Turn to the Right

'I wouldn't undo a single one of the important decisions', said Viktor Orbán on election night in 1994, when it became known that Fidesz had performed miserably.[20] He blamed the failure not on a flawed political strategy, or on the financial 'headquarters scandal', but on the fact that there was no 'Fidesz-friendly' press and on the polarization of Hungarian politics. 'Our alleged right-wingedness was not our chosen course; we were forced onto this path methodically and deliberately, twisting our intentions', said László Kövér indignantly in a statement.[21]

Kövér was right about the polarization, which was emphasized by the fact that the liberal SZDSZ went into government with the Socialist Party in 1994. However, the move to the right wasn't nearly as big a problem for the Orbán group; after all, it was they who had designed this strategic direction years earlier. When I left the party, my issue was that the Orbán wing had given up too soon on Fidesz's original centrist politics, which had aimed to steer Hungary's political elite away from historically entrenched divisions. My personal view was that Orbán had shifted to the right more because he thought the centre would not be able to gain traction independently. Moreover, Fidesz would have had to share the field with the other liberal party, the SZDSZ, and Orbán didn't think it would accept him as leader. On the left, as in other countries in the region, the post-communist MSZP had regained its former support. On the right, however, under the burden of governing in the first years, the coalition parties were in complete disarray, opening the way for Fidesz to come to the fore. Although the government fell, taken together the right-wing parties won 30% of votes in 1994. Orbán saw the possibility inherent in this and, with a firm hand, moved Fidesz from the centre to the right. 'The six-party system is not suitable for setting the destiny of our country in the right direction ... rather, we need the alternation of two large rival groups of power ... our place is on the side of a civic Hungary', he said in 1995,[22] contrary to his earlier opinion that saw the success of the country in the creation of a strong centre.

In the next few years Fidesz set about consolidating its carefully structured power, the purpose of which was to strengthen the political block on the right wing against the left. Orbán encouraged the split in the MDF,[23] which fell into crisis after Antall's death, and then formed an alliance with one wing of the divided party. Fidesz also made overtures to politicians of the Christian Democratic People's Party, which suffered from serious internal divisions. In 1997 eleven of its MPs joined Fidesz's parliamentary group of twenty, and later created a satellite party, the Christian Democratic People's Party (KDNP), which thereafter ran on Fidesz's party list.

In the spirit of this ideological U-turn, Fidesz made many gestures in order to be accepted on the right. Previously belligerently liberal, the party openly embraced religion as a tool. Fidesz leaders, including the party president, had their children baptized. Orbán was confirmed in the Reformed Church. From 1994 Orbán regularly took part in events of the Alliance of Christian Intellectuals, and the Christian Democratic politicians who moved to Fidesz helped him to get close to the head of the Catholic Church in Hungary.

These neophyte efforts were not in vain: the churches entered into a political alliance with Fidesz. Orbán always thought of the churches in a political context, and for the church leaders too it was important to be in contact with well-functioning political parties. As it veered to the right, Fidesz proved to be a good partner. In 1998 during the election campaign, after an encyclical to bishops in the Catholic Church, several parish priests encouraged believers to vote for Fidesz, which had previously been unthinkable.[24]

In 1997 at large Fidesz events, sitting in the first rows were politicians from the smaller right-wing parties who had moved to Fidesz, conservative intellectuals, and celebrity actors and sports people. By adopting these grand symbolic gestures, the party became more persuasive and attractive than any of its right-wing predecessors. The Fidesz of three years prior had disappeared into thin air.

The most virtuoso aspect of Fidesz's U-turn was the renewal of its political language (see Chapter 8). The architect of this was Fidesz's communications consultant András Wermer, who coined the expression 'civic union'[25] to define the party, which was sufficiently positive and sufficiently general for moderate conservative-liberals, Christian democrats, and more radical anti-communist nationalist voters all to identify with it.

In his speeches, Orbán drew a sharp line between the 'post-communist liberal elite supported by international capital' and the 'civic union' where, as a result of their strengthening, the middle classes represented the national interest. He claimed that the communist system of clientelism was still alive and kicking, because the liberal SZDSZ had helped it back to power.[26] He united the camp of 'civic forces' with a powerful anti-communist message: 'in 1994, the Hungarian people who had won back their freedom for four years, once more of their own accord took on the yoke of their former oppressors, who ruined them', or so he interpreted the socialists' victory.[27] These phrases and strong political symbols sharply polarized public discourse, and enabled the broad spread of right-wing voters to identify with Fidesz as it donned its conservative mask.

Orbán's supporters considered the creation of 'civic forces' the greatest achievement of the party leader. A few years later, however, the strategy director of the Századvég Institute lifted the lid on Fidesz's trick: 'Many right-wing intellectuals are under the misapprehension that the slogan "civic Hungary" is a political reality, but by nature it is a political product. Even today, they think that between 1998 and 2002 Hungary was actually a civic Hungary. This is an enormous error'.[28] The narrative of 'civic Hungary' was nothing but a slogan of the moment used to unify right-wing voters, while in government Orbán pursued etatist policies.

By 1998 Orbán had pushed Fidesz irrevocably to the right, and after the liberal SZDSZ coalition with the Socialist Party, the Hungarian political centre lost ground and the political arena became essentially bipolar. In less than ten years, the centuries-old division of the Hungarian political elite had reproduced itself; this opened the way for further polarization. Orbán had an active role in this change.

The reason why Orbán and his peers managed to transform the political profile of Fidesz so radically was that in the first few years after the regime change, political parties and the party system lacked stability. Voters did not yet have a stable party preference. The parties that triggered the regime change were themselves constantly in flux, and went through many internal crises in these years.

In addition, in Western European politics, which the 'regime-changing' parties took as a model, important changes were under way. By the 1990s, throughout Europe there was gradually less of a need to have strong representation of a particular worldview, and the legitimacy of traditional parties was weakening.[29] Orbán could count on being able to build up a people's party with a broad platform, on which significantly differing groups would be accommodated side by side. Parties became increasingly centred around personalities, and modern populist leaders appeared. Silvio Berlusconi had a great influence on Orbán: 'It's fantastic what this man has done in two and a half months in Italy', he enthused in 1994, when Berlusconi won the Italian elections.[30] The Italian media tsar inspired him to unify the right wing, and also to work out a modern populist campaign strategy. The top-down organization of Berlusconi's movement, Forza Italia, the network of political clubs modelled on football clubs, reference to political opponents by name, and the simple, symbolic language 'of football changing rooms' were all echoed in Fidesz's political logic and language.[31]

Why did Fidesz's membership follow, without dissent, the radical political path mapped out by Orbán? This was possible because the politicians who were openly critical of Orbán, and who represented a substantial alternative to him, had left the party in 1994. The moderate, pragmatic politicians still remaining in Fidesz had been given a very clear message that it was risky to go against Orbán, because you could find yourself marginalized. Everyone who stayed in Fidesz in 1994 or who joined the party later accepted Orbán's dominant role and the informal decision-making mechanisms he had created.

In the 1998 elections Fidesz won the most seats and formed a government with the now shrunken Hungarian Democratic Forum and the Independent Smallholders Party. Europe's youngest prime minister, Viktor Orbán, was welcomed enthusiastically by the continent's political leaders, and his quick thinking and outstanding political acumen were respected far and wide. At the time, few were concerned that if Orbán was able to force through such an unusual, rapid and radical political U-turn, he might do this again if it was in his interest. With hindsight the election victory justified Fidesz's volte-face.

Europe's Youngest Prime Minister

During the 1998 election campaign Orbán stated:

> We do not wish to change the pillars of the constitutional system. It is a great merit of the regime change that it created the institutional system within whose framework a Western European-type society can operate, from the stock exchange to the Constitutional Court. It would not be wise to undo this; on the contrary.[32]

True, at the time he did not have the necessary political power. Nonetheless, the change of government started in the spirit of an all-out attack, first and foremost in the choice of people for positions. Orbán and his team wanted to build up 'civic Hungary' in place of 'post-communist Hungary', and so they implemented a mass replacement of officials in the state apparatus. 'Wherever possible, we put our own people, because otherwise everything would stay the same', Orbán told his inner circle.[33] Orbán appointed his friend and closest ally, Lajos Simicska, as president of the National Tax and Customs Office. Then the chief prosecutor, Kálmán Györgyi, for reasons still unclear, unexpectedly resigned, and a Fidesz loyalist, Péter Polt, was appointed in his place.

Many former Fidesz people, like György Bence, the philosopher and former adviser to Orbán, judged these developments to be a cause for concern. His view was that in 1998 Fidesz found itself up against a suspicious and mostly hostile state administration, where most of the civil servants were of the old regime. But Orbán's people did not have the necessary self-confidence, flexibility or ability to weigh each case on its merits, to work together with people who did not agree with them one hundred per cent.[34]

Orbán settled down to a chancellor-type leadership, more centralized than before. Although Fidesz gave many governmental positions to its partners in the coalition, shadow cabinets were formed in the Prime Minister's Office. This structure made governmental decision-making less transparent, and was further aggravated by the fact that—unprecedentedly—Orbán discontinued the practice of keeping minutes at cabinet meetings.

The Fidesz-led coalition tried to restrict the opposition's room for manoeuvre by weakening the role of Parliament. The government parliamentary group made it impossible to set up ad hoc select committees in Parliament. They introduced the practice of having sessions only once every three weeks, which significantly reduced the opposition's visibility. All these steps were unusually aggressive, but at this time Orbán did not yet lay a finger on the bases of the constitutional order.

Compared with his predecessors Orbán appeared less often before a plenary parliamentary session, but he held more 'extramural' rallies with his own believers. Following the example of the American president, he introduced the custom of a 'state of the nation' speech each year, which was held in the impressive Vigadó Hall in the heart of Budapest, and broadcast live by the media. Present at these exclusive 'state of the nation' speeches were members of Fidesz's growing business, clerical and cultural circles.

The prime minister neglected the spaces of democratic political debate, and built the illusion that he was greater, that he was different, and that as leader of the nation he stood above day-to-day political battles.[35] The 'Orbán project' was moving on and a new image of the leader was being constructed. The prime minister turned up among his people: at boxing and football matches, at Masses and village sausage-making events, and he always took a sizeable crew to film his travels abroad. Symbolic politics became the norm.

In this professionally media-made role Viktor Orbán embodied a modernized national Christian conservative right-wing ideology (see Chapter 2), which was no longer old-fashioned but on the offensive and modern. The government used the thousandth anniversary of the founding of the Hungarian state to hold a year-long series of commemorative events in Hungary in 2000. Political ceremonies and sacred events were organized all around the country, and a large exhibition on great people of the Hungarian nation entitled 'Dreamers of dreams: Hungarians for the world' served to make people believe that under Viktor Orbán Hungary would again be great, strong and successful.[36]

Orbán's first term in government was undeniably successful. The Fidesz-led coalition was also aided by the fact that it took over government at a felicitous time: austerity measures implemented in 1996 by the socialist–liberal coalition had significantly improved the economic position of the country. The national debt had fallen, and the economy had begun to grow. In 1999, under Orbán's premiership, Hungary joined NATO, and the government conducted the negotiation process to join the

WITHOUT ORBÁN, THERE'S NOTHING

European Union (EU) in a responsible, professional manner. Everyone took it for granted that in 2004 Orbán would lead the country into the EU.

The Nation Cannot Be in Opposition

But Orbán's party failed to win the elections in 2002. In vain did Orbán switch strategy between the two rounds of the election and 'ploughed up the country' to mobilize his believers: Fidesz won only 48% of the seats in Parliament. 'We were many, but we were not enough', said Orbán in dismay on election night.[37]

After the unexpected election defeat Orbán withdrew from the public eye and the party quickly became demoralized. But it was impossible to speak about the lessons to be learned. 'Orbán has always set out from the view that Fidesz lost in spite of governing successfully', said a Fidesz politician in a conversation with a journalist.[38] Even in private, Fidesz leaders never acknowledged that in all probability a significant role in the defeat was played by Orbán's arrogant and divisive politics, the corruption allegations that had come to light, and Orbán's confrontational politics towards liberal-led Budapest, because it alienated voters in the capital from Fidesz. Right-wing publicists blamed the campaign manager for the defeat; Orbán was untouchable.

One month after the elections Orbán called his disappointed believers together in the Buda Castle district, where he gave a powerful speech that represented the overture to a new era.

> We are not going away. [...] The homeland is there even when it comes under the influence of foreign powers, if it is overrun by Tartars, or Turks. The homeland is there even when shaken by the storms of history. The homeland is there even if the responsibility for governing it is not ours. [...] It may be that our parties and MPs are in the opposition in Parliament, but we here in this square are not and can

never be in the opposition, because the homeland [nation] cannot be in the opposition.[39]

Orbán questioned the political legitimacy of his rivals to run the country and claimed for himself the right to represent all Hungarians. He called on his believers to create 'civic circles' all over the country, so that 'if necessary, they [could] move together'. Orbán then stepped aside from the defeated Fidesz, resigned from the post of party leader, and started to create a broader national movement, which he united with his personal authority and respect. As a result of a year-long, unprecedented mobilization campaign, under the slogan 'one camp, one flag', 11,000 civic circles were formed.

The civic circles movement was joined by many local circles for nurturing traditions, church groups, smaller trade unions, organizations fighting poverty and local environmentalists, and the movement even drew in activists from the other disintegrating right-wing parties, including many far-right groups, from which Fidesz previously had kept its distance.[40] The civic circles organized thousands of events: they held discussions and talks, and wrote petitions. The events were usually about issues of identity—nation, religion, Europe—and they organized protests against the bias of the press.[41] At the meetings, Orbán adopted a manner of speaking reminiscent of that of sect leaders: 'It is not globalization that spans the nations, it is Christian love', he said.[42] In his anti-globalization, collectivist talk, he said there was a new situation in the world, because some people 'proclaim increasingly forcefully [...] that you should only care about what you can get quickly, for what you don't need to think about, or feel deeply, or sacrifice for, make a commitment for, be faithful to, for which you don't need to love others and trust others'.[43] By keeping a distance from specific issues and adopting collectivist thinking, very different groups of people could connect to Orbán without coming into conflict in choosing values.

WITHOUT ORBÁN, THERE'S NOTHING

The disintegration of the boundary between the moderate and the extreme right caused concern among Fidesz politicians. At the same time, the civic circle activists looked with animosity on Fidesz politicians, whom they considered elitist liberals; they accepted only Viktor Orbán as an authentic right-wing politician.[44] Meanwhile, a debate developed between the forlorn leaders of Fidesz and the party's intellectual supporters over whether for the next election they should try to win over voters from the moderate centre, or whether they should entice the more radical right wing with welfare promises.[45] The debate was decided by Orbán, when one year after the lost elections, he was voted back to the helm of the party as the unshakeable leader of a national movement that went far beyond Fidesz. The party assumed the name Fidesz—Hungarian Civic Party (Fidesz-MPP). The new right-wing 'union party' dreamed of by Orbán accommodated supporters from the centre to the far right, who, unlike the disappointed Fidesz activists, revered Orbán as a hero.

The revised statutes of the party gave the leader greater authority than ever before. There were only two vice-presidential positions in the party, which were elected directly by the congress, and Orbán had significant influence over all other positions.[46] In this transformative period, when Orbán was tightening his grip on the party, many politicians whom I had once worked with lost their positions, 'retired' to mayoral posts or left politics.

As a result of this heavy-handed transformation, Fidesz's organization was reinforced: via the network of civic circles it reached into every corner of society, and could now compete with the broad national network of the Socialist Party. By means of the Fidesz-faithful media the party had created a dozen or so outspoken right-wing columnists, and the system of public debate was made more balanced, but it also became more polarized.[47] Fidesz-MPP was now exclusively Orbán's party, and his believers viewed him as an especially talented man, a model, and even as a god. Orbán pursued openly populist politics. His speeches were permeated with a powerful anti-elitism, and he explained the country's problems as a crisis of both morality and morale. Among supporters of the party, several people criticized this social demagogy conducted in populist language, because they thought it might backfire when they got into government. But nobody dared to say so out loud.[48]

In 2004, when as a new member of the EU Hungary participated in the European parliamentary elections for the first time, Fidesz won half of the Hungarian seats. It seemed Orbán had been right, and his scheme had paid off. Meanwhile, scandals broke out in the incumbent Socialist Party, and in mid-term the party changed the prime minister, which gave a further opportunity for Fidesz to win a victory at the next election. Since 1990, there had been a rotation of government in Hungary: every election brought a change in the governing coalition, which analysts interpreted as a sign of the stability and maturity of the Hungarian political system. One month before the general elections in 2006, figures also bore this out: apparently Fidesz would win, and the party entered the election campaign on a wave of confidence.

Unappeasable Desire for Revenge

However, to everybody's surprise, in the elections the socialist–liberal coalition won again. Under the leadership of Ferenc Gyurcsány, the MSZP gained a greater victory than ever. The same number of votes went to Fidesz as four years previously, and this proved once more that Orbán's personal mobilizing power had reached its peak. For the leader and the policies he symbolized, and with the unifying strategy of 'one camp, one flag', it was not possible to win over any more people. The failure of the campaign showed that the extremely centralized organization and the mistrust running through the party had eroded the party's capacity for self-correction. These facts aroused a genuine

WITHOUT ORBÁN, THERE'S NOTHING

deep concern in Fidesz politicians and the party's business and intellectual supporters.

Internal criticism of Orbán grew once more. 'While after the 2002 defeat the majority looked on Viktor as a "tragic hero", in 2006 some of the intellectuals saw him as an obstacle to development', said one important right-wing thinker.[49] For the first time in fifteen years, there was doubt in the party about whether the right wing would ever manage to get into government under Orbán's leadership.

Orbán as a person was a huge problem for the party. In the circle of committed right-wingers, the Fidesz leader was surrounded with adoration, but in the centre many would not accept his radical personality.[50] At the same time, he was the only one who could unite the right-wing groups, which often had conflicting views on issues. One Fidesz MP described the party in the following way: 'Here there is space for shamanists and bigoted Catholics, for Atlanticists and those against NATO'.[51] There was nobody to replace Orbán. The months after the 2006 defeat brought Fidesz's deepest crisis yet.

Without Orbán, it was impossible to decide anything. After the repeated election defeats Mária Schmidt, a Fidesz theoretician and director of the Twenty-First Century Institute, started a relaxed, informal series of discussions on the future of the party. A couple of Fidesz leaders (for example, János Áder) took part. They analysed the reasons for the defeat, showing some self-criticism, and discussed possible directions for right-wing politics.[52] Orbán was not present at the meetings, but he knew everything that was said there.

At the same time, in the months following the election the victorious socialist government announced a set of economic austerity measures, in many cases in stark contradiction to its own election promises. In Fidesz's famous summer school in Bálványos, Orbán blamed the Socialist Party for 'committing' a lie in its election campaign and misleading people. He reached the conclusion that 'Fidesz lost [the elections] because the government withheld the truth about the economy'.[53] He launched a campaign with the message that the 'political lie' had robbed people of their freedom of choice, and thus the elections were not democratic. An enormous rally was announced to protest against the 'political lie'.

Orbán's campaign was reinvigorated by the leaked speech made by Ferenc Gyurcsány in Balatonőszöd (as we have described in the introduction), in which the prime minister admitted that his party had lied in the election campaign. Straight away Orbán set in motion a well-planned campaign, which mobilized his believers in the name of democracy, encouraged groups on the far right, and tried to bring down the government. Instead of facing up to election defeat, Orbán once more found the way out of a politically awkward situation by radicalizing Fidesz.

The Balatonőszöd speech was a gift to Orbán, and he deployed his party to defend the threat lying in wait for Hungarian democracy. Many thought that Orbán's latest manoeuvre was a stroke of genius. 'He was able to say what he had been longing to: that we have to join forces against a common enemy' explained one political analyst sympathetic to Fidesz.[54] Self-critical analysis within the party ceased immediately: Fidesz once more closed ranks as Orbán pressed forward. Action took the place of talking; action and street politics. Orbán announced a mass demonstration and gave Ferenc Gyurcsány, head of government, a seventy-two-hour ultimatum to resign. On 6 October 2006 he said in Parliament:

> Members of the House, I ask you to look around. Who could resist such forces? What power, or what force? These many thousands of tense arms would be capable of moving every stone. Many thousands of people, linked together, are able to sweep away any power. But my

friends, our power, the power of democrats, is different, and is not physical in nature.⁵⁵

This threatening speech shows the extent to which Orbán had become radicalized over the preceding months. He was pushed to deny democracy not by victory but, as before, by not accepting defeat.

But some of Fidesz's other leaders took a dim view of these extreme tendencies. In March 2007 a strange article appeared in one of Lajos Simicska's newspapers which shed light on the controversy within the party. Entitled 'Mária Schmidt *ante portas*' and published under a pseudonym, the article accused the organizers of the previous discussions, including several more moderate politicians of the party, János Áder for instance, of conspiring against Orbán. The message of the piece was clear to everyone: 'Hands off Viktor Orbán'.

One year after this second election defeat, the increasingly aggressive Orbán had again won back his power from the moderates. Through the crusade against the 'lying enemy' to protect democracy and the nation, he had restored his tarnished glory, and he presented himself as a heroic leader who never gives up in battle. From this point on Fidesz kept up a constant barrage of attacks and campaigns against the government parties, which were unable to escape from the assault for a minute.

The Chieftain Comes to Power

On 5 September 2009, well-dressed women and men arrived keen and expectant for a cheerful, family-friendly picnic. Politicians, artists, journalists, priests, business people and their excited children gathered in the garden of the manor house of the small village of Kötcse to discuss the future of the country over typical Hungarian food cooked in a cauldron over a fire. Those present numbered about five hundred, and included members of the many scholarly and public societies formed in the previous years, the 'entire intellectual power of the right wing', as Orbán put it.[56] Unlike in previous years, when the aim of the meeting had been to encourage and unify the frustrated company, another mood now reigned. They were preparing for Fidesz to win in the elections six months later, and they would be the people on whom Orbán based his new era.

In his speech at this meeting, the text of which was later published under the title 'Retaining the Hungarian quality of life', Orbán said that post-socialist power politics and the governance of the liberal elite had ultimately failed and a new era would begin, and the right wing should prepare to govern for the next fifteen to twenty years. He recommended that 'instead of politics designed for constant battle, we must choose politics for constant governance [...] to represent certain national issues with persuasive power'. Speaking of the task of the government, he said: 'The ideal incumbent Hungarian government must be guided by the recognition that the community of Hungarians, and even the Hungarian quality of life, derives partly from the fact that we have a unique way of seeing things, the way we describe, understand, perceive and express the world around us'.[57] Orbán's enigmatic ideas outlined a radical concept: the replacement of an entire elite, using the power and tools of government.

Fidesz's landslide election victory in 2010 overrode Orbán's earlier errors, concealed the frustration arising from his awkward radicalism, and confirmed belief in the leader's special capabilities and infallibility. In 2010 the way was open for the creation of an elite that met the needs of the regime.

Orbán considered electoral victory as being given a personal mandate by the will of the people to implement a regime-changing form of governance: not to implement a specific programme in the conventional sense, but to govern as a leader in the interests of the people as he saw it, and if necessary to rewrite the rules.[58]

At the same time, the majority of Fidesz MPs, whom Orbán had chosen for the task, had neither professional nor significant political achievements to show for themselves. As an opposition MP, I later had a few rare opportunities to gain insight into Fidesz's strange world. I learned that the leader of Fidesz's parliamentary group asked various MPs to submit amendments but gave them minimal information about the bills. The MPs often received the text of the submission speech only on the morning of the day of the debate, which meant that sometimes they had hardly any idea of what the amendment bearing their name was about. Fidesz MPs are disciplined party soldiers. In their own small towns, they may be the lords of local life, the distributors of government funds and of cosy local positions of power, but this power lasts only as long as they adhere to the iron law of Viktor Orbán's party. The rules are simple: follow the leader's decisions, fight tooth and nail for the goals he sets, and carry out the tasks assigned to the utmost, whatever they may be. One of the main characteristics of Orbán's use of power is keeping things constantly in motion, which means chronic unpredictability not just for rivals, but for his followers too.

With the 'revolution at the polls', Orbán strove for the construction of a new order, generated by and linked to him, in key segments of the country. There was a far-reaching replacement of staff in the government apparatus. Orbán ensured that no independent power could be accumulated in the hands of anyone in either the political or the business domain. So that nobody could interfere in his decisions, Orbán kept his thoughts on appointments secret until the last minute. Orbán's characteristic informality demanded nerve-racking flexibility even from his own political clientele.

In Fidesz circles, the influence of players depends not on their skill, abilities or position in the institution, but only on their personal relationship to Orbán. The Fidesz elite explains this level of informality by saying that since Orbán is the exclusive embodiment of heroism and the national interest through the mandate gained in the elections, loyalty to him is the only standard of merit. Orbán trusts people, not institutions, and this is precisely why he has entrusted the most important state institutions to his own friends, who go back further than the foundation of Fidesz.

Meanwhile, even among the members of the cabinet there were few who had direct access to the prime minister. 'Everyone is under the misapprehension that people Orbán allows close to him must be influential, but it's just the opposite. Those close to Orbán are consumable goods', explained a veteran Fidesz politician.[59] In the twelve years of Orbán's regime, the rise and fall of politicians thought to be the strongest has been apparent even to outside observers.

Also very typical is how Orbán 'left nobody by the wayside'. When they are shown the door, politicians and standard-bearers are given a considerable position in the wide-ranging institutional network of the party-state, which guarantees them a stable livelihood. Exploited and humiliated politicians and business people are carefully paid off: this is Orbán's way of buying their silence.

The other characteristic of Orbán's use of power is the constant fostering of competition between clients. In Fidesz's enormous conglomerate, there are now many power groups based on ideology or personal or business interests, whose aim it is to increase their influence within the system. These interest groups do not join to form a counter-elite, because the prime minister plays them off against one another, one by one, as we will see in forthcoming chapters. Just as the 'national business people' set up in the business world are forced to compete with one another for Orbán's favours, a similar modus operandi plays out in the political arena. When filling each post, Orbán dangles the position before a few people and decides on the basis of their reaction. A couple of months before his mandate expired, a Constitutional Court justice confided to me that he feared Orbán would tell him only on the last day of his term of office whether he would nominate him for another term or whether he would recommend someone else. He desperately wanted an extension and couldn't contemplate not being able to continue in his office. In the end his term was not renewed. The elite of the Fidesz regime is full of frustrated people, and yet everyone tries to remain in the system, which depends purely on Orbán's favours.

As Orbán confronted Hungary's Western allies more frequently, he put more confrontational politicians in the diplomatic battle lines. In 2014 he placed Péter Szijjártó, an able, ambitious politician, ready to go on the offensive abroad, as foreign minister, and Judit Varga, a well-trained lawyer, as minister of justice, and tasked her with representing the frequently indefensible policies of the Hungarian government. The almost incomprehensible commitment of these young and often well-trained experts shows that there are plenty of people willing to subject themselves to Orbán's questionable methods, because beside the leader they can taste the intoxicating flavour of power.

Without Orbán There Is Nothing

After Orbán replaced both the government and the leaders of state institutions with people faithful to him, the Fidesz party became indistinguishably one with the government and the state. In this system, the significance of political parties, Parliament and advocacy groups has diminished, and the visible boundaries between institutions have disappeared. This obscurity and uncertainty, the creation of relative order, all serve the personal power interests of Viktor Orbán.

From the late 1990s, Fidesz militantly supported the reinforcement of the right-wing elite, because it was convinced that the cultural elite consisted of a majority of left-wing, liberal figures. After a series of successive Orbán governments there is now a system centralized to the extreme. A new party elite has been built up where a few highly powerful people dominate the business, cultural and social worlds far beyond their official scope of authority.[60]

Although Fidesz has expanded and entrenched its own power to an unprecedented degree, the wide-ranging and opaque system is held together by the person of Viktor Orbán. His rule rests on two factors: heroics and the autocratic exercise of power. The heroic myth is fed by the belief that the leader never backs down; in fact, the enemies he takes on get bigger and bigger. The crusade against George Soros (see Chapter 8), or the years of carefully designed combat with the EU, all serve the purpose of showing that the leader can flex his power again and again, and reinforce his believers' conviction that he is invincible.

If there is one thing that characterizes Orbán's power and ability over the past decades to surpass every player in Hungarian politics, often cleverer and more pleasing than he, it is that whatever he does, he does so with 1,000 per cent conviction. He believes that if he wants something, then sooner or later he can get it. He takes on huge risks and is prepared to pay a great price for them, drawing into this the people around him, his party and the entire country. This is the one thing that has been constant throughout his political career.

* * *

WITHOUT ORBÁN, THERE'S NOTHING

Fidesz's founding generation entered politics at a transformative historic moment. Being in power in government so young created the idea that Fidesz was born to lead Hungary, and that for its leaders politics is not just a profession: it is a destiny. Orbán's self-image as a chosen leader and his tenacious personality weighed decisively on how the party has transformed over the decades. Far beyond Fidesz, he built a political tribe that consider him a hero.

For his supporters, Orbán's charisma is not eroded by the scandals that break out in Fidesz from time to time, whether they be lies, allegations of corruption or accusations of violence. But over time they may accumulate, and it may become difficult to manage them, and the charisma of the leader might disappear in a flash. A change like that would rapidly undermine Fidesz's still apparently indisputable strength and power.

Those in the party are optimistic about the future. 'Fidesz sticks to a tried and tested system. When the time comes for a successor, the competition will not be about what to replace Orbánism with, but about who will represent it most faithfully, perhaps even against Viktor Orbán himself. [...] The prime minister has put together a durable system'.[61]

But given the fundamental uncertainty and informality in the party, it is difficult to imagine anyone in the Fidesz elite becoming the successor of the leader. Far more likely is that eventually Fidesz will face a grave succession crisis, and a cruel battle for power or for survival will ensue.

2

'MY WORLDVIEW IS HUNGARIAN'
THE IDEOLOGY OF ORBÁNISM

In August 2021, Tucker Carlson, the notorious political commentator on US Fox News, took the unusual step of broadcasting his popular politics programme from Hungary for four days. The background of his studio showed one of Hungary's finest panoramas, the banks of the Danube and the Buda Castle.

Carlson had been invited to Hungary by Mathias Corvinus Collegium (the talent management centre that Fidesz financed from the state budget with €1.5 billion)[1] and was given a state welcome: in the course of five days he met Viktor Orbán three times. He also accompanied the deputy minister as they flew in a helicopter along the 175-kilometre Hungarian–Serbian border, and noted with surprise that he saw no refugees, even though it was no hi-tech wall, simply a cheap barbed wire fence protecting the Hungarian border from aliens. The conclusion he drew was that this was the result of decisive political willpower.[2]

When he sat down with Viktor Orbán for an interview, his first question was why, unlike other European countries, Orbán decided in 2015 to close the border to refugees. Orbán's reply was that this was the only reasonable behaviour 'coming from the God, the nature [*sic*]'; after all, 'we had to protect our country, our history, and our language'.³

The two men hit it off well together. For days, the Hungarian government-friendly media conglomerate featured Carlson's doings in Hungary and presented him as the most influential conservative thinker in America. Carlson in turn expressed his gratitude by confirming that Viktor Orbán, whom the Americans already respected as a hero thirty years previously as one of the leaders of the struggle against Soviet occupation, was a true fighter for democracy.⁴ He pointed to Orbán's Hungary as a positive example for Americans, saying that 'a country based on traditional values, national identity, and Christian traditions can be successful, sometimes more successful, than a left-wing liberal government'.⁵

Despite Orbán and Carlson managing to contradict each other, for instance, on Covid vaccination,⁶ homosexuality, and Orbán's China policy, they swept these contradictions aside. These two men found common ground in the unrelenting culture war against liberals.

Carlson's visit was part of a campaign in which Orbán tried to sell his regime as a successful project to the world, one with an independent ideology. To construct and disseminate this ideology, Orbán's government has spent hundreds of billions of forints of public money. Internal contradictions pose no difficulty within the ideology of 'Orbánism'; after all, it draws on many different, conflicting sources and has the primary aim of supporting the changing political goals of the Fidesz leader. The fact that ideology is merely a political product whose purpose is to support considerations of power politics took hold in Fidesz in the mid-1990s when the party repositioned itself as a right-wing party, a move that required a considerable redefinition of its values. Still, it was bewildering to watch how successfully Orbán shifted a great number of progressive and agnostic Hungarians in the direction of political Christianism and radical intolerance.

Nationalism in Hungary

Many people who visit Hungary for extended periods will be familiar with Hungarians' special brand of nationalism, which is based on a deep-seated sense of grievance. This has its origin in the fact that Hungary, as part of the Austro-Hungarian Empire, was defeated in the First World War. Two thirds of Hungarian territory was given to neighbouring countries, along with one third of the ethnically Hungarian population. During the peace conference in Versailles, in the Grand Trianon chateau, the Treaty of Trianon, so tragic and humiliating for Hungary, was signed. To this day, the Trianon trauma is a determinant element of Hungarian political thinking.

In the reactionary conservative period between the two world wars, the ruling elite tried to reverse the past by pursuing nationalist and revisionist politics based on grievances and losses. It maintained the myth of a glorious, strong and great Hungarian nation, while trying to defuse collective frustration by looking for external and internal enemies, such as progressives, communists and the West. It hoped for a brighter future by regaining the lost territories. As a result of political nationalism, in the 1930s anti-Semitism gained ground, as did xenophobia directed at neighbouring peoples. Because of the grievance-based revisionist politics, Hungary sided with Nazi Germany in the Second World War. Much of the hostility and intensity of the ideological conflict in Hungary, as well as some of the Hungarian right's animosity towards the West, originated in this period.

During communism, even the Kádár regime had to make something of the concept of the nation and national sovereignty in order to stabilize its position. Because the Trianon grievance was taboo until the 1970s, the regime developed a concept of nation not based on national sovereignty, but on a rise in the standard of living, and the liberation of the private individual as a surrogate ideology for a post-national social order.

The core of the Kádár 'consensus' was that you could live freely in your private life but should not strive to intervene in public matters; in return, the government constantly raised the standard of living. With this 'goulash communism', Hungary became the merriest of barracks in the socialist bloc.

In the 1980s the cracks in the socialist system were starting to show in the countries of the communist bloc, which led to a rise in the oppression of Hungarian minorities outside Hungary. The cause of a Hungarian nation united across borders was promoted most actively by a small group composed mainly of writers, the so-called traditionalist thinkers. My grandfather Péterfia, who raised ten children, was very active in this intellectual circle.

But in Hungary under Kádárism, only a few shared these concerns. In the Hungary of 'goulash communism', the regime was built on welfare chauvinism: most people believed it was better to be Hungarian than one of the other peoples in Eastern Europe, because life was better in Hungary. The belief that 'we are the best' as opposed to 'everyone is attacking us' was reassuring and filled people with pride, something I felt even as a child.

The Renaissance of Nationalism after 1989

By 1989 it had become clear that the only way to build a successful nation was within a democratic framework. But at the time of the regime change, thinking about the nation was split into divergent camps. For the nascent right-wing democratic parties the idea of the nation was of utmost importance, while liberal parties organized their ideas more around modernization. The liberal and socialist parties were unable to exploit the power of national identity and nation to build a community, partly for historical reasons, and partly because in the 1990s the intellectual elite in Europe (to which the intellectual groups of Eastern European countries wished to belong) had an overall negative attitude to nationalism.

József Antall, Hungary's first freely elected prime minister, was well aware that the emergence of an emotional attachment to the idea of the nation was a crucial issue in the new Hungary. But as a historian, Antall also knew that the trauma of Trianon, dormant for seventy years, might revive the interwar nationalism based on feelings of cultural superiority.

However, the heavy burdens of the first years of regime change eroded the position of moderate conservatives. The right-wing politician István Csurka, a former playwright, was the first to open the can of worms with its old, dark myths: the spirit of nationalism and anti-communism in 1992. He believed that the failures of his own governing party were due to communists and Jews. In one of his political pamphlets he wrote:

> Back then, behind the communist henchmen, killers, those who urinated in mouths and tore off fingernails, lay [Soviet military officer Kliment] Voroshilov's Allied Control Commission and the occupying Red Army, while behind the regime change's financial elite lies the International Monetary Fund. The squad members of the former nomenklatura are lurking in the wings.[7]

This article stirred up an enormous political storm. On behalf of Fidesz, László Kövér gave an excellent speech in Parliament, in which he stated that Csurka's article:

> reeks of anti-Semitism, a deep disdain for democratic tinkering, a striving for exclusive power, an intention to deploy state forces for political ends, the stigmatization of political opponents as enemies, and the exclusion from the nation of those who consider the interests of the country are to be served in a different manner.

He said the text 'laid down the foundations for a new generation of Hungarian Nazism'.[8]

In contrast to Fidesz's current strident nationalism and exclusionary politics, in the early days of Fidesz we thought very soberly about the issue of the nation. We were aware of Hungary's political development, which included both the post-Trianon ethno-nationalism that thrust the country into a historical dead end and the oppressive communist experience that negated the nation.

Fidesz shaped its concept of the nation within a democratic framework of modernization. We believed that a democratic and free Hungary based on a market economy would be able to help Hungarians in neighbouring countries in their striving for autonomy. We were confident that in the open world of the European Community, national boundaries between us would become virtual. As regards national identity, our national slogan was 'a Hungarian is someone who declares themselves to be Hungarian'. We proposed that the Hungarian state should represent the entire community of Hungarians and take steps to resolve the problems of minorities—for instance, the social exclusion of Roma.[9] First and foremost, this was a vision of a democratic, egalitarian society based on individual freedoms and rights, supplemented with a stance on the collective rights of the Hungarian community.

In 1990 Fidesz held a 'free university' and student camp in Bálványosfürdő (Băile Bálványos), a beautiful town in Szeklerland in Romania with a majority Hungarian population. The aim of the meeting was to promote cooperation between Hungarians across the border, and the exchange of political ideas between Romanians and Hungarians. The changes in the tone and structure of the camp, which has been held annually ever since, give an accurate picture of the evolution of Fidesz's thinking.

At the beginning of the 1990s, the new Hungarian identity was contradictory. The issue of the nation was incorporated into

Hungarian political discourse, and there was much open, modern and democratic thinking and discussion of attitudes to the nation, organized around the idea of Europe. Despite a sense of xenophobia, anti-Semitism and economic nationalism, promoted only by some minor political groups, there was a theoretical possibility that a modern national consciousness might emerge in Hungary.[10]

When liberal Fidesz shifted to the right in the mid-1990s, it tried to co-opt the floundering 'traditionalist'–right-wing (*népi*) coalition. To reach its voters the party had to undergo a large-scale ideological transformation, but it could rely on the liberal-national intellectual and relationship capital it had accumulated earlier.

The ideology-free, technocratic, post-communist MSZP government was unable to provide a powerful image of the Hungarian nation. The liberal SZDSZ rejected the traditionalists' nationalism and anti-Westernism, and thus the question of Hungarians living in minorities became marginal. Fidesz moved in to fill the gap. Shifting to the right, the party identified its new political opponents as the parties of the 'nationless' socialist and liberals. Fidesz's new attitude had an ethno-cultural basis.

Orbán's assessment was that national identity met important socio-psychological needs at a time of frustration with the post-communist transformation, when society had to bear both an economic crisis and a culture shock. The emotional ties that created the Fidesz political camp were cemented together with patriotic feeling and traditional right-wing anti-communism.

My Worldview Is Hungarian: In the Guise of Rhetoric about 'Nation'

In his first term in office between 1998 and 2002, Orbán defined Fidesz as a centre-right party with civic, national sensitivities.[11] In government, it pursued a culturally traditional right-wing politics, complementing it with measures like raising the minimum wage and introducing a home-building programme, student loans and family subsidies. In its narrative, Fidesz used civic and etatist, nationalist and pro-Europe, socialist and conservative elements, depending on the demands of realpolitik. This gave it enormous flexibility in the battle for power.

This ideological miscellany was concealed by successfully constructed rhetoric about the nation. With the millennium celebrations and the national exhibition 'Dreamers of dreams', it may have seemed that Orbán's government was genuinely realizing Hungarians' dreams. On 20 August 2000, at the main ceremony celebrating the millennium of the founding of the Hungarian state, Orbán said:

> There has to be a Hungarian dream once more: a wealthy and strong Hungary, which we, confident in ourselves, have built. [...] The shared dream of Hungarians stranded outside, and those living in the mother country—the dream of us all to whom it is given to belong to this nation. Because no limits can be set to dreams![12]

In parallel with this, the Fidesz-led coalition opened new opportunities to Hungarians living in neighbouring countries. In order to promote identification with national culture and the 'unification of the nation' across borders, in 2001 the Parliament passed what was known as the status law. This eased the conditions for those of Hungarian ethnicity living abroad to travel to Hungary, study and work, and promoted the founding of transnational Hungarian cultural and educational institutions. The response of opposition socialist politicians was insensitive and demagogic: they said the agreement enabled 23 million Romanian workers to come to Hungary.[13] These maladroit political utterances contributed to the view that the issue of Hungarian minorities meant nothing to the left-wing and liberal parties.

'MY WORLDVIEW IS HUNGARIAN'

By 2002 Orbán had managed to achieve what Antall had failed to do: he complemented the national narrative with professional political communications and impressive accomplishments. Powerful symbolic gestures were linked to the government's everyday politics, and the success of the nation was made into something anyone could experience. 'My worldview is neither liberal nor conservative, neither retrograde nor progressive; it is simply a Hungarian worldview', said Orbán in an election campaign speech in 2002.[14] By the end of his first term as prime minister, Orbán had addressed many very different social groups with this 'Hungarian philosophy', groups bound together not by shared interests, but by a strong emotional tie. It appeared this was the perfect recipe for victory.

The Theft of the Cockade

The 2002 elections took place two weeks after 15 March, the anniversary of the 1848 revolution and the War of Independence. On this day, following the tradition of the bourgeois revolution, we Hungarians wear a cockade in the national colours on our overcoats. This is perhaps the only national symbol of which every Hungarian is equally proud.

On the anniversary, Orbán gave a speech as usual, and started an unexpected mobilization campaign. 'Whoever is Hungarian is with us!' he shouted, and he asked people to join the 'national ribbon movement' and not to remove the cockade after the anniversary, but to wear it right up to election day, thereby demonstrating their national feelings.[15] I remember how embarrassing it was in the following days at work, at my children's kindergarten, on the tram and in shops, when it became explicitly obvious who was one of Orbán's believers and who was not. The scandal was not just that Orbán had appropriated a symbol important to all of us, but that he forced people into publicly adopting a political position. With the wearing of the cockade Orbán pulled his supporters into a political battle, where they found themselves on the 'national side' against the forces 'alien to the nation'. Many people found it uncomfortable having to decide at Orbán's command which camp they belonged to. In 2002 politics crept into everyone's life and divided and polarized the country.

However, in the short term, the cockade campaign did not bear out the hopes pinned on it. The appropriation of the national symbol as a party badge went beyond the issue of choosing democratic values, and rather than Orbán's believers, it was his opposition who were angered and mobilized into taking part in the elections. Fidesz lost. Although nationalism had become a basic element of Orbán's 'power toolkit', it was in vain supported by government policies and professional campaigning: it proved to be insufficient to retain power. As a means of uniting the Fidesz camp, however, it proved to be a good tool and deepened Hungary's political divisions.

The nationalist mobilization emboldened more radical groups than Fidesz. In 2004, an NGO called the World Federation of Hungarians, which has as its main aim to keep alive the 'spirit of Trianon', proposed that Hungarians living outside the borders should receive dual citizenship, with the right to vote. In this awkward and confrontational situation, the political parties were forced to show their colours: until then none of the parliamentary parties had supported this policy, not even Fidesz. Now, however, the tables were turned, and Fidesz, which considered itself the only representative of the Hungarian nation, took up the cause of a referendum on the introduction of dual citizenship for ethnic Hungarians. In this issue, the socialist prime minister Ferenc Gyurcsány, who wanted to show that he could triumph over Viktor Orbán, also put forward his national programme. He said that 'the government has a duty to Hungarian citizens, it has responsibility for those living beyond the borders, but responsibility cannot override duty, and retaining one's duty cannot reduce responsibility'.[16]

'MY WORLDVIEW IS HUNGARIAN'

However, this point of view was too complex, and so the party eventually used a demagogic form of reasoning that could be put across simply: 'No to paying 20,000 HUF a week from the family money! No to paying with our jobs for cheap workers from beyond the borders! No to paying with our dreams, because the housing situation will be more difficult!' The Socialist Party flyers carried these alarmist texts all over the country.

Despite Gyurcsány's effort to devise a concept of the nation within state borders, the demagogic campaign, built on the memory of Kádárist 'welfare socialism', was alienating compared with Fidesz's nation-based approach. The legacy of Kádárist 'welfare chauvinism' had become rooted in the Hungarian collective psyche. Years afterwards it appeared in the far-right Jobbik party, which whipped up sentiment against the Roma, and ten years later Viktor Orbán played on the same feelings in his anti-refugee campaign.[17]

The view put forward in the 2004 referendum utterly destroyed the credibility of the socialist and liberal parties when they spoke about the nation. Fidesz, on the other hand, presented the issue of dual nationality as an emotional, moral question. While the campaign was in full swing, Orbán said: 'On 5 December two worldviews collide, and we have to decide whether we measure everything in money, or if there are things more important [...] such as freedom, the freedom of Hungarians beyond the borders. [...] This is a question to which every self-respecting Hungarian can only answer: yes'.[18]

Despite Fidesz having opposed dual citizenship three years earlier, in this campaign it branded 'no' voters as traitors of the nation. People were once more put in a conflicted situation. It seemed problematic to give citizenship en masse to people who had never lived in Hungary and had no share of public responsibilities, yet at the same time an outright rejection of this welcoming gesture seemed uncomfortable.

In spite of the huge mobilization, the referendum did not deliver the number of votes required to be valid, although 'yes' voters had a small majority: in 2004, it was not (yet) possible to win with moralizing identity politics.

Congealed Structures: Anti-Communism after the Regime Change

At the time of the regime change the reviving right wing, the liberals and the critical left wing were all anti-communist. The post-communist party, MSZP, was a mixed group of populists and ideology-free technocrats, and joined the Western European social democratic bloc. Owing to the often uncritical hopes placed in the market economy, a traditional socialist party could not find a foothold in post-regime change Hungary.

At the same time, because of the negotiated transition and lustration laws (which would have excluded leaders of the old nomenklatura from high office), there was no clear distinction between the old and the new elites in Hungary. As I will discuss later, in many cases influential figures in the media and the economy from the previous period remained in their positions.

As a young politician, I was irritated when socialist MPs portrayed themselves in international forums as fighters for social democratic values and democracy. I thought they were inauthentic. The rapid return to political power of the Socialist Party in 1994 was difficult for many of us to swallow. At the same time, it was clear that this party was adapting extremely well to the expectations of multi-party democracy: it was developing democratic institutions and was not trying to restore the one-party system. To emphasize this, the MSZP admitted the liberal SZDSZ into the government even though they had enough of a majority to form a government without it.

'MY WORLDVIEW IS HUNGARIAN'

However, this political development triggered a deep fear of an existential crisis in the right-wing elite. One theorist, Gyula Tellér, argued that the 'congealed structures' remaining from the communist past ensured a powerful economic background and degree of social embeddedness that allowed for continued Kádárism, with the purpose of paralysing the democratic transition.[19] For the right wing, 'post-communist' meant not someone who believed in communist principles (after all, such people were very rare in Hungary), but the officials and functionaries of the former elite and the hidden network linked to them. The paranoid reasoning of the 'congealed structures' or 'deep state' theory had an elemental influence on the imagination of the right wing after its loss of power in 1994. They declared that in contrast to morally contemptible communism, they represented the truth, and so an all-out war was to be fought against communists. This visceral anger and fear made any appraisal of the realistic risks and dangers of a return of a socialist party quite impossible.

As Fidesz turned to the right, a key goal was to amplify anti-communism. Most of the media and intelligentsia considered this change of ideology a betrayal of Fidesz's original liberal principles, one that could not be defended by reasonable arguments. But after we left the party, in 1994 Orbán's people immediately began to rewrite the original history of Fidesz, shifting the focus to anti-communism rather than liberalism. From the texts, films and photos about the formation of Fidesz and its first years, they 'edited out' the liberals who had left the party, and who no longer fitted into its rewritten history. Seen from this point of view, the ideological switch was no longer so grave: anti-communism was the bridge that enabled Orbán to walk over to the other side. Party leaders, MPs and the wider membership could believe that Fidesz had remained true to itself.

Even in 2010, anti-communist feeling, coupled with the fear of a return of the Kádárist elite, was able to forge the party's believers into a united body, even while Fidesz co-opted former state party leaders and apparatchiks by the dozen into its own elite ranks.[20]

The New Right Wing and Illiberalism

The 2000s was considered by many, rather simplistically, as yet another U-turn and a manifestation of populist politics, but in actual fact it reflected a deeper change in Viktor Orbán's thinking about the essence of politics. In this, he had a number of intellectual bedfellows.

Ideologists of Radical Conservatism

In 2002, conservative philosopher András Lánczi published a piece entitled *Konzervatív Kiáltvány* (Conservative manifesto).[21] According to him, a true regime change had not taken place, because communist ways of thinking were still rooted in people, for instance, notions of economic equality, the perception that social peace could be attained without politics, and the idea that progress brings a solution to every problem.

According to Lánczi, a true regime change could only be achieved through conservative politics, which, in contrast to communism, has morality as its foundation, enabling human values to flourish to the greatest possible extent. He believed that conservative ideals such as objective truth, traditions upheld by natural communities (that is, the family, small communities and the nation), and order and authority based on hierarchy could not flourish because the conservative ideal had been identified as unenlightened and brought into disrepute. After Fidesz's defeat, Lánczi concluded that since traditional conservatives had not managed to overcome post-communism, true regime change could come about only by more radical means, and conservatives must be prepared to take steps alien to them.[22]

'MY WORLDVIEW IS HUNGARIAN'

Lánczi's work represented a 'realist' turn in conservative thinking, which proclaimed that politics first and foremost is about power, that political action takes priority over institutional checks, and that the collective choice of values of the political community is more important than the choice of the individual. Political leadership emphasized the significance of power and authority, and the importance of citizens' duties and obligations.[23]

Lánczi's radical conservative creed went against the liberal consensus that had hitherto been followed by political thinkers in Hungary, and it did so in order enlarge the toolkit in the political struggle against the governing socialist and liberal parties, thereby opening a way for Orbán's power-centred, anti-liberal, revolutionary brand of politics.[24] This approach can be seen in Orbán's political logic, in which the essence of Hungarian politics is nothing but the struggle between post-communist forces linked to the old regime and the regime-changing 'national' forces. This approach to politics lay closest to the anti-liberal tenets developed in the 1920s by Carl Schmitt, a controversial German legal theorist who joined the Nazis in 1933, which proclaimed a strong state and the sovereignty of the leader.[25] Schmitt declared that the most important task of politics was to retain the ability to act. In politics Schmitt drew a distinction between friends and enemies, and he saw politics as a war. He argued that parliamentarianism (government by discussion) belonged to the world of liberalism and was not part of democracy. The leading threads in Schmitt's theory can be found in anti-pluralism, the unity of the state, and the defence of the state.[26]

Schmitt's ideas are reflected in Fidesz's assumption of the 'unified will of the voters' and the cult of power, and this was coupled with a strong anti-communism. Because Fidesz was in opposition in the years after the 2002 electoral defeat, Orbán created a sense of political power through constant mobilization and campaigns, for instance when Fidesz politicians dismantled the cordon around Parliament in the winter of 2007 so that protesters could get closer to the Parliament building. The notion of radical conservatism contributed to the outbreak of an increasingly brutal cold civil war in the first decade of the 2000s.[27]

Following the model of American radical conservatives, who argued for conservative counter-culture,[28] to accustom folk to the new thinking, Fidesz innovated in its use of political language, and founded institutions and publications.[29] Radical conservatism, although it was based on the opposition of 'us and them' and mobilized people against the elite, was not actually populism, since it did not want to put anything at all in the hands of the people; rather, it deliberately aimed to put a new economic, political and cultural elite into power.

In the early 2000s radical conservatism was also being kindled in other countries in Eastern Europe.[30] Bulgarian political scientist Ivan Krastev believed at the time that this politics criticized not liberalism as a whole, but only the form in which it was manifest in Eastern Europe: namely, the state; here voters can replace the government, though they cannot replace the neoliberal policies that are in line with the European zeitgeist.[31] Initially this was indeed the case, and Fidesz strove primarily to even out the balance of power. In the meantime, however, the world changed fundamentally. The 2008 financial meltdown reinforced the radical conservatives in their conviction that the liberal West had moved into a state of final crisis. When Orbán returned to power in 2010 his new political lexicon included terms such as the state, force, political greatness, public good, patriotism, and national interest. In the name of the Schmittian 'just state', the government legitimized retroactive legislation and deliberately discriminatory laws with a two-thirds majority. Orbán set to work with openly anti-liberal policies, and believed that he would not meet serious resistance from the West.

'MY WORLDVIEW IS HUNGARIAN'

An Open Rejection of Liberalism

Fidesz's internal transformation was exemplified by the trajectory of the Bálványos summer 'free university', once a forum for open debate and reflection, latterly a one-man show. In the years after 2010 one programme of the festival in particular triggered a great deal of interest: when Viktor Orbán's philosophical lecture explained the world to his believers. A pivotal moment occurred in the summer of 2014 when Orbán's speech created a stir in the international political arena.[32] The prime minister openly stated that the regime being built in Hungary did not follow liberal ideas of the organization of society. It was based not on a set of individuals, but on a community, Orbán said, which ultimately was an 'illiberal state'.[33] As examples, he held up Singapore, India, Turkey and Russia. This was the moment when most of the Western world faced up to what was happening in Hungary, even though anti-liberal politics had been forming within Fidesz for ten years with the intellectual support of radical conservatives.

The concept of 'illiberal democracy' was originally introduced by Fareed Zakaria to describe non-Western systems that call themselves democratic but where democracy and the rule of the people based on elections are not coupled with liberalism.[34] In these countries there are no legal guarantees for the rights of the individual; the separation of the branches of power does not function, and thus power is not counterbalanced by the necessary institutions; and the rule of law does not guarantee freedom of the press, of speech or of religion.

In his speech in Bálványos, Orbán depicted the system of checks and balances as superfluous and aired the conspiracy theory according to which the surveillance and registration of NGOs was justified because 'here we are not facing NGOs, but political activists financed by foreign interests' (see Chapter 9). The speech was surprising even for us in the Hungarian opposition, although we knew very well that Orbán had already built up the means to maintain excessive power in Hungary. After another two-thirds majority victory in 2014, the Hungarian prime minister considered the time was ripe to proclaim the centralized state and anti-liberal politics to the international public too.

Although Orbán borrowed the expression from Zakaria, his thinking shows much greater similarity to the radical right-wing ideas of the American political scientist Patrick J. Deneen and the English conservative philosopher Roger Scruton, who both subscribe to the view that the world is in such deep economic, political and moral peril that only a radical change can save it. Characteristic of both thinkers is that they speak of liberalism as a unified ideology which, after the failure of fascism and communism, was the only ideology still on the stage at the end of the twentieth century but has now reached a state of crisis.

Deneen suggested that turning back to the rules of community and traditions, and to responsibility to the nation and the natural hierarchy, will give an answer to questions in the future too.[35] Scruton considered authority and law to be the most important factors in conservatism; freedom was thus made subject to higher-ranking values. In his view, the aim of the state was to protect the existing hierarchy and ensure social order. He insisted that conservatives were at a disadvantage, and thus needed to be stronger, more cunning and more Machiavellian than their opponents.[36]

In the 2000s Hungarian radical conservative outlets began to publish works by Deneen and Scruton, which, in addition to the points above, lambasted multiculturalism and the culture of political correctness, and emphasized the importance of family and religion. Orbán met Deneen personally in 2019,[37] and awarded Scruton a Hungarian state decoration the year before

'MY WORLDVIEW IS HUNGARIAN'

he died.[38] Deneen and Scruton provided good ammunition for Orbán, though this did not mean that they were on the same wavelength regarding nationalism and the strong state.

Anti-Immigration with No Immigrants in Sight

For a long time Fidesz distanced itself from open xenophobia. In Hungary it was Jobbik, a party with anti-Roma slogans and intimidating campaigns, that in the first decade of the 2000s revived and reinforced the radical far-right movement, which had previously been considered an oddity. While it was not particularly strong, Fidesz had nothing against Jobbik's activity, and this allowed Fidesz to assert that it was positioned in the centre. But as Jobbik grew stronger and, restraining its most extreme politicians, moved to a more moderate politics, it became a threat to Fidesz. After the 2014 elections Fidesz's popularity began to wane, and Jobbik's grew. When a year later refugees arrived in Hungary, Orbán suddenly switched to an anti-immigration line, and the country was covered with Fidesz's posters: 'If you come to Hungary, you can't take Hungarians' jobs!' (see Chapter 8). This xenophobia was partly a tactical manoeuvre: Orbán decided that with harsh anti-immigration slogans the party could outdo Jobbik on the right.

Orbán spoke of a clash of civilizations, while criticizing the West for being dishonest about the dangers of immigration, and demanding they remove the muzzle of political correctness.[39] Opposing the plan for a common refugee policy, in his battle against the European Union Orbán demanded national sovereignty and turned it into political action: he built a border fence, criminalized unauthorized crossing of the border, and made it practically impossible for refugees fleeing to Hungary to enter the country legally or get refugee status.

Presenting Migration as an Existential Threat

In 2015 government-financed pundits came forward as experts on migration, demographics and terrorism prevention, and flooded the Fidesz media with their pseudo-scholarly opinions. Mária Schmidt, a Fidesz historian quoted several times in this book, spread the conspiracy theory that someone had 'set an enormous demographic surplus on an experimental journey'.[40] Soon Fidesz had established a Migration Research Institute, which churned out op-ed pieces on matters such as 'the security risks of Swedish immigration',[41] the link between migration and terrorism,[42] and no-go areas in Western Europe. Their 'analyses' focused on topics such as the relationship between progressive parties in Western Europe and Muslim voters.[43] This misinformation spread through Fidesz's media like wildfire.

The ruling party put across the message that while Fidesz protected the country against dangerous intruders, left-wing parties and human rights organizations were 'on the side of the aliens'. As the prime minister put it: 'the Hungarian left wing [...] would now welcome the illegal immigrants with open arms. These people, these politicians quite simply do not like Hungarians, and the reason they do not like them is because they are Hungarian'.[44]

Orbán coupled deep xenophobia with appeals to national sentiment, bringing out the existential fears voiced earlier by the Hungarian radical right wing. The first to lay out such theories on paper was István Csurka in 1998:

> The ultimate goal is to destroy the Hungarian community. [...] This time in which we live and especially the one to come in the coming century is the era of Migration of Peoples. Peoples with coloured skin living in immeasurable poverty but multiplying by the dozen migrate from east to west, from south to north. International big capital and banks assist in this migration of peoples, because it is in their interest.[45]

At the time, this text put him on the far edge of the political spectrum. By 2015 this frenzied fabrication had now become the official standpoint of the Fidesz government. Moreover, Fidesz proposed a broader, 'great replacement' discourse, similar to that of the European and US radical conservative right.

Although the demographic panic fitted into the traditions of the Hungarian right wing, the systematic messaging of the danger affected a considerable part of the population. When the Fidesz campaign set up 'unnatural' liberal notions such as liberty or humanity against the natural order, it aimed primarily at these people. The anti-Enlightenment and also anti-West sentiment that placed national collectivism before individualism and human rights turned Scruton's and Deneen's ideas into practice, and it reinforced the concept of an authoritarian state.[46]

Orbán combined the themes of ethnical nationalism, xenophobia, demographical panic and anti-liberalism, portrayed it all as a battle between right- and left-wing ideologies, and thus opened the way for an influx of ideas from radical right-wing forces active in the West. According to the anti-Islam and anti-immigration parties that appeared in multicultural societies from the 2000s, fighting immigration and multiculturalism served to protect Christian values and the European civilization built on them.[47] This chimed in with Orbán's narrative of a conflict of civilizations, first declared during the migration crisis, which thus went beyond the traditional Hungarian nationalism focused on differences with neighbouring peoples. This universal approach made it possible for traditional Eastern European nationalist parties to forge alliances with the Western European anti-immigration radical right and American radicals within the Republican Party.

With the refugee crisis, anti-migration parties all over Europe gained ground, anti-immigrant language became cruder, and even moderate centrist parties shifted to a more pragmatic immigration policy. The election of Donald Trump as US president gave more momentum to exclusionary political forces. The 'civilizational crisis' theme continued to spread.

Orbán's conspiracy theory, in which he accused Hungarian and the West's green, socialist and liberal politicians of working to flood Europe with Muslim immigrants, was incredibly successful. Many extremist Western politicians considered Orbán a hero. Geert Wilders, the leader of the Dutch anti-Islam Party for Freedom, said, 'Orbán has more backbone and character than all the cowards of the EU combined'.[48] The reason Orbán became particularly popular was that, in its position of power, Fidesz was able to mobilize the entire apparatus of the Hungarian state to put its radical ideas into practice. Western extremists were also in awe of Orbán's confrontational personality, the way he stood at the fore of the uprising, continually testing the patience of politicians who adhered to the liberal fundamental values of the European Union, and constantly attacked the bases of liberal democracy. Although Orbán's aggressiveness repelled many Europeans, when he spoke of saving European civilization which rested on a Christian basis, his words rang true for many people in Western Europe. In interviews in the German press, Orbán spoke more cautiously, and, instead of conspiracy theories, he focused on the culture war between ethnicities and religions, because he knew that a more radical line would be unacceptable in German political culture.[49]

Although in 2015 the Hungarian government temporarily found itself face to face with a genuine migration crisis, and reacted to this, that situation very soon changed, because the crisis ceased and the refugees left. But the nativist, exclusivist rhetoric remained. The main reason Orbán appropriated anti-immigrant ideology and maintained it over the years as a political product was to further cement his power. As a result of this destructive politics, even after the 2015 crisis waned it was not possible to form a rational refugee and migration policy that reflected the reality of the twenty-first century either in Hungary or in the European Union.

Political 'Christianism'

Anyone who visited Budapest on 20 August 2021 had the chance to see a very strange event. During the celebration of the foundation of the Hungarian state, there was as usual a street party, a handicraft fair, a wine festival, a Catholic procession, and fireworks to entertain the crowds coming to the city. That year, however, the curious public was enticed with a grand state show called the Feast of Saint Stephen. Spread over several days, the occasion was touted by the government as the greatest festival ever. As well as the usual events, there was a huge, spectacular procession along the streets of Budapest. At the head of the procession were half-naked, muscle-bound men with painted bodies (supposedly representing the ancient Hungarian tribes), hauling a huge shining metal *turul* bird[50] through the city, while shamans chanted. The *turul* was followed by yet more ancient legendary figures, then there appeared an enormous replica of the holy Hungarian crown, and finally a giant statue of Saint Stephen, founder of the state. Between the metal statues were folk dancers, acrobats and fire-eaters, to entertain the audience who had flocked to the streets. On concert stages coloured with clouds of smoke, musicians sang eulogies to the earth, the homeland and the nation. At the end of this mystical techno-show preserving traditions, sixty riders trotting on horseback extended the Hungarian national flag. The highlight of the evening, as usual, was the fireworks, at the end of which a gigantic cross was depicted by drones in the sky over the Danube.

Public opinion on this grandiose show, like everything in Hungary, was sharply divided. In one camp people laughed at the kitsch decorations of the procession, were disgusted at the burden of symbolism associated with the *turul*,[51] and resented the government pulling out all the stops to put on a celebratory show instead of commemorating the 30,000 who had died of Covid-19. But commentators in the Fidesz media viewed the event as one of devotion, deeply moving and spiritually uplifting. In their view, the iconic image of the cross displayed over the Danube and the Parliament was a fitting representation of what the government claimed to embody: Christian Hungary.

The 'Christian Hungary' regime was proclaimed by Viktor Orbán in 2018 in his customary speech at Bálványos. The 'illiberal state' introduced four years previously had become toxic in Europe, and Fidesz was exposed to increasingly serious criticism even from the family of conservative parties in Europe. So Orbán set about building a new brand, with which he clearly opened up to the radical right-wing forces in Europe. 'Illiberal politics is correct, we just need to find another word for it', he said. In a long speech peppered with witty remarks, he finally found the new slogan: 'Let it be said clearly that Christian democracy is not liberal. Liberal democracy is liberal, Christian democracy is, by definition, not liberal; it is, if you will, illiberal'. Then he went on to say: 'Liberal democracy is pro-immigration, Christian democracy is anti-immigration, which is a true illiberal idea. And liberal democracy rests on the basis of variable family models, while Christian democracy is based on the Christian family model, which is also an illiberal idea'.[52]

All this was a clear provocation for moderate Christian democratic and conservative parties in Europe. Orbán no longer cited the conservative predecessors once important to him when he wanted to gain support from the right wing. And with good reason. József Antall's Christian democratic convictions rested on a very different basis from those of Orbán at the end of the 2010s. 'The only kind of Christian democracy we can accept is one that believes parliamentarianism and in its political programme adheres to all the values that we have noted as liberal values', Antall had said in 1991.[53]

Orbán's Christian identity, by contrast, was basically a negative creed, which served the purpose of dividing the 'good' from the 'evil'. For him, Christian democracy had nothing to do with Christian belief. In his speech he explained this as follows:

> Christian democracy is not about protecting articles of faith, in this case articles of Christian faith. Christian democrat politics means protecting the way of life that arose from Christian culture. [...] such things as human dignity, the family, the nation. [...] This is the job of Christian democracy, not the protection of articles of faith.[54]

Orbán deliberately misrepresented the fundamentals of Christian democracy and the concept of the nation, which was created by nineteenth-century liberalism, not by Christianity.

When Fidesz purposely turned to religion in the mid-1990s to obtain the support of the churches, it was in all likelihood counting on tapping into their community-building capability, which the party leaders may have seen in the example of the Polish Catholic Church. The Catholic tradition in Hungary is not as strong, yet Fidesz was able to build on it, because there is typically greater social trust between members of the same faith than in atomized secular society.[55] Fidesz tried to exploit this society-organizing potential, which was particularly important in a country where only a tiny minority view religion as an important part of their life.[56] Fidesz's scheme paid off: the party was able to mobilize a broad segment of believers in building political communities, for instance in setting up the civic circles movement.

When Orbán proclaimed a 'Christian state' devoid of Christian dogma, he was able to emphasize criteria important for his own politics, all in the name of Christianity. This selective politics was on spectacular display during the migration crisis. Citing Christian values, Orbán's government introduced draconian and often inhuman regulations against refugees, and made it impossible for aid organizations to do their work. For the government the refugee problem was about shaping identity, and Fidesz spoke about the people entering the country in exclusively negative terms, tarring refugees and immigrants with the same brush as terrorists. 'We do not believe that everyone who comes from there is a terrorist, but we do not know, nobody can say, how many terrorists have arrived with the migrants so far. [...] Even one terrorist is too many',[57] Orbán said enigmatically. 'Anyone who brings masses of unregistered immigrants into the country from the Middle East is importing [...] terrorism, crime, anti-Semitism, and homophobia into the country',[58] he said accusingly. The prime minister's manipulative talk robbed Christianity of its moral content and posed serious moral dilemmas for true believers.

Orbán's harsh policies citing Christianity were also at odds with the views of Pope Francis, who at the time of the migration crisis spoke out firmly in support of taking in and helping refugees. In the Fidesz-ruled media, the Pope was stigmatized as a demented old fool and a communist.[59] In this context, very few Hungarian religious leaders spoke up openly for refugees.

In 2017, two Hungarian bishops, one Evangelical Lutheran, one Catholic, featured in a film encouraging people to help refugees, as part of a campaign organized by the UN High Commissioner for Refugees, as a result of which they both later came under heavy attack.[60] 'The dam broke. We were overwhelmed by a tsunami of hate coming from deep down', said one of them in an interview.[61] 'The hearts of many people have hardened, so that they fear not just those of a different religion, but even their Christian brothers and sisters, rejecting even their persecuted neighbours. In mass-produced hate we do not see the face of the refugees, or their Jesus-like aspect'.

When in 2018 Orbán brought in the idea of a 'Christian state', as well as reinforcing identity politics, his aim was to change mainstream liberal European politics. His hard-line politics paralysed the debate about a joint European immigration and refugee policy. Orbán accused his fellow party members in the European People's Party of betraying traditional conservative values and espousing the view of cosmopolitan liberals.[62] He himself proclaimed the founding of a new 'genuine' Christian democrat movement.

In summer 2020 during the Covid pandemic, instead of the usual Bálványos speech, Orbán published a sarcastic essay in which he made it clear he was fighting an ideological battle.[63] For him, the greatest opponents of Christian democrats today were once more liberalism and liberals. He argued that 'for just governance based on morals' it was not sufficient to have a liberal-style rule of law, but that 'absolute values declared by God and the religious, biblical tradition that arises from them' are necessary. He justified this by saying that more important than accountability in the rule of law was governance based on Christian morals, which place a genuine check on political leaders. This was a deliberate misinterpretation of the concept of the rule of law.

Orbán's politics also contradicted the central principles of the Christian democratic movement, which had always nurtured natural communities like the family and professional, religious and other civil bodies, but also protected them from any group trying to force its will upon them in the name of collectivist ideology. Christian democrats are upholders of the rule of law against autocratic rulers: they stand for the principles of the separation of powers and decentralization, and they reject nationalism. Orbán's authoritarian regime is actually a denial of Christian democratic principles.

In order to use Christianity for political purposes, starting in 2010 Orbán provided more financial support than ever before to the main Hungarian churches, in order to buy their commitment and prove his Christian credentials. The number of institutions maintained by the churches multiplied; in 2018 twice as many children studied in church schools as in 2010. However, the expansion of religious education institutions was not the result of greater demand, but was generated by a series of government incentives. Although money flows freely, the churches are struggling to serve the institutions in their charge, because there are not enough religion teachers, deacons or theologians. Cardinal Péter Erdő said in an interview, somewhat ambiguously, that the tasks assigned to the churches were given by politics, but they did not request them, and nobody asked them if they wanted them.[64]

Family as Ideology and 'Gender Madness'

Fidesz launched his ideological use of religion with a radical recasting of the family, sexuality and the social role of women. When I was a member of Parliament, I worked for years trying to get the Hungarian National Assembly to ratify the Istanbul Convention on action against violence against women and domestic violence.[65] As a staff member of the Council of Europe, working on the ground-breaking convention had been an important life experience for me. While in Parliament, I consulted with women's organizations and visited prisons and shelters that cared for women and children who had escaped from domestic violence. Learning of their miserable experiences, I felt even more obliged to stand up for women's rights and against any form of violence.

'MY WORLDVIEW IS HUNGARIAN'

In 2014 the Hungarian government signed the international treaty but did not ratify it. I pushed this issue in Parliament but the government dragged its feet. For a long time, Fidesz had represented family-friendly politics, but a 2015 speech by László Kövér, speaker of the Parliament, opened a new direction in the party's message. At the Fidesz annual congress he said that the 'female principle' was to have children, and he rejected 'gender madness'. 'We would like our daughters to consider bearing us grandchildren as the highest form of self-realization', he said.[66]

I was astonished to hear Kövér speak on gender issues, because at this point hardly anybody in Hungary understood the term 'gender', which does not even have a clear Hungarian-language equivalent. Until then, the Hungarian gender debate was particular and sporadic, restricted mainly to academic discourse.

Fidesz politicians began to hammer home a pre-existing idea: that the reason behind the falling birth rate was the disintegration of the tradition family model and neglect of the day-to-day roles of mothers. In parallel with the strengthening of the anti-migration campaign in 2015, Fidesz reconceptualized its narrative on family as an opposing theory to solve Europe's demographic problems.

Family had a key role in Fidesz's social policy already in 2011, expressed by the introduction of the family tax system. This conservative idea was in harmony with the regime's concept of a 'work-based society', which also introduced a radical, obligatory workfare programme for those unemployed for more than three months.

The more ideological family policy campaign was launched by Kövér's speech: 'We do not want to see Hungary in the futureless vision of men-hating women and feminine men fearful of women, who see in childrearing only an obstacle to self-realization. Men should be men, and women, mothers'.[67] Orbán appointed a state secretary and then a minister for family policy. Under her watch an extremely broad range of family policy subsidies was launched to incentivize parents to have more children.

The minister for families, Katalin Novák, published a video in 2020 in which, as a woman, she encouraged young women not to fight for equality and not to compete with men for positions or for equal pay.[68] Instead, she suggested that women take pride in embracing the fact that they are able to bear twice the burden of their male peers as mothers and workers. This 'novel traditionalist' view flew in the face of the approach even of conservative European parties, which had long since recognized equal roles for women and men in the family and society.

Fidesz's traditionalist approach was rejected and often ridiculed in the free media and rejected by many women and men, for whom the struggle for equal opportunities was self-evident. This demonstrated that there are limits to how anti-gender narratives can be exploited in the public space against women's rights.

Fidesz navigates between anti-feminism and female voter expectations by glorifying the figure of the woman, who is both the core of the family (and a source of life) and also an active participant in the job market. This coexists with calls for masculinity. Using the word 'gender' as an unnatural 'ideology' followed the traditions of current extreme-right movements, in which traditional sexual roles, masculinity and femininity, are used as symbolic capital. Any departure from the traditional is portrayed as a threat to the natural state.[69] Orbán has said several times that 'gender' lies somewhere between man and woman, and therefore cannot be used.[70]

The expression 'gender ideology' was originally coined by the Vatican, but became a political movement around 2005 in firmly Catholic countries in South America and southern Europe. From 2010 onwards, extreme-right movements and populist parties adopted the idea, and the term became less associated with religious groups. The appearance of this anti-gender movement took us by surprise: it seemed utter nonsense, because for decades in Hungary relatively pragmatic policies had been followed regarding the role of women—policies which, for the most part, even Fidesz supported. There were no radical anti-government right-wing groups, and the identity of men was never questioned. The activism of trans and queer movements in Western Europe gave a new impetus to anti-gender movements worldwide.[71] Unlike in many other countries, in Hungary it was the ruling party's own think tanks, journals, pseudo-NGOs,[72] and the party itself that propounded anti-gender ideas. In 2017 one of Fidesz's vice-presidents stated: 'The Istanbul Convention is not about women's rights; it contributes to the stealthy encroachment of gender politics'.[73] The issue of equality for women was irredeemably blurred with propaganda against the gay community and trans and queer subcultures.

In 2017, the World Congress of Families, an ultra-traditionalist and obscure American and Russian anti-gender organization, held its annual gathering in Budapest, with leaders from the Hungarian government also taking part.[74] In fact, the event was merged with the Second Demographic Congress hosted by Katalin Novák. Orbán spoke of the showpiece family-friendly policies of the Hungarian government, and proclaimed the successes of natalist ideology,[75] while speakers from abroad used the conference as a platform for radical speeches.

In these years Fidesz grew more radical, and it adopted anti-gender ideas wholesale. At a similar forum held in 2021 Orbán warned that 'control is being taken over in the West at lightning speed by the neo-Marxist new left, the woke movement, as they say in America', and that 'even in the kindergarten they want to lead our children astray [...] and popularize free choice of gender'.[76] Orbán's exaggerations were mendacious, because in Hungary there was no such activity, and there was no woke movement to speak of.

Fidesz used the word 'gender' as a symbolic glue to bind together markedly different groups, such as committed Catholics, the less educated elderly, and even radical football hooligans, in their rejection of the idea.[77] Anti-gender ideology became the leading ideology of politics rebelling against the liberal status quo and the achievements of progressive politics, such as 'political correctness' and multiculturalism. Extreme-right 'anti-gender' movements, such as CitizenGO, which specializes in manufacturing an image of the enemy in order to maintain fear, gained a foothold in Hungary at the end of the 2010s and supported the Fidesz government's ideological warfare.

Fidesz linked its anti-gender narrative to its new 'Christian state' idea. In the name of Christianity, Orbán broadcast simplistic and manipulative ideas, while the topics that he spoke of constituted issues of debate in almost every church in the world. What is more, quite a few churches, mainly Protestant denominations, recognize homosexual relationships. The anti-gender stance was a deliberately ambiguous approach that brought out homophobia, but also affected people who were tolerant of homosexuality yet rejected what they saw as the Western 'trans trend'.[78]

This battle against 'gender ideology' in Hungary went beyond the confines of rhetoric. In 2020, Fidesz passed an amendment to the Hungarian Fundamental Law, adding to the text that 'the mother shall be a woman, the father shall be a man', and stipulating that every child has the right to the identity of their birth sex. The real repercussions of the wording could only be understood in light of the omnibus bill approved at the same time, amending the Civil Code and Child Protection Act, which made it difficult to become an adoptive parent as a single person, in particular for those living with a same-sex partner.

Then in 2021, the Hungarian National Assembly passed a law originally intended for safeguarding children against paedophilia, to which certain provisions were added at the last minute.

According to this addition, it was dangerous for children's development to receive information about sexual minorities before the age of eighteen. This deliberately misleading law, which before the additions had fairly broad support, went against the rights of children and drew scalding criticism from European institutions, which launched legal actions against the Orbán government.[79] This law also played a key role in the 2022 parliamentary election campaign, where, in the form of a referendum, it served to mobilize conservative voters to vote for Fidesz.

These hypocritical policies, however, were not without risk. In 2020, in the midst of the Covid-19 pandemic, József Szájer, one of Fidesz's founders and an important politician as the leader of the party's group in the European Parliament, was discovered at a gay sex party organized in Brussels while a curfew and ban on all gatherings were in force. His case triggered a scandal even beyond Hungary's borders, and Orbán immediately condemned his friend and comrade-in-arms, forcing him to resign, even though they had worked side by side in the party for thirty years.

Heaven for the Far Right

In the years following the refugee crisis and the victory of Donald Trump in America, Orbán clearly hoped that radical right-wing parties similar to Fidesz would triumph in Italy, Germany, the Netherlands and France, and as a result of this tectonic shift the European status quo would break down. Orbán believed that there was another 'national' uprising taking place in the assertion of sovereignty against international networks and federal regimes, against believers in the United States of Europe, a struggle which was bound together by 'an intellectual uprising against political correctness, isolation, and stigma'.[80]

In 2019, when Europe was preparing for the European Parliament elections, Orbán called on his believers to fight not against the minor opposition parties, but the international network-cum-empire, global media concerns and the NGOs enlisted as George Soros's agents. 'Hungarians, hold the flags high, march and fight, onward to victory!' ran the rallying cry at the end of his speech.[81]

To perfect its European strategy, the Hungarian government conducted regular opinion polls in important countries in Europe,[82] and placed opinion articles and advertisements in leading European papers. In the years following the refugee crisis, every known extreme-right theoretician and political leader was invited to Budapest.

In 2018, Milo Yiannopoulos, one of the troubling figures of the British alt-right, began a speech as the keynote speaker in a Budapest conference on the future of the European Union with the words: 'The devil is real. And he lies. And his name is Soros György!' The speech, every sentence of which regurgitated Fidesz's usual campaign slogans, praised Viktor Orbán at length, and urged Hungarians: 'Hungary is doing a nice job of telling everybody else to go fuck themselves. You are the vanguard, you are the front line [...]. Don't mess it up!'[83]

Other illustrious speakers were also given a platform, such as Douglas Murray, the provocative British conservative writer, and Steve Bannon, Donald Trump's former strategic adviser, who called Orbán a world political figure.[84] Bannon planned to work together with Orbán on the European alt-right movement.[85]

Although in 2019 this endeavour was not successful, Orbán did not give up on the plan. After being forced to leave the European People's Party (see Chapter 11), Orbán went about finding allies with renewed strength. Thus in 2021, Tucker Carlson, then Marine Le Pen, Éric Zemmour, and Marion Maréchal, exponents of the French radical right, all came to Budapest. In 2022, the most spectacular event was the Conservative Political Action Conference held in Budapest, featuring the most important radical right-wing politicians of the world.

* * *

Fidesz has built on the experiences of the traditional, intolerant Hungarian right, but has incorporated much from the narratives of the radical right in the West. From the American conservative counter-revolution operationalized by President George W. Bush's influential adviser Karl Rove,[86] it has learned how to win by representing the interests of a minority but using the votes of deceived citizens in a society embroiled in a culture war. The innovation of Orbánism lies in the way it successfully combined American-style self-confidence with a politics of indignation, transforming ethnic nationalism into an angst about civilization; delegitimizing civil society and in its stead building a strong state; exploiting the narratives of political Christianity in opposition to Christian principles; and renewing the language of populism so that it can be deployed from a position of government.

Over time, Orbán's politics have merged with the teachings of Western European far right and the American alt-right, which are contradictory in themselves, but which in every case serve the endeavours of a political clique to gain power. They manipulate the significance of the left wing, with its radical identity politics, artificially exaggerating it to legitimize their own extreme opposing views. The radical right wing, as everywhere else in the world, is a tool with which the camp of the disaffected can be stirred up.

If Fidesz once had a coherent ideology, this is no longer the case, as I have demonstrated in this chapter, and in this respect it fits perfectly into the international trend of the radical right wing. After all, back in 2006 Orbán made it clear that the power forging his ideology is not ideas, but constant battle.

TAINTED DEMOCRACY

> The path I have travelled leads not from liberalism to conservatism. [...] I believe I have sensed how relative ideologies can be, how limited their importance. [...] I do not need my views, my thoughts about the world, even if they touch on the world of politics, to be forced into the cage of any ideology that can be summarized in a book.[87]

Nevertheless, as we have seen, one of the secrets of Orbán's strength was that he was always able to link his rhetoric to the crisis discourse in the world at any given moment. For a long time he continually sought out the conceptual framework for a right-wing uprising until he reached the extreme right. He put unprecedented sums of money into building a whole series of ideological campaigns, making ideology an important base of his power.

3

'ALONE WE WOULD FAIL, BUT TOGETHER WE WILL WIN!'

ORBÁN'S POLITICAL OPPOSITION

'This government has to go!' Gordon Bajnai declared in a speech on 23 October 2012 at a huge demonstration on the anniversary of the 1956 revolution.

> Change of government is not enough: we need a change of regime! [...] We need a new political centre that is strong enough to eradicate from our lives a power that is founded on dividing the nation. [...] So we have decided to lay the foundations of a collaboration to organize a new, strong centre. [...] I know it will be difficult, because they want to divide us. And also because there really will be hundreds of issues we don't agree on. [...] But there are four important things we do agree on: the homeland and progress, solidarity and Europe!

He ended with the exhortation 'Alone we would fail, but together we will win!'[1]

That day Bajnai, who led the technocratic government in 2009–10, stepped onto the scene, and announced the political movement Együtt 2014 (Together 2014), a coalition of recently formed opposition groups.[2] Együtt's aim was to unite the extra-parliamentary movements and the parliamentary opposition so that together they could defeat Viktor Orbán's party at the 2014 elections.

Two and a half years after Fidesz's huge victory, the government party was already ruling the country through the institutions it had transformed to suit its own interests. As a result of the government's conflicting decisions Fidesz's popularity had dropped considerably,[3] and it seemed as though the time had come for opposition forces to organize to challenge the ruling party. But the opposition parties in Parliament were weak. The former governing parties defeated in 2010 had suffered a serious loss of credibility. The Hungarian Socialist Party had split in two. The new parliamentary parties—the far-right Jobbik and the green party Politics Can Be Different (LMP)—were still finding their feet under the pressure of Fidesz.

Bajnai, however, was well known and very popular,[4] and in two years Orbán's popularity had plummeted from 50% to 15%.[5] Moreover, Bajnai's personality was the polar opposite of Orbán's confrontational, radical style: with his calm, judicious statements and his search for consensus, he presented an attractive alternative.

Bajnai's initiative was aimed at creating a broad democratic opposition alliance, without the far-right Jobbik. Cooperation between left, green and liberal parties and groups was necessitated by the fact that (as I will describe in Chapter 4) after 2010 the balance of power between parties in Hungary underwent a fundamental change. Previously, two competing blocs of similar size, the right and the left, had occupied Hungary's political space. But in 2010 Fidesz took the 'centre field of force';[6] Jobbik grew on the right, and on the left were several smaller liberal, socialist and green parties. It was in Orbán's interest to maintain this central power, and in order to do so Fidesz reinforced the 'winner-takes-all' electoral system and sharpened the competition

'ALONE WE WOULD FAIL, BUT TOGETHER WE WILL WIN!'

between its right- and left-wing rivals. Independently, none of the opposition parties was any match for the Fidesz giant, and the opposition was trapped as a result.

In 2010, Fidesz had won almost every single-member constituency, and we were worried this would continue if candidates from smaller parties were to compete against one another. Együtt aimed to build a coalition. Despite our efforts, Fidesz managed to repeat its feat of winning a supermajority in Parliament in 2014 and even in 2018. Only in 2019 at the municipality elections did the opposition to Orbán become capable, after several huge failures, of creating a broader, cross-party coalition and of winning in a number of cities.

Although Együtt 2014 was unable to realize its original goals at the time, some of its politicians managed to enter Parliament. I was one of them. Under Fidesz's ever-growing dominance, we in the opposition political groups continually sought new forms of political action and persistently looked for new ways of creating a united force that offered a realistic chance of defeating Fidesz.

Resistance Is Reborn

The Fidesz government's all-out attack started in 2010 and had a crippling effect on the country, perhaps even on those who had voted for Fidesz. The victorious party pressed ahead with incredible self-confidence, while the opposition lay in ruins. The noisy accession to power and the spectacular transformation of the structure of the state, which I described in the introductory chapter, generated feelings of gloom and overwhelming helplessness. My acquaintances used to say in resignation that Fidesz was settling in for twenty years in power.

The situation shocked the political opposition too. The only party I had any sympathy with, the green party LMP, had formed but a year previously, and with 4% of the seats, in the shadow of Fidesz, it was barely visible in the National Assembly. It was dismaying to see the far-right racist Jobbik alongside LMP, with 12% of seats. Never before had such an openly discriminatory party won so many votes in Hungary. The two right-wing parties, Fidesz and Jobbik, accounted for 80% of members of Parliament. The Hungarian Socialist Party had shrunk drastically: its share of the popular vote dropped from 43% in 2006 to 19% in 2010,[7] and after this massive failure, it was torn by internal battles. Like many others, I believed that being in power in previous years had greatly corrupted the Socialist Party, and serious errors in government had led to Hungary being particularly badly hit by the 2008 financial crisis, while democratic consensus had broken down. The liberal SZDSZ, which had been in government with the Socialist Party, had been eroded almost completely, which was a huge loss for the country.

Former prime minister Ferenc Gyurcsány, whom many held responsible for the transformation of the political field, left the socialists in 2011 and founded a new party called Democratic Coalition (DK). My major problem with Gyurcsány was that, like Orbán, both his personality and his political actions were divisive. Not by chance was Gyurcsány the most unpopular politician in Hungary in 2010.[8]

In this depressive atmosphere several civil groups were born and began organizing debates about what could be done to counter the growing power of the government party. The largest movement, One Million People for Press Freedom, known as Milla, was the most successful in organizing mass demonstrations, which created a mood of euphoria. I also participated in Milla's protest events.

Together We Will Win! Együtt Steps onto the Scene

In summer 2012 I was contacted by Gordon Bajnai, a long-time friend. He explained he was preparing to return to politics

'ALONE WE WOULD FAIL, BUT TOGETHER WE WILL WIN!'

and asked if I too would like to enter the ring. His plan to pull together opposition forces seemed sensible, because at the time 80% of people believed that things were going in the wrong direction in the country. Fidesz had lost 1 million voters since the elections, and its popularity was at a low of 19%.[9] Against this, in the opposition the Socialist Party had the support of 16% of the population, the Greens 4%, Jobbik 8% and Gyurcsány's DK 2%. Although this gave stronger support to the opposition parties, because of fragmentation there was a good chance that Fidesz could easily win again in 2014. The idea Bajnai shared with me, of creating an opposition umbrella organization, first with the extra-parliamentary political groups and later with parliamentary parties, seemed both sound and exciting.

The plan was not without risks. In two decades, Fidesz had built up a robust nationwide organization, while opposition parties had grown weak, and the new parties and movements were not sufficiently embedded in society. I was concerned that a lightweight network-style organized campaign would not be able to tackle Fidesz's strong base. The other big question was whether this broad opposition collaboration was actually feasible. Would Bajnai manage to rally behind him the political parties as well as civil groups? Would the new civil groups, such as Milla, which followed Bajnai's call be willing to collaborate with the Socialist Party and DK, the parties of the 'old elite', which they held responsible for the decay of democracy? We had to find answers to all these questions.

But there is no such thing as risk-free politics. Since I had stopped working at the Council of Europe in 2010 and was now a freelance consultant, I had much more flexibility, and I was very concerned about the future of Hungary. After some thought, I said yes to Bajnai's invitation to return to Hungarian politics within the organization Homeland and Progress Foundation, which he led. Homeland and Progress consisted of progressive, centrist-liberal thinkers, and had drawn in an excellent team of experts with political know-how who would be needed to implement the plan. The most suitable moment to announce the election alliance seemed to be the next Milla demonstration, scheduled for 23 October 2012.

Expectations were running very high, because the news had been leaked. Tens of thousands wanted to see Bajnai return, and many regarded him as the only person who could possibly save Hungary. At the demonstration, Bajnai announced the Együtt movement, formed by Homeland and Progress, Milla and Szolidaritás, a trade union-based group. The demonstration was held in a spirit of civil resistance, and sent an open invitation to political parties to join the initiative.

Just weeks after it was announced, Együtt's popularity surged, with pollsters measuring its support at 10%–14%.[10] They predicted that with Bajnai the opposition could mobilize 4%–6% of voters who had grown disillusioned with Fidesz. Things started off well.

We soon began probing the parties in the National Assembly. Naturally, Jobbik was not considered as a partner. Above all, we wanted to involve the Socialist Party and LMP in the election collaboration. In the MSZP Bajnai was very popular after having led the government in 2009, following Gyurcsány's fall, and because he was able to consolidate the economy. In addition, in LMP there was a significant group who believed their small party would not be able to put down roots alone, and would have to cooperate with Bajnai in order to change the government.

Although nobody questioned the wisdom of cooperating, the formation of the Együtt movement presented a serious challenge to both parties. As a young party, LMP was still very much preoccupied with building its own identity, and in its leadership there was a strong desire to break with the past, namely, the 'old elite', which the Socialist Party represented.

'ALONE WE WOULD FAIL, BUT TOGETHER WE WILL WIN!'

The appearance of Együtt was unsettling for the Socialist Party too. Formerly a large organization, after the election it had shrunk, its leaders were in crisis, and fears were spreading among the party elite that Bajnai wanted to 'occupy' the party from outside. Many were irked by Együtt's statement that it was open to the centre right. The party members, on the other hand, were extremely sympathetic to Bajnai, and so the leaders decided to wait it out.[11]

Együtt drafted a statement containing its fundamental principles and suggested manifesto, and sent it to LMP first. At the LMP congress held in mid-November 2012, two divergent opinions were expressed: to initiate cooperation with Együtt or to concentrate on independent politics. The congress took an even more dramatic turn than expected. The long debate went on into the night. The party was bitterly divided. In the small hours a decision was made, by a majority of a few votes, that LMP would not join Együtt's opposition movement. The situation was so explosive that after the decision, Benedek Jávor, leader of the LMP parliamentary group, said: 'We have made a decision that bears no relation to reality. We have relinquished the chance of putting an end to the Orbán regime. [...] We have made a decision which, I believe, is fatal to LMP and detrimental to Hungary'.[12] Years later, every word proved to be true. Jávor and his two deputies resigned from their positions there and then. For their part, the pro-coalition members of LMP[13] founded an organization called Dialogue for Hungary, and joined Bajnai's Együtt movement.

One far-reaching consequence of the result regarding LMP was its effect on the behaviour of the bigger opposition party, the Hungarian Socialist Party. One of its leaders said to a journalist:

> It will turn out that there will be no such thing as the centre, which everyone is talking about now, and which [Együtt] thinks is an

indispensable condition for defeating Viktor Orbán. There won't be because it's not in anyone's interest for it to take shape. Neither for Viktor Orbán, nor for the MSZP. You've got to face it.[14]

The majority of the MSZP leaders still thought of themselves as one of the two large parties in Hungary, and insisted on keeping things this way. The newly elected president of the party, Attila Mesterházy, belonged to a new generation of MPs, and wanted to prove that the Socialist Party was viable and strong. While publicly he showed interest in the coalition, in reality he strove to hinder Együtt's alliance building.

Fidesz understood very well that there was a danger in Bajnai's initiative. A failed MSZP was no problem for them, but they saw in Bajnai an integrating figure who had stepped onto the stage, who could unite the opposition forces and put pressure on Orbán's party. Fidesz thus made it a basic strategic aim to ruin Együtt's initiative. This became immediately clear when Civil Union, an organization created by Fidesz, ran a crude smear campaign against Bajnai. Two weeks after Együtt was launched, all over the country, buses and columns were plastered with posters of Bajnai and Gyurcsány, bending their heads together, and above them the text 'Together [Együtt] they ruined the country, and once was enough! We won't forget!' Both visually and verbally, the poster linked Bajnai to the extremely unpopular Ferenc Gyurcsány. The aim of blurring the line between the 'old elite' and Együtt was to undermine our efforts to build the image of a new political force. This character assassination campaign tried to shake the trust of the various civil actors gathered in Együtt, who themselves felt antipathy to the person and politics of Gyurcsány. This crude, negative campaign against Bajnai went on for years, right up to the elections in 2014.

Although many in the MSZP leadership were pleased that Fidesz was concentrating on Bajnai, and not on them, they were

'ALONE WE WOULD FAIL, BUT TOGETHER WE WILL WIN!'

under pressure from their own party membership to cooperate with Együtt. The idea of a coalition between parties was very popular among opposition voters as well. MSZP's interests spurred the party leadership to take charge of the planned coalition themselves. Sensing that anyone who uttered the word 'coalition' increased their popularity, Ferenc Gyurcsány also started to speak about cooperating with other opposition parties, even though public support for his party, DK, was negligible. His entry on the scene complicated the picture, because antipathy towards him was so great that opposition parties had a basic interest in distancing themselves from him. For Bajnai's Együtt, a big problem was that the nascent cooperation was open to some opposition parties, but not to others. Moreover, the ambitions of the socialists to lead the opposition coalition and of Gyurcsány to participate in it carried the threat that Együtt wouldn't be able exploit its potential and attract liberal and moderate conservative voters, for whom choosing the 'old left elite' was difficult to imagine.

When we created Együtt we underestimated that what was at stake for the parliamentary opposition parties was their very survival, and cooperation was not on their agenda, at least not yet. They saw Együtt's initiative as a provocation, not a means of support. The behaviour of LMP and MSZP was motivated by the narrowest of party interests, which hindered their ability to think in a broader context. Six months after launching the Együtt 2014 movement, we found ourselves in the vortex of rivalry between opposition parties. In order to realize our original plan and make an election coalition with the parties, we were forced to establish a political party. Együtt-PM was formed from the Együtt 2014 movement and the small green party Dialogue for Hungary (PM), which seceded from LMP.

With the elections in sight, we immediately concentrated on planning a campaign. We based the image of the party on

Bajnai's character. We set about drawing up a political manifesto, and started a nationwide campaign. We travelled systematically around the country with Bajnai and held very successful rallies. Our working together and touring nationwide tour propelled the initiative, and positive feedback from all over the country confirmed our conviction that we were on the right track.

A Union with a Sneer[15]

Finally, ten months before the 2014 elections, negotiations between Együtt-PM and the Socialist Party began to give shape to an electoral coalition. The idea was that we run joint candidates in single-member constituencies, but that each party runs its own separate party list. This was the basis for what we called our 'coordinated' campaign. One of the big questions was in what proportion each of the two parties should put forward candidates in the 106 constituencies with the support of the other party. Negotiations dragged on excruciatingly, because we also wanted to prevent the MSZP from putting forward discredited candidates who represented the 'old elite'. However, the party's leaders were not strong enough to keep their corrupt colleagues in the background.[16]

Another sore point was the candidate for prime minister. Obviously, we wanted the socialists to support Bajnai, who was a popular and unifying figure. But the MSZP thought that their party was the leading power on the left, and wouldn't accept playing second fiddle in a cooperation pact, so they postponed the decision. After negotiations had dragged on for months, we agreed that the socialists would put forward candidates in 75 constituencies, and Együtt-PM in 31, and both parties would support each other's candidates. We had to make many compromises. I was one of the 31 of Együtt-PM candidates. Seven months before the elections we started working on a joint campaign together with the Socialist Party's local chapter in

'ALONE WE WOULD FAIL, BUT TOGETHER WE WILL WIN!'

Budapest's fourth electoral district. Fortunately, by this time I had recruited a truly excellent and committed team.[17]

Initially, cooperation with the socialists at the local level was immensely challenging. Smoothing out differences in tactics and strategy used up huge reserves of energy. The socialists had been in government for years, and they spoke the language of the politics of power, which was repugnant to us, as well as inadequate, given the situation. On occasion, the socialists even asked me not to talk about certain topics in public that might be awkward for them. I wasn't to talk about property speculation, which would have lifted the lid on the fact that certain of their leaders were still in cahoots with Fidesz in economic matters. They recommended consultants that I didn't trust. I rejected these suggestions, and this resulted in many conflicts. However, many of the Socialist Party activists entered my campaign team, and gave me a great deal of support. Just as six months previously, it once more became apparent that party activists grasp the essence of cooperation much better than the party elite, which is burdened with personal power interests. Preparation for the campaign took place in this contradictory way, with frustrating arguments alternating with buoyant campaign meetings.

The campaign preparations were well under way locally, but there was still no national-level agreement between the two parties on the candidate for prime minister. A ruthless character assassination campaign dented Bajnai's popularity and helped the socialists in the negotiations. Moreover, Gyurcsány's party become more popular and demanded a place in the opposition coalition. Együtt-PM was forced into another serious compromise by cooperating with the 'old elite'.

Three months before the elections, the coordinated collaboration of democratic parties led by Bajnai came to nothing: we stood on the same platform as the most compromised of parties, the Socialist Party, and Gyurcsány. A foreboding atmosphere stirred within the Együtt-PM party.

In early January 2014, when the president of the republic announced the day of the elections, there was a final opportunity to decide on a joint candidate for prime minister. The potential for another Fidesz victory struck such panic in the core opposition voters and in intellectual circles that we came under enormous pressure. Our supporters asked Együtt-PM to accept that Bajnai would not be the candidate for prime minister, to agree on a joint electoral list, and to involve every existing opposition group, even tiny fringe parties, in the coalition. Once, when Bajnai met important liberal public figures, and I accompanied him, I saw that pundits who understood little of politics were trying to persuade him to step down. It was a terrible conversation, because what they said contradicted political sense.

On the last night before the decision, the extended leadership of the Együtt-PM party sat down and thought through all the possible scenarios. By then, it was obvious there would be a joint national list led by the chairperson of the Socialist Party as candidate for prime minister, with Bajnai in second position and Gyurcsány in third place. Együtt-PM was defeated on all fronts, just as Fidesz would have wanted.

Bajnai considered not giving his name to such an odd coalition, but that night we convinced him that we had to go through with the campaign to the end. When, one week later, I saw the first billboard poster in my district with Attila Mesterházy (candidate of the united opposition for prime minister) pictured behind me instead of Bajnai, I asked myself whether I would really vote for this opposition coalition if I were not on the poster. It was a most depressing feeling.

'ALONE WE WOULD FAIL, BUT TOGETHER WE WILL WIN!'

Collapse

After a year of arduous negotiations, public rivalry and poor compromises, we did not manage to win the voters we were aiming for. Meanwhile, the economy stabilized, feeding into Fidesz's narrative (see Chapter 5) about its success, at a price, in managing to pull the country back from the 'brink of insolvency', and enabling everyone to share in the wealth of a flourishing country. Ten months before the elections Fidesz's popularity began to climb. On nationwide TV and on billboards, we saw Fidesz's carefully composed slogan: 'We will keep utility fees down!'

In addition to the huge smear campaign against Bajnai (which worsened our negotiating position month by month), Fidesz media always showed Gyurcsány as a decisive politician, who could stabilize his party. By bolstering him, Fidesz clearly intended to alienate voters critical of Fidesz from the opposition coalition. The way negotiations dragged on, and the eventual unfavourable result (in terms of votes), gave rise to the suspicion that Fidesz was trying to influence the negotiation process not just from outside, but also from within. It was rumoured that some opposition politicians had been prevailed upon by people close to Fidesz in order to hamper any agreement. One businessman who operated around Fidesz told me in 2019 that he regularly sought to influence a leading MSZP politician in order to put a spanner in the works of the negotiation process. Although I had my reservations about his reliability, it seemed indisputable that one could demoralize the contending parties from within, through certain people.

In the final weeks of the election campaign, Fidesz's victory was no longer in doubt; the only question was by how much they would win.[18] The public too felt that nothing was really at stake: never had there been such a low turnout at elections. The final result was crushing. Fidesz won with 44.8% of the popular vote and 66.8% of seats, once again attaining a two-thirds supermajority. Jobbik grew too, winning 20% of votes, and LMP, who rejected the left-wing alliance outright, also got into Parliament, with 5.3% of the vote. We in the left-liberal coalition of several parties gained 25% of the votes, but because the electoral system favoured the winner (see Chapter 4), this gave only 19% of the seats, a mere thirty-eight in number, divided between seven small parties. This was the galling outcome we had to face on election night, 6 April 2014. Almost certainly, we would not have been able to prevent a Fidesz victory, but we might have stopped them gaining a supermajority. The supremacy of the government party in terms of resources and media, and the disproportional workings of the Elections Act which advantaged Fidesz, were not enough to justify our failure.

Although more parties had joined forces to defeat Fidesz, there was strong rivalry between these groups too. Every party was striving to build its own identity and squeeze its rivals out. In a normal multi-party democracy these are perfectly legitimate endeavours. For parties to form a coalition without any kind of test actually contradicts the basic logic of political competition, and is ultimately an abnormal requirement. By altering the Elections Act (see Chapter 4) and forcing parties to form a pre-election coalition, Fidesz robbed Hungarian parties of the opportunity for democratic competition.

In 2014, eventually only four Együtt-PM politicians entered the National Assembly from the joint opposition list. This was not even enough to form a party group. After the defeat, our relationship with the other parties deteriorated so much that there was no talk of forming a joint group either. Bajnai decided he would leave politics and trusted his closest allies, who had stuck beside him all through the one-and-a-half-year struggle, to move on with the party.[19] This was the shambolic state in which we started the new parliamentary term.

'ALONE WE WOULD FAIL, BUT TOGETHER WE WILL WIN!'

Opportunities and Dilemmas in Opposition Political Action

While we were preoccupied with the overwhelming and critical legislative work in Parliament, my party made efforts to build narratives that captured the essence of Orbán's regime and showed an alternative vision for Hungary. The opportunity arrived when we learned from Russian press sources that Viktor Orbán had secretly signed a treaty with Russian president Vladimir Putin for the Russian company Rosatom to build two new reactors at the Paks Nuclear Power Plant, which Hungary would fund through a thirty-year, €10 billion loan from Russia.

News of the secret deal sparked outrage. The construction of new Russian nuclear reactors went against the strategic aim of diversifying of Hungary's energy sources and, in financial terms, it put the country catastrophically in debt to Russia. Orbán's new-found commitment to Russia was incomprehensible as just a few years earlier he himself had said: 'Energy is a key issue, not just an economic one, but a question of security, foreign policy, one that is connected to our freedom'.[20]

We were worried that the hidden deal concealed a commitment highly disadvantageous for Hungary, in exchange for securing low energy prices. These were absolutely crucial for Orbán's ruling party when it launched the 'lower utility bills' campaign in 2013, which provided fixed low energy prices for households and proved to be essential for Orbán's election victory in 2014. In Parliament I said: 'The "Paks agreement" is [...] a historical error, which determines our fate for decades. [...] The point of the "Paks agreement" is that Putin wants to export nuclear power plants to Europe, and the Fidesz government is helping him. He is leading us by the nose'.[21] We presented the case as a fateful issue of choosing between the West and the autocratic East. We pointed out that being at the mercy of Putin's regime distanced Hungary from the core of Europe. The case triggered a broad wave of street protests, and we pummelled the government with questions in Parliament.

To our astonishment, this offensive, which lasted months, had little effect. From the minute the Paks story came to light, Fidesz released hundreds of different news items and dozens of legislative initiatives which, after a while, distracted the focus of the opposition. Finally, the Paks story, the most important issue for us, fell apart and faded away in the surrounding noise.

Another effort of ours was to build a visionary narrative for a modern model of the family, in contrast to Fidesz's traditional image of the family.[22] The family can always be projected onto society as a whole, and Orbán as a national leader modelled a patriarchal, authoritarian father role. In Orbán's authoritarian family model, the father, by virtue of his position, has power over the rest of the family, just as the leader of a country, because of his status, stands over the nation like a chieftain. Ultimately everyone depends on the head of the family.[23] The Fidesz regime strove to tighten these dependency relationships.

In contrast to this image of family and nation, we represented a more democratic vision, where the relationship between women and men was equal and family members were bound by love, mutual care and cooperation. Interestingly, whatever basic critique of the system these ideas reflected, and however they could have been capitalized on in political communication, we never managed to elaborate this narrative and use it as a framework for our thinking. I think my male colleagues simply didn't understand the potential communicative ammunition this would give us. The Hungarian political elite as a whole, albeit not as explicitly authoritarian as Orbán, has a rather dated attitude to relations between men and women, though liberal and left-wing politicians would never admit this.

The greatest efforts eventually went into building a narrative to present the overwhelming, systemic corruption Fidesz

'ALONE WE WOULD FAIL, BUT TOGETHER WE WILL WIN!'

had built up. The patron–client arrangement, as the overall characteristic of the Fidesz regime, poisoned political and social life. For years we aired the most incredible stories: the shocking property speculation in the centre of Budapest,[24] the unscrupulous syphoning off of European development funds, and the spectacular accumulation of fortunes in the Orbán family (see Chapter 6). We tried to make it clear that the system was operated from the top down, and that ultimately it was a mafia state.[25]

Despite our efforts to build comprehensive narratives, we could not move forward. The suffocating media supremacy of the regime (see Chapter 7) and the distraction of the government propaganda machinery, in addition to the competing narratives emerging on the side of the opposition, made our efforts inadequate and worthless. With our messages we were locked into the camp of Orbán's critics, and were unable to attract a wider and more depoliticized public.

In fact, competition between opposition parties was limited to attempts to drain off voters from each other. The rivalry consisted in showing who was most anti-Orbán, and who could deliver the harshest condemnation of one or other absurd move of Fidesz. Breakfast political briefings focused on what the 'zeitgeist' was, what we should strike at first. This reactive, defensive behaviour, the 'daily criticism of Orbán', was sufficient for us to survive from day to day, because it got us into the non-Fidesz press.

Coherent, long-term ideas were always overridden by the rivalry between the opposition parties, which in the short term paid off better. Perhaps it was wrong to expect more. Rivalry in the opposition and the limitations of political communication shed light on even deeper problems.

Opposition to the Government or to the Regime?

Until 2010, there operated in Hungary a liberal democracy where the system of checks and balances, along with a free press, restricted the elected government from abusing power, even if it was not perfect. For the opposition at any given time, the aim of elections was to oust the government and get into power, bearing in mind that four years later there would be another contest for power. Thanks to this rotation system, in spite of considerable differences of opinion, rival parties did not transgress the democratic framework; they accepted each other as opponents and from time to time were able to compromise. By 2006 this democratic consensus had unravelled, once Fidesz changed its strategy and aimed not simply to oust the government but to morally incapacitate it (see the introduction). Finally, after 2010, citing the democratic mandate of the nation, Fidesz abandoned the system of the rule of law built on checks and balances. We in the opposition considered this development undemocratic, and beyond defeating Orbán's party our political aim was to redemocratize Hungary.

At the same time there was a contradiction: if we did not consider the system democratic, then why take part in the workings of a Parliament that had lost its function? Why write a letter to the president of the republic, why demand an inquiry from the Constitutional Court, when we considered these bodies and positions illegitimate, the empty trappings of democracy? In 2016, when Fidesz held a referendum against European Union refugee quotas, we were convinced that it was unconstitutional, and it was then that we first decided to declare a boycott (see Chapter 8). But was it possible to boycott Orbán's entire political edifice? How far should one play a part in the political circus arranged by Fidesz, whose rules were written by Orbán alone?

In Europe, we were basically facing these dilemmas alone. I took part in countless European initiatives as an MP, and when I entered discussions with my colleagues, I realized that they simply could not conceive the strategic dilemmas we had to face in the restrictive Hungarian political environment.

'ALONE WE WOULD FAIL, BUT TOGETHER WE WILL WIN!'

Orbán's regime could be considered a democracy for the reason that parliamentary elections were held, and the opposition was genuine, because it had at least half of the voters behind it. However, after 2014 the elections were no longer fair, because the ideas of the political forces challenging Fidesz never reached a significant part of the electorate, and the Elections Act skewed the extent of Fidesz's victory. In moral terms, the right response would have been to reject the system and engage in extra-parliamentary politics.

An outright rejection of the entire system would have demonstrated very clearly that we considered it illegitimate. Yet it was doubtful, even if we could have persuaded all the opposition parties to unite and refuse to participate in the elections, what we would have achieved through this. If we had marched out of Parliament, our parties would have lost the ground under their feet. Without the remaining rights of parliamentarians, which, for example, made it possible for us to monitor public institutions and question the government, the visibility of the opposition would have soon disappeared. Without the resources to which parties were entitled, opposition political forces would have rapidly become insignificant. Moreover, Fidesz would most probably have set up fake parties to its liking. The risk of a total boycott was enormous.

Nevertheless, we knew that if we took part in the elections, we were behaving as if they could be won, and so we couldn't call the regime a dictatorship. In this sense, then, there was no way to create a consistent politics of opposition to the system. Pragmatic considerations led us to mobilize our extremely meagre means both in and outside Parliament to scrutinize the use of power, and to express our protests with regard to the system.

Between a Rock and a Hard Place: To Compete, or to Unite?

It became increasingly obvious that Orbán's regime, although clearly distinguishable from purely authoritarian regimes, had diverged fundamentally from Western democracies. As political scientists Steven Levinsky and Lucan A. Way have shown, this type of system can stay in place for decades, particularly if it is able to rely on a stable political infrastructure.[26] In Fidesz's second term with a supermajority, the party consolidated its social network and institutions, and used every possible means of the government to bolster and keep this voting conglomerate united. The stability of the system could be felt very clearly, already during my term in Parliament. The basic political fault line was now between Orbánism and anti-Orbánism, although at the time opposition parties didn't recognize this.

After 2014 MPs from seven parties sat on the opposition benches in the National Assembly, and another party, Momentum, made up of young people, was established. This figure shows how splintered we were, and that the opposition was not providing any central force. The regime's rules of play were less restrictive when it came to rivalry in the opposition, and in fact this was a gift to Fidesz. Cross-party willingness to cooperate was diminished by the knowledge that (as I wrote above) from time to time a party would cooperate with Fidesz in order to get the edge over other members of the opposition.

At the same time, in the given framework, the struggle between opposition parties was determined by what was practicable. There was still space in Hungary for pluralistic democratic public life, however confined. At stake in this competition was which party would become the leading force in the opposition. Without some degree of leadership in the opposition, an electoral victory was unthinkable, and the viability of a post-Orbán coalition government seemed hopeless without this.

The splintered opposition also meant that even though there were popular opposition politicians, none of them had the political strength to persuade other opposition parties to combine efforts. This led party leaders to focus on pursuing a polarizing, anti-

'ALONE WE WOULD FAIL, BUT TOGETHER WE WILL WIN!'

Orbán message. This tactic bolstered their names and popularity in their own camp but did not help to build a broader community or integrate politically.

The Road to Another Electoral Defeat

'Fidesz's two-thirds majority can be defeated!' 'Fidesz has failed!' 'Fidesz has lost all moral basis for leading the country!' ran the headlines on 22 February 2015. The previous Sunday there had been by-elections in Veszprém, a city in western Hungary, after the district's Fidesz MP was delegated to the European Commission. To the astonishment of the whole country, a totally unknown independent candidate, Zoltán Kész, won the seat by a considerable majority. For the first time in Hungary, a number of opposition parties (apart from Jobbik and LMP) backed the civil candidate. Because Fidesz only held a supermajority in Parliament by one seat, the result also meant that the government party lost its constitutional majority.

A few weeks later, Jobbik's candidate won a by-election in another town, Tapolca, also taking a seat previously occupied by Fidesz. Other opposition parties could not openly support the far-right party, but Jobbik's candidate stood the best chance at victory. Therefore, in order to defeat Fidesz, the parties adopted the following tactic: they put forward candidates, but did not campaign for them. Meanwhile, Jobbik's candidate showed that the party was moving increasingly to the centre, and had barred its more extreme politicians. This victory was a breakthrough for the right-wing party, because it had never before won in a single-member constituency.

These events clearly showed that through coordinated collaboration, the opposition could defeat Fidesz politicians even in their own safe seats. Leading public figures immediately began to call for the opposition to join forces, once again. These unexpected victories for the opposition also taught Fidesz that it should do everything to prevent the opposition from uniting at the elections in 2018. The ruling party developed several methods to hinder the opposition from cooperating. For example, if one party wanted to withdraw a candidate in a single constituency for the sake of another, it had to repay a large amount of campaign funding to the state. These new rules hampered reasonable coordination between the opposition parties.

Another tried and tested method of Fidesz was to amend the conditions of political advertising. Ten months before the elections in 2018, a new set of legal amendments aimed to limit party advertisements to a three-month election campaign period, and to punish parties which secured advertising at prices below the official rates. In 2017 only Jobbik had the means to advertise well before the elections, as the party enjoyed the generous support of media oligarch Lajos Simicska, who at that time was engaged in a political war against Orbán (see Chapter 6). However, for this amendment a two-thirds majority was needed, which Fidesz lacked at the time. Thus, the ruling party began to scout among the opposition parties seen as rivals to Jobbik, promising them advertising space in exchange for supporting the amendment. This apparently advantageous offer caused serious internal conflicts in the opposition parties, because there were politicians who thought that an occasional deal with Fidesz would be a good idea.

Although finally none of the parties collaborated with Fidesz, this weeks-long affair had very serious consequences. Deep fault lines appeared between the opposition parties and within the parties themselves, and relationships went sour. Moreover, Fidesz eventually found a legal stratagem, so that they wouldn't need the opposition to pass the amendment.[27]

It was galling to see with my own eyes how easily Fidesz could use simple means to create confusion in an opposition divested

'ALONE WE WOULD FAIL, BUT TOGETHER WE WILL WIN!'

of its resources: by tempting them with money, or advertising space, corrupting opposition politicians became child's play. In this case common sense finally prevailed, but the last crumbs of trust between the parties were ground down, and a gloomy mood held sway. Opposition parties were growing further apart, and organized coordination with regard to the upcoming elections went out of the window.

As hope of fair cooperation with other parties was gone, and my party, Együtt, was too small to run alone, I decided not to stand in the elections in 2018.

There was another unexpected by-election victory six weeks before the elections, when Péter Márki-Zay, a political outsider, managed to win a mayoralty by an impressive 15% of votes in a Fidesz stronghold. This created a spark of hope that the opposition could win if parties cooperated. But by then time was too short and the political will too weak to build systemic cooperation.

The 2018 elections were a total fiasco for the opposition. Fidesz once more won a two-thirds majority. The days following the elections saw demonstrations with hundreds of thousands protesting against Fidesz's latest victory. Crowds of disappointed people called for a new opposition made up of non-partisan candidates, because the current opposition was unfit to defeat the government. In the weeks following the elections, almost every opposition party president resigned. The opposition had been annihilated, both politically and in terms of morale.

The Opposition Comes Down onto the Pitch

In spring 2018, after Fidesz's election victory, those who wanted change were overcome with despondency. People began to wonder whether there was any sense in opposition. Demonstrations and petitions over the years had all been in vain, and couldn't even prevent the regime from becoming more radical. Political dependency, vulnerability and anxiety had become part of our everyday life, and it seemed that a large portion of Hungarian society was resigned to this state of affairs.

The huge spontaneous wave of protests after the 2018 elections conveyed the message that the people now had to take control, because the parties had proved to be unfit for purpose. But the reality was that despite five and a half million people participating in elections, only a few hundred thousand were ready to take action and go on the streets. Hungarians had a vote, but they didn't have a voice. The opposition parties were forced to re-examine their aims and strategies in order to defeat Orbán.

The first signs of this self-review became apparent at the end of 2018 when the government put an amendment to the labour law before Parliament that would significantly raise the number of overtime hours employees could be required to work and change the way overtime was calculated. At that point all the opposition parties sided with the weak trade unions and took to the streets in total unity. As the proposal threatened to increase the vulnerability of workers in the private sector, protesters nicknamed it the 'slavery law'. Fidesz said, hypocritically, that the law allowed people who wanted to work more and earn more money to do just that.[28] Every day the protests grew stronger, and led to the opposition initiating a filibuster by submitting 2,925 amendments in order to change the bill. At this, the speaker of the house decided that Parliament could vote on all the amendments in one single vote. After this unprecedented decision, at the stage of the final vote on the law, the opposition occupied the speaker's podium and MPs created tumult in the hall, moving around, whistling, shouting, and broadcasting events with their mobile phones. A few had banners reading 'Year of slaves 2018—Thanks, Fidesz!' while others scattered leaflets (declaring 'Decent wages instead of slave labour!') from

'ALONE WE WOULD FAIL, BUT TOGETHER WE WILL WIN!'

the balcony. In spite of the obstructions the speaker forced through the vote, leading it from the benches, with manual voting. Because all this was live-streamed on Facebook, a spontaneous demonstration started in front of Parliament in Kossuth Square, followed by protests in other towns in the country. The Budapest demonstration went on until late in the evening: a coloured smoke bomb was ignited, and conflict broke out between protesters and the police.

The following day a dozen MPs went to the headquarters of Hungarian Television and demanded the public TV present events truthfully. The station's president, Dániel Papp (see Chapter 7), declined to engage in any discussion with the MPs. Following this, the politicians refused to leave the building, and the next day they were removed by force. For the first time in many years, the opposition determined the Hungarian political agenda for two weeks, showing all the hypocrisy that lay behind Orbán's 'work-based society' and providing a systematic framework for addressing questions of labour law, freedom and democracy. In these weeks the dynamics of political events changed, and actions that previously had been impossible became conceivable: obstruction, open opposition to the regime, civil disobedience, and confrontation with the police.

These events were the first occasion when the right and left opposition organized joint action against the ruling Fidesz. When in autumn 2019 there were municipal elections, the opposition parties were together able to put forward candidates for mayor in hundreds of municipalities, which was an unexpected success. In half of the bigger towns in the country, opposition candidates won, even though previously 80% of these had been ruled by Fidesz. The greatest triumph was the opposition's taking of the capital, Budapest, where Gergely Karácsony won a huge victory and where the opposition also won a sizeable majority in the Budapest assembly.[29]

TAINTED DEMOCRACY

Faced with this result, Fidesz broadcast the message that here was proof that Hungary was a democracy and that elections were fair. But the truth was that opposition victories took place in the uneven circumstances of the local elections. In essence, Fidesz made it impossible for the opposition to advertise in public spaces, which left only social media and personal contact. Meanwhile, the government party deployed its huge media and advertising supremacy in smear campaigns against opposition candidates, from Budapest to the smallest villages.[30] Fidesz had the entire government apparatus behind it. Fidesz's offensive bore fruit: it managed to increase the number of people who voted for it, despite the gains of the opposition.

Nonetheless, after 2019 the political space changed markedly, and the 'central space of force' that Fidesz had occupied for a decade collapsed. A relatively large and diverse anti-Orbán bloc of voters formed, which unified supporters of the 'old' and 'new' oppositions and all ideological sides.

Six opposition parties declared in 2020 that they would put forward jointly supported candidates in every one of the 106 single-member constituencies in the elections in 2022. In order to find the most suitable candidates, they organized something hitherto unheard of in Hungary: primary elections in September 2021. Ten per cent of all voters participated in the process.[31] The primary for the prime ministerial candidate resulted in the victory of the relatively unknown Péter Márki-Zay, mayor of the small town of Hódmezővásárhely, thus demonstrating that people wanted new faces in politics. The many public debates that Hungarians had been deprived of for more than a decade, and the long queues at the voting tents, gave proof of the fundamental desire for political pluralism and democratic competition. The primaries provided strong legitimacy for the joint candidates in the elections in 2022.

The stakes of the 2022 elections were very high both for the opposition, which had already failed badly twice, and for Fidesz.

'ALONE WE WOULD FAIL, BUT TOGETHER WE WILL WIN!'

After twelve years of corruption and of building an unfair system, Fidesz simply could not afford to lose. As János Lázár, one of Fidesz's strongmen, once put it: '2022 will see the crudest, wildest, and most important election campaign of the last thirty years'.[32]

While an outright opposition victory was but a faint prospect, there was a realistic hope that Fidesz's constitutional majority would be finally ended, and that the opposition could act at least as a strong check on the ruling party's activities. Instead, the opposition suffered a dramatic defeat and Orbán's party won its fourth consecutive landslide, securing 135 seats with 54% of the votes. The united opposition gained only 57 seats with 35% of the votes and a new far-right party, Our Homeland, entered Parliament with 5.88% of the votes. Hungary had become greatly polarized between Budapest and the large cities, where the opposition won overwhelmingly, and the countryside, which turned massively orange (the colour of Fidesz).

The defeated Hungarian opposition faced a huge dilemma: now that the united platform had failed so badly, what next?

PART II

ESTABLISHING CONTROL

4

THE ILLUSION OF DEMOCRACY
OVERHAULING PARLIAMENT AND THE JUDICIARY

Let me return to the 2014 election campaign, in order to show how the Fidesz government assisted its own party's chances by changing the election rules.

We were filled with excitement as we left behind the city of Kecskemét after a busy day in early March 2014. A large crowd had gathered in the dance hall of Hotel Aranyhomok for Együtt's campaign rally. The town of Kecskemét was a Fidesz stronghold, so even we were surprised at how many people wanted to hear us a few weeks before the 2014 parliamentary elections—at how many people wanted political change.

My fellow party members and I had already attended three hustings that day, and our tour of the country was going full steam ahead. We travelled home feeling positive, while we dissected the afternoon's events and surveyed the latest opinion polls. The figures were varied, but the trend was encouraging. Fidesz was leading with 30%, but the partial opposition alliance we had created with difficulty in January 2014 stood at 23%.[1]

As the campaign proceeded, I fell increasingly under the spell of campaign fever. I felt as if the energy of several people was concentrated in me. New activists joined our team, we spent more and more time at the street campaign stalls, and many people came to our hustings. All reasonable signs pointed to a Fidesz win, but we were nevertheless optimistic.

Fidesz invested enormous resources in their campaign. According to calculations by Transparency International, 'the government's parliamentary campaign cost almost 4 billion HUF', despite the fact that 'according to the law, a party can only spend a maximum of 995 million HUF on its parliamentary election campaign'. Fidesz, however, claimed to have complied with the law, only acknowledging campaign spending of 984 million HUF.[2] In addition, it ran a crude, hostile campaign against us. Fidesz portrayed the opposition parties as a communist scheme. Gordon Bajnai faced a systematic smear campaign. Fidesz's paid demonstrators marched in front of the hotel in Kecskemét to slander Bajnai, but there our supporters kept them away.

Constantly Rejigging the Election Law

The hostile campaign was one thing, but we had a bigger problem: with its constitutional majority, Fidesz had changed the Electoral Act governing members of Parliament in 2011. The electoral system formed in 1989 had provided a flexible political system for twenty years, albeit an absolute majority could easily be won, in a manner unique in Europe. This was what made it possible for Fidesz to win more than two thirds of the seats with 52% of the popular vote, representing only 33% of the electorate. If there was a problem with the electoral system, it was this lack of proportion.

Fidesz justified amending the law by saying that it would be more democratic. The new act could have made the election results

THE ILLUSION OF DEMOCRACY

more democratic by correcting the disproportion, but that is not what happened. First, Fidesz eliminated the two-round election system in the single-member constituencies, in terms of which the three most successful candidates in the first round competed in the second. Since 1990, between the two rounds candidate withdrawals based on agreements between the parties had gone a long way to shaping the final results. Previously Fidesz itself had made good use of this opportunity. For instance, in 1998, when the Hungarian Socialist Party (MSZP) won in the first round, Fidesz reached agreements with smaller parties between the two rounds, and thus managed to defeat the MSZP. Abolishing the second round clearly served the purpose of preventing smaller parties from collaborating against Fidesz, ensuring that the government party would secure the 'central force'.

Second, Fidesz reduced the number of electoral districts from 176 to 106 and redrew the boundaries for all the constituencies. Based on previous election results, they left the Fidesz-friendly constituencies relatively intact, but if an opposition candidate had a greater chance of success, the constituency was significantly redrawn.[3] This happened where I was standing, in a swing constituency. The bill carved out the heart of my electoral district, Széll Kálmán Square and surrounds, where for years the inhabitants had been liberal voters. Things were worked out in such detail that in many places constituency boundaries snaked around blocks in the same street. This is a typical technique of gerrymandering—the political manipulation of electoral district boundaries with the intent of creating undue advantage for a party.

A further difficulty was that instead of remedying the majority system, a more disproportional system was introduced by increasing the ratio of seats from individual constituencies. The disproportionality was exacerbated by a truly surprising system, known as 'compensating the winner', which awards further fractional votes to the party of a winning candidate in a single-member constituency. While, previously, a form of compensation existed to boost the parties of individual candidates who were at a disadvantage because of the winner-takes-all principle, now it gave even greater rewards to the winning party. These changes served the interests of the largest party, Fidesz.[4] Moreover, the Constitutional Court, which by 2011 had a majority of Fidesz appointees, found no objection to them.

What also affected the outcome of the elections was that the Fidesz government amended the act on citizenship, making it possible for ethnic Hungarians living abroad to obtain Hungarian citizenship even without being domiciled in Hungary. The government actively supported organizations in Romania, Serbia and Ukraine which promoted the simplified naturalization procedure. Hundreds of thousands of ethnic Hungarians in neighbouring countries were eligible to take part in the Hungarian parliamentary elections in 2014, and of those who finally voted, 96% voted for Fidesz.

While these newly minted citizens were able to vote by post, Hungarians studying or working abroad had to cast their ballot in person at foreign embassies. This discriminatory aspect of the law was unsuccessfully challenged in the Constitutional Court as well. While in the Romanian region of Szeklerland, Hungarians in small villages voted en masse by mail, my daughter, an exchange student in Belgium who turned eighteen that year, had to travel two hours to the Hungarian Embassy in Brussels to vote. No surprise that turnout was much lower among Hungarian expats.

A further dozen or so amendments introduced to the election law changed the requirements for putting forward a candidate and the system of state financial support to which candidates were entitled.[5] The result was the financial incentivization of 'parties' consisting of a handful of people to run in the elections without having any chance of meeting the 5% threshold to enter Parliament. They were useful for misleading voters. The ploys embedded in the law call into question the fairness of the elections.

Manipulation of the 2014 Campaign

There were also changes in the regulations governing political advertising, made just one year before the elections. Commercial media were banned from profiting from political advertising, and therefore had little incentive to air party political broadcasts. During the 2014 election campaign, not a single commercial TV or radio station gave broadcasting time to the competing parties.[6]

Meanwhile, the government spent many millions of forints on televised 'public interest' information campaigns, which did not count as political campaigning. In these ads, the government used the slogan 'Hungary is performing better', which was the same as the one on Fidesz's campaign posters. My party took legal action against Fidesz, and the Curia, the highest judicial authority, ruled in our favour.[7] But this did nothing to change the campaign, and the Fidesz government's illegal propaganda proceeded openly on both state and commercial TV stations.[8] The competitive disadvantage for us was staggering.

With television advertising out of the question, we needed another way to reach potential voters. Most of the billboard market was controlled by companies belonging to a Fidesz ally whose firms only gave advertising space to Fidesz. Electricity poles, which number in the tens of thousands, were the most affordable option. But just as we entered negotiations with ESMA, which sold electricity pole banners, the government outlawed this type of advertising, citing road safety concerns. ESMA rapidly came close to bankruptcy, and we lost one of our last remaining solutions. In a clear sign that this was nothing but a calculated move, after the election another businessman close to the prime minister bought the now worthless company. Shortly thereafter, advertising on electricity poles was once more allowed, with slight changes in the regulations.[9] Soon, ESMA's banners (now with an owner close to Fidesz) were filled with advertisements by state companies, and since then the company has been more profitable than ever, serving also political campaigns.

Ultimately, my campaign team and I reverted to the amateurish tactics we had employed in 1990, putting up posters in the street on homemade stands. We could get only two dozen billboard posters in my constituency of 80,000 people. In the last weeks of the campaign, my team swelled to 200 people. We were constantly doing the rounds on the streets in our campaign cars, and activists knocked on every door.

With campaigning rules tipped so heavily in favour of Fidesz, it was difficult to calculate the extent to which this would distort the result. Even though we were fully aware of the obstacles we faced, the results of the elections hit us like a cold shower. With less than 45% of the votes, Fidesz once more gained power. In 2010 Fidesz had won a two-thirds majority with 52% of the votes; now it had taken less than half of the votes, owing to the changes in the election law. Despite having lost a fifth of its supporters in four years, it still won a supermajority. The brutal distortions in the election rules could not have been more apparent.

On the night of the elections, our Együtt team was overcome by disappointment. I will never forget that feeling. When I stood next to party chairman Gordon Bajnai on the stage to announce the results to our supporters and the press, I felt hollow. All our efforts, sacrifices and political compromises had been in vain. We had disappointed our supporters, who weeks earlier had sent us off from campaign meetings with rounds of applause. We knew that what happened next would have direct consequences for their lives too. However many voted for us, the electoral laws had got the better of all of us.

THE ILLUSION OF DEMOCRACY

With 38% of the votes in my constituency, I lost to Fidesz's candidate, who received 45% of the vote. If there had been a second round, we could have partnered with the green party LMP, which received 11% of the vote, and defeated him. In the end, I entered Parliament on the parliamentary compensation list.

Fidesz won a supermajority by just one seat, but lost it in a by-election the following year, and could no longer alter the Electoral Act ahead of the next contest in 2018. At the same time, the governing parties gained considerable influence in the market for billboards and other media. Government propaganda, disguised as public information advertising, flooded state and commercial TV and radio stations. This unprecedented advantage in the media further distorted the 2018 parliamentary contest.

The Election Observation Mission of the Organization for Security and Co-operation in Europe (OSCE) found that the parliamentary elections in 2018 'were characterized by a pervasive overlap between state and ruling party resources, undermining contestants' ability to compete on an equal basis'.[10] The report pointed out that the media were highly biased towards the ruling party, and that intimidating rhetoric and opaque campaign financing had severely restricted the arena for genuine political debate and limited voters' ability to make a fully informed decision. Our assessment was that for the third of voters who did not have access to the internet, it must have seemed as though the opposition did not exist.

When Fidesz regained a supermajority in 2018, it once again set about altering the Electoral Act. This further restricted the opposition's room for manoeuvre. As the billboard market had for some time been concentrated in the hands of oligarchs close to Fidesz, the law focused on the opportunities to put up free posters. Under the pretext of conserving the appearance of towns, it was now illegal to display posters anywhere in Hungary. In the 2019 municipal elections, when opposition parties in the city of Nyíregyháza stuck their posters to electricity poles, the Fidesz mayor had them removed, and invoiced the opposition for the cost of the work, while Fidesz posters were bristling all around the town.[11]

During the 2018 campaign the National Election Commission, the only supervisory body of the state in which there were representatives of all parties, levied fines for several infringements, even on Fidesz. Viktor Orbán's campaign team was fined hundreds of thousands of forints after the prime minister campaigned with kindergarten children without their parents' knowledge. As the election approached, Orbán posted a cheery video on his Facebook page about his campaigning trip round Hungary, in which one scene was shot at the inauguration of the new building of the Hungarian University of Public Service. In the clip, the prime minister spoke about the court case. 'Well, Patyi fined me! Haha. Fine friend!' said Orbán directly to András Patyi, the university rector, who at the time was also the president of the National Election Commission. 'I'm very sorry, Prime Minister', said the rector, making his excuses for having simply done his job. This exchange illustrated perfectly not only the hierarchy among key actors in the Hungarian state, when the leader of an independent institution charged with ensuring 'checks and balances' humbled himself as a subordinate of the head of government. It was also emblematic of Fidesz's governance: its determination to erode the ethos of autonomous institutions, to interpret clear principles of public administration in an arbitrary manner, and, in place of a state based on the rule of law, to demand political loyalty.

The Formation of a Politically Biased State

As I was sworn into Parliament in June 2014, I found myself surrounded by Fidesz politicians. My isolation was relieved only

THE ILLUSION OF DEMOCRACY

by my husband and our three children sitting in the audience, who looked forward to our new life with cautious optimism.

Twenty-four years previously, my experience in 1990, when I assumed my parliamentary seat bursting with pride, had been completely different. Back then, as members of Fidesz's small team, we saw ourselves as the anointed representatives of democracy. In the 1990s, the rule of law was one of Fidesz's guiding principles, and not once did we critique a law without making reference to democratic norms. 'We responsibly declare that all of Fidesz's policies in all circumstances are guided by its belief in pluralism, which includes a changing [government]', we said in 1990 when debating the governmental programme.[12] Viktor Orbán criticized the government, saying: 'Stable legal principles worked out over millennia cannot be made subservient to short-term political aims'.[13] It was unacceptable, in our view, for the government to reject the opposition's criticisms: 'such scenes bode ill for the future of democracy'.

Over time, Fidesz's strong commitment to the rule of law waned. This was demonstrated when during the 2006 election campaign, Orbán encouraged his supporters to ignore electoral silence rules, in terms of which candidates are not allowed to campaign on election day. A recording was made public in which Orbán told party members: 'On Saturday and Sunday the call to go and vote will go out in my name, and for that the National Election Commission will censure me, and lawyers will defend me, and that's that'.[14] Fidesz has since shown that it is not above using legal loopholes and stratagems. But back then, it was unthinkable for a Hungarian government to openly depart from the rule of law.

In 2014, twenty-four years after first being sworn in, I had to ask myself a difficult question: what point was there in working as an opposition member of Parliament? Fidesz had a supermajority, and therefore did not need the support of other parties to pass legislation. The leaders of state institutions were chosen by a single person. Though it was difficult to imagine, Fidesz could do whatever it wanted.

In this situation the only task left for the opposition was to check the government, but the chances for doing so had shrunk considerably. The parliamentary majority obstructed the opposition's work in every way possible. Fidesz introduced a procedure for exceptional cases of urgency, which enabled a bill to be passed twenty-four hours after it had been submitted. My team and I had to work every weekend to survey reams of proposed legislation and to prepare our responses. Obviously, these changes did not only affect the opposition, but government MPs were unfazed. Without a word of complaint, they voted blindly, often on laws of cardinal importance.

Fidesz MPs also blocked committees of inquiry, and government MPs skipped hearings instigated by opposition MPs. My first speech took place on a Monday evening in summer 2014 and the benches of the ruling party were completely empty. These limited opportunities forced opposition MPs to use advertising banners and posters to attract attention during voting. The house speaker levied severe fines on the 'troublemakers' and barred several opposition MPs from Parliament.[15] These drastic steps called into question Parliament's constitutional role and democratic function. Fidesz was obviously attempting to rob the National Assembly of its ability to act as an independent branch of power, a process that was managed by the speaker, László Kövér.

The atmosphere in Parliament can be characterized by an incident when a fellow member of the opposition enquired about a corruption case regarding the Orbán family that had appeared in the press. Orbán, who was legally required to answer MPs' questions, stood up and said: 'Merry Christmas to the honourable member!'[16] The Fidesz group guffawed at the apparently witty answer.

THE ILLUSION OF DEMOCRACY

In eight years, the Orbán government passed 1,589 Acts of Parliament, 40% more than in previous parliamentary term.[17] It was incredibly hard work for the opposition to keep track of these many laws, especially because the turnaround time for a law was on average twenty days shorter than in previous years, and the most important submissions went through the house in forty-eight hours. The aim was clearly to debilitate parliamentary control and question the seriousness of the opposition.

Party Faithful at the Helm of Supervisory Institutions

By 2014, Fidesz had taken over all the constitutional institutions of the state meant to provide oversight of the government. Their leaders were replaced by people directly linked to Fidesz (as seen in the Introduction).

After Fidesz increased the number of places on the Constitutional Court, the vacancies were gradually filled by its own people, often politicians. In autumn 2014, when I was already an MP, three more places on the Constitutional Court were filled. In the National Assembly, the parties set up an ad hoc committee of MPs to debate the nomination of the new justices for the Constitutional Court. To our surprise, the sitting of the committee was unexpectedly declared closed, and the Fidesz representatives quickly voted down all the opposition's nominees. Only Fidesz's three nominees were given public hearings, as if no one else had been in the running. In response, opposition MPs boycotted the rest of the process. In the sitting, one Fidesz nominee, András Zs. Varga, who had previously been the deputy chief prosecutor, warned against the Constitutional Court becoming an arbitrary and unlimited organ of power in the name of the rule of law. He clearly was not preparing to enter a constitutional institution charged with checking governmental power. Fidesz MPs leaned back, satisfied, and asked no questions. The nominees for Constitutional Court justices made no effort to present their professional expertise or general personal skills to the public at large. After the farcical hearings they were given the green light to sit on the Constitutional Court. In Parliament, such petty, unworthy situations became the norm.

Particularly injurious was the way that, one after another, the mandate of people in the most important positions of the state was extended from six to nine years, for instance the president of the National Office for the Judiciary, the National Media Authority, and the chief prosecutor. In doing so, Fidesz guaranteed that its people would hold their positions well after the government's term of office had expired.

The position of chief prosecutor also underwent conspicuous changes. Fidesz needed a two-thirds majority to fill the position, rather than the simple majority stipulated in the Fundamental Law at the time. The Fundamental Law stipulated that if a new chief prosecutor could not be nominated with a two-thirds majority after nine years, the incumbent would remain in office. In practice this meant that if Fidesz were to lose the election, and the subsequent government did not have a two-thirds supermajority, then the Fidesz nominee could remain in office indefinitely. This move showed the long-term entrenchment of Fidesz's power, in clear violation of the constitution. MPs were no longer able to question the chief prosecutor in Parliament, with the result that the Prosecution Service answered neither to the National Assembly nor to the government. In contrast to the courts, the prosecutors worked to strict orders given by the chief prosecutor. As such, the chief prosecutor had extraordinary power over the justice system. At the time of writing, Péter Polt, a reliable, long-trusted Fidesz cadre, had occupied the post for twelve years.

The heads of the State Audit Office (SAO) are also former members of the Fidesz parliamentary group. The SAO is the highest auditing body in the state, the guardian of public monies. Working there requires, at a minimum, extensive professional expertise and impartiality. Yet for the first time since Hungary became a democracy, in 2010 the National Assembly appointed a Fidesz politician, László Domokos, as SAO president. He was awarded an unusually long, twelve-year mandate. Prior to joining the SAO, Domokos, like several other politicians, had accumulated several seats on councils at local and regional levels and in Parliament, acquiring in the process such a high income that the final sum could not be ascertained.[18]

Under Domokos's leadership, the activity of the SAO has changed noticeably. He has exaggerated the seriousness of minor discrepancies found in the audits of state institutions, such as universities, hospitals and research institutions, and thereby provided the government with an excuse to replace these bodies' leadership.[19] In the hands of the state party of Fidesz, the SAO has become a tool for centralizing government.

Creating an Unconstitutional Constitution

By the time I became an MP, the Fundamental Law, which had come into force two years previously amid long celebrations, had been amended five times. A quarter of the text had been completely replaced, with substantial changes in the content, involving the introduction of unconstitutional elements.

The process of amending the law was already in full swing before the ink on the document had dried. In December 2011, one month before the new Fundamental Law had officially come into force, Fidesz passed a strange set of laws known as the Transitional Provisions of the Fundamental Law. This flew in the face of fundamental human rights, the rule of law, and the separation of powers. It was so restrictive that even the Fidesz-friendly Constitutional Court rejected many elements of the proposed text.

The ruling did not matter to Fidesz. The Fundamental Law was amended, for a fourth time, to include those contested provisions. This gesture showed complete disregard for the Constitutional Court and the citizens of Hungary. To further humiliate the country's highest legal institution, the updated text stated that the court would have no remit to examine amendments to the Fundamental Law. This represented a major blow to the rule of law and constitutionalism in Hungary.

The decision led to considerable outcry in political and legal circles in Hungary and abroad. The president of the European Commission[20] and the US Department of State[21] both called on the government to postpone the amendment until it had received the detailed expert opinion of the Venice Commission of the Council of Europe.[22] In typical Fidesz fashion, while the Venice Commission was drafting its opinion, the National Assembly had long since passed the amendment.[23] The commission found that the Fundamental Law and its amendments, together with the several dozen cardinal laws which required a two-thirds majority to alter, endangered the system of checks and balances. In the commission's view, the Hungarian government was using the constitution as a political tool and, in so doing, it blurred the lines between governing and constitution-making.

The renowned conservative constitutional lawyer László Sólyom, the first president of the Constitutional Court and later president of the republic, wrote in 2012 that what was happening was not an amendment to the constitution, but the stealthy introduction of a new constitution.[24] 'More than a symbolic change, it is in actual fact a blow against the constitutional development of the last twenty years'.[25]

New Momentum in the Permanent Process of Constitution-Making

In spring 2015, millions of refugees started travelling through Turkey and across Hungary to reach Western Europe. The Orbán government launched an aggressive anti-refugee campaign, and in 2016 it announced a referendum. Despite constitutional concerns, the referendum was held in October 2016 with a low turnout and, thus, with no valid result.

Nevertheless, Viktor Orbán wasted no time in preparing a fresh amendment to the Fundamental Law.[26] Although the tendentious question ('Do you want the European Union to be able to mandate the obligatory settlement of non-Hungarian citizens in Hungary even without the approval of the [Hungarian] National Assembly?') in the referendum suggested that the Hungarian government would openly oppose the European Union, the proposed amendment was a cautious balance between the Treaty on European Union and the Hungarian Fundamental Law. At the same time, the Fundamental Law amendment contained the sentence 'A foreign people cannot be settled in Hungary'. Another sentence was added to the preamble of the Fundamental Law: 'We believe that the protection of our identity rooted in our historical constitution is the basic obligation of the state'. This statement was designed as a declaration of the sovereignty of the Hungarian state, but it also created a basis for future conflict between the Constitutional Court and the Court of Justice of the European Union. The constitutional amendment bill was put forward in the National Assembly in 2018, and Orbán's government came in for a barrage of criticism from international organizations.

This kind of permanent constitution-making resulted in a gradual deterioration of the guarantees of fundamental rights and an erosion of effective checks and balances. While sometimes there were ideological motives behind the changes to the constitutional system, the emerging elements were often contradictory and eclectic. Most of the changes served as an instrument in the struggle for political power.[27]

Frankly speaking, for an opposition politician it was more than difficult to act reasonably in such a debased constitutional environment. Our strategy could not be other than to act according to the law but make every effort to change it. That was exactly what the young Fidesz party had done in 1988 when facing the seemingly unbreakable power of the Hungarian Socialist Workers' Party.

The Independence of the Courts

'One hundred and fifty years ago the question was whether the Hungarian state wanted to ensure the independence of the judiciary. Looking to the future, the question is whether for their part Hungarian judges wish to ensure the independence of the state', said László Kövér, speaker of the National Assembly, at an event to celebrate the 150th anniversary of the act ensuring the independence of the judiciary, which was attended by leading prosecutors and lawyers.[28] Those present were certainly astonished, because although there had been attempts by Fidesz to influence the judiciary for some time, until then no one had openly called into question the sacred and inviolable independence of the judiciary. Kövér, a law graduate himself, was renowned for his radicalism, yet his speech still raised eyebrows.

The Orbán government began reshaping the Hungarian judiciary in 2010 when, by retiring judges with instant effect, it removed several hundred experienced judges from the system. The following year, the government started laying out reforms to modernize the justice system. After the Fidesz majority had curtailed the power of the Constitutional Court and lowered the retirement age for judges, the plans prompted concerns.

The most important step in the reform was to replace the former uniform judicial authority with a dual system. The Supreme Court was replaced with the Curia, overseeing judgements, and the National Office for the Judiciary, whose president was given the authority to select and nominate leading judges and to supervise judges. This office was supposed to be counterbalanced by the National Judicial Council, which was democratically elected by judges, but this institution did not receive the powers that would have enabled it to effectively fulfil its supervisory function. The position of the president of the Supreme Court simply ceased to exist, and the parliamentary majority voted for new heads for both the Curia and the National Office for the Judiciary. This latter position was given to Tünde Handó, wife of a leading Fidesz politician and a confidante of the prime minister. Her work was initially greeted with cautious support, although she was obviously a political appointee. Judges hoped that through her connections with the government she would be able to represent the interests of the judiciary and implement important internal reforms. But the reforms were left by the wayside, while at the same time political pressure became increasingly obvious.[29]

Handó enforced the government's interests through the nomination of judges and the distribution of sensitive cases.[30] This process violated the very foundation of judicial independence. The politicization of the judiciary grew steadily, and increasingly Handó came into conflict with members of the body overseeing her, the National Judicial Council. The latter believed that Handó's opaque tactics threatened the integrity of the judiciary and even petitioned the National Assembly for her removal, without success.[31] When the conflicts between the judiciary and political power reached international professional forums, Handó levelled accusations of treason against those judges who had represented Hungary at the European Network of Councils for the Judiciary: 'Some of our fellow judges, neglecting themselves and their duties, run abroad and betray our homeland'.[32]

I was dismayed not just that political influence over the courts was threatening Hungary's democracy, but also that Tünde Handó had taken on this role. I had known her since

Fidesz was established in 1988. The first summer we set up a women's group together, the Madzsar Alíz group. We organized women's demonstrations, and hoped that we would be able to give women a voice within the organization. When in 1990 Fidesz became a parliamentary party, Tünde Handó chose a career as a judge and we went our separate ways, but over the decades I had repeatedly turned to her for professional help. An outstanding labour lawyer, she had always given me useful advice. I was glad that she had a successful career. But in her role as president of the National Office for the Judiciary, the Fidesz government expected Handó to transform the judiciary into an organ that posed no risk to the party. She must have known this when she accepted the position. When I heard her report in the budgetary committee of the National Assembly in 2016, the only matter on which I could support her was her call for gender pay parity among judges. A sad state of affairs. After she became unsupportable, Orbán nominated her as a constitutional justice.

When the government realized that, although judges could be put under pressure, their independence could not simply be eliminated, it decided to create special courts. These were to concentrate on disputes between the government and citizens, ranging from the review of decisions by authorities to questions relating to elections, referenda, the tax authority, public procurement, the competition authority and the media authority. The aim was to remove these politically sensitive questions from the jurisdiction of the ordinary courts. Although such politically sensitive cases require unassailably independent courts, it was up to the justice minister to nominate the judges.

This brazen circumvention of judicial independence triggered fierce criticism from constitutional lawyers, the international community, and even people within Fidesz's interest groups. Consequently, in this matter Orbán's government had to retreat, and in an amendment to the Fundamental Law, the special courts were abandoned.[33]

Despite mounting political pressure on the judiciary over the years, rulings on politically sensitive questions showed that most Hungarian judges' independence was unwavering.[34] Still, Orbán's government was intent on sheltering organs of the state from the justice system.

Six months after the plans for special administrative courts were withdrawn, the National Assembly passed an omnibus law. Buried within these hundreds of pages was an amendment that enabled state institutions to turn to the Constitutional Court if they were handed an unfavourable ruling. This recourse, known as a constitutional complaint, is usually intended for citizens who feel that a legal statute or court ruling infringes their human rights. A judge commented on the consequences of this decision: 'Will there be a judge who grants refugee status to an asylum seeker if they are concerned that the Immigration Office might challenge the ruling at the Constitutional Court?'[35] The government had found a new method to reinforce judges' self-censorship.

The Orbán government has used varied and often informal means to pressure judges but in 2020, the prime minister openly rejected a court ruling. The Hungarian state had been ordered to pay compensation because a school was found to be segregating Roma children and providing them with poorer-quality education. Orbán commented, 'This whole affair is no good', and deemed it 'deeply unjust'. 'I don't know exactly what should be done, but, for sure, things can't stay like this'.[36] Parliament then passed a law that suspended the state's obligation to pay compensation for six months. As this case demonstrated, it was impossible for Hungarian courts to rule on politically sensitive cases without being subjected to political pressure.

The independence of judges is a crucial issue in the functioning of a democracy, because the equality of parties before the court can only be guaranteed by the impartiality and independence of the judges. If they act unlawfully, the authorities must be prepared to find themselves at odds with the justice system. But Orbán's government questioned even this fundamental democratic principle. The words of the speaker of the National Assembly at the conference celebrating the 150th anniversary of judicial independence reflect this attitude. 'You, the judges, can always be independent only to the extent that the Hungarian state is too',[37] he said, adding: 'The messianic endeavours of globalization [...] constantly attempt to weaken the competencies of democratically legitimate states by means of the system of jurisdiction. [...] Today's jurists and politicians must decide for themselves which side they will take: those defending and building the state, or those attacking and ruining the state'.

In 2020, when the Curia president's term came to an end, Fidesz took the opportunity to find a replacement who shared Kövér's ideas. The party settled on constitutional justice András Zs. Varga. So important was it for the governing party that Varga should become president of the Curia that it amended two laws to make him electable. This happened despite the National Judicial Council almost unanimously rejecting Varga's appointment. Its members took issue with the fact that his previous time in office had been spent in the Prosecution Service, and that he 'had never been a judge, and had never experienced judicial independence'.[38] Moreover, as a constitutional justice, he had supported cases that the Court of Justice of the European Union had later ruled to be unlawful.[39] Varga's appointment presaged serious friction in the Hungarian legal system, which was soon manifested in his statement that 'it is an urgent task to rediscover [...] the natural limits of judicial independence'.[40]

The new laws passed in the first twelve years of the Orbán government formed a coherent system in the sense that they aimed to broaden the government's power as much as possible.

THE ILLUSION OF DEMOCRACY

The Fidesz government always acknowledged, indeed proclaimed, the construction of a strong state, which it justified by saying that the interests of national governance had to be protected against the dominance of the global liberal elite. But the legal tradition, 'reheated' by the Orbán government, had no bearing on the system of European democracy set up in the second half of the twentieth century, which Hungary joined after the regime change, and according to which neither democracy nor constitutional government can exist without checks on power.

Constitutional Vandalism in the European Union

In 2010, when Orbán won the elections, the steps he took to change the constitutional order caught Brussels by surprise. It was several years before the European Parliament and the European Commission understood that the Hungarian government's actions were threatening the separation of powers. However, already in 2014 Orbán had said: 'The system of checks and balances is an American invention, which Europe, perhaps due to intellectual mediocrity, borrowed and applied to European politics'.[41]

Until then, no European Union (EU) member state had ever deliberately endeavoured to undermine democracy. As mentioned in the introduction, the first controversy in the European Parliament arose when Orbán's party voted on the provisions of the Media Act, which infringed the freedom of the press and created a one-party media authority without any external supervision. Shortly afterwards, the act on the compulsory early retirement of judges came onto the agenda. There was a debate in the European Commission about how to approach the problem, and finally Brussels initiated its traditional infringement procedure against the Hungarian government. In the first conflict, just as in every similar subsequent case, Orbán spoke of an insult against the Hungarian people. 'I cannot accept from anybody, not even from the Germans, that just because the Hungarian people lived in a dictatorship for 40 years, anyone can question the democratic commitment of the Hungarian people'.[42]

Orbán's government posed an unprecedented challenge not just for the Hungarian opposition, but for the EU's institutions and member states.

The Tavares Report

In 2013, the European Parliament published the first in-depth examination of fundamental rights in Hungary. The report was drafted after the Hungarian National Assembly passed the controversial fourth amendment to the Fundamental Law. According to what is known as the Tavares Report,[43] systemic changes had happened in Hungary that departed from the fundamental values of the EU. After a tumultuous debate in the European Parliament, Orbán claimed the report was part of a left-wing showcase trial, and that the Hungarian government would not implement its recommendations.[44]

In response to the report, Fidesz MPs voted on a counter-declaration in which they demanded that the EU respect Hungarians.[45] This childish reaction, devoid of any legal validity, was a sad moment in the Hungarian National Assembly, and has been repeated several times since.

It soon became clear that dialogue alone would not be enough to persuade the Orbán government to uphold the EU's fundamental values. Brussels lacked an effective tool for defending the freedom of its citizens. Policymakers were reluctant to trigger Article 7 of the Treaty on European Union, according to which a member state's voting rights can be suspended if it breaches core EU values. Though the Tavares Report had demonstrated that Orbán's policies were a series of deliberate steps towards authoritarianism, European politicians trusted that they would be able to keep the Hungarian government within certain limits through political negotiations. After the debate on the report, however, the EU started to think about developing a more effective mechanism to protect fundamental rights.

The debate also demonstrated how Orbán's contradictory, autocratic politics divided European political parties. Social-democratic, green and liberal political groups had from the beginning criticized his government for its anti-democratic measures, while far-right groups had stood up for him. The situation was particularly delicate for the centrist-conservative European People's Party (EPP), to which Fidesz belonged. The group was split into three factions: harsh critics, strong supporters, and the pragmatists. Among the pragmatists there were influential leaders, like Joseph Daul, the president of the EPP, who in 2015 stated that 'Orbán likes to provoke, he is the "enfant terrible" of the EPP family, but I like him'.[46] Manfred Weber, representative for the German Christian Social Union and leader of the EPP group in the European Parliament, had campaigned personally in Budapest alongside Fidesz several times, even in 2014. From my view in Hungary, it was shocking to see this moderate and cultured German politician standing up for Orbán.

It would be difficult to say to what extent the EPP leaders really liked him. After all, Orbán often outmanoeuvred them and sparked division in the political group. At the same time, they thought that as long as they kept Orbán onside, they could influence him on important European issues. In return, Fidesz members of the European Parliament (MEPs) merged obediently into the EPP group, and voted for most proposals, often going against the Hungarian government's rhetoric. The pragmatists were motivated mainly by the fact that as the largest group in the European Parliament, the EPP possessed the most senior posts in the EU, and without Fidesz it might have lost this powerful position. They needed Orbán's party in the EPP group, and this meant they had an interest in not splitting from Fidesz. Orbán could rely on his supporters.

Nevertheless, Fidesz faced constant questioning, even in the EPP group. Orbán's people developed several methods to gain the support of fellow conservative parties, even amid doubts over constitutionality in Hungary. Firstly, Fidesz insisted that each question be examined individually, and in every critical issue it cited examples outside Hungary.[47] Taken out of context, these examples were irrelevant. At EPP meetings, Orbán lined up a troop of young, well-trained and well-dressed lawyers who assured their fellow party members that the legal procedures adopted by the Hungarian government were not unique. As the MEPs did not examine the constitutional context, Orbán's people were able to persuade many of them. That the critical laws were examined individually also prevented experts of the European Commission from being able to understand their true political consequences in the context of the continually changing Hungarian legal framework.

Legal Trickery

To get a true picture, it was necessary to examine these laws in terms of their outcome. For instance, the results of the 2014 election were influenced not only by changing the Elections Act, but by altering the system of party financing, abolishing payment for campaign advertising on television, and radically restricting the appearance of the opposition in state media. If the European Commission had assessed the 2014 elections, it would have found that these were neither free nor fair. But the commission did not have the political mandate to do so, and Fidesz lobbied strongly for it not to have this authority. In every debate on governance, Fidesz argued that the party had gained great power as the result of democratic elections, and thus everything that was happening in Hungary was democratic. The leaders of EU institutions never questioned this statement, even though in 2014 and 2018 it was clear that the Hungarian elections were unfair.[48]

Another Orbán tactic consisted of introducing radical measures which went far beyond the red line of tolerable democratic rules, and retreating slightly when Brussels raised objections. Lawyers in the Hungarian government knew full well that the significant lowering of the age of retirement for judges, or certain aspects of the Media Act, would clash with European regulations. This did not prevent Hungarian politicians from approving these laws, because in the years that passed until the European Commission and the Court of Justice made their decisions, they could effectively change the context. Two steps forward, one step back.

The Hungarian prime minister not only normalized aggressive, belligerent behaviour; his radical measures also continually pushed the boundaries of what the organization considered acceptable. Orbán became the pioneer of changes that represented a model to other member states. In 2015, when the Law and Justice party won the Polish general elections, it followed in Orbán's steps as it set about reining in the justice system, primarily by restricting the activity of the Constitutional Court.

Orbán's risk-taking and radical politics became obvious throughout Europe during the 2015 refugee crisis. This was the first time when, in relation to the sharing of refugee quotas, the Hungarian prime minister openly opposed a European Council decision and persisted in obstructing a joint European solution. Orbán's harsh anti-refugee policies and openly anti-Muslim campaign (see Chapter 8) made an impression on many European politicians. But the divisive, exclusionary rhetoric he used was unacceptable in Western Europe. There it was spouted only by far-right parties, with whom moderate politicians could not share a platform. Orbán was a different kind of prime minister, and although his harsh policies were publicly rejected by many, in the course of the crisis every country in Europe tightened its refugee and immigration rules. Compared with Orbán's unrelenting and radical solutions, other European governments seemed humane. Embracing the role of 'useful idiot', Orbán did Western politicians a service. It is unsurprising, then, that institutional criticism of him dwindled that year, even though in Hungary profoundly anti-democratic legislation was still being passed. After 2015, Orbán's government put critics of the system under greater pressure than ever, stigmatizing politicians, journalists and NGOs.

In 2017, two new laws stirred controversy in Western European political circles, with Orbán once more the centre of attention. The first, known as Lex NGO (see Chapter 9), was aimed at organizations monitoring government policies—looking at corruption or freedoms, for instance—that received financial support from foreign donors.[49] The law forced these organizations to register on a public government webpage as 'organizations with foreign support'. The government's aim was simply to pillory organizations that criticized it. Media close to Fidesz soon started to feature these NGOs and denigrate them. The second law imposed excessively onerous conditions on the Central European University (CEU), which, if implemented, would have made it impossible for the CEU to operate.[50]

Protests against the two laws in Hungary soon turned into a global outcry. The European Commission launched infringement procedures regarding both matters, which were carried over to the Court of Justice of the European Union. It took the court three years to publish its rulings condemning both laws, but by then it was too late. The university had already left Hungary (see Chapter 9).

Fidesz's politics attracted wider European attention following an investigation by OLAF, the European Anti-Fraud Office, which found that there had been 'serious irregularities' and 'conflict of interest' in the way Viktor Orbán's son-in-law had acquired millions of euros in EU development funds.[51] This was scandalous news to Orbán's fellow conservative party members, but after the Hungarian chief prosecutor dropped the case, it became increasingly apparent that justice in Hungary was not impartial. This episode was instrumental in returning the Hungarian question to the European parliamentary agenda.

The Sargentini Report

On 11 September 2018, there was a great bustle in the imposing glass building of the European Parliament in Strasbourg. MEPs were preparing for a historic debate. According to a report by Judith Sargentini,[52] despite the EU's many attempts to resolve the systematic problems of constitutionality and democracy arising in Hungary, there had been no progress in protecting the rule of law. The report recommended initiating the strict Article 7 procedure against Hungary, and called on the European Council to establish whether there was a clear threat to the rule of law in Hungary and to make recommendations to the government.

The tone of the parliamentary debate was acerbic. Orbán saw the report as deeply unjust: 'You will be condemning the Hungary that for one thousand years has been a part of Christian Europe. The Hungary that with its work and when necessary with its blood contributed to our splendid European history'.[53] He saw the entire procedure as stigmatizing and exclusionary, and at one point he added, to the great surprise of those present: 'We would never go as far as to silence those who disagree with us'. This statement, coming from someone whose government had spent the previous decade stripping thousands of their freedom of expression, reeked of hypocrisy.

The vote on the Sargentini report was due one day after the debate. Its adoption required a two-thirds majority. Orbán met with the EPP parliamentary group to discuss its position. He was questioned at length by MEPs. He viewed the report as a party-political witch hunt, and with his team of lawyers, in the customary manner, he criticized many details of the report. Orbán conceded nothing.

The hearing took a dramatic turn when MEPs asked Orbán how his son-in-law was able to receive EU development funds. By then the legal team had departed, and Orbán dispensed with all formalities, saying: 'Really, who cares what you say? Hungarians voted us back to power with a two-thirds majority to boot, that is all that matters'.[54]

The EPP group members were astonished by Orbán's arrogance. The following day the majority of the group—including its leader, Manfred Weber—decided to vote in favour of Sargentini's report, and so it was passed. It seemed as though a giant step had been taken in the history of the EU.

But what actually happened was that after the vote, the affair died down for a while. Although the European Parliament had the authority to trigger Article 7, only the European Council could conduct the process. The council, however, was unprepared and unwilling to launch the lengthy, unprecedented process which, at the end, requires unanimity among member states. This was inconceivable, as the Hungarian and Polish heads of government had declared that if this procedure were initiated against either country, the other would veto it.[55] Shortly afterwards, politicians left Brussels to campaign for the 2019 European elections. To Fidesz's incredible good fortune, the Hungarian question came off the agenda again, but only for a few months.

The Report on the Rule of Law

At the beginning of October 2020, the European Commission made public its first comprehensive report on the rule of law in EU member states. This pointed to serious problems in Hungary. When presenting the report, Věra Jourová, vice-president of the European Commission for Values and Transparency, called

THE ILLUSION OF DEMOCRACY

Hungary an 'ill democracy';⁵⁶ this angered the Hungarian government. 'I am obliged to turn to Madame the Chair because of Commission Vice-President Věra Jourová's offensive words about Hungary. The Vice-President [...] insulted EU citizens of Hungarian nationality, saying they are "not in a position to form an independent opinion". [...] The commissioner's [...] resignation is indispensable',⁵⁷ said Orbán in a complaint to Ursula von der Leyen, president of the European Commission. Speaking at an event to celebrate the independent judiciary, the speaker of the National Assembly levelled the following accusation at the EU:

> The aim is to eliminate democratic nation-states and to form supranational centres of power without electoral legitimacy. [...] This is the result of an aggressive spread of abnormality, a total loss of values and a denial of the natural order, that, how shall I put it, knows neither man nor God, in the name of liberalism and human rights.⁵⁸

A decade after Fidesz had come to power, its worldview was clearly incompatible with European democracy.

Orbán's regime reasoned that, compared with the liberal democracy prevalent in Europe, the Hungarian system embodied an 'alternative version of constitutionality', and attempted to engage the EU in this debate. Fidesz asserted that the rule of law was a dynamically changing construct. Each member state should accept other members' regulations as equal, so that cooperation among states could continue unperturbed.⁵⁹

The grave crisis of democracy that had come into being during Orbán's decade in power was described in a European study as involving 'the process through which elected public authorities deliberately implement governmental blueprints which aim to systematically weaken, annihilate or capture internal checks on power with the view of dismantling the liberal democratic state and entrenching the long-term rule of the dominant party'.[60]

For a long time, the EU was not able to confront the danger that Orbán's regime represented to its norms and principles, because the political will to do so was missing. By failing to arrest the systematic constitutional problems, the EU actually supported Orbán's government institutionally, morally and financially.

Orbán's regime was nothing other than an illusion of democracy, which shook the very foundation of trust between European states. Just as it would have been delusional of Fidesz to think that the trust of pragmatic European politicians would hold out forever, so it was delusional to imagine that the EU would survive if it tolerated authoritarian regimes within its ranks.

5

'NEITHER THE IMF NOR THE EU IS MY BOSS'

UNORTHODOX ECONOMIC POLICY

Viktor Orbán was in a good mood when he took the stage at the Focus on National Interest conference in June 2012.[1] Hundreds of business people, politicians and academics had gathered to hear the renowned speakers, who included ministers, constitutional justices and distinguished academics. The event had added lustre with the presence of former Austrian chancellor Wolfgang Schüssel and the contribution sent by video from former governor of the State of New York George Pataki.

Prime Minister Orbán started his speech with an anecdote: one day, the mice got fed up with being eaten by cats. They went to the wise owl to ask for advice about what to do. The owl suggested that since cats are scared of dogs, the mice should turn into dogs. When the mice said, okay, but just how should we change, all the owl said was: 'I don't deal with questions of tactics'. From Orbán's cheery story, the audience understood that the prime minister didn't think much of the advice of international organizations on economic policy.

The distinguished audience were receptive to Orbán's words, and he went on to say that his predecessors, who always followed the advice of the European Union, didn't get anywhere. The conclusion he reached was that 'the ability to triumph lies in acting differently to those we defeat', and added that his government would do everything differently from previous ones. He added that those who shared his view that Hungary was a nation of victors 'can see the fact they were born here as part of a greater plan, and this gives them a task. This is something foreordained, not something chosen'. After this, he began to explain his new 'unorthodox economic policy', which his government introduced to resolve the problems that still existed after the 2008 financial crisis.

Orbán and his close circle had for a long time been convinced that politics was the highest form of knowledge, and since politicians decided the order and direction of the life of the community, politics was always ahead of the economy.[2] As you read this chapter, it is worth bearing this in mind; it means that behind every economic step, the prime interest to be sought is the political power interest of Orbán and Fidesz.

But before discussing what Orbán calls his unorthodox economic policy, let us examine the legacy from which Orbán so wished to break free.

Economic Legacy

The new democratic Hungarian government that came to power in 1990 inherited an economy suffering from crisis. Central economic planning and the system of trade defined by the regional cooperation of socialist regimes had all collapsed, bringing down many large socialist conglomerates and causing enormous unemployment. In the first few years the transition was accompanied by huge economic losses. The first government offered early retirement pensions and long-term unemployment benefits to millions as a compensation for loss, and to avoid mass poverty. After a while, the economy stabilized, but subsequent governments maintained these wide-ranging social benefits for two decades. This concealed the fact that education and labour reforms were unsuccessful in helping the poorly trained unemployed masses find jobs. Wide-ranging welfare benefits, however, did not promote retraining or returning to employment, and millions became dependent on the state in the long term, something which was ingrained in society, as it had formed the basis of the communist system. All this put a great strain on government finances.

The other crucial issue of the 1989 regime change was how to move companies from state ownership (which needed modernizing) into private hands. Hungary inherited a particularly high public debt burden from socialist times. As a result, the first freely elected government aimed to attract as much foreign direct investment as possible to the economy, selling strategic manufacturing plants and public service corporations, mainly to foreign owners. This process saw many firms which had been state monopolies, such as telecommunications, utility companies and energy providers, pass to foreign investors: in the energy sector E.ON and RWE dominated, while Deutsche Telekom took the lead in the telecommunications market. Privatization, of course, came with tensions. It was frustrating for society to see that the technocratic directors of socialist companies were able to acquire ownership rights in the firms they directed, and that a wide range of assets passed into the hands of foreign businesses.

But with foreign capital, manufacturing companies could access the most modern technologies, and this was indispensable for the Hungarian economy to develop. The process was reinforced by the creation of the institutions of a market economy, and the rapid adaptation of companies, which thus laid the foundation for change and for convergence with the developed West. Macroeconomic indicators stabilized, thanks in great part to the economic austerity measures introduced in 1995, and foreign loans made economic policy more prudent. By the end of the 1990s economic growth had reached 4%, making Hungary the front runner in the Central and Eastern European region.

But after 2000 economic growth lost its momentum, the rate of increase in exports slowed, the ability to attract foreign direct investment weakened, and the problems of international competitiveness mounted, because of lax fiscal policies. Before the 2002 elections, Orbán's first government introduced wage increases and subsidized mortgage loans. The next government under Socialist Party leadership continued with fiscal alcoholism[3] throughout the decade. The country was living on more money than it could reasonably afford. Hungary's advantage over neighbouring countries shrank, and the economy's convergence with the West stalled. A dual economic system emerged, in which antiquated Hungarian companies existed side by side with modern, competitive, foreign-owned companies, and without any skills or knowledge transfer between the two. High taxes and bureaucratic obstacles dissuaded people from establishing new enterprises and the new democratic institutions were only partially able to keep the grey economy in check.[4]

In the two decades following the regime change, few people were actually able to acquire meaningful private property. Most people lacked the capital to participate in privatization. About one quarter of the population was employed by the state, and a significant group of the working-age population was living on welfare benefits. The emergence of a middle class with a strong bourgeois mentality, independent of the state, proved to be a slow process. Moreover, despite the ill-planned reforms that started in the 1990s, the education system was still unable to support social mobility and instead tended to reinforce existing class divisions.

'NEITHER THE IMF NOR THE EU IS MY BOSS'

In terms of education, this was a step backwards, even compared with the years of socialism.

Albeit with great effort, by the end of the 1990s the high state debt had been reined in to less than 60% of GDP, but by 2008 it had jumped to 74% again. Because in these years both the state and households took out loans denominated in foreign currency, the 2008 economic crisis dealt a destructive blow to the Hungarian economy. Caught in the crossfire of political attacks and with continuously waning popularity, Ferenc Gyurcsány's socialist government introduced considerable fiscal austerity measures in autumn 2008. This improved government finances, but runaway debt incurred before the austerity measures kicked in brought the threat of national bankruptcy, and so the government approached international organizations for stand-by loans.[5]

The months of the economic crisis saw the culmination of the political chaos that had been brewing since 2006, forcing Gyurcsány, whom the opposition Fidesz had been pressuring with street politics for years (as described in the introduction), to resign. The ruling Socialist Party formed a technocratic government led by Gordon Bajnai, which managed to stabilize the economy within a year. At the same time, Hungarian economic policy had to focus on reducing the fiscal deficit, and so, unlike other countries, it lacked the resources to mitigate the effect of the 2008 crisis for businesses and families. The 2010 general elections were held in this situation, and Viktor Orbán won with a large majority.

The government debt-to-GDP ratio (80%), the poor international competitiveness indicators, and the still relatively high government deficit presented a great challenge to the new administration. But Orbán's new government was aided by the fact that because of the Bajnai government's crisis management, the economy was already moving in the right direction, and economic growth returned in May 2010.

The Orbán government had its work cut out for it, and the prime minister had a strong political mandate to continue the reforms. Additionally, after the crisis, fiscal discipline had slackened worldwide, and it was possible for governments to intervene more boldly to control the economy than previously. Many believed that as the crisis receded, Orbán would be able to modernize the economy. But that is not what happened. The power logic of the Fidesz government aimed primarily to shake off the monitoring role of international organizations. It also wanted to have a free hand to promote its own elite in amassing wealth, and to create a well-defined voting block with a strong material interest in maintaining the new regime.

'We Shall Not Be a Colony!'

'Neither the IMF nor the EU are my bosses', declared Orbán confidently at the international press conference held the day after the 2010 elections.[6] He thus made it clear that he would not follow his predecessors, who during the crisis had only been able to avoid sovereign bankruptcy by taking loans and following recommendations from international organizations. In actual fact, already during his first term between 1998 and 2002 he had looked for new methods to kickstart the economy, with budget incentives rather than austerity policies. In 2010 he appointed the fringe economist György Matolcsy to the helm of the Ministry of the Economy, so that together they could experiment in implementing Orbán's 'unorthodox' economic policy.

The plan was to start the motor of economic growth by loosening the budget, reducing taxes, and driving up consumption. The government trusted that the Hungarian economy would 'grow out of' the temporary deficit spike without serious austerity measures. Orbán took this proposal to Brussels, but during the negotiations it became clear that the creditor organizations would not allow an increase in the budget deficit. Hungary has been under the Excess Deficit Procedure of the European Union ever since it joined the EU in 2004, because the deficit was continually in excess of 3% of GDP, and it increased further when the country borrowed significantly in 2008. Thus, the government was unable to avoid austerity policies. This experience merely reinforced Orbán's desire to reduce the deficit to under 3% as soon as he could, so that he could have a free rein in managing the economy.

But in 2010 he had to implement plan B. Orbán submitted a package of twenty-nine austerity measures to the National Assembly, but he was adamant that he would reduce taxes. The most striking element of the plan was moving from progressive taxation to a flat-rate personal income tax, and an extremely low one at that of 16%.[7] The proposal generated huge controversy among experts and opposition politicians. The introduction of a flat-rate tax deprived the budget of 2% of its revenue, or 600 billion HUF, from a budget that was already struggling with a deficit. No wonder that all the other austerity measures aimed to increase revenue.

But in its public communications, Fidesz highlighted only two elements. One was that the pay of senior state officials would be drastically reduced. The other step, which genuinely brought in much more revenue, was the introduction of a 20% bank levy. In his speech in Parliament, Orbán managed to give the impression that he would hold banks and large companies to ransom, while everyone else would benefit greatly. Naturally the banks passed on a significant part of the levy to their customers, but that was not the prime minister's problem. Even in the opposition, many thought Orbán's sleight of hand in his messaging was brilliant.

These corrective measures included an apparently insignificant point which, however, played a crucial role in the implementation and success of the 'unorthodox' economic policy. One of the provisions stipulated that those working in the public sector had to pay 98% tax on the severance pay they received.[8] Orbán's party communicated the message that it wanted to put an end to the brazen sums of severance pay disbursed to departing employees of the previous government, and this was a popular policy. In practice this meant that several thousand people had to pay back their legally disbursed severance pay. This retroactive tax was seen as illegal by legal scholars, and the opposition said so in no uncertain terms. László Sólyom, president of the republic, immediately sent the law to the Constitutional Court for scrutiny. In spite of this body already having been filled with Fidesz faithful, it found the law to be unconstitutional and annulled it. Fidesz knew the bill was illegal, yet everyone was aware that Orbán wouldn't back down. But what happened next was without precedent. With its two-thirds parliamentary majority, Fidesz simply deprived the Constitutional Court of the authorization to exercise normative control in financial matters. After that, it submitted the unconstitutional bill once more, unchanged. This was planned like clockwork, so that while the controversy was in full swing, László Sólyom's mandate as president of the republic came to an end, and the new president, Pál Schmidt, quickly voted in and appointed by Fidesz, signed the unconstitutional law without any qualms.

This was the first instance when Fidesz used its supermajority to change the democratic rules when it encountered a legal obstacle, and to dismantle the legal constraints and weaken institutions to assert its will. This strategy opened the way for Orbán's people to implement whatever they wanted, without restrictions, in the economy. The case proved to be a watershed moment in Fidesz's construction of its power base.

Why was it so important for Fidesz to fly in the face of the constitution in a symbolic matter of little importance, and curtail the authority of the Constitutional Court? This was

'NEITHER THE IMF NOR THE EU IS MY BOSS'

soon to become clear. The bank levy proved to be insufficient to compensate for the huge loss of revenue arising from the flat-rate income tax. The government levied new special taxes on the energy and telecommunications sectors and on large retailers. But the government finances were still in a critical state, and within a year the government introduced twelve new special taxes, particularly in the services sector. These measures made the economic environment utterly unpredictable and seriously distorted. The government became engaged in an enormous conflict with foreign investors in the sectors that suffered from the special taxes, but Orbán came out of it well: his supporters looked on him as a hero and believed that the government was punishing not them, but the big foreign-owned companies, the ones with capital.

Despite all these efforts, a large hole was still gaping in the budget, and the government needed to raise more revenue. Orbán decided to use people's contributions to private pension schemes to repay the government debt. Alongside the state pension, private pension funds had also been present in Hungary since 1998. Employers paid 75% of their workers' pension contributions into the state scheme, and 25% into the private schemes. Thus every worker was accruing employers' contributions on their own account, which they supplemented with their own contribution. The Orbán government initially introduced strong incentives for members of private pension funds to return to the state system, together with their payments. When this failed to produce results, it passed a new law stating that anyone who did not return to the state system would lose the right to a state pension—a right they had been earning over decades.[9] The Orbán government thus forced 3 million people to give up their private savings, and simply nationalized their money. It justified this enormous expropriation, totalling 3,000 billion HUF, or 10% of GDP, by claiming that the budget deficit had forced its hand, and in exchange promised to whittle down the debt service and reform the pension system.

Only a few years later did it transpire how good a steward of this astonishing sum the Orbán government had been. The reforms made private pension funds impossible to operate, and overturned important achievements in the modernization of the pension system and the initial buds of a culture of self-sufficiency. Although the pension assets should only have been used to pay out pensions and reduce debt, in 2011 the government used some of it to finance its current spending and buy shares in companies. The reduction of debt proved to be a one-off event, and at the end of 2013 state debt once more stood at 79%.[10]

The expropriation of private pension savings raised serious constitutional issues, but by the time this bill was before Parliament, the Constitution Court no longer had the authorization to review financial issues.

In the first years of the 2010s, the Fidesz government clashed with almost every stakeholder in the economy. The constant escalation of conflicts strengthened the image of Orbán as a strong leader. In fact, by exacerbating the conflicts he was able to start from a strong position when he was forced to negotiate with players in the economy. The first steps the government took in economic policy were baffling and irrational; only in terms of maintaining power did they form a unified system. It came as no surprise that the country sank back into recession by 2012. Although Fidesz chanted day and night that everything bad was the result of the 'last eight years' (referring to the previous, socialist-led government), the party's popularity waned greatly. This is why Orbán needed to find a miracle weapon for the 2014 elections: 'lower utility bills'.

'NEITHER THE IMF NOR THE EU IS MY BOSS'

Economic Policy and the Accumulation of Capital

Reinforcing the Power of the State through Nationalization

To achieve his political aims, Orbán was strident and aggressive in his use of devices to redistribute income and assets. The original reason for the Orbán government's introduction of the exceptional taxes on certain sectors was to use the revenues to stabilize the budget after it had introduced the flat-rate income tax. The exceptional taxes were levied on companies that typically were in foreign ownership, and that, because of their infrastructure, could not withdraw from the country. The level of these taxes was many times the customary level in Europe, and in 2013 they accounted for 5% of budgetary revenue.[11] The exceptional taxes were called 'crisis taxes', but year by year they grew in number. For a long time, the sectors affected shouldered the burden while their financial position deteriorated.

That was exactly what Orbán wanted; after all, one of the purposes of the exceptional taxes was to improve the state of the budget. The other, even more important strategic goal was to strengthen big capitalists in Hungary, and the way to do this was to bleed foreign-owned companies. Already before the elections, the prime minister had made it clear that in the new world, there would be a successful banking system, and dynamic energy, land and food market sectors, all in Hungarian ownership, because without strategic sectors in Hungarian hands, the national economy would be weak and vulnerable.[12]

The government used the exceptional taxes to weaken entire sectors and nudge foreign owners to leave. Orbán's voters, who had viewed the market economy with suspicion since the 1989 regime change, looked favourably on this debilitation of foreign companies and the steps towards renationalization. These companies often ended up as the property of certain Hungarian business people generously subsidized by state banks (see Chapter 6).

To squeeze foreign investors out of the market, other forms of coercion were necessary. The first opportunity for the government to put pressure on service providers arose in the gas sector. Citing the economic crisis, the cabinet temporarily restricted the licences of gas trading companies, and at the same time put a company known as Hungarian Electricity (MVM) in a monopoly position. The market position of gas traders soon deteriorated, and before long MVM bought out the gas business of the German company E.ON.[13] The state had not renationalized the gas trading market, but had handed it to an interest group close to the governing party.

The big gas deal continued to develop. In spring 2013 the government announced a 'lower utility bills' campaign for households. These services in Hungary were provided by foreign-owned companies, so the campaign could be coupled with the issue of sovereignty. 'The year 2014 will be the year of the utility fees battle', announced Orbán at a Fidesz congress. 'We have been fighting for Hungary's independence for a quarter of a century. We just have one more battle to win, the battle of economic independence, the battle of economic self-determination'.[14]

The government imposed a cap for gas and electricity fees in law, causing the service providers to suffer a significant drop in revenue. For instance, the revenue of gas service providers fell by a quarter in three years.[15] Another blow to the companies was a law stipulating that all public service providers had to operate as non-profit entities. This large additional drop in utility bills for the public served as the basis for an unprecedented political campaign, and became the main topic of the 2014 general elections. The government went all out to promote its 'utility fees battle campaign': there was not an electricity pole or bus in Hungary that did not boast the Fidesz government's slogan: 'We'll protect the reduced utility bills!'

Following this, the cabinet created a vast 'utility holding company', the National Utility, which acquired the right to gas and electricity service provision for most of the country, and even obtained a significant part of the gas network and electricity grid. With minimal competition, changes in utility fees lacked transparency. Millions of consumers could not follow whether the famous 'lower utility bills' had in fact come to pass, because eight years after the campaign Hungarians were still paying gas and electricity prices frozen in 2014. At the same time the price for gas worldwide fell considerably, and in this competitive environment household energy prices declined. In Hungary, however, given the expensive increases in capital in the network of state companies and a series of pointless buyouts, it was costing much more to maintain the system than it would have done in a competitive framework aiming to make a profit.[16]

Under pressure from the law on compulsory fee reduction and non-profit services, widespread nationalization and centralization also took place in the water works and waste management sector. Exploiting its power with a two-thirds parliamentary majority, the government enshrined the deals in law, and squeezed many of the mostly foreign private service providers out of the market. This cornering of private service provision and the 'low utility bills battle' were pivotal in Fidesz's winning a two-thirds majority in the National Assembly in 2014.

In order to increase the state's role in public utility services, the government purchased assets of enormous value (gas reservoirs, pipe networks, gas trading companies), and increased its share in the Hungarian oil company MOL. By 2017 the German company E.ON and the Italian company Eni had been completely squeezed out of the market for public energy service providers in Hungary. In parallel, a process began in which business people close to the government acquired a share in this market.[17]

In the first ten years of Orbán's regime, the government systematically exploited one or other important public good (such as energy security or health protection) in order to introduce a state monopoly. It then redistributed the given market to its own cronies.

We Want a Bank!

'The bank levy in Hungary is ten times greater than in other countries, and it's like an expropriation, because it is independent of profit', said the German owner of one of the largest Hungarian banks, the Hungarian Credit Bank (MKB), when confronted with the introduction of the bank tax in 2010.[18] The bank tax placed a huge burden on this financial institution which, because of its large portfolio of real estate, had suffered particularly great losses during the 2008 crisis. But the German owner of the bank, Bayerische Landesbank, kept MKB afloat, and it continued to operate even after several loss-making years.

However, in 2014 EU competition regulations forced Bayerische Landesbank to sell MKB, and the Hungarian government was ready to buy it. It seemed incomprehensible that the Hungarian state would use public money to buy a bank that was making a serious loss. A government representative tried to explain the contradiction by saying that 'when the government supports a bank owned by the nation, it is supporting a business model, because locally owned banks do not follow a global strategy'.[19] Naturally this argument cannot be borne out by economic evidence.

In acquiring MKB, the government laid out a significant sum of public money for an asset which they knew would require further capital injection. In effect, the government paid the German owner to leave Hungary. The government's plan was to sell the bank after a capital injection.[20] But the government did not have the funds to improve the bank's balance sheet, and so, in an unusual move, it passed ownership to the Hungarian National Bank (MNB). Under the direction of one of MNB's vice-presidents it recapitalized the bank's portfolio, and then two years later sold it for 37 billion HUF. MKB was bought by an international consortium with an offshore background and unknown owners.[21]

Subsequently, MKB joined forces with the Savings and Mortgage Bank (Takarék Jelzálogbank), which was created from a network of 180 small savings cooperatives over six years through a complicated series of government regulatory measures, making it the fifth-largest bank in the country. By then the network had long dropped out of state ownership, and had become part of the Lőrinc Mészáros conglomerate, of which we shall learn more in Chapter 6. Finally, these two banks merged with the nationalized Budapest Bank, to create a mega-bank, Magyar Bankholding, which serves one fifth of the Hungarian public and operates half of the network of bank branches in the country.[22] The owners of the giant bank include Mészáros and his business partner József Vida.

With this grandiose transaction, Orbán's decade-long dream of having half of the banking sector in Hungarian hands was finally realized. For good reason, this transaction was not publicly celebrated. The merger of private banks was classified as being of national strategic importance, barring any kind of check to ensure that it conformed to competition law.

Good Foreigner, Bad Foreigner

I remember a conversation with a German company director who said how glad he was that in the Ministry of Foreign Trade and Foreign Affairs a special member of staff was available to help his company find its way in the Hungarian environment, and, if necessary, he could phone the minister at any time. True, this was the director of an electronics machine factory. His corporation was one of those the Orbán government classified as 'good foreigners'. These were typically industries requiring high-tech know-how and manufacturing for export, which could operate anywhere in the world but chose to do so in Hungary. They included automotive, electronics, food industry and pharmaceutical multinational corporations. They provided a substantial portion of Hungarian tax revenue.[23] The multinationals accounted for nearly 35% of Hungarian exports, and their contribution to GDP was also very high.[24] Since they were crucial to the Hungarian economy, incumbent governments since the 2000s have incentivized multinational investments with subsidies and favourable taxes based on individual governmental decisions.

On the other hand, retail and telecommunications companies, and the firms hounded out of the gas and bank sectors, were regarded as some of the 'bad foreigners', against whom the Fidesz government conducted an ideological and political campaign. These companies provided the public with profitable services, which Orbán's circle believed should have been supplied by Hungarian companies. Subsequently Fidesz governments changed the laws back and forth, creating monopolies to put pressure on these sectors and to transform the ownership structures in a manner that was questionable in terms of economics, fairness and legality. Citing the public interest, Orbán's circle strove to control the strategic points of the economy.

When the government introduced the first punitive exceptional taxes in 2010, I thought that the banks in the banking alliance would represent a powerful economic and lobbying force, and I assumed the three telecommunications companies with a multinational background, Telekom, Telenor and Vodafone, could together push back against the government's steamrolling. Strangely, this is not what happened.

The government negotiated with the actors one by one and managed to reach a different bargain with each. This was not the first time I had seen Orbán's 'divide and conquer' principle at work in politics, but I was surprised that the leader of a small government could corner significant international companies.

'NEITHER THE IMF NOR THE EU IS MY BOSS'

The Orbán government was able to acquire ownership from corporations like Axel Springer and some subsidiaries of Deutsche Telekom, probably because the Hungarian market was not worth the trouble for them. But they were big in Hungarian terms, and I thought that if strong corporations could not agree on a joint negotiation strategy, then how would civil and political players, who have no economic power, be able to put up any resistance to the brazen and aggressive exercise of power?

In the first two terms after 2010, the Orbán governments mobilized vast assets: they bought more than 200 companies worth over 1,600 billion HUF, equivalent to about 5% of GDP.[25] In addition to the energy and bank sectors, the list included power stations, shipyards, machine factories, garbage collectors, telecommunications companies, film production companies, restaurant chains, tobacco traders, textbook publishers, and many news outlets and media products.

On the other hand, the government followed a completely different strategy with the companies of 'good foreigners', which were treated with great attention. The government created so-called individual strategic agreements when the economic environment after 2010 was extremely unpredictable and threatened to drive the 'good' foreign companies out of the country. The first agreement was signed with Coca-Cola amid great celebration in 2012, and it was followed by dozens of others. In 2022 there were ninety-one such agreements in place.[26] These contracts were from the beginning shrouded in secrecy, because they were all based on individual private agreements, and it was impossible to know whether in addition to the public agreement there was not some informal deal.

In a 2014 study, Transparency International Hungary reported that large companies expected these agreements to reduce political risks.[27] The political authorities meanwhile used them to retain big investors in processing industries important to the Hungarian economy, and keep them in the country. These were naturally understandable considerations, but since the government made arbitrary distinctions between the good 'manufacturer' and the bad 'speculator' in the market, the working relationship between companies and government office holders became politicized. Because the companies tried to make unique strategic agreements, the risk of corruption increased. Moreover, the system of treating each case individually curtailed initiatives to self-regulate sectors. Thus, although the position of some companies stabilized, the system of individual strategic agreements overall weakened the market environment and created a new network of dependencies.

From the government's point of view, the strategic agreements proved to be an effective tool in terms of both economic policy and power politics. The foreign companies it favoured were also satisfied. The managing director of the German–Hungarian Chamber of Commerce and Industry, when asked in 2018 about problems with the rule of law and corruption in Hungary, said: 'We are a business organization. The figures speak for themselves. Since 2010 German corporations have invested about nine billion euros in Hungary. So, as you see, companies do not apply ideological criteria when making investments'.[28]

Important corporations manufacturing exports set themselves up in the country, making a large contribution to Hungary's positive trade balance. Despite this, the government's contradictory economic policy caused demonstrable damage to the Hungarian economy. If we compare the extent of individual government subsidies that Fidesz governments gave to multinational companies with those of their predecessors, we can see that in the first ten years of Fidesz rule this sum was on average annually three times the amount previously given. In 2019, the figure was 105.3 billion HUF (€300 million).[29]

'NEITHER THE IMF NOR THE EU IS MY BOSS'

The growing governmental subsidies show that competition for multinational companies in Central and Eastern Europe was becoming fiercer. However, the Fidesz government created an economic environment in which far more had to be paid for the trust of Western companies than previously. At any rate, the government must have thought so, because several studies have shown that half of the large corporation subsidies going to multinationals were spent on projects the companies would have realized in any case.[30]

Giving special government subsidies to foreign companies was extremely disadvantageous for Hungarian companies. An average Hungarian company could but dream of such generous resources, and they fell behind in technological development. In addition, subsidized foreign companies offered higher salaries, skimming off the cream of the workforce and creating a further competitive disadvantage for Hungarian corporations. While Orbán's government kept talking about strengthening the position of domestic companies in the economy, in reality this was true for very few corporations, most of which were linked through their owners to the current political elite. Overall, the productivity advantage of foreign-owned companies over domestically owned ones has increased since 2010.[31] The presence of state subsidies in this system sent companies the message that rather than increasing their own competitiveness, they had to get as close as possible to the power that dished them out. This ultimately led to a very inefficient economy.

Discriminating between 'good' and 'bad' companies also increased the risk of corruption. Surprisingly, the first significant scandal became public only in 2019, showing just what manoeuvres might actually be taking place, with even the largest multinational companies participating. During an American audit Microsoft Hungary admitted that with its cooperation Hungarian dealers were selling overpriced software licences to Hungarian state agencies, including the National Tax and Customs Administration and the National Police Headquarters, while telling the American parent company that they had to offer a considerable discount to clinch the deal. The resellers worked on margins of up to 30%.[32] Naturally the case was known at the highest level of the Hungarian state; and the directors fired from their position in Microsoft Hungary were soon given positions in government.

The Changing Nature of Public Assets

By 2013, Orbán and his minister of the economy, György Matolcsy, had reined in the budget deficit to less than 3% and, with a complete overhaul of the tax system, had created the basis for the new Orbánite economic policy. In 2013 the term of the previous governors of the Hungarian National Bank (MNB) expired, and their departure enabled Orbán to gain control over the central bank.

Matolcsy's job was to support the generation of economic growth by devaluing the national currency. The conditions for implementing this economic policy were favourable by 2013. Indeed, after the global crisis, interest rates stayed low because of lax monetary policy worldwide. The MNB stimulated consumption and economic growth by keeping interest rates low, aided by deflation in the eurozone. While the central bank made aggressive use of lowered interest rates, it was unperturbed by a considerable short-term fall in the forint's exchange rate.

However, the low interest rates helped the bank to make a considerable exchange rate gain. Although making a profit is certainly not the remit of a central bank, it soon transpired why the chief of the MNB was so keen to weaken the forint. By amending the act on the central bank in 2013, the Orbán government annulled the section which obliged the bank to pay any exchange rate gain into the central budget as a dividend.

'NEITHER THE IMF NOR THE EU IS MY BOSS'

As a consequence, in 2013 the 270 billion HUF exchange rate gain, which was equal to the entire public budget for higher education, was not paid into state coffers.[33] It turned out that that the MNB's economic policy far exceeded the role of an independent central bank.

In 2014, Mihály Varga, the minister for the economy, a conflict-averse politician, whom I knew well from the Fidesz of old, gave a report to the National Assembly's budgetary committee. As an MP, I asked him whether his ministry had missed the several hundred billion forints from the budget, when the government was struggling to pay back its debt services. I wondered why the minister for the economy had not insisted that such a large public revenue be redistributed within the framework of the budget. I was also curious about what purpose the MNB might have had for such a large sum. Varga sidestepped my questions, saying the bank was independent of the government. But obviously Varga, who was constantly having to balance the budget, sorely missed this enormous sum. However, in Hungary such an important decision could not have been made without Orbán's approval, so there was little he could do.

With the massive sum arising from the exchange rate gain, the central bank rather strangely created a group of charitable trusts called the Pallas Athéné foundations, ostensibly to support Hungarian higher education. The boards of directors of the foundations included members of György Matolcsy's family and others close to the government. From this point on, they operated as private foundations in total secrecy. As opposition politicians, we found this situation unacceptable, and we launched dozens of lawsuits in the public interest against the MNB in order to find out how this public money was being used.

Fidesz, in typical brazen fashion, submitted to Parliament an amendment bill stipulating that the assets transferred to the foundations of the MNB were 'of such sums that it can be ascertained that they "lose their nature as public assets"'.³⁴ In other words, the funds placed in the foundations were so large that they no longer counted as public money. Fidesz's actions caused huge outrage in the National Assembly. Before the vote, in a corridor in Parliament a journalist from the news portal Index asked several Fidesz politicians how they would vote on the law making confidential hundreds of billions in MNB assets. 'I'll be honest, I'm not familiar with the proposal, but tomorrow I'll be in Abu Dhabi, so I am excused from voting', foreign minister Péter Szijjártó told the press. Other MPs were not so lucky, and had to vote. They said things like: 'Oh sorry, I'm in a rush, I have to greet a Polish delegation'. Or 'I'm not fully in the picture'. Others said: 'If people don't like it, they'll change the government'. The president of the justice committee announced indignantly: 'I refuse to say, because at seventy-three years old, after forty-five years of being a lawyer, I know that speech is mere chatter, whereas the text of the law is law. Goodbye'.³⁵ All of these MPs voted for this astonishing, unconstitutional bill. The direct upshot of the affair was that house speaker László Kövér banned journalists from the Parliament building, to spare Fidesz politicians voting for such embarrassing legislation being shamed in public.³⁶

However, this bill, exceptionally, did not make it past the Curia and the Constitutional Court. The text of the law was not sufficient to cause public assets worth 0.8% of GDP to 'disappear'. In 2016 the foundations of the central bank were forced to reveal their tenders and financial reports and declare what they had done with this public money. The outrage did not die down, however, not just because it was not the task of the MNB to accumulate assets, but because the total outlay on luxury real estate and artwork items amassed by the foundations fell far short of the vast sum of assets the foundations had acquired. It was reasonable to presume that what we saw was merely a cover story, and that the foundations were actually created to conduct other large-scale economic transactions.

Because of the increase in public interest and the series of scandals, the Pallas Athéné foundations made increasingly complicated investments. They invested the money in government bonds and placed significant sums in banks, particularly in the recently sold MKB bank. By mid-2018 the foundations' monies were gradually passing to a subsidiary, Optima Investments, and the real estate project companies under its wings. Unlike the foundations, these companies now cited business secrets and gave out even less information, and the path of the originally 270 billion HUF of assets became utterly impossible to trace. Finally, notwithstanding the Constitutional Court ruling, the enormous state revenue from the devaluation of the forint did eventually 'lose its nature as public assets'.[37]

Opening to the East

'Diplomacy and cultural diplomacy have lost none of their beauty, but in an export-oriented country, the foreign ministry is oriented to the economy', said Viktor Orbán in summer 2014, after taking part in a meeting of ambassadors at the newly founded Ministry of Foreign Economy and Foreign Affairs. He explained that 80% of Hungarian exports went to the EU, which made Hungary too dependent on one market, and that it was necessary to open up 'to markets many perhaps consider to be less refined and have lower standards'.[38] The government set the goal of increasing fivefold within four years the number of small and medium-sized enterprises able to export, and of having one third of Hungarian exports destined to non-EU countries. Orbán told the ambassadors that they should find foreign markets for the products of Hungarian companies, and made it clear that from then on this would be the measure of an ambassador's success.

Orbán became convinced that the key to Hungarian sovereignty was to loosen economic ties to the West by opening up to the East. In 2012 the government founded an agency called the Hungarian National Trading House, which opened more than forty offices in Latin America, Africa and East Asia. Excitement grew around the trading houses because the government launched the system with billions of forints of state subsidies. Hundreds of companies put in bids for these opportunities and, one by one, companies of Fidesz politicians and consultants also gained a share of the plentiful subsidies.[39] However, a considerable proportion of the subsidized companies were not able to export, and although they had taken the subsidy, they were unable to meet the requirements. Problems increased: Viktor Orbán's relatives cropped up among those listed as owners of subsidized but non-performing companies.[40]

Because of the scandals accompanying the project and the spectacular failure of attempts to expand the market, after three years the government closed a string of trading houses. But by then it had already spent eye-watering sums on offices and subsidies: hundreds of billions of forints, which only came to light after research by opposition politicians.[41] In spite of all the spending, in 2020 almost 90% of Hungarian exports were still going to European countries, and all Asian countries together accounted for only 5%, which was less than a decade earlier.[42] In 2021, foreign direct investment and the lion's share of Hungarian trade abroad were just as European in nature as they had been ten years earlier.[43] New markets were effectively opened only in Caucasian countries (Azerbaijan, Turkmenistan, and Kazakhstan) and the Philippines, but the revenue deriving from this was minuscule: 0.003% of exports as a whole.[44]

Over time the expansion in exports was replaced by subsidies for imports and investments from Eastern markets, and in 2019 the government spent several billions of forints on enticing

'NEITHER THE IMF NOR THE EU IS MY BOSS'

Eastern investors to Hungary.[45] But Orbán's original plan, of diversifying Hungarian trade and subsidizing the export of Hungarian products, did not bring resounding results for the national economy. This was not surprising. For the subsidies to work, the government would have had to direct them to medium-sized enterprises able to export, not to its own cronies. The policy of opening to the East was guided not by rational considerations, but by hubris, individual interests and greed, and the entire process was inevitably riddled with corruption.

Another scandalous element of the 'opening to the East' efforts was the residency bonds programme launched in June 2013, which the government created, supposedly, to help finance the national debt. Most interest in purchasing the Hungarian residency bond, through which one could obtain a residence permit in the European Union, was shown by citizens of countries in the East: Chinese, Russians and Iranians.[46] Right from the start, many questions were raised regarding the residency bonds. The companies which received the right to sell the bonds were chosen not by the government, but by the National Assembly's economic committee, and they were almost all companies registered in offshore countries, with headquarters abroad. These intermediaries made an extraordinarily high commission on the sale of the bonds, 162 billion HUF, while owing to a peculiar interest structure, the Hungarian budget recorded a loss.[47] The bonds were also a source of considerable profit for a certain law firm, which was the legal representative for Antal Rogán, the minister in charge of the Prime Minister's Office. Incidentally, when the residency bond programme was launched, Rogán was the president of the National Assembly's economic committee.

All this happened while I was a member of Parliament. With other opposition MPs, we convened the National Assembly's budgetary committee several times over the dubious transactions, and invited the minister for the economy to report on the results of the bond programme. This never took place, because neither Fidesz MPs nor the minister once attended the sessions. My party, Együtt, filed a complaint over the bond programme, citing suspicion of embezzlement, but the Prosecution Service found no evidence of criminal activity.[48] The National Assembly's economic committee had not broken the rules, because there were no rules.[49]

According to Transparency International, the bond programme involved an extremely high risk of corruption and enormous sums of taxpayers' money were lost.[50] Selling residency bonds was also a matter of concern in terms of national security, because of the unusually short period given for the security screening of bond purchasers. In view of the serious reservations about the programme, the government discontinued the bonds in 2018, but by then 20,000 foreign citizens had acquired the right to permanent residency without either their persons or the sources of the money they invested being thoroughly screened. We cannot know for sure if there were criminals among the beneficiaries of the project, but what is certain is that during the programme, residence permits were given to a suspicious Syrian businessman, a convicted Russian tax evader, and the son of the chief of the Russian Foreign Intelligence Service, whose identity came to light in spite of all the secrecy.[51]

Perverse Redistribution: 'Work- and Family-Based Society'

'People should save, and build, brick by brick. If someone can't do that, if they have nothing, that's all they are worth. That's what I think. That's all his life is worth', said János Lázár, leader of Fidesz's parliamentary group, in 2011.[52] Lázár's artless words were a crystal-clear translation of those in the preamble to the Fundamental Law, which states: 'The basis for the strength of the community and each person's respect is work'. As I pointed out at the beginning of the chapter, Orbán believed that a shift

'NEITHER THE IMF NOR THE EU IS MY BOSS'

from the benefit-based economy to a work-based economy was the essence of his 'Hungarian model' and the cornerstone of the regime's social policy.

The first pillar of the 'work-based social policy' was realized with the introduction of the flat-rate income tax set at 16% for everyone, while it also abolished the tax-free band for income below a certain threshold. As a result, those with a higher income did very well, while the poor had to shoulder a much greater burden than before. The main characteristic of the flat-rate tax in Hungary was that it did not take into account any social considerations.

In order to prompt the 'lazy' to work, as the second pillar of its policy, the government reduced the job-seeker benefit from nine months to three—the shortest period in the EU— after which the unemployed person had to participate in a state workfare programme. The government claimed that the workfare programme was successful in terms of society's sense of what is right: at least the unemployed were doing something useful, working for their money. However, without active labour policies this programme made it effectively impossible for people to acquire new skills and return to regular work. In 2016 the budget poured 1% of GDP into the workfare programme, even though over a few years this sum would have been enough to set up a complex service system that could have taken into account the needs of both people and employers.[53] Nevertheless, these measures did succeed in reducing unemployment from 11% in 2010 to 3.5% by the end of the decade, a reduction that was also the result of labour shortages amid dynamic economic growth in the region.

The other key element of Orbán's social policy was the introduction of the family tax system, which benefited families with more income, because families with unstable labour market positions, who earlier were exempt from personal income tax, could not benefit from the flat-tax system and were not advantaged through other family policy means. One of these is a parental allowance for mothers who work full-time after the first birthday of their children.[54] In the spirit of a 'work-based society' this family policy meant that within a few years the children of poorer, often Roma families became even poorer. Twelve years later the consequences were clear: chances for social mobility had weakened significantly.[55]

Putting the 'work-based society' and the population-centric family policy in the spotlight was useful to Fidesz not just because it displayed a clear ideology and an opportunity to show a strong hand. We can see extremely practical reasons behind the achievements of the radical transformation of the redistributive policy. The government supported the middle classes because in this way it secured a committed voter base ensuring a supermajority victory in the next parliamentary elections.

How Come There Is Money for Everything?

'The Hungarian fairy tale, or the Hungarian example, will be a successful one in a year['s] time', asserted György Matolcsy to Richard Quest, CNN presenter, when asked about the quirks of Hungary's unorthodox economic policy.[56] International markets did not appreciate the Orbán government's initial steps, the battles in economic policy, and for a while they turned their back on it. But in 2016 international credit rating agencies raised Hungary's rating to investment grade. By this time the budget deficit was stable and under 3% of GDP, and by 2019 the national debt had fallen to 66.3% of GDP.[57] Economic growth started slowly post-2012, but after 2014 it reached 4%–5% per annum, which was good even by global standards. In 2010, GDP per capita in Hungary was 65% of the EU average, but by 2019 this had risen to 73%.[58] People's income had risen significantly in ten years. Unemployment fell to a very low level (albeit by classifying those on workfare as employed). Between 2010 and 2017 export revenues poured in from trade with the West. Meanwhile, the government kept pursuing the policy of raising the share of Hungarian owners in productive assets. The tax revenue shortfall due to the introduction of the flat-tax system was compensated for by the introduction of other taxes mentioned above. Because of the boom and the rise in income, people spent more. The rise in consumption and the higher VAT income brought enormous revenue to the state: compared with 2,200 billion HUF in 2010, in 2019 the figure was 4,500 billion HUF.[59] Through various measures to turn the informal economy into a formal one, including the digitalization of taxation, the government managed to collect taxes more effectively, and this too helped to increase tax revenues.

The decade 2010–20 saw a boom in public investments too. Several thousand kilometres of roads and railways were modernized, hundreds of public buildings, schools and kindergartens were built, churches were renovated, as were castles and main squares in towns, mostly with EU funds.[60] And football stadiums, small and large, were built in numbers hitherto unseen.

On the Wave of the European Boom

At first glance the achievements of the Orbán governments' economic policies seem striking. Fidesz claimed that a country on the brink of state bankruptcy was saved because of its commitment to national sovereignty and unorthodox policies, breaking with the global liberal order. In fact, one of the fundamental sources for creating macroeconomic stability was the enormous sums flowing in from the EU. In the seven years following 2013, the EU funds arriving in the country were equivalent annually to 4%–6% of Hungary's GDP. Never before in its history had Hungary had access to such large funds that were not loans.

In terms of size, these funds can be compared only with the Marshall Plan disbursed to the war-torn countries of Western Europe after the Second World War. This was an extremely good outcome even if, in exchange for EU development funds, Hungary opened its market, from which Western European companies profited very nicely.

The Hungarian economy also benefited from the transfers by Hungarians working in other EU countries. The sheer size of this resource promoted economic growth and exercised a positive effect on the budgetary balance. Paradoxically, the masses who went to settle abroad, many fleeing Orbán's regime, contributed to the economic success of the regime by transferring money home.

One government-commissioned study showed that without EU funds the Hungarian economy would not have grown at all.[61] In addition to the enormous good fortune of the Orbán government, a few after the 2008 crisis a cycle of growth started in Europe. By 2018, compared with the last year before the 2008 crisis, productivity in EU countries had risen by 8%; in Germany this figure was 14%.[62] Since the Hungarian economy is extremely dependent on German manufacturing, primarily through automotive, machine and electronics manufacturing, growth in Germany had a knock-on effect in Hungary. Finally, in 2014 oil prices on the world market fell, which also had a favourable effect on economic growth.

These particularly fortunate circumstances naturally affected not only Hungary, but the whole Central European region. If we compare economic growth in countries in the region with the economic crisis in 2008, we see that Hungary's achievements lagged behind those of its neighbours by 1%–1.5%.[63]

The unique Orbánist 'unorthodox economic policy', the 'Hungarian way', brought no special success to Hungary whatsoever. The Hungarian National Bank kept interest rates even lower than other European banks did, so the regime wasn't even 'unorthodox'. The government's measures in economic policy merged into liberal European trends they so liked to attack. Orbán's government was rarely at loggerheads with EU institutions on economic questions; in fact, in line with expectations, it kept the budget deficit below 3% and reduced the government debt until 2020. It spent enormous funds on keeping within the country manufacturing multinationals crucial to the Hungarian economy, and the country's main export partners continued to be European countries. For an economy so deeply embedded in Europe, a radically different economic way of thinking would have been inconceivable.

Government propaganda glossed over the fact that the good results were not (or not only) due to the performance of the Hungarian economy, but to favourable external conditions and EU subsidies. The funds disbursed raised the standard of living of the public, and dampened the population's indignation at the enormous wealth amassed in the orbit of their political leaders. The long-term interests of the country would have been better served in this exceptionally favourable, plentiful period if the government had reduced the deficit far more, thus strengthening the position of the budget, improved the competitiveness of small and medium-sized enterprises on the basis of excellence, and invested in developing a knowledge-based economy and in the diversification of Hungary's energy sources. This did not happen. The country's best economists warned in vain that the Hungarian economy, with its structural problems, was unprepared to ride out an unexpected crisis. This was demonstrated by the Covid pandemic and the subsequent crisis generated by Russia's war in Ukraine. These hit Hungary very badly starting in 2020.

Orbán's Economic Crisis Management

During the Covid-19 pandemic, the government's toolbox for economic crisis management was largely similar to that of other states in the EU, although it had special characteristics. Orbán looked on every crisis, on every troubling situation, as an opportunity to further consolidate his power. Meanwhile, citing the pandemic, the government bled large sums from its real or perceived political adversaries.

As soon as a state of emergency was introduced to cope with the Covid-19 pandemic, the cabinet introduced an automatic loan moratorium for all debtors. As a result, far more debtors made use of the delayed repayment measure than actually needed it, and this step landed the banks with an unjustifiably large burden. Another inexplicable decision was that the Orbán government centralized the collection of various taxes and made parking free throughout the country. As a result, municipalities, whose responsibilities grew significantly during the pandemic, lost a large share of their income. The government was clearly trying to use the crisis to push Budapest and other town councils, most of which were controlled by the opposition, into financial ruin. This became evident when dozens of towns led by Fidesz received large financial compensation funds from the government, but most of the cities led by the opposition did not.

The lack of parliamentary oversight during the emergency helped the government set up the Economic Protection Fund, as a protective shield against the negative economic effects of the Covid pandemic. After the European Commission waived its strict limit of 3% of GDP for the budget deficit, by the end of 2020 the Orbán government had handed out over 3,977 billion HUF from this fund, a sum equivalent to 8%–9% of GDP.[64] Whereas the fund helped to balance the budget, it did not strengthen the long-term resilience of the Hungarian economy. At least 40% of this fund was handed out for unjustified projects, such as the construction of the expensive Budapest–Belgrade railway financed by a loan from China; sports facilities; and reconstruction work on the Buda

'NEITHER THE IMF NOR THE EU IS MY BOSS'

Castle to restore its pre-1945 state. A significant part of state funds was spent on social groups and business circles, which did not really need this income.

In summer 2020 the government focused on saving the tourism sector. The budget of the already existing hotel development programme (the Kisfaludy programme) was quadrupled and monies were paid out within weeks. Twenty per cent of the entire sum, 17.7 billion HUF, went to the Hunguest Hotel chain, the interest of Lőrinc Mészáros (see more on him in Chapter 6). Another 30% of the fund went to Mészáros's and Tiborcz's circles, with the result that Fidesz oligarchs collected half of the entire sum.[65] By way of comparison, the support Mészáros received for his fourteen luxury hotels was equal to the sum disbursed for 5,166 smaller hotels and *pensions* in twenty-five provincial towns.

All over the world, governments were the main protagonists in managing the crisis, and they spent record-breaking sums of money in doing so. In its 2020 report Transparency International Hungary found that the Covid crisis had accelerated the hollowing out of democracy, because the permanent adoption of government by decree provided the executive power with especially broad room for manoeuvre.[66]

One day before Christmas 2020 the government decided on a 860 billion HUF stimulus package, which accounted for 3.5% of the entire Hungarian budget for 2019. The largest item of this fund, 94 billion HUF, went to a barely known private foundation, the Tihanyi Foundation,[67] which was set up by a businessman linked to Fidesz.[68] This foundation ran an elite college, the Mathias Corvinus Collegium (MCC). A good few students have moved straight from the college into the ranks of the Fidesz party apparatus. In spring 2020, the government quite inexplicably declared the Tihanyi Foundation to be what is known as a 'public-benefit asset management foundation', and donated to it two valuable state-owned properties and other assets. By the end of 2020, the state's offerings to the foundation amounted to 500 billion HUF, equivalent to 1.7% of the annual budget of the country.[69]

This unprecedented donation of public assets to a private foundation was clearly unconstitutional. To ensure this move could not be legally challenged, the government again amended the Fundamental Law, for the ninth time.[70] The amendment changed what is considered a public asset and limited it to the state's revenue, expenses and claims. The law draws a line between the concept of public assets and the performance of public services, and states that the activities and management of asset managers cannot be overseen by either state agencies or courts of law.

The Fidesz government had long tried to make public funds disappear in the legal sense, ever since the founding of the Hungarian National Bank's Pallas Athéné foundations, but that failed because the court insisted that public funds remain public even if they pass into private ownership. However, this constitutional amendment swept all obstacles out of the governing party's way, enabling it to transfer unprecedented numbers of public assets into private hands.

The government was so brazen in this matter that the bill was submitted by Balázs Orbán, state secretary of the Prime Minister's Office (no relation of Viktor Orbán), who was also the president of the board of trustees of the Tihanyi Foundation. When during the debate in Parliament the opposition MPs protested vehemently against this obvious conflict of interests, the state secretary said simply: 'I have two hats. Even in the West it is customary for a politician to take part in running foundations'.[71] And with that, the matter was settled, and the bill was passed. In December 2020 when this debate took place, I was no longer an MP, but I still felt helpless anger.

In spring 2021, the running of 70% of Hungarian higher education was entrusted to newly formed public foundations, as

'NEITHER THE IMF NOR THE EU IS MY BOSS'

were castles, museums, resorts, harbours, parks, land, theatres and clinics. Receiving nothing in compensation, the state gave these foundations several thousand billion forints of public assets, and their boards were occupied by Fidesz politicians. If a change of government were to happen in Hungary, it would be impossible for the new government to exercise oversight over the activities of these foundations.[72]

The party that came to government after 2010 had secured economic power to stay in political power in the long run.

* * *

Orbán has used a particularly fortunate period of economic growth to build a self-sustaining system of power. An abundance of funds and growth made it possible for him, through targeted redistribution of incomes, to secure a broad group of voters in support of the regime. At the time of writing, Fidesz's 2.5-million-strong voter base has been enough to raise Orbán's party to absolute power every four years since 2010. Like other modern autocrats, the Hungarian prime minister has understood that it is better to buy off the middle class than to openly oppress them.

No wonder Orbán told the Austrian paper *Kronen Zeitung* that, if necessary, he would make all regulations unchangeable: those of the pension system, the tax system, and budget management: 'I make no secret of the fact that in this respect I tie the hands of the next government. Not just the next one, but the next ten'.[73]

At the pinnacle of the system stood Orbán, surrounded by his narrow circle of 'national business people'. Orbán deliberately misinterpreted the idea of national sovereignty, which ultimately he identified with his own room for political manoeuvre, but at the same time, if it suited his interests, he subscribed to the opposite principle. Not only was this politics mendacious; not only did it present no successful alternative to the politics of previous Hungarian governments; but it seriously jeopardized Hungary's future.

The real novelty of Orbán's twelve-year reign was the calculated reorganization of the structure of ownership. Anyone who looked at the 100 richest people in Hungary in 2010 and 2020 would see the difference. The circle has significantly changed and in 2020 two thirds of the business people on that list were among the top beneficiaries of Orbán's regime. They had an interest in maintaining the system. A sentence written by András Lánczi, an important consultant for Fidesz and former rector of the Corvinus University, has become a maxim in Hungary: 'What they call corruption is practically Fidesz's main policy'.[74]

6

'I DON'T DEAL WITH BUSINESS MATTERS'
CORRUPTION, SCANDALS AND CRONYISM

In early June 1993 local Fidesz leaders, government councillors and MPs gathered for an extraordinary meeting. I was among the hundred attendees wanting to hear an accurate financial report from the chairman of the party, Viktor Orbán. There was one year to go before the elections, the second free elections since the regime change. However, an enormous scandal had broken in the press just a few days beforehand.[1] Through a secret government resolution six months previously, Fidesz had received a highly valuable real estate property from the state to use as headquarters, and had immediately sold it for 700 million HUF (the equivalent of 7 billion HUF today). We Fidesz politicians knew nothing of this: only Orbán and a few others had been aware of it. We didn't even know what had happened to the revenue, an extraordinary amount at the time. News was flying around that the money wasn't in the party coffers but had landed in private companies, one of which dealt with leasing luxury cars. The transaction and the shroud of mystery around it shook us deeply. We were all in our twenties or thirties, and the main characteristics and attraction of the Fidesz we represented were that it was irreproachable and scrupulous. Orbán had a lot of explaining to do.

Unexpectedly, two men—looking totally at odds with the young company in attendance—entered the room. They wore dark suits and dark glasses, with gold rings on their fingers, and marched through the long room with a briefcase, like something from *The Godfather*. It was Lajos Simicska and Tamás Varga, two notorious lawyers, who we knew were working as economic consultants alongside Fidesz. The meeting was tense, with showers of questions, because we wanted to know all the details, but the briefing was limited to minimal information. Simicska explained that everyone could rest assured that nothing illegal had taken place. The party director explained that Fidesz did only what other parties did, because Fidesz too had to create a solid financial base.

In the early 1990s there was a genuine need for financial resources to build up the new democratic parties. An agreement was made in 1991 that the new parties had to be given utilizable real estate, at the expense of the assets of the Hungarian Socialist Party (MSZP), in order to compensate for the vast material superiority of the MSZP in the post-communist period. The allocation of the headquarters to Fidesz was the consequence of this political decision. In the affair that had blown up, the problem was that the building acquired by Fidesz was unsuitable as headquarters.

As Fidesz's twenty-two-member parliamentary group, we demanded to know more, and pressed Orbán to share the details with us. We learned that the money from selling the headquarters had been spread over various companies owned by the two financial consultants, Simicska and Varga, and they had reinvested the income in other businesses. All these companies were owned by a narrow circle: the two financial consultants and their family members. We simply could not believe our ears.

'I DON'T DEAL WITH BUSINESS MATTERS'

Simicska, Varga, Orbán and László Kövér had known each other from their days at the Bibó College and had formed a close-knit group. In 1988 Simicska and Varga, rather than joining Fidesz, started building careers as lawyers. After Fidesz became a parliamentary party and was entitled to regular state subsidies, Orbán hired his old friends as advisers.

Over time it transpired that Simicska and his cronies had identified every one of Fidesz's local councillors overseeing the properties of their municipalities and had tried to pressure them to get on their municipal asset management committee. If any refused to comply, their names were noted. But those who were up for the 'game' had to live with the constant presence and demands of Simicska's people from then on. No wonder the reputation of these two men in the party grew steadily worse.

Orbán's opinion on the matter was that the party must be independent financially and try not to rely on external players—whether the state or individual donors. As Orbán explained in an interview in 1994:

> Our legally owned property must be managed in the way most advantageous to Fidesz. [...] Our opponents have been taking pickings for the last forty years, they have saved up for hard times, or they have used their current position in government to create a financial basis. [...] We only have ourselves to rely on; all we have is what we acquire ourselves.[2]

If this statement sounded familiar to anyone decades later, it is no coincidence. Breaking free from dependency, the desire for 'room for manoeuvre', has lain behind Fidesz's ideas of 'sovereignty' ever since.

Only years later did we find out that the dozen or so companies Simicska and his cronies created in which to invest the revenue from the headquarters sale had been set up long before the money arrived, and they had made lucrative deals.[3] The network of private companies that emerged around Fidesz in 1992 have ever since been known as 'companies close to Fidesz'. The headquarters scandal was traumatic for all of us. Fidesz, the party of the young, which had built its entire image on a politics of 'clean hands', had lost its innocence. This affair deeply split the party, and many critics of Orbán left (for more detail, see Chapter 1). The Fidesz 'headquarters affair' was a model of Simicska-style legal–business innovation, which became part of the party's operations for decades.

Boomeranging Back into the Opposition

Although these complex legal–business projects were cooked up by Lajos Simicska, nothing would have worked without Viktor Orbán. From 1990 Orbán had an important role in managing Fidesz's financial matters, first as parliamentary group leader and later as party chairman, and he shared only the minimum information with the party's elected officials. In Orbán's hands, the finances of the parliamentary group and the rest of the party started to overlap. The party's financial transactions became more opaque when Orbán charged his friends outside the party to deal with Fidesz's financial matters. It never occurred to us MPs that any problems might arise. Orbán was from the beginning aware that whoever controlled the finances held greater power in the party. In this respect, he was two steps ahead of us, while the party's elected MPs and party leaders mainly in their twenties were caught up in the euphoric days of the democratic transition as part of a historical process.

The essence of the collaboration between Orbán and Simicska was that Orbán got access to public money via the party, Fidesz, and Simicska invested it in private companies with good returns. The income was put back into the party coffers and spent on political campaigns and other necessary expenses. Meanwhile, they diverted as much profit as possible from the private companies to themselves. According to a former colleague,[4] Simicska and Orbán shared 50–50 in the companies registered in Simicska's name, but no reliable information on this has been made public.

In the 1990s the Hungarian law on party financing was extremely restrictive in the way political parties could use state and private funds, and consequently parties' actual needs were never really met. Parties thus took the step of paying for a significant part of their political campaigns through external, private companies, which blurred the boundaries between politics and business. The unresolved problem of party and campaign financing became, in Hungary as in many other countries, a breeding ground for corruption.[5]

When Fidesz split in 1994 and Orbán's critics left the party en masse, the party chair gained free rein over the party's finances. Fidesz's remaining members and the leaders that closed ranks behind Orbán were uncomfortable that 'the lads had had their hands in the jam jar' but they conceded that, given the disadvantageous situation, Simicska's method would help strengthen Fidesz financially, and that they were not transgressing the official law. The line between party interests and the personal interests of those directing the party became blurred, and Orbán was clearly behaving as though he was the party.

This Is Our Due

In these years, Fidesz and the other parties accessed financial resources mainly through the municipal governments. For instance, if the leaders of a small town gave work to a company, in exchange they expected the company owner to support the mayor of the town or the campaign of the mayor's party.[6] From the 1990s onwards this kind of give-and-take became a typical form of political corruption, and all the parties in power had recourse to it. One study of company directors showed that the 'corruption fee' accounted for 10%–20% of commissions, and went not to public servants but in almost every case directly to politicians. Naturally not every politician, public servant or company director was corrupt, but enough partook in the system to sustain it.

By 1998 Fidesz had a solid financial grounding. These were the years in which the companies founded by Simicska and friends in 1992, which had invested the money from the headquarters sale, mysteriously went bankrupt. It transpired that by 1995, after they had been drained and had accumulated public debts, these 'phantom companies' were eventually sold to two foreigners, Kaya Ibrahim and Josip Tot. Police discovered that these two foreigners' names and papers had simply been used. The companies had officially been sold to these individuals, but that in practice they hadn't actually bought them. In this manner the old owners rid themselves of their debts, taxpayers' money disappeared, and many years later the case was closed. By then Orbán was prime minister, and his confidant Péter Polt was the chief prosecutor of Hungary.[7] By the second half of the 1990s, thanks in no small part to the activities of Simicska, Fidesz had staked out its ground in the right wing of the political arena, and after the 1998 elections Orbán was able to form a coalition government. This new political success opened further prospects for putting down financial roots.

The newly invested prime minister appointed his friend Simicska as the director of the National Tax and Custom Administration (NAV). This decision shocked the public, because by then Simicska was sufficiently notorious as a result of the sale of the phantom companies. From the very first minute there were grave accusations that at the helm of the tax authority he played a part in spiriting away the traces of official investigation into the companies which he had previously owned but had later disappeared. A year later Simicska was forced to resign. After this he withdrew from the public eye, but his informal influence remained considerable, and his reach went far indeed. He went on to exploit his talent as a consultant to the CEO of the Hungarian Development Bank (MFB).

In government, the leaders of Fidesz made efforts to build up companies that could compete for public tenders. Within the MFB, Simicska assisted in the birth of the motorway construction programme, which this state bank financed. Between 1998 and 2002, almost every motorway construction contract was won by a company called Vegyépszer, which brought subcontractors in to do the work, and so all the money flowed through the main contractor.[8] Hungarian motorways were much more expensive to build than those in other European countries. The opposition dubbed Vegyépszer the 'in-house motorway construction company of the Orbán government', assuming that Vegyépszer passed large sums to companies or private individuals close to Fidesz.

Alongside the construction industry, Fidesz's other priority was to expand financial and political influence in the media. When Fidesz got into power, Mahir, a large advertisement company in the portfolio of Simicska, acquired the publication rights of *Magyar Nemzet*, the largest conservative daily newspaper, and a conservative weekly called *Heti Válasz* was established from public funds.

While they were in government between 1998 and 2002, there was visible growth in the wealth of leading Fidesz politicians. When I met an old colleague at an event (he was then a state secretary), the conversation touched on shady financial deals. He said: 'This money is our due'. Even though the declarations of assets made by Fidesz politicians did not show a significant increase in wealth, their spouses, siblings, parents and children all founded companies, which grew on the back of municipal and state contracts.[9] The profiles of the family companies stretched from mining to wine-making, from sports papers and textbook publishers to the pharma industry and communications companies.[10]

Seventy Per Cent–Thirty Per Cent

In 2002 Fidesz lost the elections, but by then it had built a considerable financial cushion. Many former government politicians were employed by the various companies close to Fidesz. Moreover, Simicska's companies did so well that they were able to launch television and radio stations while Fidesz was in opposition. These media ventures helped enormously to influence public opinion in respect of political issues raised by Fidesz. They also did a great service to the Fidesz mayors who were still in office, who gave large contracts to companies close to the party.

These forms of corruption, which political parties used while in government and in opposition, were rent-seeking methods typical of those times. Companies close to political parties grew fat not by competing on the market, but on state and municipality contracts. The culture of public procurement only became widespread with Hungary's accession to the European Union in 2004, but even after that parties found a way, through invitations for tenders, to give an advantage to the companies they preferred, which in return 'expressed their gratitude'. In the 1990s a few cases of corruption were uncovered, and the parties involved suffered badly in political terms. After the headquarters scandal in 1994, Fidesz endured serious losses. In 1998, the Socialist Party and the Alliance of Free Democrats lost the elections after corruption allegations surfaced. The so-called Tocsik case led to the resignation of numerous socialist and liberal politicians, but the only person convicted of any offence was a lawyer called Marta Tocsik.[11] The large parties had a mutual interest in covering up corrupt deals financed with public money, and these mechanisms were applied on the basis of 'you scratch my back, I'll scratch

'I DON'T DEAL WITH BUSINESS MATTERS'

yours'. Two investigative journalists discovered that the treasurers of the two largest parties, Fidesz and MSZP (who both happened to own holiday homes in the picturesque village of Szigliget, on the shores of Lake Balaton), had agreed that the business circles close to the incumbent government and the opposition would split state contracts in the proportion of 70% and 30% respectively.[12] This system remained in place right up until 2010, when Fidesz won the elections with a two-thirds majority.

Only in 2005 did the MSZP government draft a comprehensive package of bills to regulate party financing, but by that time the political struggle between the two main parties had intensified and the bills were never approved. Between 2000 and 2010, in Transparency International's Corruption Perceptions Index, Hungary slid from twenty-ninth place to forty-seventh.[13] According to the organization's director, in the 2000s the legal environment that regulated public money was more or less in order, but the loopholes in public procurement made large state investments opaque and impossible to audit. Moreover, the decision-makers did not abide by rules on conflict of interest, and party financing remained unresolved.[14] Corruption disrupted social and economic relations and, in the long term, was bad for the country's competitiveness.[15]

Before the 2010 elections, a number of corruption allegations linked particularly to the governing socialist and liberal parties came to light.[16] Fidesz promised to put an end to corruption. In a background conversation with business people, one Fidesz politician said, 'Lads, you can forget the "constitutional expenses". There won't be such things under the new government'.[17] What he meant was that there would be an end to the graft paid to win tenders.

Rich Pickings All Round

An Offer That's Impossible to Refuse: The Simicska Era

In spring 2010, after Fidesz's overwhelming election victory, Lajos Simicska spent many weeks at Viktor Orbán's country house, so they could decide on the ministers and holders of other important government offices. Orbán allowed his ally to be part of the decision-making process not just because of their decades-long close friendship and Simicska's shrewd business thinking, but rather, in the words of an influential government politician, 'because that much was owed to him, not just by [Orbán], but by the party too'.[18] When the government was formed, Simicska's people cornered key positions in the apparatus of government, including the management of the National Development Agency, which oversaw the distribution of EU funds, and the Public Procurement Authority. Simicska himself did not take on any governmental position, but he was so important that the minister leading the Prime Minister's Office and the leader of the Fidesz parliamentary group consulted with him daily on legislative matters. News leaked that Simicska, holding court in the headquarters of one of his companies, quite simply summoned various ministers and state secretaries and 'informed them that this or that case should be dealt with in such a manner'.[19]

Since Simicska did not hold public office and could not be held to account, his vast influence was a particularly serious problem. The most critical economic bills were proposed to the Parliament as private members' bills, which made it difficult to identify which business group's interests were actually being served by any given proposal. Government decisions became entirely inscrutable.

After Hungary's accession to the European Union, important state investments took off, especially in construction, the most dynamic sector of the economy. Like its predecessors, Fidesz gave special attention to this sector. Two years after Fidesz came to power, 70% of large investments were being won by new companies on the scene.[20] Whether it was motorways, railways, public utilities or urban rehabilitation programmes, above a certain value the same companies cropped up all over the country.

One particular company stood out for the dizzying success it had in securing public procurement contracts: Közgép, with its opaque circle of owners.[21] In the form of consortia, the company won public contracts worth hundreds of billions, resulting in its revenue increasing tenfold in three years.[22] In the construction industry, Közgép became the unavoidable 'alpha predator'. It became clear that the company was one of the government's favourites, just as Vegyépszer had been in Fidesz's earlier term. With more and more investigative journalists looking into the company, and the parliamentary opposition constantly questioning ministers about Közgép's affairs, the director of the company conceded that the 'actual owner' of the company was Lajos Simicska.[23] The position of president of the board was held by the businessman Zsolt Nyerges, a close personal acquaintance of the Orbán family. The companies that submitted public procurement tenders with Közgép in 2013 won 15%–20% of all state construction tenders.[24] Simicska and Nyerges managed to persuade Fidesz municipalities to approach them for anything that needed building. The owners were so sure of securing future state contracts that they didn't put any of the profits back into the corporation, but took dividends worth several billion forints out of the company for personal use.

Beyond the construction industry Simicska's business empire included media and advertising companies, and he acquired excellent land and profitable agricultural companies as well. Businesses tied to Simicska formed a tangled network, in which corporations often changed owner, companies owned other companies, and those companies owned other companies in turn. Information was completely hidden in the public registers. As a result it was almost impossible to estimate how much Simicska and other business people close to Fidesz were actually worth. Characteristically, in 2014 a magazine which listed the richest business people tried to get around this confusion and lack of information regarding the actual and informal players in the economy by creating what they called an 'influence barometer'. On this list the first place was occupied by Viktor Orbán, and the third by Lajos Simicska.[25]

Where are the tax inspectors?

The public viewed the enrichment of business people around Fidesz with increasing frustration, opposition politicians protested by resorting to civil disobedience, and there were grumbles even in the inner circles of Fidesz.

The public procurement issues surrounding Közgép and others were glaring indeed, but not necessarily illegal. The companies around Fidesz had, after all, won the work through tender procedures, and although, according to estimates by Transparency International, a company close to Fidesz won seven out of every ten public procurement tenders, 'all the paperwork was taken care of'.[26]

In a 2011 analysis, Transparency International Hungary showed that the Orbán government has transformed the institutional environment to make possible state capture.[27] The most important state institutions for the control of public money—the Constitutional Court, the State Audit Office and the Competition Authority—had directors who were beholden to Fidesz, and they curtailed the scope of authority of these organizations. For example, László Domokos, who moved from being a Fidesz MP to becoming the president of the State Audit Office, could not be expected to censure Hungarian Electricity (MVM) for making a disadvantageous contract with one of

'I DON'T DEAL WITH BUSINESS MATTERS'

Simicska's companies, because Csaba Baji, the MVM president, had previously worked for Simicska. In 2013 a tax inspector in the National Tax and Customs Administration resigned and subsequently stated publicly that some business people were regarded as untouchable by the authority, even though the office knew full well that their activities caused an annual budget shortfall of thousands of billions of forints.[28]

The role of the chief prosecutor was also crucial in this system: Péter Polt, a confidant of Orbán, assumed office for the second time in 2010. Statistics from the Prosecution Service show that after Fidesz came to power in 2010, reports of corruption-related crimes fell by half, yet the proportion of complaints not pursued by the prosecutor's office tripled. The number of investigations that were terminated prematurely doubled.[29] Between 2014 and 2020, parliamentary parties and opposition politicians filed complaints in 119 cases in which corruption was suspected, but proceedings were initiated only in a few cases, and never against members of the government.[30]

Another Fidesz innovation was that the government not only gave its business cronies a competitive advantage through legislation tailor-made for certain people or companies, but it liquidated entire previously competitive markets and redistributed them anew. For example, in 2013, with the purported aim of reducing smoking, the government drastically reduced the number of 'kiosks' selling tobacco, and made opening a shop dependent on a new licence. A leaked audio recording revealed that the decision about who won the new licence to sell tobacco products was made not in the designated state office, but in the local Fidesz party offices.[31] The government party actually used the redistribution of the profitable tobacco market (worth 500 billion HUF a year) to enable its local politicians to build their own crony network. With a similar sleight of hand, the ownership structure soon changed in land, retail, gambling and even liquidation companies.

Before 2010, corruption, albeit frequent and involving large sums of money, was diffuse, reflecting a 'look for a loophole' mentality. But under the Fidesz regime everything became centralized and 'legal'. This made it possible to appropriate larger sums than ever before, colossal fortunes, from public money.[32]

Apart from Simicska's business empire, innumerable cases involving various government politicians became public knowledge, right from the start of the regime. The opposition's accusations that Orbán was building his own oligarchy were countered by the prime minister's claim that these people were not oligarchs but 'national business people', whose rise and growth served the interests of the country. The truth about oligarchs was probably best expressed by the bank director Sándor Csányi, one of the richest people in the decades after the 1989 regime change. According to him, an oligarch is a rich person who is able to influence politics, but 'tell me one person in Hungary who is able to influence Viktor Orbán!'[33] The unique characteristic of Orbán's system was that in Hungary it was not outside actors but the prime minister and the governing party themselves who took the state captive.[34]

Assets in Your Name Must Be Left in the Party Coffers

In February 2015, the editors-in-chief of the daily papers, television and radio owned by Simicska unexpectedly resigned. This move by leaders of the media empire supporting Fidesz surprised everyone, even the owner himself. The media mogul, who shunned the public eye, almost immediately stood before the press and said, 'Now I'll go into the editorial offices and tell them to fuck off! I know very well who is behind this. Orbán is a scumbag!'[35] From this shocking, vulgar interview, we all learned that the decades-long lord of Fidesz's corporate empire, the man whose name was not to be uttered in Fidesz circles, had not been on speaking terms with the prime minister for months. In the following weeks, the oligarch gave many entertainingly angry interviews, and stated he would start an 'all-out war' against Orbán's government.

At the time, I was an MP and, together with fellow party members, for weeks tried to untangle what lay behind this previously unthinkable turn of events. It seemed the conflict broke out because state companies were slowly withdrawing their advertising from the media owned by Simicska, resulting in a significant loss of income. Moreover, it turned out that the government was planning to amend the law on advertising, which would have led to Simicska's news television station paying five times as much tax, further weakening the company's financial position on the market. In response, the media mogul's papers started to publish an increasing number of pieces critical of the government, thereby starting the 'all-out media war' against Orbán. Most of the news editors and editors-in-chief of his media companies did not, however, wish to take part in the Simicska–Orbán battle, especially not against Orbán. Their resignation made the conflict public. It was a mystery why the 'blood contract' between the two old allies had unravelled.

This conflict, beyond causing widespread amusement because of Simicska's obscene language, was important politically too. It gave a rare insight into Fidesz's extremely secret internal relations, and it presaged a change in the economic status quo. An armed battle was extremely risky for both men, because for decades they had not only known everything about each other, but were linked by the staggering fortune they had jointly acquired. But Simicska was a warrior by nature. In intimate circles he was reported to have uttered things like 'I made this man great, and, if necessary, I will crush him'.[36] But the events of the following months and years did not bear out this threat.

After Fidesz's 2014 election victory, Orbán removed Simicska's people from the government and from leading positions in state agencies and state companies—in other words, all those who had previously had any role in ensuring that state funds rolled in Simicska's direction. Next, state advertisements disappeared from the businessman's media companies, and their financial position therefore became increasingly difficult. Next, the crowning glory of Simicska's empire, the construction company Közgép, started to lose public procurement tenders. But his extended corporate network had reserves aplenty, and his media companies were ready for battle. They hired new people, new programmes started, and a much more open and critical period began in journalism. As an opposition politician, I found it rather comical to see how television and radio channels once tied to Fidesz, which previously had never reported on our work, were now continually inviting us on to their programmes and giving airtime to views critical of the government.

Simicska tried to prevent Orbán from depriving him of his fortune, while also attacking him politically. In select company Simicska spoke of how he felt guilty for 'letting Orbán screw the whole country'.[37] Regarding his own role, he remarked, with self-criticism, 'We had to pick up the commies' methods, because they were suffocating us'. When I tried to piece together why, ultimately, Simicska and Orbán had set upon each other, I reached the conclusion that the two players in this 'game of thrones' had the same problem. They both thought that the other wanted everything for himself: power and money.

For decades, while Fidesz was either in government or in opposition, the economic–political collaboration between the two men was perfectly rational and extremely productive. But when Fidesz gained a supermajority for the second time in the National Assembly in 2014, Orbán acquired the power necessary to control the economic–political system of Hungary himself. His main ally had become a burden. The aggressive Simicska represented an increasingly large political risk to Orbán and

'I DON'T DEAL WITH BUSINESS MATTERS'

Fidesz. The prime minister, who had acquired the long-term financial security necessary for the party, had actually already set about finding other economic players alongside Simicska much earlier, and other financiers began to grow wealthy on the system's artful benefits.

Being clever, Simicska saw through things and (as far as we know) decided that if Orbán no longer needed him, then he would buy him out. But this attitude irritated Orbán and his entourage because, as one of them put it, 'there was a tacit agreement in Fidesz that what had been created was in Lajos's name, but it didn't belong to him, it was the community's'.[38]

After this conflict erupted in February 2015, the 'de-Simicskaization' speeded up, and the government pounced on the financier's economic interests. The new minister of development halted the construction of the M4 motorway from one day to the next,[39] after Közgép had been working on it for months. The greatest blow was that, citing irregularities in tenders, the ministry barred Közgép from all public procurement tenders for three years.[40]

The media which had hitherto served Fidesz's and Orbán's purposes also became a target. After the government and state corporations withdrew all their support from Simicska's media empire, the oligarch's advertising and brokering companies were bled dry. Finally, the government dealt a blow to the oligarch's agricultural enterprises. The agricultural production company Mezort, which had been the greatest beneficiary of EU agricultural subsidies in Hungary, was suddenly removed from the list of subsidized companies as the result of a change in the law. The area of land rented from Simicska also shrank, because the authorities did not extend the rental contracts.[41] Finally, tax inspectors descended on the former oligarch's companies, beginning several investigations that went on for years.[42]

It was a surreal experience to see the very same methods that Simicska had helped to develop, which had been used by the governing party to immobilize business people and entire sectors, now being deployed against their creator. In Parliament it was noticeable that some bills had the sole purpose of weakening Simicska's companies. This process was so blatant that a significant number of people took the side of the previously feared oligarch. Opposition politicians turned up in company with Simicska, saying they would support him if necessary—though, of course, mainly for money.

Simicska's struggle lasted right until the 2018 elections. The day after Fidesz's new election victory, Máté Kocsis, a politician who acted as intermediary between the prime minister and the businessman, went to Simicska to negotiate a truce. But this time he had no choice: Orbán demanded total capitulation. That day Simicska announced that he would sell everything to his business partner, Zsolt Nyerges, and step aside.[43] The former confidant and billionaire moved to his house in the country and spent his time breeding horses and other animals. He completely retired from public life.

Not only had the prime minister rid himself of a rival for power; he had proved to his own camp that no one could oppose him. This was a particularly potent message within Fidesz, because the party had managed to conceal the Simicska-related scandals by means of the anti-migration campaign, and for many in the party this kind of step was unpalatable. There were voices of criticism, but another electoral victory for Fidesz in 2018 reinforced Orbán's position in the party. In addition, a new generation of Fidesz's economic–political elite had emerged whose entire careers had been built up under Orbán's two-thirds majority regime. They had learned all the ins and outs of politics from him, and had only Orbán to thank for their position. These young people would do anything for their leader.

'I DON'T DEAL WITH BUSINESS MATTERS'

With the Help of Good Fortune, the Good Lord Above, and Viktor Orbán

'That I've got this far, certainly the good Lord above, good fortune, and the person of Viktor Orbán all played a role in it, but I've never privatized, I've never filched things, I've always acquired things by working and being clever'.⁴⁴ So Lőrinc Mészáros told the weekly magazine *Heti Válasz* in 2014, when, as mayor of the small village of Felcsút, he was coming increasingly under the spotlight. At the end of the 1990s he had set up a company as a plumber and gas fitter, but at the beginning of the 2000s he nearly went bankrupt. After he recovered, he began to take a professional interest in football, and became manager and financial donor of the village football team. His utilities company took off, and after a while he became involved in the construction of blocks of flats. After 2010 he turned to public life, and in 2011 he was elected mayor of Felcsút. This marked the beginning of a new period in Mészáros's life, and within a couple of years he had amassed a fortune.

Between 2008 and 2019, Mészáros and his company Mészáros Kft increased their revenue almost thousandfold, especially after the conflict with Simicska.⁴⁵ The village mayor acquired a football team (the Puskás Akadémia Football Club, founded by Orbán), land, a road construction company, and then, after 2015, a castle, a media company, a chain of hotels, a bank, a power station, and an energy service provider. In 2015 he made his first appearance on the list of the richest Hungarians, in thirtieth place. Three years later, he topped the list, his wealth having increased tenfold.⁴⁶ And in 2019 the gas fitter–entrepreneur made it onto *Forbes*'s list of billionaires.⁴⁷ By then, Simicska's former companies had found their way to him as well. Naturally, he used an old recipe: not everything was under Mészáros's name. A huge group of corporations grew around him, with three or four people as owners alongside the village mayor, typically his old acquaintances, partners or employees. When he was asked in an interview how it was possible that the growth of his corporate empire had overshot that of the Meta company owner Mark Zuckerberg, Mészáros said cheerily: 'Perhaps I'm cleverer, don't you think?'[48]

The rise of Lőrinc Mészáros illustrated how the post-Simicska system worked. Between 2010 and 2014, with Simicska as practically the sole ruler of Közgép, the company earned 500 billion HUF. In the new era, Fidesz-linked business people won four times as many investment subsidies, which were distributed between several people. In a smart power move, Orbán built up a new elite from players linked directly to him. There would be no chance of a new Lajos Simicska rising from among them, and there would be no power nexuses with a hankering for independence.

Mészáros's business model was very simple. He has made himself rich exclusively through Hungarian state contracts. A number of political contacts and a series of state loans given on favourable terms helped him to win these deals.[49] Then he invested the assets, and on this basis the companies grew further. By the end of the 2010s, not only was Mészáros the wealthiest citizen in Hungary, but his weight was felt in the Hungarian economy. Compared with the gigantic corporate empire of Mészáros, the former company network of Simicska's seemed a very small slice of the cake.[50]

An investigation by a conservative internet portal critical of the government into the construction companies sponsoring Puskás Akadémia FC revealed a telling conclusion.[51] The sponsoring companies turned out to be exactly the same ones that occupied the top places on the Hungarian public procurement list between 2015 and 2019. Among the ten most successful construction companies, seven were linked to Mészáros, one

'I DON'T DEAL WITH BUSINESS MATTERS'

involved the business circle of Viktor Orbán's son-in-law, and two were Austrian companies that have long been present in the Hungarian market, Strabag and Swietelsky. The top leaders of government and the biggest winners of public tenders essentially form one clique of owners. The research also showed that the closer a construction company is to the pinnacle of power, the larger the profit on revenue it produces. Construction companies independent of the government typically work with a profit margin of 2%–3%. In the case of companies formerly belonging to Simicska, this rate was 6.8%. But profit for companies in which Mészáros had an interest hit the 15%–16% mark.

In my time as an MP, I grew accustomed to witnessing the wildest scandals, but apart from uncovering these affairs and speaking out, my colleagues and I could hardly do anything. Still, in 2016 I was personally deeply dismayed by one of Mészáros's deals. Unexpectedly, he bought the Ramada hotel in the lakeside resort of Balatonalmádi, the town where I was born. When I was a child, my friends and I would frequently play in the hotel's beautiful garden, which was then open to public. At that time the multi-storey lakeside hotel was called Auróra and was one of the landmark buildings in the resort. The windows upstairs offered one of the best views of the picturesque Lake Balaton and the surrounding hills. After the hotel was privatized in the 1990s, the building and garden became private property, and the beach was closed to locals.

Mészáros turned up as a property investor in the lake region in 2016. This hotel was one of his first tourism investments on the shores of Lake Balaton, soon to be followed by a dozen or so others, all in the finest locations in Hungary. The Balaton is the largest freshwater lake in Central Europe: in summer the water is warm, and in winter it freezes over, making it a favourite spot for holidaymakers and sports lovers for over a century. During the communist era it was a focal meeting point for families from East and West Germany. To this day, many sections of the lakeshore are open to the public, with their beaches, parks, campsites and harbours. On the volcanic hills of the northern shore grow excellent grapes for wine, famed throughout Europe. Business groups around Fidesz set out after 2010 to buy, first, the yacht and sailing harbours, then the quality wine-making areas. When they began targeting the hotels, it became clear that they also wanted to lay claim to the areas on the shore.

Occupation of the Balaton took place, as usual, with help from the government. In 2019 the state, using a large amount of capital, unexpectedly bought into Balaton Shipping (Bahart), a company operating properties, harbours and water traffic formerly owned by the lakeside municipalities. Within a mere four days, the municipalities' share became suddenly a minority share in relation to the state's. The ownership rights of the company were taken over by the Hungarian Tourism Agency, overseen by Antal Rogán, the minister in charge of the Prime Minister's Office. The mayor of one of the lakeside towns expressed his concern: 'Where Antal Rogán appears, it's wise to be cautious'.[52] One year later, in summer 2020 during the Covid-19 pandemic, within just a few weeks the municipalities were presented with a reorganization plan that made it possible to sell valuable lakeside properties and outsource the operation of the most valuable yachting harbours. Privatization began right away, using the subsidies paid out to mitigate the economic effects of the Covid pandemic. In the most blatant manner possible, the president of Bahart, who was Lőrinc Mészáros' partner in other projects, received 2.8 billion HUF in the form of non-repayable subsidies to his own companies.[53] One online study estimated that companies linked to Fidesz circles, including those with ties to Mészáros, invested in forty-two mega-projects in the Balaton region in 2021. These investments received 63.5 billion HUF from the state for developing hotels and jetties—half of the entire sum awarded nationwide.[54] By

'I DON'T DEAL WITH BUSINESS MATTERS'

2021 private companies close to Fidesz had encircled the entire lake, and in the most beautiful areas, including some protected areas, previously used by local inhabitants and holidaymakers, they built luxury harbours, gated communities, adventure parks and hotels.

Local inhabitants and municipalities fought in vain against the government's actions. NGOs started petitions; political parties filed complaints against construction in the protected areas. But the protests were in vain. The mayor of Szigliget, a historical town on Lake Balaton, resigned after twenty-two years of service, together with the entire council, and declared bitterly: 'We feel that we are defenceless against certain business people and investors. The way we see it, we can no longer put a stop to these processes as leaders of the town, and this is how we wish to draw public attention to the dangers'.[55] When I heard this, there were no words to express my despondency. They had held out for a long time. The central embankment areas of my home town, Balatonalmádi, had long fallen prey to companies close to Fidesz. It was exasperating to know that the number of free beaches, fishing areas and green spaces around Lake Balaton were steadily decreasing. The shore, the water, and the fertile vineyards and wine *pensions* in the hills were all passing to a narrow circle close to Fidesz.

His Name Is Worth Gold

Mészáros's growing corporate empire included some failures. In 2017, he bought the Mátra Erőmű, a coal-fired power station supplying 15% of Hungary's energy. It was difficult to conceive why Mészáros needed an out-of-date power station which would have to be closed anyway in a few years because of EU regulations. But the new owner's confidence must have known no bounds, because in spite of the company making a loss, at the end of the first year he received a considerable dividend.

However, things didn't go well: two years later he had a change of heart and was searching for a buyer for the 'power station wreck'. And who should the buyer be but the Hungarian state, more specifically the state-owned Hungarian Electricity (MVM). The deal was kept so secret that the purchase price came to light only when opposition MPs took the state energy company to court.[56] It transpired that in addition to the purchase price, the corporation demanded three times that amount from the state for expenses, in order for MVM to settle outstanding debts and balance the loss-making company's books. The leaders of MVM asked the supervising minister to authorize the purchase, because they considered it high risk. Because of this transaction, which cost the state tens of billions of forints, opposition politicians filed complaints of embezzlement, but the National Bureau of Investigation terminated inquiries since they detected no crime.

Mészáros was right when he said the architect of his success was the good Lord above, good fortune and, most of all, Viktor Orbán. At Mészáros's name, banks and credit institutions open their doors, ministry employees stand to attention, and state auditing institutions draw a veil over his deals. But Mészáros never slams the door on anyone, nor does he shout. He is no Lajos Simicska. His name is enough for a company to be successful. The Vivien mineral water factory, which Mészáros saved from bankruptcy, turned profitable in a couple of days when Hungarian State Railways immediately ordered several million bottles of mineral water to hand out to people at railway stations on hot summer days. Mészáros didn't even have to pick up the phone.

Fidesz-related companies in the 'Mészáros period' have gone far beyond the Simicska era, in terms of both funds involved and the diversity of their portfolios. They have naturally retained the classical trinity of construction industry, agriculture, and media and advertising, the third being a basic tool for wielding power, which state companies fatten with generous advertisements. Mészáros and his partners also acquired a significant share in sectors where state monopolies help to ensure a continuous growth in revenue, such as energy service providers and the defence industry.

Heading into the Future

Mészáros's companies first appeared on the stock market in 2017, not in the traditional manner, by issuing shares or through his buying up valuable companies, but in a rather 'unorthodox' way. Mészáros would buy a share in an ailing company, for a much higher price than its condition warranted, and after that the share price of the company mysteriously began to rise significantly. Investors in the stock market looked on astonished. The secret behind this 'unorthodox' arrangement was simple: the companies become valuable not through traditional growth, but because of the participation of a man close to the prime minister.[57] In 2022 it was not yet clear whether these companies, which were overly dependent on the state, would be able to prove themselves in a competitive market.

The most spectacular example of this was the infocommunications company 4iG. This small company had been generating a loss for years when Mészáros's group bought it in 2018. It can hardly be a coincidence that at exactly the same time the government set up the Digital Government Agency with the aim of making a central assessment of the IT needs of ministries, state institutions and companies, and deciding how to meet the orders. After ten years, I was rarely surprised by the behaviour of companies close to Fidesz, but the extent to which this deal was coordinated astounded me.

Within a year, 4iG became the number one beneficiary of state IT public procurement, and its profitability grew 1,700-fold in one year.[58] Under the lead of Mészáros's partner, Gellért Jászai, the company won a contract to develop the Hungarian Treasury's accounts system, which, in addition to being massive, was also a confidential project. With large-scale acquisitions in 2022, 4iG become the second-largest telecommunications company in Hungary with a regional outreach and was ready to become a global service provider even in space telecommunications.[59]

As well as the emblematic Mészáros companies, dozens of business groups have grown up around the government party during Orbán's twelve-year rule. Over this time the profit of these companies grew tenfold, and the dividends paid to the owners rocketed twentyfold.[60] Orbán's line was that their owners were 'national business people', whose vocation was to build the country, and thus they were deserving of state support. The truth, however, was very different. The Hungarian government was not helping entrepreneurs who were developing the country and moving it forward with marketable services and products. Among Orbán's 'national business people' there was nobody whose company would be able to stay afloat without government monopolies and subsidies. A prime example of this was the corporate empire of Lajos Simicska, which seemed vast at the time but collapsed within a year when it lost subsidies and support from the government and state companies.

In Parliament, not a question time passed without opposition MPs, myself included, questioning the prime minister about the latest fabulous deals of Mészáros and his partners. And Viktor Orbán always has the same answer: 'I don't deal with business matters'.

We Don't Win the Most!

Each year, 1 February is an exciting day in Hungarian politics: this is when MPs' annual declarations of assets become public. Orbán's affairs, as usual, received special attention in 2022,

'I DON'T DEAL WITH BUSINESS MATTERS'

though to judge from the document, this was unjustified: on paper, Orbán is one of the poorest politicians in the country. He has a moderately large house in his childhood village of Felcsút, and shares a flat in Budapest with his wife. He has no savings. Even for summer holidays, the Orbán family go no further than the Croatian coast, just like many middle-class Hungarians. Orbán lives apparently modestly, and it is clear that work means everything for him. I have known his wife, Anikó Lévai, for thirty years, and we often bump into one another in the Vasas Sports Club in Budapest. When we meet in front of the gym, we pause for a moment to ask how the kids are, then we smile and say goodbye. But it is difficult to believe the illusion that the Orbán family live like any other Hungarian clan. Although they take care not to display wealth in their public appearances, the growth of the extended family's wealth is increasingly noticeable.

At the beginning of the 2000s, light was thrown on the family's growing wealth through a venture involving Viktor Orbán's wife. Together with others, in the late 1990s Anikó owned vineyards in the famous Tokaj wine-growing region. During Fidesz's first term in government, she and her partners extended this land significantly, using various state subsidies. One document that became public shows that on several occasions the directors of the company held their meetings at the prime minister's residence, and the prime minister gave the owners specific instructions on how to apply for state subsidies. 'Let's not gain all that we ask for; let's not get the most ourselves',[61] he recommended. It is true that Viktor Orbán has never in his life purchased a business company in his own name. However, contrary to his assertion, he does deal with business matters, both in government and in opposition, and not just matters around the party, but the business matters of the companies of his own family.

TAINTED DEMOCRACY

The Daughter and the Son-in-Law

Viktor Orbán's eldest daughter, Ráhel, got married in 2013 to entrepreneur István Tiborcz, in a wedding open to the tabloid press, which was quite a novelty for figures in Hungarian politics. Months before the wedding, carefully planned snippets of news and photos of the young couple were leaked. The wedding day was accompanied by lively media attention. The front pages of newspapers were covered with photos of the prime minister and the bride. Accompanied by all the trappings of peasant romanticism, including Roma music, the enormous and exclusive wedding reception in a homestead on a horse farm was supposed to symbolize everything the prime minister wanted to convey to 'his people': that they were an authentic Hungarian family, where the father knows his family duties, and the family eat the same food and listen to the same music as everyone else.

With the wedding, the economic interests of the Tiborcz family immediately came under the spotlight. This young man in his twenties was already the owner and managing director of several of his father's companies. However, one business stood out, which the young groom had founded earlier with Lajos Simicska: Elios Innovatív, a subsidiary of Közgép, dealing with renewable energy. In 2013, the year of the wedding, the company became independent, and from this point on it won an increasing number of public procurement contracts, mostly for modernizing urban street lighting. After Simicska's fall, Tiborcz gained a majority share in the company. By then the company had contracts with thirty-four Hungarian towns to implement an innovative LED street-lighting system. At the time LED lighting was in an experimental phase worldwide, causing problems in many places because the light was not strong enough. This fact drew attention to risky municipal investments.

'I DON'T DEAL WITH BUSINESS MATTERS'

Investigative journalists followed the trail of contracts and discovered that in most towns the calls for tenders were identical word for word. They had been drafted by the same company, which was led by a former business partner of István Tiborcz. In more than half of the municipal procurements, Elios had been the only contender, because it was the only company to meet the specifications.[62] After opposition politicians filed a complaint about the public lighting works won by Elios Innovatív, a police investigation was launched, but the probe was inconclusive.

Because these developments were implemented with EU money, the European Anti-Fraud Office (OLAF) also began to investigate. OLAF found 'serious irregularities' in thirty-five public procurement tenders won by Elios Innovatív between 2011 and 2015, as well as 'evidence of conflict of interest'.[63] OLAF recommended that the entire sum of the subsidies won from the European Commission, €43.7 million, be withdrawn from the Hungarian state.

In this extremely embarrassing affair, Viktor Orbán's government did not wish to quarrel with the EU. The Hungarian government managed things by not invoicing these projects to the European Commission but paid for the company's works out of the Hungarian budget. What happened, then, is that István Tiborcz's company foisted poor-quality work on dozens of Hungarian towns for enormous sums of money and was remunerated in full from Hungarian taxpayers' pockets. This affair caused a great stir in Hungarian politics, and was still upsetting people years later, in 2020. Orbán continually had to face awkward questions from journalists. On one occasion he said: 'My view is that there is no such thing as EU money. It is our money. Hungarians' money. The EU disburses it, but it is our money'.[64] Not only is Orbán's statement false (since most EU subsidies arrive in Hungary from the taxes of citizens of other

EU countries) but it also reveals the prime minister's belief that the government can do what it likes with EU money.

On the basis of the OLAF report and the complaint by Hungarian MPs, the Chief Prosecutor's Office had no choice but to start an inquiry. Needless to say, the National Bureau of Investigation found no evidence of criminal activity and closed the investigation after a few months.

After the Elios affair the young couple disappeared from the public eye for a while. Tiborcz sold his share in this company and moved into real estate and tourism. This came to light when, in the town of Keszthely on the shores of Lake Balaton, friends of István Tiborcz acquired the town harbour and valuable old buildings in the vicinity from the municipality.[65] It nevertheless caused a great stir, and the people of Keszthely and opposition politicians protested in vain against the privatization of the harbour. Since then, Tiborcz and Mészáros have opened hotels in these valuable buildings. The method of business circles close to Fidesz, pressuring municipalities to sell them important public parks and real estate, served as a model for other lakeside real estate development projects.

Tiborcz's new company, BDPST, a real estate development group, acquired several dozen extremely valuable hotels, palaces and historic buildings in the centre of Budapest, almost all financed by loans.[66] In 2018, BDPST also purchased the listed real estate development company Appeninn from Mészáros. This was the first time that assets passed directly from Mészáros to the Orbán family, but it was not clear whether the deal involved a financial transaction.[67]

The development of Tiborcz's property empire was assisted not just by a handful of friendly construction companies but also by plentiful state funds, derived from EU tourism subsidies. No wonder the Orbán government declared activities related to tourism and catering 'strategic sectors'. This important activity

'I DON'T DEAL WITH BUSINESS MATTERS'

was coordinated by the Hungarian Tourism Agency, whose director 'constantly asks the expert Ráhel Orbán's opinion'; in her free time and for no recompense she gives advice to the state organ.[68] Ráhel Orbán learned the trade in one of the world's most prestigious private hospitality management schools, the École Hôtelière de Lausanne, in Switzerland. Naturally, the prime minister's daughter did not occupy a position in a state office but had considerable influence over the development of tourism and the distribution of funds. The fashion industry met a similar fate: there, too, a state office was set up to support it, the Hungarian Fashion and Design Agency, which was led by a classmate and friend of Ráhel Orbán.

As a result of these developments, in 2016, at the age of twenty-seven, Ráhel Orbán made it onto the *Forbes* magazine list of the most influential Hungarian women, which was led that year by her mother, Anikó Lévai. In 2020, Ráhel ranked second on the list; she was said to be the 'invisible hand behind the tourism and fashion sectors'.[69] If you wanted to achieve something in the tourism sector or the fashion industry in Hungary, it was pointless going to the government agencies; much better was to go straight to Ráhel Orbán—so I have been told by acquaintances working in the best Budapest fashion houses.

In 2012, when I went back into Hungarian politics, I ran into a dear old friend, who for a long time had worked as a diplomat in post-Soviet Eastern European countries. As we chatted about events in Hungary, he suddenly said: 'Just how corrupt a politician is mostly becomes visible in the following generation, with his children. Until then he can conceal his fortune, but the children want to spend'. My friend proved to be a wise seer. Ráhel Orbán and her husband, unlike her parents, did not conceal their fortune or their luxury lifestyle. Starting with their sumptuous wedding reception, they liked to show off their expensive cars and dress in clothes by the world's leading designers; this was a far cry from the lifestyle of the average Hungarian. In the list of the richest Hungarians, István Tiborcz was the youngest, and in 2020 he was thirty-fourth in the rankings. Ráhel Orbán led a lively social life, and was often followed by the press. Once, after a criticism levelled at the couple, a brazen post appeared on her Facebook page: 'My husband and I have an independent family, we stand on our own two feet, we make a living from our own resources, we live our own lives'.[70] It was no problem for them that their path to riches started with deals behind closed doors, and that their extraordinary influence was due to her father, the prime minister.

A Country without Consequences

Between 2010 and 2022 Viktor Orbán had achieved his aim: in his party-state, power fused with the largest economic interest group. Not only was political power centralized in the prime minister's hands, but so too were economic decisions. For this reason, there was no lobbying in the traditional sense of the word, because the system itself built up the companies for which it then smoothed the path to prosperity.

Behind the prime minister at the top of the pyramid, there were the party's 'big fish', who controlled considerable economic networks from positions in government.[71] Around them, on the next level, were several hundreds of party MPs, mayors and other officials, who enriched themselves primarily through state and local public procurement tenders, often financed by the EU. At the same time, government MPs had minimal influence on the course of public affairs and legislation because, as I showed in Chapter 4, most of the MPs were mere voting fodder for the Fidesz group, devoid of any autonomy whatsoever. These MPs, who hid behind the parliamentary benches to the extent that I did not even note their names in the years we spent together, were the lords of life and death in their own counties. This

'I DON'T DEAL WITH BUSINESS MATTERS'

Fidesz political class was aided and served by a considerable network of institutions, tender-writing companies, transactional lawyers, liquidators and tax experts, whom the system provided with well-paid work. All this cost Hungarians an inestimable amount in terms of taxpayers' money.

The other key element that differentiated Orbán's system from that of the preceding period was the removal of state institutions' functions of scrutiny. The Chief Prosecutor's Office, the State Audit Office and the Competition Authority were all degraded even though they still formally existed and had the authority to scrutinize the government. In practice, however, they simply did not make use of their powers and became willingly subservient in the system. There was no need for anyone to telephone from the Prime Minister's Office regarding an awkward affair. The carefully selected leaders, faithful to Fidesz, knew very well which companies and transactions needed to be scrutinized, and which did not. They did not scrutinize the central government; they conveyed the will of the central government. A prosecutor's office that systematically turns a blind eye in certain cases might as well not exist. There was hardly any country in Europe where the authorities charged with scrutiny and control were in such a dilapidated state as in Hungary. So all the complaints and reports were in vain: charges and sanctions never sullied those who were 'protected' by the government. The risk of being found out in corruption, at least for players sufficiently close to the government, was almost zero. Hungary had become a country without consequences, and the effect of this was devastating, both economically and morally.

Why Didn't Hungarians Rebel?

Quite justifiably, the question arises: In such an impossible situation, where were the incensed Hungarians? Why did they not hold mass protests, why did they not replace the party which was plundering the country? Why didn't corruption mobilize the people?

One EU survey found in 2020 that, of all member states, Hungary had the highest proportion of those who thought it was possible to live with corruption: only 38% of the population rejected abuse of political positions outright.[72] At the same time, 87% saw it as a grave problem.[73] The vast majority of Hungarians therefore were aware of corruption, but they believed that if they reported it there would be no consequences.[74] In Orbán's regime, Hungarians had simply resigned themselves to corruption. This was shown by a conversation I once had with a provincial agricultural entrepreneur, who said,

> Well, I found a niche for myself in this system in a couple of years. I don't like it, but I get by. I supply to one of the big dogs, but I've got work, I've got orders, I'm getting on. I don't want to upset things, because then I'll have to start over from scratch.

The development of this sad state of affairs was reinforced by other factors. Viktor Orbán often referred to the cooked frog syndrome. If you put a frog in water and begin to heat it, the frog first feels how warm the water is, but by the time it realizes it is boiling and it will die, it is too late. As we have seen in this chapter, the level of political corruption has gradually increased since 2010. In 2012 things didn't look the way they did in 2016, and by 2022 enormous changes had happened even by those standards. With this gradual deterioration, people withdrew from collective action.

Moreover, most people could not even conceive of the sheer size of a thousand billion forints, or of an institution that supplies electricity to half the country. Typically, the few corruption cases that did after all provoke scandal were actually petty matters, such as Roland 'Voldemort' Mengyi's budgetary fraud,[75] some politicians' summer yachting and 'sex party',[76] or Ráhel Orbán's 10-million-forint watch.[77]

'I DON'T DEAL WITH BUSINESS MATTERS'

Interestingly, political loyalties in the country also held greater sway than misgivings about corruption. In their judgement about state-level corruption, Fidesz voters proved notably more lenient than opposition-leaning people.[78] Orbán's believers had accepted that the support of 'national business people' was an act of nation-building; it was at least better than the enrichment of foreigners. Moreover, since the Prosecution Service, which was supposed to exercise control, hardly ever initiated proceedings, it was difficult to judge what was a problem and what was not. The Hungarian system of law no longer enshrined the principles of social justice or morality, and the social system of norms had been completely overturned.

Sociologists have long stated that the mistrust entrenched in Hungarian society made evasion of the rules more acceptable. Coupled with an ideological charge, this environment provided an opportunity for political corruption to spread. But emphasizing cultural characteristics provides an excuse not to act, and leads us to resign ourselves to the present state of affairs.

Hungarian corruption research institutions and anti-corruption organizations made several recommendations about how to put a stop to abuses of power. Taking a stand against corruption, however, requires an enormous effort. Successful anti-corruption campaigns all over the world show that in order to cleanse public life, the commitment of the entire political elite is necessary. For this, we in Hungary need a change of government and a new elite for whom the future of the country is more important than, or at least as important as, its own power. Corruption accompanies power and is present in every country. But a transparent institutional environment has a greater chance of filtering out the abuse and sends the message that corruption is unacceptable.

7

PRESS-GANGED INTO SERVICE
THE ASSAULT ON THE FREE PRESS

One morning in July 2020 the entire staff of Hungary's leading online news portal, Index, snaked in long lines towards the office of the chairman of the board. Each of them was clutching a letter of resignation. Instead of the usual daily news, interviews and witty exposé videos posted to Index, that day one million people accessing the portal watched a live stream of this dramatic event.[1] Index was Hungary's most important news portal for current affairs, first set up when most people were just getting to grips with the internet. In 2020, it was read and watched by 1.7 million people out of a population of 10 million.[2]

After the journalists had submitted their resignations, they explained in a press conference that for many years they had been working independently without outside interference in the published content or in the choice of the editorial staff. However, two days previously the editor-in-chief was fired for obviously political reasons and the staff felt that with his dismissal the very basis of their independence had been attacked. They viewed the future so bleakly that almost all ninety of them resigned.

TAINTED DEMOCRACY

The spectacle of the resignation was shocking for me, partly because I was an avid Index reader and had just been interviewed for the portal's podcast, *Kibeszélő* (Speak out).[3] But the spectre of the 'annihilation' of Index had long been looming. Since 2010 the Hungarian media market had been dramatically transformed. Dozens of press and media organs had ceased to exist or had been rebranded over the previous decade as a result of intervention from the authorities or pro-government business people. Index was the latest in a long line, and the most significant organ of the media to be endangered. But as in previous cases, it was impossible to know what the final nail in the coffin would be, the signal that a media product no longer existed or was no longer what it used to be.

In 2022 the International Press Institute found that the Hungarian government had systematically eroded press freedom, independence and diversity, hijacked the media market, divided journalists, and obtained an unprecedented level of political control over the country's media ecosystem.[4] Contrary to this, members of the Hungarian government claimed that the press was balanced. According to Viktor Orbán, it was even freer and more diverse than the German press.[5] 'If we look at Hungarian media, we see that the left wing has at most 60%, more like 50%, and the Christian Conservative right has 40%–50%', he proclaimed in 2019.[6] The Mérték Media Analysis Workshop meanwhile found that in that year 77.8% of news published in Hungary could be traced back to Fidesz.[7]

After 2010 my fellow politicians and sociologists abroad asked me whether there were journalists in prison, whether any were threatened with physical violence, and whether the government used administrative means to silence those critical of its policies. This chapter shows that these things are not necessary for press freedom to be seriously curtailed. Press freedom does not just mean that the press is diverse; it also means that broad masses of people can access ideas and opinions that differ from their own.

PRESS-GANGED INTO SERVICE

The Decade-Long Build-Up of a Diverse Media Market

The first time I was ever on TV was in 1990, at peak viewing time. On the night of Hungary's first free elections, when news came in that Fidesz had made it into Parliament, Viktor Orbán and I went into the studios of Hungarian Television to comment on this fantastic result. We were in a euphoric mood—not just us, but the entire crew, from the producer to the camera operators and the lighting crew. György Baló, one of the country's best-known broadcasting journalists, who was well respected even before the regime change, hosted the election programme. Baló was a member of the generation of journalists who, in the second half of the 1980s, when the Kádár regime's political control over the press began waning, broadcast late-evening programmes critical of the regime.

At the end of the 1980s, the communist power elite could no longer keep the media under control, but the new democratic forces were not yet strong enough to overturn them. In this power vacuum, statements by journalists could influence political events: their reports uncovered scandals and brought down public figures. This made for an extreme change compared with the boring, monotonous, propaganda-flavoured party media of earlier decades.

In 1989, hundreds of independent papers, local publications, and city radio and TV stations were founded, and a diverse media market, in terms of both ideology and language, emerged. When Veszprém Television[8] broadcast the first multi-party election candidate debate in 1990, I immediately became known because the whole city saw the programme. Never before had television broadcast such a debate; after all, in the years of communism, there were simply no multi-party debates.

Among the young people who founded Fidesz and took it to victory, there was a group who were reluctant to take on a political role. They founded a liberal weekly, completely novel in format and language, called the *Magyar Narancs* (Hungarian Orange). *Narancs* aimed to adopt the traditions of the journalism and investigative rigour of the English-speaking world but, following the Eastern European literary journalistic tradition, lending a satirical tone to accounts of events in public and cultural life. To secure its freedom, *Narancs* deliberately cut ties with Fidesz and any other political party. The two to three years after the regime change were the golden era of press freedom.

A generational gap appeared. Journalists successful in the previous authoritarian regime, even the best ones, lacked the professional experience to be impartial and balanced as a matter of course. In public life during the regime change, these journalists often overstepped the mark of what constitutes an independent role for the press in a democracy. They started influencing not just public opinion but also politics. This transgression of their professional role and lack of professional ethics contributed greatly to the polarization of intellectual and political life in Hungary, as discussed in the introduction.

For a while, media players freed from the oppression of state-party dictatorship enjoyed the illusion that they could operate beyond the influence of the political or economic spheres, but instead as their equals, as a kind of fourth estate. This was, however, at odds with the interests of power politics. The battle for control of the most influential media, the national TV and radio channels, began immediately after the first free elections in 1990. The government expected the public media to be instrumental in informing citizens about the historical tasks of the regime change. A sizeable part of the press, however, had no intention of meeting this expectation, and took a critical stance towards the government. Members of Prime Minister Antall's government felt that the mainstream press was not on board with them and claimed that most of the media remained under the influence of the former communist elite. Without a doubt, there had been no process of lustration aimed at either the political elite or the press. As in the case of politicians, there remained some journalists planted by the communist secret service, who tried to attain political influence by means of the press. The struggles for influence imposed a moral burden on journalists to hold political power to account, and this had an effect on Hungary's nascent democracy.

In the political–economic struggles for influence over the media, one of the players was the media industry itself, which was fighting for its own emancipation. In parallel with political tensions, journalists were also divided. In the early 1990s, as in all countries in the region, Hungary had its own 'media war', the key question being whether the primary task of the press was to hold the government to account or to support the government's task of changing the system.

The relationship between the governing parties and the media ultimately soured. Citing their majority in Parliament, governing party politicians tried to curtail the independence of critical television and radio stations. István Csurka, a radical politician in the governing MDF party, stated in 1991 that 'today anywhere in the world, only someone with their own television [station] can be said to have power. [...] Given that elections are a question of power, it is logical that the winning parties should exercise an influence on the national media'.[9] The government coalition put pressure on the heads of Hungarian Radio and Hungarian television (who had been appointed with cross-party consensus), until they resigned. In their place, the government planted its cronies. The governing party also established daily and weekly papers, which openly conveyed the government's point of view.[10] A new TV channel was launched to create a common media space with Hungarians living abroad.[11] Direct government intervention in the operation of the public media took place in a similar manner throughout the post-Soviet region, and aimed to subordinate news channels to the ruling parties. However, the classic tools of propaganda (mindless repetition, use of stereotypes, and stigmatization of rivals) had a serious boomerang effect when the right-wing governing parties lost the elections in 1994.

Laying down the framework for press freedom took years, and happened imperfectly and through countless conflicts. The first media law, which regulated television and radio, was drafted in 1995. This finally created the institutions which became the guarantors of journalistic independence and balanced information in the public service media.[12] Each political party in Parliament appointed members to the supervisory bodies, and although controversies remained, the situation was consolidated. In part because of the privatization of some media outlets and their sale to foreign owners, by the end of the 1990s open government interference in the media had dwindled, and ideological diversity became the accepted norm.

Fidesz's First Struggles with the Media

In the early 1990s, the press was generally friendly towards Fidesz. I remember how consciously we tried to keep our distance from the media war, which we felt was alien to us. Journalists appreciated this, and let us say anything we pleased. Our special treatment only became apparent with the scandal surrounding the sale of the building housing Fidesz's headquarters, as discussed in Chapter 6. At that point, Fidesz came under a barrage of criticism, and we faced difficult questions from the press. The controversy heightened tensions within the party, which was precisely the picture some journalists wanted to paint. As newly elected party president, Orbán took control of Fidesz's communications, and became increasingly hostile to representatives of the press. I noticed how Orbán and a narrow circle around him responded to the critical press with the same indignation as the right-wing government coalition had done. Previously we had looked down on this behaviour and mocked it. Orbán attributed the right-wing parties' 1994 electoral defeat to the failure of the first head of government to leverage his position of power with the media.[13] When Fidesz shifted to the right in 1994, it joined the club of those who claimed there was a liberal–socialist dominance in public service media. While I think this was an over-reaction, it cannot be denied that there were moments of provocation, for example when one publicist wrote in 1991: 'We pulled you out of the bin and we will let you get back there'.[14] This quote became fixed in Fidesz's mind ever afterwards.

In 1998 Orbán formed a coalition government and immediately changed course on media policy.

> The civic government [...] unlike its predecessors, is preparing to take an active role for the public good in shaping supply and demand on the media market. With this intention in mind, the government declares positive discrimination of the civic press. [...] The government can no longer be so naive, waiting for [the opposition's] agreement, as to dispense with even the slightest opportunity to exercise pressure, which might move us closer to [...] the creation of a genuinely impartial public TV with a strong public service function, from the ruins of MTV [...][15]

In power Fidesz would not trust the independent media but aimed to amplify its own right-wing voices. Thus it appointed openly biased allies as editors-in-chief in the public media, and pro-government programmes multiplied. Hungarian Radio started broadcasting a weekly interview with the prime minister, which was more like a speech than a series of genuine answers to genuine questions, with the reporter often merely playing the role of a microphone stand—a state that has not changed to this day. Fidesz invested public money in the conservative papers[16] and created a conservative weekly called *Heti Válasz*.

The advertising company Mahir Cityposter, owned by Lajos Simicska, expanded, thanks to generous government orders. Yet the Fidesz-led coalition was defeated in 2002, and Orbán's team once more blamed the press for this. Fidesz became even more determined to strengthen its allies in the media. Simicska founded a television station, Hír TV, while another Fidesz-friendly entrepreneur entered the media market with Echo TV, which broadcast programmes with explicitly far-right content. As a result, the press became more diverse but also more polarized, though the political tone was not vulgar, and shows featuring debates gave airtime to genuine disputes.

In the 2000s, as with the secret economic agreements, media policy was also marked by cross-party bargaining. For instance, as the result of a cross-party deal, commercial radio frequencies were distributed between the respective cronies of the ruling and the largest opposition parties.[17]

Radio and television news broadcasters were under constant political pressure in the 2000s, though no one party was able to implement its own will without constraint. The institutions supervising the media worked well, acting like a buffer deflecting attempts at political influence, and they prevented the concentration of power. The varied structure of media ownership created a diverse news press which, although dominated by politically biased organs, still provided many sources of information for consumers wanting a balanced picture. Another contributory factor was that a generation of journalists had matured who, drawing on the spirit of *Magyar Narancs*, were not tied to any political party and were committed to the ethos of independent journalism. At the end of the 1990s they also launched two online news portals, Index and Origo, opening a completely new dimension for independent journalism. This productive period came to an end ten years later, in 2010, with startling speed.

PRESS-GANGED INTO SERVICE

The Spread of Pro-Government Media in Hungary

By chance, I came across a Facebook group that was launched one day after the Fidesz-majority Parliament had passed the new media law in 2010. The group was the 'One Million for Press Freedom' Milla (see Chapter 3), which was created by a civil activist. In just one day, the group gained more than 30,000 supporters. Many people said the time had come for action. 'We always wait for someone to solve problems. Nobody will solve them. That's why I joined', wrote one supporter.[18] The group organized the demonstration (described in the introduction) on 15 March, the Hungarian national day, in Budapest, in Szabad sajtó útja (Free Press Road). At this mass demonstration everyone sang the song 'I don't like the system', which became a slogan of the budding movement.[19]

The Transformation of the Institutions

Their anger was justified. In autumn 2010, Hungarians were confronted with an all-out attack by the Orbán government. Within the space of just a few months, the Fidesz government had interfered with the institutions regulating the media three times. By December a system was in place that no longer guaranteed a diverse press and press freedom. The media law submitted 'under the Christmas tree'—three days before Christmas—was approved by Fidesz MPs after a three-day debate. The president of the republic signed it immediately, and one week later it was already in force.[20]

The scope of the law extended to every branch of the media, including radio, television, print and online. A vast body was set up to regulate the media, the National Media and Infocommunications Authority (NMHH), which was charged with overseeing the regulation of the telephone market and managing broadcasting frequencies. As part of the NMHH, a

Media Council was set up to supervise the media, consisting exclusively of Fidesz appointees. Orbán appointed a Fidesz MP as president for a nine-year term, which led to public outrage.

The new law established a behemoth service corporation, the Media Services Support and Asset Management Fund (MTVA), which brought all of the public media under state ownership.[21] Uniform control of content was introduced in public service media right away, and 600 editors and journalists were fired.[22] The Hungarian News Agency (MTI), which enjoyed considerable state subsidies, made its news services free of charge, and as a result smaller news agencies that functioned on a commercial basis went bankrupt in a few months. From then on, the entire Hungarian press had no choice but to compile their news from the news service of MTI (although it should be noted that MTI already had a dominant role).

The Media Council and the NMHH implemented politically biased measures when distributing radio frequencies. For example, they limited, then withdrew, the frequency licence of Klubrádió, which was critical of the government, while many new church and conservative stations were able to launch new channels all over the country.[23]

Fidesz made a sharp break with previous media policy, which had divided power between the two leading parties. Instead, it set up a confrontational strategy, in which the winner took all: official posts at the helm of public media, state resources dedicated to advertising, frequencies, and broadcasting time. Checks and balances were completely eradicated from the supervisory system as they would have prevented the ruling coalition of parties from gaining supervisory control over the media. The media institutions created by Fidesz institutionalized political pressures.[24]

PRESS-GANGED INTO SERVICE

The Disappearance of Public Media

When Fidesz came to power in 2010, Orbán believed the country was in an ideological vacuum, and that he had gained an opportunity to exclusively shape public opinion. He shared this idea in an internal forum:

> A political power system has three sources. It has to be fed with three things, in order to regenerate: money, ideology, and votes. A great governing party [...] has to be capable of putting national issues into words—and not in constant debate, but it represents these matters as a matter of course.[25]

Through creating ideological hegemony, Orbán was preparing to win voters' long-term loyalty and consolidate his power. In order to realize this political goal, Fidesz assumed exclusive control of the state media. However, this aggressive takeover did not go unnoticed in Europe.

In spring 2011, during a debate in the European Parliament on the state of the Hungarian media, Orbán got into a heated exchange with French-German green MEP Daniel Cohn-Bendit. Not long afterwards, when Cohn-Bendit was in Hungary and gave a press conference, a journalist from Hungarian Television asked a provocative question about a book Cohn-Bendit had published forty years previously. The question pertained to accusations of paedophilia.[26] After Cohn-Bendit answered, he added that he found it dismaying that the journalist had reheated a years-old political attack by the French far right.[27]

That evening, the Hungarian Television newscast broadcast footage that gave the impression that Cohn-Bendit had refused to answer the question and had left the press conference. This news item was broadcast repeatedly and picked up by Hungarian Radio and many newspapers. After this distortion came to light, several media called Hungarian Television's editor-in-chief, Daniel Papp, a founding member of the extreme-right party Jobbik, a 'news-faker',[28] leading Papp to initiate court proceedings against them. The court found that Papp had indeed distorted reality, and could be called a 'news-faker'. In another case, the court declared that criticism of the state media was in the public interest.

One year after Orbán's victory in 2010, the public media were already dominated by the government. In 83% of news items, government representatives spoke, while opposition parties were heard only sporadically.[29] As Fidesz's power swelled, distortions of content became even cruder in the state media. In one investigative report, journalists working at the public television station gave anonymous accounts of how pressure on them had increased over the years.[30] Initially, they simply had to be careful of how issues were presented. 'We could do items on gays, NGOs or the refugee crisis, but in a suitable way, and after consultation', one journalist recounted. Over time, more and more topics were banned, for instance those featuring various human rights movements or climate activist Greta Thunberg. For these subjects, special permission was required from the editor-in-chief. The producers 'guided' the journalists with euphemisms to explain the angle to take with each item. But sometimes it happened that an explicit request came from the director-in-chief of the channel, whom the journalists referred to among themselves as Pitbull. They were also instructed that when a scandal involving a foreign politician was discussed, they always had to state if the subject was a 'left-wing' politician, while for right-wing politicians they were to avoid mentioning the politician's affinities. The French president Emmanuel Macron was to be mentioned not as a centrist, but as a 'former socialist minister'.

The state media were so biased towards the government that during the 2018 election campaign not once did they interview an opposition politician. When the opposition parties made a constitutional complaint against the state news channel, the television's news editing room replied that 'the media service provider cannot be expected to explore every single stance in regard to a given case, it is not obliged to give air space to every single opinion expressed, together with their proponents'.[31] The Media Act states unequivocally that the public service media content provider must, in regard to current political events, strive to allow viewers and listeners to become acquainted with parties' different opinions, and to give a balanced account of them in line with the requirements of the public interest.[32] True, Fidesz had amended the text of the 2010 act several times, and the requirement for balanced news had become increasingly vague. The text of the law no longer gives such clear guidance on what qualifies as impartial presentation of opinions. All of this threatened the very basis of the elections, but legal remedies were addressed only much later. Four days before the elections, the Constitutional Court ruled that the National Election Commission and the Curia were justified in censuring state television for these grave disproportionalities.[33]

Bursting with self-confidence, Fidesz ascribed great importance to the European Parliament elections in 2019, because it hoped that similar illiberal parties would also make a breakthrough in the rest of Europe. This expectation was apparent in state media too. Two months before the elections, Balázs Bende, editor-in-chief of the foreign politics department of Hungarian Television, and Zsolt 'Pitbull' Németh, director of the channel M1, summoned members of the department to a special meeting. Unusually, before the meeting the journalists were relieved of their mobile phones. Still, a secret recording was leaked of the meeting, the purpose of which was for the editor-in-chief to inform staff of what was expected of them during the campaign.[34] Bende told those present: 'Everyone is aware that at the end of May there will be the EP [European Parliament] elections. I'm sure nobody will be surprised if I say that in this institution, it's not the opposition alliance that is supported'. Never before had anyone said so clearly and openly in public what line should be followed in state television. After this, Bende warned his staff in no uncertain terms that their jobs would be on the line if they spoke out: 'If this statement comes as a surprise to anyone, they should go home now. [...] This is what we are all working for. No questions'. Then he explained what was expected in more detail: 'Mainly migration, mainly Brussels, and other things. [...] Those on duty have to take their turn, to put together material with the right narrative, following the right method and direction. If anyone doesn't like it, they can hand in their resignation'.

This instruction not only put an end to freedom of speech but also revealed the extremely threatening atmosphere in which the TV staff had to work. But when MPs reported the matter, the police closed the case after three days, saying that 'there was no verbal threat or threat of violence'.[35] In a statement, the National Media and Infocommunications Authority brushed off the inquiry, saying that 'any infringements of the law that may have been committed during programme making are not covered by laws on media management', and that this was part of journalistic freedom.[36]

The Hungarian Journalists' Association and the political opposition demanded that Hungarian Television impose heavy sanctions on the producers and leaders involved, and called for a shake-up of the state media—but in vain. Neither Hungarian Television nor the cultural committee of Parliament found anything to object to in the matter.

The institutions supervising the media no longer fulfilled their supposed tasks, and state media had become a mere mouthpiece for the government.

In the meantime, over the ten years of Orbán governments, the budget for the state media had doubled and in 2021 it stood at 115 billion HUF. All this money was spent by the centralized programme production company, the Media Services Support and Asset Management Fund. But this was not enough for Fidesz. Political parties had learned that control over state media, even when it is generously financed, is no guarantee for political success in the complex media world of the twenty-first century. To establish the ideological hegemony necessary to hold on to power, the ruling party wanted to control commercial media too. And, for this, what it needed most was money.

The Key Ingredient in Partisan Media: Money

By the time Fidesz came to power in 2010, the business people close to Fidesz, primarily Lajos Simicska and his partners, already owned newspapers, radio stations and small TV news channels, and had purchased another two advertising companies[37] and a free daily paper.[38] After the 2008 financial crisis when corporations cut advertising expenses, several foreign owners reckoned that they could not maintain their media outlets profitably,[39] and sold them to business people close to the government. This resulted in a considerable expansion of the portfolio of Fidesz-loyal media companies—both personally and ideologically—which were also linked to the governing party at a business level. Other entrepreneurs close to Fidesz launched into the online media space, and new forums and blogs came into being with special purposes.[40] For instance, the online portal Pesti Srácok portrayed itself as a news site with a conservative slant, yet from the beginning it became notorious for carrying derogatory and offensive articles. It normalized an unbearably crude tone in Hungarian politics, which Fidesz then spread further even in Parliament.

But operating this considerable media portfolio and making it profitable was challenging even in the hands of owners close to Fidesz, and advertising revenue fell massively. Nevertheless, the media companies forming around the governing party could build upon the role that the state sector had assumed. A system took shape which, in its own way, was supremely well thought out and organized. This system, which appeared perfectly legal, used state resources to build up a Fidesz-friendly private media empire.

The financing model can be described as follows: Simicska's people in ministries, in state companies like the National Lottery, or on the board of directors of Hungarian Electricity (MVM) ensured these institutions frequently paid for advertisements, and their public procurement tenders for communications would be won by the same six agencies.[41] These agencies then spent the state's advertising money not on the basis of business calculations, but on press products linked to Fidesz. These media outlets thus not only survived the period when advertisements were sparse, but became so profitable that the owners were able to pay out a sizeable dividend from the first year.[42]

Over 70% of the entire state advertising outlay was won by six agencies at a time when over a hundred advertising agencies were operating in Hungary.[43] But Simicska's people were present in the Public Procurement Authority, responsible for fair competition, and the Competition Authority, and they prevented any investigation into important deals. Although a similar phenomenon had occurred under previous governments, never before in Hungary had there been this level of bias. Before 2010, state advertisements were spread across a broad range of the media, contributing to their secure business operation and ensuring media pluralism. After Fidesz came to power, the system became so shockingly disproportionate that in 2013, when almost half the companies in the Hungarian media market were still making a loss, the return on sales in the media empire close to Fidesz was 20.5%.[44] Within two years, in 2010–12, taxpayers' money funded a major media portfolio, which dominated the market and conveyed the news according to Fidesz's requirements.

The independent media were forced to bow to pressure from the government. Major advertisers including foreign companies became reluctant to advertise in media that were openly critical of the government. With the drop in advertising revenue, the independent press was increasingly at a competitive disadvantage.

The only thing that the government was unable to implement because of unexpected protests was the introduction of an internet tax aimed to limit social media.[45] So many people took to the streets that drone shots of demonstrators' smartphones lighting up the night were shown around the world. The idea of the internet tax backfired spectacularly. Many young people who perhaps had never raised their voice immediately understood that the internet tax would limit their freedom of speech and even basic human relationships and entertainment. In a few days, the government backtracked in the face of mass protests and even reversed the policy: a government commissioner was appointed to develop digital culture in the country.

Building Fidesz's Media Empire by New Owners

In 2011, the editors-in-chief of Origo, the main online news outlet, were unexpectedly fired.[46] Origo was created in 1998 by Magyar Telekom with significant financial support, and the company's director, Miklós Vaszily, justified the move by saying that after fourteen years consumer demand had changed, and new blood was needed to renew the magazine. At the time, only a few people suspected the editors had been fired for political reasons.

But the Origo team continued to work in the original, independent spirit. And yet, beginning in 2011, journalists at the portal noticed that Vaszily was making requests about content, something that had not happened before. For instance, they were asked to omit certain details from an article about the accumulation of wealth by the leader of the Fidesz parliamentary group. Sometimes, during interviews, Fidesz politicians would offer to supply information, on condition that the magazine refrain from writing about certain topics.[47]

Origo journalists did not take these requests seriously. In fact, in 2012 one of the portal's journalists, András Pethő, started legal action to get information about the amount of public money spent on journeys abroad by János Lázár, because the Prime Minister's Office (of which he was minister) had not given any financial information in answer to a question.[48] After the court ordered the Prime Minister's Office to issue the requested information, and Origo wrote an exposé about the minister's expenses,[49] editor-in-chief Gergő Sáling was immediately fired. The owner once more cited habits of media consumption, but the evidence of direct political pressure was clear.

The Origo case was the first clearly documented instance of the Orbán government interfering in an independent media outlet. This was merely a sign of greater changes to come. One year after Sáling was fired, in 2015 Magyar Telekom sold Origo, saying its German parent company, Deutsche Telekom, was reducing its media interests all over Europe. Many parties showed an interest, but the portal was sold to New Wave Media, which belonged to the business interests of the cousin of György Matolcsy, the president of the Hungarian National Bank and a former minister of the economy under Fidesz. At the same time it transpired that this company had received 500 million forints in subsidies and loans from the Hungarian National Bank's Growth and Credit Programme.[50] This astonishing conflict of interests was surpassed a year later when ownership of Origo passed to Matolcsy's son, and it began to receive even more state subsidies.[51]

Origo changed completely: it struck an increasingly government-friendly tone, and carried derogatory articles on the political opposition. More and more staff left, one of whom said that the editing room had become servile,[52] while another said,

'They've turned the magazine into a worthless lie factory, and they had no idea what it was worth'.[53] Origo underwent brutal changes: one of the first Hungarian online news portals, which was proud of its independence, became an online tabloid, a source of fake news about public life. During the 2018 election campaign, the courts obliged the portal to publish corrections thirty-four times.[54]

I felt genuine sadness when I removed Origo from my browser favourites. Up to that point, it had been my computer's home page. Over the next few years I looked at it only for work purposes, to find out what nonsense or untruths they had written about my work or about the party I represented.

The complete transformation of Origo was the first step in an astonishing operation by Fidesz to strengthen its media position. The Orbán government mobilized great resources to make things impossible for other foreign media owners to do business profitably in Hungary.

TV Acquisition with Front Men

Despite the expansion of the media market, Fidesz was without a large, nationwide commercial television channel. The two major stations in Hungary had suffered huge losses in early 2010 because of the shrinking advertising market, and there was a glimmer of opportunity for Fidesz to purchase at least one of them. The party bosses chose the TV2 group, which was owned by the German company ProSiebenSat.1 Media (P7S1). The channel began to make a loss in 2010, but the public never found out why the media owner, which had plenty of capital, should have sold it after expanding it considerably as recently as 2013.[55]

In 2013 Lajos Simicska and his business partner, Zsolt Nyerges, suggested buying the channel; the media portfolio they owned was awash in state advertising and gave them much confidence in the negotiation process. Simicska and his associates managed to get a purchase option on the media company. But, as we have seen in Chapter 6, in 2014 Orbán and his oldest friend and ally fell out, and it was no longer important for Fidesz that Simicska should buy TV2. To our great surprise, two individuals, the TV2 group's CEO, Zsolt Simon, and its CFO, Yvonne Dederick, founded a company in order to buy TV2, supposedly to prevent Simicska from doing so. This bizarre development gave way to months of public farce permeated with statements and leaks worthy of a banana republic: it was all part of a business and political battle to remove Simicska from the group of buyers. The one-time almighty economic lord of Fidesz, who was himself a master of legal conjuring tricks, was in the end unable to acquire the station, because the complicated web of companies around TV2 had been reorganized so that his purchase option applied only to a shell of a company, with nothing left inside.

Finally, the TV2 media company was bought by the company's two top managers, well below the market price and thanks to a loan from the owner. They promised to pay off the instalments from the company's revenue. It seemed quite obvious that the two directors were not the genuine owners. The big secret of who had actually come up with the purchase price was revealed a year later. It was Andrew G. Vajna, government commissioner for film and member of the prime minister's confidential circle, who had bought the station, making use of a 6.7 billion HUF (€21 million) loan from the state-owned Eximbank, which the foreign minister personally supervised.[56]

In the change of ownership of TV2, the Orbán government not only exercised unacceptable pressure behind the scenes, as in the case of Origo, but even intervened in the business transactions with legal instruments. While negotiations were in progress, the government announced that it would levy an advertising tax on media products, to increase progressively in line with revenue. Since this tax contributed very little to state income, it was clear that the tax was intended to put the TV2 owners in a tight corner, bring down prices and scare off interested foreign parties from purchasing TV2.

Fidesz proposed the bill on this advertising tax to Parliament after the 2014 elections. In the most brazen manner possible, at the last moment before the vote, the advertising tax bill was amended so that RTL Klub, a competitor of TV2, would have to pay 80% of all the taxes. The government did not even attempt to conceal the fact it was a punitive tax. When it was put to a vote, one Fidesz politician admitted: 'Things like this happen. [The advertising tax] has now been used as a political weapon'.[57] The law clearly interfered in the competition between two private television stations and set off a war against the other commercial media.

After the change of ownership, as was customary with media close to Fidesz, advertising started to drift towards TV2. An anonymous diplomat from the embassy of a European country spoke of how companies from his country operating in Hungary had been approached by Fidesz's politicians, asking them to move their advertising to TV2.[58]

Just like Origo, TV2 immediately became a mouthpiece for the government's propaganda. Its leading programme *Tények* (Facts) became a hotbed of fake news, constantly whipping up hatred against the homeless and refugees, and becoming expert at smear campaigns against opposition politicians. Although TV2 regularly lost the cases brought against it because of fake news, this did not for one moment dissuade it from this unethical method.

When the owner, Andrew G. Vajna, died unexpectedly in 2019, TV2 did not stay in his heir's possession for a minute. Within weeks, the station drifted further off, ending up in the business interests of gas fitter-cum-billionaire Lőrinc Mészáros.[59] It turned out that Vajna was not the true owner of this important medium; it had merely been lent to him for safekeeping.

TAINTED DEMOCRACY

Devastation in the Dailies' Market

On 9 October 2016 a strange announcement appeared on the Facebook page of *Népszabadság*, the largest Hungarian news daily. The announcement ran: 'Dear Followers, the editors of *Népszabadság* have learned simultaneously with the public that the paper is shut down with immediate effect. Our first thought is that this is a coup. More news soon'. It was impossible to know whether this was a joke or the result of an attack by hackers. More information came later that day. Journalists at the paper said that from one day to the next, they were unable to log into the editors' webpage or their email accounts, and a motorbike courier had delivered a letter telling them that they were being temporarily relieved of their duties. The announcement struck them like lightning out of the blue. The journalists gathered on the street in front of the locked building of the publishing house and held a press conference there. The owner of the paper, on the other hand, issued only a brief statement saying that after buying the publishing company of the paper, it would be rethinking *Népszabadság*'s future. These events were incomprehensible and confusing.

Népszabadság was one of the oldest daily papers in the country, with a long and eventful history. In the communist years, as the official paper of the Hungarian Socialist Workers' Party, it had a circulation in the millions. After the regime change, ownership of *Népszabadság* passed between several foreign corporations, ultimately ending up as part of a company called Mediaworks, which by 2015 was wholly owned by an Austrian, Heinrich Pecina, with links to business people close to Fidesz.

In 2016 it was the only nationwide daily paper that Fidesz had not yet got its hands on. I should note here that it was bizarre to look on *Népszabadság* as a representative of press freedom, the very paper that had always been politically biased. Under Mediaworks ownership, political pressure on the editors increased, but they believed the paper could never be subjected to the kind of hostile makeover that had befallen other media because of its wide readership and prestige. This was probably true and, instead, the owner simply shut down the paper.

At the same time, Mediaworks continuously expanded, and in 2016 it became the second-biggest media owner in Hungary with three nationwide dailies, all nineteen county dailies, several magazines and digital media products. The daily press by then was almost entirely dominated by Mediaworks. Two weeks after closing *Népszabadság* and making all these acquisitions, the Austrian owner sold this gigantic media corporation to a company called Optimus Press, which belonged to the sphere of interests of Lőrinc Mészáros.

Between 2010 and 2016 most of the foreign owners had been eliminated from the Hungarian media market. The Swiss company Ringier sold its Hungarian interests, as did the German Axel Springer, the Swedish Modern Times Group, the Finnish Sanoma, and the German ProSiebenSat.1 and Funke-WAZ publishers. The fact that foreign investors fled the country demonstrates how weak and vulnerable the Hungarian media industry had become.

After the prime minister and Simicska broke up, the latter recalled that Orbán 'divided media players into three groups: those in complete agreement with the government, the critical ones, and the enemies, and the aim was for only those in the first category to remain. He makes things impossible for the rest'.[60] Orbán's ambition for complete dominance of the media market represented an existential threat to every independent publication. And, yet, those that had not already fallen into the claws of the governing party believed that they could escape.

A Complete Turnaround in the Media Market

Building up Mediaworks represented the beginnings of a new era for the Fidesz media empire: in one and a half years, a new Orbánist media portfolio was created out of nothing.

During the years of the Orbán–Simicska battle, other trusted people came forward as media owners, hoping that if they owned a stake in the media, their influence within the governing party would grow. Alongside Origo and TV2, the tabloid portfolio, the provincial network of papers owned by Mediaworks, and the radio stations formed a media empire of an unprecedented size, with a politically homogeneous ownership structure. The expenses for acquisitions and operations were partly resources channelled from the Hungarian budget, and partly covered by profits from projects financed by EU funds directed to the oligarchs.[61]

The complicated media financing system dreamed up and implemented by Simicska also became unnecessary. The Fidesz government created a much more efficient system for state funds to find their way to a suitable beneficiary. Under the aegis of the Prime Minister's Office, the government set up a National Communications Office, which centralized the 40 billion HUF in state spending of the government and state companies. The Office put independent media players and Simicska's media interests at a serious disadvantage by cutting state advertisements in these organs to zero. Fidesz also took care that as a result of the advertising tax law, the Simicska-owned Hír TV, the free paper Metropol, and the oligarch's remaining advertising companies would face a disproportionately large tax burden.

Hungarian press history had this farcical intermezzo: after Orbán and Simicska went their separate ways, the oligarch made an effort to turn the media under his ownership away from Fidesz and to create a critical press. Journalists hoped they could finally rebuild independent, modern conservative journalism in Hungary, free of political influence, which until then the Fidesz communication machine had steamrolled and corrupted. This period of war between the two men lasted from 2015 to the 2018 elections. But after Orbán's repeated victory, Simicska's companies could not sail against the wind, and so he was forced to sell all his advertising and media interests to his former business partner, Zsolt Nyerges, who remained loyal to Orbán.

During Orbán's second term, between 2014 and 2018, there was an informal convergence in Hungary of most private and state-owned media. Such concentration had been seen before, in Italy, under Silvio Berlusconi's rule, and especially in Russia, where state funds were also used for media accumulation.[62]

The independent press market was shrinking, and news sites like Index, 444 and HVG fought a heroic battle in the shadow of Fidesz's power, which tried by both economic and legal means to incapacitate them. What is more, the independent press organs were not only constantly threatened by the possibility of a hostile buyout or bankruptcy, but each year information became more difficult to extract from the government.

To enable the government to keep control over political news, its communication office served up carefully worded weekly digests to the Hungarian News Agency and, through it, to the government-friendly press. These were adopted word for word on the radio and in papers. But government politicians almost never appeared in public; only a few thoroughly trained 'talking heads' had the authority to do so. The prime minister's infrequent press conferences could be accessed with entrance permits—which went only to the slavish Fidesz media. In his weekly radio interview, carefully choreographed, the reliable radio cadres offered him questions, while he held forth freely. Moreover, as we have mentioned, journalists were regularly banned from the Parliament building.

To help Fidesz MPs hide from journalists, the act on freedom of information was continually amended. In my time in Parliament, the information law was amended three times. First, government bodies were given the right to ask for payment for the release of information in the public interest. The second amendment banned the release of public information that would form the basis of a future decision.⁶³ The third amendment stated that certain state companies, such as the Hungarian National Bank and Hungarian Post, were exempt from the obligation to provide information to the public. In this way, people were prevented from, for example, finding out how much the Fidesz government had spent on the so-called national consultation with each citizen. Through countless, often anti-constitutional ways, the government has managed to force journalists to apply to courts and international forums for the most elementary information, such as government contracts or public spending figures.

On top of this, the government has made the decision-making process opaque in the long term. From 2010 to the time of writing (March 2022), no written minutes were taken of the Orbán government's meetings; only a summary was drafted.⁶⁴ Moreover, the government classified hundreds of resolutions as confidential, citing national security risks as it hid away information important for the public.

A Fidesz Media with 'National Strategic Importance'

On 28 November 2018, newspapers close to Fidesz carried an interesting piece of news. One of Lőrinc Mészáros's companies, Talentis Group, had purchased several important media companies and immediately donated them to an organization founded just months before, the Central European Press and Media Foundation (KESMA). A few hours later more business people were lining up to offer the media outlets they owned to the unknown foundation. It was difficult to see any sense in what had happened: the owners of 476 Fidesz-friendly outlets had, one by one, dutifully ceded the interests held in their name, some worth 10 billion forints, and given them without recompense to a private foundation. It was clear as daylight that these people were not genuine owners but simply functioned as the governing party's strawmen. In the framework of KESMA, all of the county daily papers, the most-read news portal and many smaller ones, the second-largest tabloid paper, the only free daily, and two nationwide news TV stations all passed into the hands of KESMA. Directing the foundation were familiar Fidesz figures, with Gábor Liszkay (formerly Lajos Simicska's leading manager, then CEO of Mediaworks) acting as president of its board of trustees and Miklós Vaszily (former chief executive manager of Origo and of the MTVA) as its CEO.

The reason for this complete centralization, according to a person close to the prime minister, was that 'Orbán had had enough individual strawmen and designated owners looking on the assets entrusted to them as their own property, and arbitrarily carrying them off'. According to the unwritten rules of the government's companies, 'You can put money aside, but only as much as you've agreed on with the boss; if you take more profit than that, you're finished. Even the plundering economy has its own highwayman's code of honour'.[65] If one looks at the annual increase in state advertising expenses, it is apparent that maintaining the government media universe was consuming more and more public money, and the 'owners' were taking out billions in dividends.

The 'owners' did not cede their press interests of their own free will; this is clear from the fact that several of them turned to the Hungarian Competition Authority, asking it to investigate the legality of the deal and any conflict of interests. The office initiated an investigation, but a couple of days later the government issued a decree that classified the series of transactions as being of 'national strategic importance', thus ruling out any inquiry in terms of competition law. To justify the decree, the government declared simply that it had decided this 'in the public interest'. The following day, citing the fact that it had no authority, the Competition Authority closed the investigation and authorized KESMA's acquisition.

The government's actions were clearly unconstitutional, because the giant company it had created had too great an influence on the market.[66] This gravely distorted the media market, made fair competition impossible, and essentially put an end to media diversity and the possibility of freedom of information. According to a calculation by the Mérték Media Analysis Workshop, KESMA received 40%[67] of the sales revenue of the news and public media market. However, the merger of the conglomerate was in financial terms too small for the intervention of the European Commission, as European competition law is designed for bigger mergers.[68]

According to Zoltán Kovács, the Orbán government's state secretary for communication, KESMA was 'of national strategic importance' because it had enabled 'nearly 50% of the Hungarian press to put across the government's point of view'.[69] Soon centralized news editing became visible right away. For instance, all nineteen county daily papers often carry the same articles on their pages, with just one or two pages left for local journalists to fill up with provincial news.

A survey conducted in 2020 showed that the Hungarian public was aware that Fidesz had greater influence in the country's media than the opposition.[70] Even 65% of Fidesz voters agreed with this. Only 13% of adults and 23% of government party voters believed that the media world was balanced. Altogether, only a quarter of Hungarians believed that the truth could be discovered from the Hungarian press—a very dismaying finding indeed. And although an overwhelming majority of people found it unacceptable that politicians interfered in the contents of the news, 39% of Hungarians still got their information from the pro-government press, partly because they did not have much choice.

After all this, if anyone were to think that this enormous dominance in the media were sufficient for Fidesz, they would be wrong. It looked like Simicska was actually right, and Orbán's aim was to control all of the Hungarian press.

Index

It is against this backdrop that we return to the events that took place at Index in 2020, with which this chapter began. Index was founded in 1999 in the golden age of the internet by the editors of a forum for internet professionals. Like the journalists at Origo, they were very quick to see the opportunities inherent in the internet. Behind the experimental workshop of Origo was Magyar Telekom, which was strong in capital, but Index was launched as a genuine Hungarian start-up.

To make the company grow, financial investors had to come on board. An injection of capital in 2003 gave a huge boost to the paper, and it soon became extremely profitable. The original investor sold the portal in 2005 to CEMP (Central European Media and Publishing) whose owner, it later transpired, was Zoltán Spéder, a businessman close to Fidesz leaders. Through Spéder, politics became a factor in the life of the editors, even though he said that he had no more say in the contents than any media owner in Europe and the US.[71] For ten years, Origo and the provocative Index shaped the Hungarian online media market.

After Fidesz's victory in 2010, the owner leaned more heavily on the portal, and its independent, strong-headed journalists found this difficult to accept. The founding editor-in-chief, Péter Uj, left and set up a new internet portal called 444, run by a small team of editors, which operates to this day.

But Index retained its critical stance and navigated skilfully between independence and the growing requirements of the government. After Origo's 'liquidation' in 2014, Index became the largest news portal. It was no wonder Orbán's people started to covet the paper. Simicska, when he was still all-powerful in the governing party's financial and media matters, obtained a purchase option for Index. He could have exercised his right to ownership at any time. One investigative report showed that Orbán was impatient with the independent media and already back in 2014 wanted Simicska to take Index and then close it.[72] In a private conversation he said: 'You see, the press has changed its position, and they see that it is more natural for journalists to adopt a more critical stance', then added that he would do everything possible to create a kind of media that would support him unconditionally.[73]

But in 2015 Simicska fell out with Orbán, without having taken over Index. The portal was threatening for Fidesz not just because of its million or so readers, but also because its owner, Spéder, had founded a close alliance with János Lázár, minister in charge of the Prime Minister's Office. Together with Simicska, they formed a dangerous power group for the prime minister. The years 2015–16 saw grim battles for TV2 and *Népszabadság* as well. By 2016, Spéder, who had worked on creating a Fidesz mega-bank (see Chapter 5), also fell out of Orbán's favour, and was subjected to public slander.[74]

From that moment on, there was constant uncertainty around Index, and the political and economic battles within Fidesz made the editors more vulnerable than ever to politics. Finally, in 2017 Simicska used his option to buy Index. To ensure the portal's operation and its independence from Fidesz, Simicska and Spéder created a foundation which they entrusted to three people who had the support of the editors. Ownership rights were exercised by one person alone, László Bodolai, formerly Index's lawyer. This was necessary because many of the journalists would not have been willing to work directly for Simicska.

The attempt to maintain Index's independence and save the paper was thus made by oligarchs trying to break ties with Orbán, not for the sake of democracy (naturally) but for revenge. With the change of ownership, however, Index lost the strong

PRESS-GANGED INTO SERVICE

financial backing which the CEMP media holding had provided, and this put the portal in a more vulnerable financial situation. After Orbán's victory in 2018, Fidesz gathered strength. Under pressure Spéder sold his shares in CEMP to two little-known, minor investors, Zoltán Ziegler and József Oltyán, who were close to Fidesz. The sale included the agency Indamedia, which was the exclusive seller of Index's advertising space. From this point on, Index's economic position was defined, via the advertising, by players linked to Fidesz. In March 2020 Miklós Vaszily, a powerful leader loyal to Orbán, entered the advertising company as owner. In the editing room, everyone was shocked, as they knew that Vaszily was linked to what had happened at Origo and the complete change of direction of the state media.

And, sure enough, economic rationalization soon began. The plan was to place the journalists in outsourcing companies. Index journalists interpreted this as the beginning of the fragmentation of the editorial community, and believed this plan was in contravention of the editorial principle of independence. On the Index news page, they set up an 'independence monitoring barometer', which they moved from 'independent' to 'at risk'. After this, the director terminated the contract of the editor-in-chief, Szabolcs Dull. However, he hadn't counted on the solidarity of the staff, who dug their heels in. 'Don't be silent!' the fired editor-in-chief advised his team. Two days later, almost the entire newsroom handed in their resignations.

In summer 2020, after a long battle, Fidesz swallowed up Index, the largest public bastion of independence in Hungary. The event shocked the public, because Index was such a large and important medium that its fate determined the life of not only its fans and readers, but also those who hated it, and its rivals in the market.

Just as with other independent media, the takeover of Index was given a cover story. There was no trace of Fidesz having had anything to do with these deals and power games. In actual fact, the events were shaped by Viktor Orbán's closest stewards and advisers: Simicska, Spéder, Mária Schmidt and Miklós Vaszily. Index passed to the ownership of Lőrinc Mészáros, and was swallowed up by the government party's media empire.

The underlying moral of the story of Bodolai and Vaszily will be familiar to thousands of people working in a variety of institutions—the press, schools, state offices, private companies—who thought that by being chummy with people in power, and making compromises here and there, they could avoid having to cave in to the demands and interests of Fidesz. But the story of the last decades has taught us that in Hungary this is impossible. In Orbán's regime, there is no middle path. For the Fidesz power elite, nothing is enough, they are never satisfied, they will never stop.

The new owner of Index, which was now integrated into the Fidesz media empire, continued the portal with a new team. Just like Origo, it continues to operate, but the spirit behind it has gone, and what is left is something completely different. The portal fought against Fidesz's attempts at influence, fragmentation and annihilation for fifteen years, and all the while it retained its independence. Today, when my journalist friends mention Index, they always have to clarify whether they are talking about the old Index or the current one. In just the same way, I always have to clarify when I talk about the old Fidesz, which it was good to be a member of and cool to represent, and when I speak of today's Fidesz, which is brazen and power-hungry.

The findings of a decade of research by the Átlátszó (Transparent) team showed that in the ten years after 2010 all regional daily papers and radio stations became pro-government.[75] Half of the national dailies and online news portals are loyal to Fidesz, as are 52% of TV news programmes. The only forum where the independent press has a majority is the weekly political magazines (80%), but their readership cannot be remotely compared with figures for TV or online portals.

Strong Power or Free Press?

By 2022, a media universe had formed around the ruling party, and it operated as a news factory working in line with Fidesz's political aims, using the tools of propaganda and fake news. This media empire reached the entire population of Hungary. This is why it was in the governing party's interest to restrict the press that lay outside, to undermine its credibility, and to withhold information from it.

The way the Fidesz government gained political control over the media was not with open violence and outright censorship, but through informal structures, administrative and legal restrictions, and the distribution of government money in the form of advertising spending. In the dominant one-party Fidesz media, a patron–client system came into being. This punished ethical journalism that provided a decent service to the public at large, and rewarded the press that collaborated with the government party. In the Maslow pyramid of journalists' needs, job security preceded self-realization or ethical conduct.[76] One journalist who left the government media put it this way:

> For a while, [you say] they pay well. Then [that] I don't have to deal with politics. Then [you say] I didn't write that. Then: I wrote it, but it got altered. Then: I've got to do something to support the family. Then: I don't have any choice. From now on, I don't have to say these things.[77]

Over the last decade, thousands of journalists have chosen ethical journalism, by leaving the framework of the Fidesz media or by being thrown out, and they have made a significant sacrifice in terms of making a living. Yet there are many more who have accommodated themselves to being well-paid servants of the Fidesz media empire, to serving up slander and lies. It would be stretching things to call them journalists, but they were the ones who operated this world.

In this decade there were sweeping changes in the media world globally. Regardless of politics, mainstream media faced a challenge from radical changes in ownership structures, the shrinking of the advertising market, technological changes, opinion journalism, and the ubiquity of fake news. This shook general trust in news providers and discredited journalism as a vocation. The environment magnified extreme and demagogic messages, and affected politics, catalysing the emergence of populist parties. Orbán's intervention in Hungarian media hastened these processes and weakened the ability of the democratic system to protect itself. Even minimalist interpretations of democracy hold freedom of speech and information to be the basic prerequisites for a democratic system. The pressure on a free media is not unconnected to the spread of corruption, because the restraining power of public scrutiny is gone.

At the time of the parliamentary elections in 2022, the Hungarian press could no longer be called free, but there was not yet complete censorship. It was not all propaganda, but a large chunk of it was no longer journalism. The media market was not free, but it was not entirely subjugated to the governing power.[78] The Hungarian media world was a grey zone that changed year by year, and the situation was always getting worse. The restrictions on free and independent media, especially TV stations and local papers, resulted in a state where there was a considerable number of people in smaller settlements in Hungary who only had access to government propaganda. Still, research shows that only 10 percent of Hungarians follow exclusively pro-government media, and most people consume government-critical sources as well.[79] Fidesz's modus operandi was in line with twenty-first-century autocracies, especially the Putin model in Russia. First, the authorities attack independent media and NGOs scrutinizing the government, then polarize society emotionally, create and spread false information, and ultimately undermine fair and free elections.

At the same time, even within the framework of Orbán's patron–client media system, there were journalists and editors who, in defiance of the narrowing opportunities, still tried to practise ethical journalism. New media have emerged: online portals, podcasts, and self-printed news reviews trying out the latest technologies and formats. The YouTube channel Partizán, for example, has grown into a multi-channel television channel within a few years. Journalists are constantly trying to find ways to share news about reality with the public that are accurate, witty and interesting. In a future system based on competition, this will be an enormous advantage.

The issue of press freedom in Hungary is of grave concern, but a fundamental change can only be expected when Fidesz's political dominance ceases and future governments use their power to install a stronger system of checks and balances.

8

FROM COMMUNICATION TO PROPAGANDA
THE MAKING OF THE PERFECT CAMPAIGN

'Economic migration is a bad thing in Europe', stated Viktor Orbán on 11 January 2015 at Charles de Gaulle airport. 'We shouldn't look on it as having any benefit, because it brings problems and danger to European people. This is why migration must be stopped. We will not allow Hungary to become a destination for migrants, at least not while I am prime minister'.

Orbán was on his way home from a mass march in Paris, in which millions of French citizens took part to express their determination not to allow jihadist terrorists to erode the values of the republic: freedom of the press and mutual tolerance. The demonstration was held after a terrorist attack against the editorial staff of the French satirical magazine *Charlie Hebdo*. A total of seventeen people lost their lives in the incident and subsequent police chase. The attack was carried out by armed extremists who were born to immigrants.

This happened months before the first Syrian refugees appeared at the Hungarian border in April 2015. Later, they were followed by tens and hundreds of thousands, ushering in a refugee crisis of unprecedented scale in Europe. But even earlier, after the *Charlie Hebdo* attack, Orbán had drawn the conclusion that the issue of immigration would become a focus in European politics, and it could be used for political ends in Hungary too. Hungary had never been a destination for migrants; in fact, people are more like to emigrate from Hungary. But in 2015, when the so-called Balkan immigration route opened, for a few months Hungary became a transit country for refugees, and the world press carried powerful images of this. Already when the first group appeared, Orbán adopted a stern anti-refugee stance, and during crisis negotiations with other European Union leaders, he recommended that no refugees at all be allowed into the bloc. His opinion was underlined by the construction in summer 2015 of a fence 175 kilometres long, on the Hungarian–Serbian border.

Meanwhile, the government put in place a billboard campaign with slogans (in Hungarian) such as 'If you come to Hungary, you can't take Hungarians' jobs!' Even a simpleton could see that the message was not for refugees—it was for the general public. The fear-mongering campaign that began in 2015 eventually grew into a comprehensive conspiracy theory. This became so politically beneficial to Fidesz that the party used the topic even in the 2018 general election campaign, when there were no longer any refugees in Hungary and the situation in Europe had stabilized. This wide-ranging political campaign was planned and financed by the ministries of the Fidesz government, and was implemented by the entire state media and the ever-growing private media empire controlled by the ruling party. This media campaign, which was unlike anything modern Europe had seen, contributed greatly to Fidesz's election victory in 2018 and 2022.

FROM COMMUNICATION TO PROPAGANDA

Recipe for the Perfect Campaign

Ever since it was founded, Fidesz had paid special attention to professional political communications. Already in 1990, the party's amateurish 'communication strategists' won respect when they based Fidesz's 1990 campaign on the song 'Listen to your heart' by the Swedish band Roxette.[1] Election posters showed the famous image of the communist leaders Leonid Brezhnev and Erich Honecker kissing, alongside a couple of young lovers, and encouraged voters to choose whom they wanted.

When Fidesz moved to the right in the late 1990s, the party started to build a new, neo-conservative political language, which created a discontinuity with the past, built on the everyday experiences of people, and openly spoke about conservative values. This was more 'user-friendly' than the technocratic language employed by the socialist and liberal parties. The new language was followed by a new communications strategy, launched during the 1998 election campaign. The communications team, headed by András Wermer, set out to convince Fidesz leaders that marketing is everything, and that politics is a product to be sold just like washing powder. Fidesz leaders were advised to behave as though they had already won, because voters love someone who looks successful. That was when Fidesz politicians mastered the art of talking not to their rivals but outwards, to the public, whether on television or in face-to-face debates. Behaviour, gestures and dress were all aligned with the text, and this made the political message easy to digest.[2] Another step towards political propaganda was the strict centralization of party communications and the parroting of messages ad infinitum. This non-stop offensive enabled Fidesz to shape the public agenda.

This superiority in communication contributed greatly to Fidesz's unexpected election victory in 1998. When four years later Fidesz lost its majority as a government, Orbán disbanded the party's team of communications advisers. Something new was needed. This is when another adviser, Árpád Habony, appeared. He helped the party president build up a new Orbán image: as a 'man of the people' who wore a tweed jacket. Habony became a key player in the party in spite of never holding an official post. He was a provocative, often arrogant person, and Orbán kept him constantly by his side. From 2000 to 2010 Habony consolidated the cult of personality around Orbán. Fidesz's educational and research centre, the Századvég Foundation, was reorganized and became a centre for political strategic communications. By 2010 Habony had become more important than the political ideologues around Fidesz or even the party's vice-chairmen.[3]

Alongside Habony, another important ally of Orbán at this time was Arthur J. Finkelstein, an American communications adviser. He had worked for the US Republican Party since the 1970s, and became notorious for working on three campaigns for Jesse Helms, the openly racist, homophobic and anti-feminist senator for North Carolina. But Finkelstein's main skill was building campaigns on databases. At the end of the 1970s he was among the first to use this technique, which made it possible to convey different messages to various groups by means of microtargeting techniques. He did not believe in ideologies but in numbers. He said that voters are not primarily rational beings, but make their decisions on the basis of instinct and emotion; consequently, politicians have to outsmart them.[4]

In addition, he was a master of the smear campaign. He perfected his method of identifying opponents' vulnerable points and using these to build a negative campaign. The first time we were confronted with the brutality of this method was in 2012, when Gordon Bajnai entered the public sphere with the political movement Együtt. Fidesz's communication teams cherry-picked unrelated elements from Bajnai's past, which they juxtaposed and overemphasized to incapacitate him morally and politically.

When I was an MP, I once ran into one of Fidesz's leading politicians, who had been a good friend twenty-five years beforehand. He proudly told me that he was organizing campaign training for politicians in Fidesz's conservative sister party in Spain. He boasted of how he had learned the craft from Arthur Finkelstein. When I asked him what the most important thing was that he had picked up, he said: Finkelstein was a pure professional. He lived with a man but had no qualms about building a campaign against same-sex marriage for a Republican senator. After they won, Finkelstein and his partner travelled to Massachusetts, got married, and adopted a child. My former friend saw the professionalism of this operation in the way that Finkelstein was able to utterly separate his personal values from the political product he sold; this he tried to persuade others to adopt as a conviction. I was astonished when he said this, but it helped me understand the values and patterns within which Fidesz politicians operate. Finkelstein played a leading role in building up Fidesz's government campaigns as from 2010. One Fidesz adviser said of him that all the strategic issues were in his hands: he drew the connections between the numbers; he made proposals for drafting messages and the techniques for broadcasting them. 'Finkelstein was the brains'.[5]

The essence of the American campaign adviser's recipe was that you have to focus on the opponent, not on your own candidate. Use any trifling detail from the opponent's past to label them a liberal, use simple, strong words, and warn voters about the chaos that will ensue if he or she is elected. Repeat the slogans non-stop on every TV channel. This negative campaign method pins the opponent in a tight corner, and makes it almost impossible for them to defend themselves.

Finkelstein's other great achievement was that he managed to turn the term 'liberal' into an insult. In the 1990s all his campaigns in the United States focused on the existential fears of the white middle class and targeted liberals, and he always won. Finkelstein's method is to choose a minority who face wide-ranging prejudices in a given society. By magnifying the negative feelings and seeds of fear, it is possible to reinforce the antipathy, and finally the image of the minority invested with these negative contents has to be pinned on to the liberals. If somebody had told me ten years ago that this was a trick that could be learned, I would have laughed out loud. But 2015 and the following years proved just how quickly such a strategy can be implemented.

Orbán Launches an Anti-Refugee Campaign

In spring 2015, when the first refugees from the Middle East unexpectedly turned up in Hungary, the governing party was already prepared with its messages that Fidesz politicians repeated daily in Parliament: 'These people are flooding into Europe uncontrolled, in order to find a better life for themselves. Hungary does not need economic immigrants!' The country was soon covered in billboard posters: 'If you come to Hungary, you have to adhere to our laws!' Whatever the subject being discussed, government politicians ended up talking about refugees. They systematically confused the terms 'refugee' and 'immigrant', and portrayed the immigrants as parasites, dangerous criminals and terrorists.

I tried to get my information first-hand and understand the phenomenon in all its complexity in terms of its economic, security and humanitarian aspects. Because it was impossible to trust information received from the government, I visited many of the regions taking in refugees. I managed to travel to the Greek island of Lesbos (one of the islands most affected by the crisis), to find out about the broader context of the problem from the authorities and aid organizations there. But in Hungary, it was impossible to reason with people on the basis of facts. The interpretative framework and concepts forced by the government on public discourse were hammered home for weeks and made any kind of debate about the refugee crisis impossible.

The Fidesz government's poster campaign repeated almost verbatim the anti-Roma slogans that have long been common in Hungary. Ten years previously, the far-right party Jobbik had campaigned successfully with these very same ideas.[6] Fidesz's campaign took the anti-Roma prejudice of sections of the public, a rejection built on welfare chauvinism, and turned it against the refugees. Meanwhile, the Immigration Office announced daily the increasing numbers of new arrivals, now simply termed 'migrants'.[7]

The barbed wire fence hastily erected by the Hungarian government closed the border with Serbia in the first days of September 2015, arousing enormous interest from the press. While the sense of physical threat was being constantly evoked, Orbán switched messages, saying that 'mortal danger threatens the life principles on which we built Europe'.[8] From then on, he portrayed the refugee crisis as a civilizational threat to European values, which further increased the sense of vulnerability.

In its own way, the choice of refugees as scapegoats was a brilliant decision by Fidesz to create an enemy that aroused fear.[9] Anti-Semitic and anti-Roma views were rather passé ideas in Hungary, as ethnic minorities are ostensibly protected from discrimination by law. But Fidesz found a new enemy, the 'migrants', which the party was the first to construct in Hungary, and the topic was linked to them. The choice of 'migrants' in transit,[10] of unknown foreigners who made up a faceless enemy, was, to put it cynically, a stroke of genius, particularly since prejudices against other groups were already incorporated in the public psyche.

'Migrant', a term which did not even have a Hungarian equivalent, became the root of a whole set of completely new linguistic constructions, such as migrant-petting, migrantophile, pro-migrant, migrant pact. These sarcastic expressions, which Fidesz used to mock the party's critics, had a very negative tone and defined how not only people from other countries but also the opposition were seen. This was the perfect implementation of the Finkelstein-style language war.

When in September 2015 the German chancellor Angela Merkel made her famous speech when the greatest wave of refugees reached Europe, 'Wir schaffen das' (We will manage [to take many refugees in Germany]), Orbán found an adversary. From then on, he embodied the antithesis of Merkel's *Willkommenskultur*, and his name and policies became known all over Europe. The Hungarian prime minister forced his European peers to react to his own radical ideas—ideas previously espoused only by extremist politicians. Orbán's views and methods were now dividing public opinion not only in Hungary, but also internationally. For Orbán this was an ideal environment: it didn't matter that the context was negative; he was able to set the agenda for public discourse, even though he was unable to dominate European public opinion. Through this he gained supporters abroad. No matter that over time the number of refugees fell; the political waves of the migration crisis were unstoppable. European public opinion changed, and radical right-wing political groups throughout Europe were emboldened.

At the start of 2016 Orbán's party held a referendum (as seen in Chapter 4) in Hungary to further heighten the tension of the fear-mongering campaign. The plan was for the referendum to show that the government's hard-line anti-quota stance, which was difficult to defend in the discourse between EU member states, was supported by the majority of Hungarians. The question posed in the referendum ran as follows: 'Do you want the European Union to be able to mandate the obligatory settlement of non-Hungarian citizens in Hungary even without the approval of the [Hungarian] National Assembly?'

FROM COMMUNICATION TO PROPAGANDA

Immediately, billboard posters appeared in Hungary, with the patronizing slogan 'Let's tell Brussels, so they get the message too!' In the first step, the government projected society's fear of the Roma onto the refugees, and thereby evoked antipathy towards them. The next step was for Fidesz messaging to link the 'migrants' to European politicians who criticized Orbán. In this crafty campaign, Fidesz distinguished Brussels ('bad Europe') from 'good Europe' (which was, appropriately, embodied by Fidesz itself). The repetition of 'Brussels' suggested that EU bureaucrats and liberal politicians formed a homogeneous group with its own interests, a kind of deep state that could be mobilized against the nation-states of Europe. This was necessary to make the attack on EU leaders palatable to the Hungarian public, who were firmly pro-EU.

The upshot was a full-fledged language war, which Fidesz used not only to dominate the agenda but to completely reframe the debate to suit its own position. The party managed to portray its position not as a political construction but as common sense. We in the opposition were completely unprepared for such an attack and were baffled. It was particularly challenging to avoid using Fidesz's language to describe the situation, because we knew that if we copied their expressions, we would adopt their frame of thinking, and so we struggled to figure out an alternative political approach.

The referendum was also an enormous political challenge for the opposition because we were convinced that the question was unconstitutional. It was extremely manipulative, because common sense dictated that only one answer could be given— 'no': the answer Fidesz wanted. After much discussion and debate, we decided in agreement with the other opposition parties to advertise a boycott of the referendum. The first immediate problem was how, faced with the government's steamrolling campaign, we could get our message across to voters at all. State television and media close to Fidesz showed images of masses of refugees pouring in, day and night. Each day there were reports of conflict between immigrants and locals in cities in Western Europe. Government slogans sounded from every possible radio and TV station, and the streets were full of them too.

The propaganda insinuated that Europe was being besieged by Muslim immigrants, whose clear intention was to populate and occupy our world. The government media aired fake interviews, for instance, showing Hungarians who had fled back to Hungary for 'refuge', and claiming how impossible it was to live in cities in the West.[11] In another report, the subject of an interview introduced as a 'person on the street' turned out to be a German politician for the far-right AfD, and the use of misleading contexts, sometimes with images shot years previously in America, produced the narrative that the government required.[12] The public TV channel launched a programme called *Weekly Terror*, in which 'experts' (in fact, propagandists paid by Fidesz) explained staggering crimes attributed to immigrants. The fake 'reports' were legion in number. According to one survey, the news site Origo alone carried thirteen migration-themed items every day, all painting immigrants in a negative light, and never carrying a byline.[13]

This referendum was such an important political issue for Fidesz that the government spent an incredible sum, 8.6 billion HUF, on the anti-migrant quota campaign. This sum was at least as much as the party, the government and organizations supporting Fidesz had spent jointly on the 2014 election campaign,[14] and more than the UK government spent on the entire Brexit campaign.[15] The difference was that while London divided the sum between campaigning parties and NGOs, in Hungary the entire sum was spent by the government party itself, to popularize its own point of view. Other parties and organizations did not get a penny of campaign funding.

FROM COMMUNICATION TO PROPAGANDA

The other problem we had to face had to do with our call for a boycott. Ultimately, a boycott is a device usually employed in the absence of rational options. It was hard for us to campaign knowing we had made this decision because we were helpless. 'Don't go to vote, don't take part in this evil sham!' was our message.

In the end, the completely uneven competition produced an invalid result, because only 44% of voters took part in the referendum.[16] As 6% of all votes cast were invalid, this meant that only 41.3% of eligible voters cast a valid vote; and 98% of them said 'no'. We felt that the opposition boycott had won after all: the majority of people could not be duped. The picture was nuanced by the fact that those who voted almost all affirmed Fidesz's point of view. Politically rather than legally speaking, Fidesz had achieved its aim: it had mobilized its voter base, it had kept its anti-migrant propaganda on full volume for months, and it had given Orbán an opportunity to stand firmly for his uncompromising point of view in the European Council. The prime minister naturally interpreted the result as a victory and, 'to meet the demands of the people', announced that he would initiate an amendment to the constitution.[17] 'A foreign people cannot be settled in Hungary', was the proposed text (see Chapter 4). This was suitably elusive, legally speaking, but was certainly well adapted to inciting xenophobia.

The constant hate-mongering campaign, which played on the worst aspects of human nature, worked wonders for Fidesz. The party's popularity grew continually,[18] fear and xenophobia were reinforced in a way never seen before,[19] and most Hungarians saw the refugee issue as the country's biggest problem. Finkelstein's hateful and divisive recipe worked perfectly even without the 'master', who at the time was seriously ill.

TAINTED DEMOCRACY

An Unscrupulous Conspiracy Theory Campaign

In spring 2017 another sea of posters flooded the country. The new campaign was initiated as usual by Orbán in a big interview he gave at Easter. He said, 'The whole issue is that George Soros, who stays out of the public eye, is, through organizations in Hungary, putting huge sums of money into supporting illegal immigration'.[20] He reminded people that Hungarians, as always, were still fighting for freedom, and at the centre of the field of battle was the issue of migration. In this battle, he claimed, the enemies of the Hungarian nation were those subsidized by the American financier George Soros.

Anyone with an ounce of common sense could see that it was the prime minister himself who was devising a conspiracy theory, painting George Soros as the global orchestrator of the refugee crisis. This was the spirit in which the second anti-migrant campaign kicked off. 'Don't let Soros have the last laugh!' shrieked the posters, which showed the laughing face of the philanthropist Soros. The Fidesz media machine overstepped the line once again. 'Soros is cheating at the game!' 'Soros pulls the strings that work the Brussels politicians!' 'Soros wants to influence the whole world!' 'Soros may have killed his mother!' 'We can expect a wave of extreme left violence from Soros in Budapest'. Nobody could escape hearing Soros's name every day. Within Parliament there was a constant, disdainful chanting of 'Soros'. Naturally we opposition MPs all became 'Soros's hirelings', allegedly trying to destroy Europe with a flood of refugees. Government politicians and Fidesz media trumpeted Orbán's crazy theory and magnified it a thousand times.

After people had been bombarded with these absurdities for months, the government set about organizing a new so-called national consultation. The first question posed to voters was: 'George Soros wants to persuade Brussels to settle at least one million people from Africa and the Middle East in European

Union territory, including Hungary. Do you support this part of the Soros plan?'[21] Ostensibly a questionnaire, the consultation contained the latest creation dreamed up by the Fidesz communications think tank: a series of lies they dubbed the 'Soros plan'. According to the accusations, the 'plan' consisted of Brussels wanting to force Hungarians to dismantle its border fence and pay 9 million HUF (€25,000) per capita to the immigrants. The aim of the 'plan' was, according to the letter, to limit the use of Hungarian as a language. This concocted 'Soros plan' served to reinforce the fears of the population and create a basis for the Hungarian government 'having to protect' the country against 'external enemies'. Moral panic was stirred up to fever pitch by the Hungarian government. This all-out campaign lasted right up to the day of the 2018 elections.

The scapegoating of Soros as well as the attack on NGOs associated with him was not the idea of Orbán's people. Finkelstein and his partner George Birnbaum had already tried it in Israel,[22] but in Hungary it worked like a treat. In an interview he gave to a Swiss magazine in 2019, Birnbaum boasted of how the invention of Soros as the arch-enemy was the best of all their creations.[23]

> Soros proved to be the perfect choice. First, because you could stick the liberal label on him, and second, because he embodies everything the conservatives hate in a successful left-winger: a financial speculator who wants a weaker form of capitalism. Third, because he doesn't do politics, so he had no political means to bite back, and he doesn't even live in the country.

Birnbaum also described how in his work with Orbán, first in 2008 they went for the communists, then in 2010 the exponents of financial capital, in 2015 the Brussels bureaucrats, and finally in 2018 Soros and the liberals.

Although the anti-Soros campaign was not intended to be anti-Semitic, it was based on classic anti-Semitic tropes, which tapped into old prejudices. Soros became the embodiment of all evil. As Finkelstein had found earlier, the billionaire could do nothing. 'The more he rejected the attacks, the more he would have confirmed the claim that he was interfering in politics. [...] Yet Soros didn't have the remotest intention of entering Hungarian politics', explained Birnbaum.[24] The consultant also conceded that with the Soros formula, they had manufactured a strong and effective enemy that could be accessed freely and adapted with ease anywhere in the world.

According to Fidesz's own polling company, even in late 2016, 61% of Hungarians associated negative qualities with the otherwise unknown person of Soros; in fact, even half the voters for opposition parties shared this opinion.[25] In the election campaign, all that was left to do was to link the name of opposition politicians to Soros, so that they too appeared in a negative light. The country was plastered with posters that showed the leaders of opposition parties and, behind them, Soros with a wicked grin.

But the political and social damage done by the anti-refugee and anti-Soros campaigns cannot be pinned on Finkelstein. His techniques are used only by politicians who are so inclined, who for the sake of power take the seeds of fear present in society and bring them to germination by deliberately speaking of exaggerated dangers, and then ride on the crests of the waves of fear. The mega-campaign that dominated Hungarian public discourse between 2016 and 2018 was the brainchild of Fidesz's centralized system, which it implemented through the communications and media empire it had built up since 2010.

A Tried-and-Tested Machine

In the early years dominated by former Orbán ally Lajos Simicska, media financing involved many players, but after 2015 Fidesz reorganized central party and government communications, handing these directly to the Prime Minister's Office. Orbán entrusted their coordination to his reliable minister Antal Rogán. A super-agency known as the National Communications Office was set up, with several hundred workers, which not only planned and carried out political communications campaigns, but also managed the advertising spending of about 1,500 state institutions and agencies. In 2015 the government doubled its own budget for communications.[26]

When political campaigns were planned, the Fidesz-established think tank, the Századvég Foundation, on the basis of large surveys and focus groups conducted by a handpicked polling company,[27] selected the slogans and messages to be used in public, and decided on the text and visuals for TV and poster campaigns and their political contents. One of the company's former staff said, 'For campaigns they look for memorable expressions which trigger strong negative emotional reactions in Fidesz and uncertain opposition voters'. This is how they came to refer to Brussels instead of the European Union, because 'Brussels' is easier to associate with faceless, money-grubbing bureaucrats. The Central European University has to be referred to as the Soros University, opposition politicians as 'lefty liberals', and a critical NGO has to have the tag 'foreign-financed organization'.[28]

Minister Antal Rogán held a weekly briefing on the current communications trends and the messages to be used in the media by the governing party's talking heads, the responsible editors in government media, and Fidesz analysts. The weekly messages were also sent out to Fidesz's people at the local level. Although prohibited, I too got hold of such material: not only was the guide worked out to the last detail, but it also showed who was allowed to make statements on any topic. 'Each week government contact people come to us to go over who we will invite to the TV, and what we'll ask them about', said a TV producer to news site 444.[29]

TAINTED DEMOCRACY

According to journalists working at government papers, the most politically important propaganda or defamatory material was sent to the paper ready-made, passing through the hands only of trusted people, and appearing unexpectedly and without a byline in the paper. They worked out in advance which press organ would be first to present the news story that distorted reality, and then it would spread like wildfire throughout the media empire. The two centres of this system were the state media and the Central European Press and Media Foundation (KESMA), with its approximately 500 media interests.

Alongside media dealing with public life and news programmes, a special role was taken by the tabloid press, which denigrated the selected 'opponents' with simple negative messages embedded in more frivolous stories. In Habony's hands, a pro-government version of the tabloid press was formed, which specialized in mud-slinging.[30] Zsolt Bayer, a founding member of Fidesz, was an old acquaintance of mine; I remember him as a cheerful, good-humoured lad. In the 2010s he had his own show joking about Fidesz critics in order to question their credibility. Though he published short stories and belles-lettres, in his programmes he used vulgar common language and often talked like a rabble-rouser. For instance, referring to a student who spoke at a demonstration, he said: 'She can't be any more than eighteen, and she's already a right cretin, a stupid idiot. [...] Well then, dear Blanka. The thing is, you're not a hero; you're a pathetic, miserable, cheap piece of trash'.[31] Bayer and his colleagues made hate-mongering and scandalous language acceptable in mainstream Hungarian media. This suited Fidesz's divisive politics perfectly, because it was based on manufactured enemies.

The implementation of the party-government communications campaign was backed by colossal sums of money from the state budget. This involved the ministry in commissioning up to eight or ten polls a month, and continually monitoring the minutest

FROM COMMUNICATION TO PROPAGANDA

of changes in the public mood.[32] Opposition parties can count themselves lucky if they have enough money for eight polls a year. Though the National Communications Office was originally created with the aim of spending budget money economically, this agency began spending more and more money each year. In 2020 it spent 150 billion HUF on media advertising alone—more than it would cost to build an Olympic stadium.[33] This gargantuan sum sustained hundreds of private media which would have immediately disappeared in a free market environment. In many cases, the proportion of advertising revenue from the state exceeded 60%–70%.[34]

This astonishingly efficient machinery was put into action when in February 2022 Russia attacked Ukraine, which happened at the height of the Hungarian election campaign. The war showed Orbán on the side of the aggressor, Vladimir Putin, but Fidesz's communications apparatus was able to construct a narrative and reach every household within days. Spinning the opposition's message to stand by Ukraine, government propaganda showed the opposition as dangerous warmongers and Orbán as a man of peace and stability. The billions of forints spent on adverts on billboards, Meta and YouTube, and the distorted news in the hundreds of Fidesz media outlets, diluted Hungarians' natural sympathy and moral duty to help Ukraine. Orbán's simple message—do you want blood (the opposition) or oil (Fidesz)?—persuaded millions, and people voted for the ruling party en masse. The war in Ukraine showed how Orbán's propaganda machine could turn a highly unfavourable political position into victory.

Of course, every country has communication institutions serving the aims of the government, and political leaders exploit these resources to gain the upper hand. But in Orbán's Hungary, the communications apparatus of the government and Fidesz were one and the same. Campaign-related government questionnaires benefited the party's database, and state campaigns running on multiple channels helped to maintain the identity of Fidesz's voting base.

If Hungary really had a diverse and balanced media environment, as Fidesz politicians claim,[35] then conspiracy theories and fake stories would not have been able to take root, because media independent of the government would have countered them. But in Hungary, independent and opposition media can do little to stand up to the steamroller of government media.

9

A PASSIVE PEOPLE?
INTIMIDATING AND DEPOLITICIZING SOCIETY

'I remind you that we are funded by the Prime Minister's Office!' wrote the director of one research institute to staff when in 2017 there was a broad push for a referendum on the government's decision to offer to host the 2024 Olympics.

> I don't want to see staff writing or liking posts that attack the Olympics. Everyone is entitled to their opinion, but I ask you not to make this public, because by doing so you may damage the institute. If anyone wants to go independent, to support another political trend, then I inform them they are not obliged to work here.[1]

One younger member of staff in the institute had liked a Facebook post by the Momentum Movement collecting signatures for a petition, after which the director humiliated her in an email to the entire staff. The leading lawyer in the research institute spoke out about this humiliating procedure, and the next day she was fired.

This email, and the dismissal of the lawyer who stood up for her colleague, give a good snapshot of the state of things in

Hungary. Over-zealous leaders of institutions, fearful of (yet also servile to) the ruthless power of the Orbán regime, have used highly questionable means to instil fear in their staff.

Orbán's work in building the regime deliberately strove to reorganize social networks according to the interests of power. Autonomous, independent citizens and civil society actors and organizations had no place in this. The regime systematically worked to have as many people as possible in a position of dependency upon it. This dependency discouraged people from openly voicing their opinions on public life, creating a harsh, chilling effect. When I was an MP, at almost every townhall meeting I met people who said: 'I'm here instead of my son and his wife. In the place they work at, they'd get into trouble if it came out that they'd taken part in an opposition party event'. The result of this intimidation by the regime is that masses of people have retreated and keep their opinions within the private sphere, maintaining their distance from public matters.

Decades of political unfreedom may have made Hungarians more inclined to avoid active engagement in public life. An important study in 2009 showed that twenty years after the regime change, civil liberties and political freedoms were less important to the Hungarian public, and Hungarian citizens had less confidence in one another and in political institutions than those in other Central European countries.[2] Another study demonstrated that trust, tolerance and work-related autonomy, which are seen in proactive, success-oriented attitudes, were at a much lower level in Hungarian society than in the Western European countries surveyed.[3] Half of Hungarians prioritized stability, conformity and maintaining the status quo, and expected the state to provide a solution to their problems. Sadly, governments after the regime change did not consider it important to change this culture of passivity. Although civil-minded culture has revived, education in active citizenship has not become integrated into school curricula. In 2010, a typical young person would speak about politics only to family and close friends, and not more than 9% of them participated in an NGO, and only 5%–7% of them took part in public life.[4] In a comparative study made at the Budapest Sziget Festival, Hungarian young people were significantly less likely to engage in civil disobedience, strikes or protest actions than their peers in Western Europe.[5]

This desire for stability and a passive attitude to public life provided a perfect environment for Orbán to make fears self-fulfilling by systematically increasing vulnerability and using intimidation. Fears can easily become ingrained in the identity of people, and lead to the depoliticization of society.

Civil Society Organizations as an 'Obstacle' to Democracy

'There is no objective standard by which to judge the government's politics. If there is no such standard, then it's not worth making demands that the government be held to account', wrote Gábor G. Fodor, an ideologist for Fidesz.[6] Long before the party's historic victory in 2010, he and his colleagues aired the idea that the liberal concept of the state, which centred on 'good governance', the idea that the state can serve citizens best if they harmonize their actions with non-state actors, had failed. Fodor and others argued that the role of the state is not to create the conditions for good governance, but to govern well, thus 'good government', and only the state can ensure well-being, solidarity and dignity for all. If the government does not govern well, it clearly bears responsibility, and it can be ousted at the elections. That is democracy, pure and simple. However, if the government includes civil society organizations and various other interest groups in decision-making, it deflects responsibility, and the public interest is dissipated. These critics questioned whether involving non-governmental players in negotiating interests would improve the quality and social acceptance of the government's decisions. Their conclusion was that if the public interest can be represented by the government alone, then it is in the interests of democratic government for there to be an active, strong state. With this idea, they laid the foundation for Fidesz's policy of power concentration.[7]

With this in mind, as early as in 2011 the Fidesz government abolished all the self-organized interest advocacy forums, which were built on the triad of government, employers and employees, and which had operated for twenty years. In their place a broad consultation council was set up with arbitrarily nominated members. In 2011 the government amended the Labour Code, weakening employees' and trade unions' rights. As a result, between 2009 and 2020 trade union membership fell from 12% to 5% of the population.[8] The amended law on strikes tightened the criteria for striking, so that in some cases employees engaging in strikes became at risk of losing their jobs. After 2011 the number of strikes fell considerably, particularly in the public sector.[9]

The vulnerability of public sector employees and civil servants become more acute when Fidesz centralized significant areas of state administration, first and foremost in public education. Head teachers were replaced by political appointees en masse. Teachers were forced to join corporate bodies instead of the previous chambers and trade unions, membership of which was a matter of free choice. For example, teachers, who had to join the National Teachers' Chamber, were made to sign an ethics code which contained contradictory expectations about their non-teaching activities. This kind of pressure on teachers led to self-censorship, and made it difficult for them to speak freely with students about current issues relating to public life.

In 2016, the Programme for International Student Assessment (PISA), which assesses educational systems in OECD countries,

A PASSIVE PEOPLE?

clearly showed a drop in quality in Hungarian education. Five years after Fidesz's education reforms, the performance of Hungarian children had deteriorated in every skill.[10] This was self-evident proof of the error in centralizing the education system. What followed was demonstrations of tens of thousands demanding the human resources minister's resignation and the creation of an independent ministry for education. A movement of teachers called Tanítanék (I would teach), and another of educationists called the Civil Public Education Platform, were formed; these made recommendations to improve education policy. These two small organizations were able to organize countless protests and solidarity events for two years, but they had no visible effect. Huge swathes of teachers dared not join the movement, and the demonstrations were not a sufficient show of force to persuade the government to reform the centralized system.

Compared with the vulnerability of the middle class, the situation of those who lived on workfare in small settlements (see Chapter 5) was even more serious. The spread of workfare meant that hundreds of thousands of people were completely dependent on the local mayors. Many local leaders tried to organize the work fairly, but many took advantage of their positions of power. 'There are some mayors who, though they pay people, tell them which shop they can spend the money in. Others are registered as being on workfare, but then they work in the mayor's company for an extra three or four thousand forints [€10] a week. It's a nightmare', said one villager to *Szabad Európa* online.[11] Even today, there is nobody to represent the interests of these vulnerable people, but Fidesz has managed to recruit them politically. Being accepted into or turned out of the workfare programme determines the day-to-day subsistence of these people, so they do what they are told, and think little of voting according to their conscience.[12]

In Viktor Orbán's system, the depoliticization of society was one of the main guarantees of the regime's survival. There were many people in Hungary who believed that the simplest expression of political activism, for instance 'liking' a Facebook post, carried an existential risk.

Shrinking Civic Space

In spite of the passivity of society inherited from communism, after the regime change civil society started to mushroom. This was thanks to a historical tradition of civic autonomies and decentralization, which, at the end of the nineteenth century, was manifested in densely networked local communities, foundations, sport clubs and church congregations. Historic events of the twentieth century seriously damaged these autonomous networks, but after 1990 free civil society was quickly revived and social organizations formed by the tens of thousands (compared with the previous few thousand during communism). In 2010 there were 65,000 foundations, associations and advocacy groups in Hungary. The legal framework followed European standards and provided great freedom for the organization of space for collective action. Decisions on government subsidies were made by democratically created bodies, and the National Civil Fund Programme (launched in 2004) made it possible to disburse subsidies for operating costs to social organizations. However, the culture of private donations was weak, and civil society organizations were rather dependent on state finances.

There occurred a great change in this trend when in 2011 the Orbán government passed an amendment to the Civil Act. The main thrust of the changes was to push the social organizations towards public services, that is, to identify those organizations able to take on the tasks of the state, and to support them with central financing. This measure implied that NGOs were expected to 'earn' their state subsidies. This approach was a turnabout from the time when the state considered the civil sector as involved in activities based on people's free self-organization. A new body set up in line with this new thinking, the National Civil Fund, discontinued funding for thousands of organizations that did not align with the government's aims. For others, it undertook to provide stable, long-term cooperation in the form of subsidies. For example, organizations dealing with the provision of family assistance, or international humanitarian activities, saw their subsidies increase significantly. The government included humanitarian assistance in the tools of Hungarian foreign policy, and for this it needed the experience of NGOs specializing in development. Although even these NGOs were concerned about the way the government was reshaping the civil sector, the increase in funding deterred them from voicing their criticisms.[13]

Unlike authoritarian states such as Russia or Turkey, which shut down NGOs and arrested their leaders, Fidesz 'merely' divided them in order to draw this space of free association under closer state control.[14]

Open Attack on NGOs

One morning in September 2014 the inhabitants of a small quiet street in the centre of Budapest awoke to a frightening scene. A dozen police officers had gone into one of the residential buildings and raided one of the apartments that functioned as an office. Everyone there had their telephone confiscated, and they were threatened with serious punishment unless they cooperated. All day long, the police buried themselves in the people's laptops and documents, then in the afternoon one person was escorted home by four police officers to retrieve more documents. By then several hundred people, including myself, had gathered in the narrow street, and photos of the incident were seen all over the country. We went to protest against the proceedings: this attack by the authorities was against the Ökotárs Foundation, which organized the Hungarian programme of the Norway Grants' Active Citizens' Fund, linked to the Norwegian government, and the person escorted away was the leader of this NGO, Veronika Móra, whom many of us knew and respected.

This intimidating action by the police was difficult to justify, because the foundation, which a state office had previously audited, had always operated in line with the law. This case was obviously a political attack. A couple of months earlier, János Lázár, the minister in the Prime Minister's Office, had written a letter of protest to the Norwegian government, complaining that his office could not audit the civil society-targeted subsidies of the Active Citizens' Fund, which he believed was subsidizing political activity.[15] He demanded that Norway suspend the operation of the fund and renegotiate its terms, so that the Hungarian government could participate in the distribution of the money. But the Norwegians refused, because the intergovernmental treaty on the civil society grants specifies that the funds shall be distributed independently by NGOs selected for that purpose.

While the demonstration against the use of police force against the Ökotárs Foundation went on, several dozen other NGOs were accused of abuse, and were subjected to special state audits.[16] Meanwhile, high-ranking members of government and the prime minister voiced serious accusations: 'these are political activists financed from abroad', who 'at a given time and in given questions want to exercise influence over the life of the Hungarian state'. In the Fidesz press, a smear campaign started against the 'Norwegian NGOs'.[17] From this point, the government kept up the attack on several dozen organizations subsidized by the Norway Grants' Active Citizens' Fund for three years. What riled the Hungarian government was not just that these NGOs were able to get funding independently of the government, but that many of them, with a broad range of knowledge at their disposal, were able to rigorously analyse the government's operations, and shed light on its contradictions and illegalities, and were also embedded internationally. They were not subject to the government in the same way as those that depended mainly on subsidies from the Hungarian state. The Orbán government, in its bid for total hegemony, was not prepared to tolerate such a situation. After years of court proceedings, it transpired that Viktor Orbán had personally ordered the authorities' attack on the NGOs,[18] while denying any knowledge of the affair in the German press.[19]

For seven years, right up to 2021, the Hungarian and Norwegian governments negotiated the conditions based on which the former could access the development subsidies due to Hungary from the Norway Grants (a total of €9.6 million). But Orbán and his allies considered it such a high risk for NGOs to receive funding not linked to the government that they preferred to relinquish the €220 million infrastructure development funds due to Hungary.[20]

NGOs supported by the Norway Grants' Active Citizens' Fund endured years of harassment by the authorities, but no illegalities in their operations were brought to light. The most vulnerable of them, including many NGOs operating in the provinces, collapsed under the attacks. Fidesz's vice-president, who orchestrated the campaign, conceded a few years later that the entire Norway affair was basically a fuss about nothing.[21]

With this ongoing smear campaign, the government party also managed to create a general mistrust of any NGOs dealing with public life. As with commercial companies and the press, the government strove for division among NGOs and drew a dividing line between the 'good' (those which adapted to the system) and the 'bad' (those which remained critical).

However, several of the NGOs, supported by the Active Citizens' Fund, survived the attacks, sought out new funds, and stood up for their beliefs with even more determination. This must have annoyed the government, because the ruling party came up with a new formula. Fidesz's politicians announced that there were some organizations that were pseudo-civil, maintained by foreign funding in order to 'push global capital and political correctness over the heads of national governments. These organizations must be held back by all means, and must be *stamped out*'.[22]

This communications campaign marked another milestone in the attack against NGOs. Fidesz submitted to Parliament a bill on the 'transparency of organizations financed from abroad'.[23] Citing the prevention of money laundering and terrorism, it demanded greater transparency from NGOs. It specified that every NGO that received more than 7.2 million HUF (€20,000) per year from foreign donors must register on the Civil Information Portal set up by the government for this purpose, and in every public appearance it must display the text 'foreign-funded organization'. This law followed the logic of the Russian 'foreign agent' law of 2012,[24] which regarded foreign support of NGOs as a national security threat, and demanded that a set of NGOs register themselves as 'foreign agents'. That the law was seriously discriminatory was proven by the extremely high number of exceptions: it did not apply to sports, ethnic or religious NGOs, or to the foundations of political parties, or to the thousands of NGOs teeming around Fidesz, which collected large sums of money from abroad. In one interview Orbán gave himself away: he said that there were sixty-three organizations in Hungary subsidized by George Soros, which made it clear that these were the dozen or so NGOs the government was targeting.[25]

The government party built up a conspiracy theory in which migrants (suspicious terrorists) and critical civil society organizations (those helping migrants) were linked with George Soros (who financed watchdog NGOs) by means of a carefully structured propaganda campaign, as we have seen in Chapter 8. The other law that laid the groundwork for this theory was the attack against the Central European University (CEU).[26] The government accused this private university, founded by George Soros, of having irregularities in its operation, and then passed a bill that stated that the university had to accredit itself again, one requirement of which was a treaty between Hungary and the United States. Thus, the government gave itself the authority to define the existence of the CEU. These two legal amendments and the communication campaign went beyond serving to stigmatize and intimidate: they also questioned the NGOs' and the university's right to exist.

When the NGO Act was in the consultation phase, five NGO activists took part as observers in the parliamentary committee on justice, and when opposition MPs spoke, they held up small boards with slogans such as 'No! to the stigmatization of NGOs!' 'We want to speak!' and 'Don't vote to pass the NGO Act!' At this, the president suspended the session, saying there had been no advance notification of the demonstration. (We regularly organized such actions, because they were a way of getting a few moments in Parliament that would create some press coverage on one important issue or another.) It was after this event that Zsolt Bayer, founder of the Civil Unity Forum (CÖF) and star presenter on Hungarian Television, said on the radio: 'If this lot appear in Parliament again, and disturb work there, they should be thrown out like a cat to shit. If they have to be yanked out by their snot and blood, then so be it, [...] if necessary, their faces should be smashed in'.[27]

Both the anti-NGO and the anti-CEU laws came before the Court of Justice of the European Union, and in 2020 in two different decisions the court found that these laws were contrary to the Treaty on the European Union,[28] and required the Orbán government to repeal them. Fidesz then accepted less repressive but still intimidating bills. Naturally, even when the laws were passed, Fidesz knew that they infringed EU legal principles and the Hungarian constitution, and would not stand up in court, but before the 2018 elections it wanted to make a show of standing up to the 'enemy attacking the nation'. During the election campaign the party notched up the tension with the promise of a law called the 'Stop Soros' package, which criminalized the provision of services to immigrants and asylum seekers, and required NGOs dealing in this field to pay a special tax. As before, this was merely a political PR stunt, because, just as no cases were ever brought against NGOs for espionage or terrorism, so the state obliged none of them to pay this tax. This expensive, destructive campaign, lasting several years, was nothing but a circus for Fidesz.

This series of intimidating measures proved extremely effective. The attacks, which were protracted for years without any end in sight, were excruciating for the NGOs. The offensive even scared off some foreign donors. Once I spoke to the director of a German foundation whose organization worked on reinforcing democratic citizenship, who said to me that the foundation didn't want to be active in a country where it was not welcome. It was incredibly dispiriting to see how the Orbán government was able to assert its will even in circles that had nothing to fear from it. Although the Open Society Foundations led by George Soros was Orbán's target, and it moved its headquarters from Budapest, it was completely unrealistic to think that the Orbán regime would attack German interests. A good relationship with Germany had always been a fundamental interest for Fidesz. Once more, the question arose: what could we expect from the resilience of NGOs vulnerable to the Orbán government, if even big, wealthy international players turned away from Hungary at the blink of Orbán's eye?

Mobilizing Pro-Government Agitprop

Although Orbán's party tried to rid itself of the civil society organizations that were critical of the government, in fact it needed NGOs in order to maintain the legitimacy of his power.

A PASSIVE PEOPLE?

As I said earlier, when the Együtt movement was launched in 2012, almost out of nowhere crude posters appeared on Budapest buses and columns. Over large parts of the city, an organization calling itself the Civil Unity Forum (CÖF) conducted a 'political information campaign', as they later put it during a court case.[29] This 'movement' was launched in 2009 by Fidesz-friendly pundits, for example the radical journalist Zsolt Bayer. CÖF became widely known for organizing giant marches in support of Viktor Orbán, called peace marches. Fidesz's most committed supporters registered in local Fidesz offices, and were then transported by buses to the demonstration to 'protect Viktor Orbán and Fidesz from the attacks of the West'.

This device—by which people employed by the regime, financed and organized by the government party, operate organizations that call themselves independent, and mobilize people in Fidesz's interests[30]—has become part of the regime's everyday toolkit. In order for Fidesz to keep its hands clean, the party outsourced its most vituperative character assassination campaigns to party confidants around CÖF. Moreover, the president of CÖF was László Csizmadia, who in a brazen move was made president of the National Cooperation Fund (NEA), which was responsible for subsidizing NGOs. During office hours Csizmadia handed out government money to NGOs who 'deserved it' (that is, according to political considerations), and after hours he went into action as leader of a pro-Fidesz agitprop organization. The NEA, which he led, supported CÖF's activities,[31] and it received funding from rich state companies, such as MVM (Hungarian Electricity). These organizations confused and misled public opinion, and they discredited autonomous initiatives. In twelve years, Fidesz created a whole series of government-organized NGOs.

For example, the Centre for Fundamental Rights, a kind of think tank, was given the task of standing up for the government's positions at international forums. This organization, while disguised as an independent NGO, is generously supported by governmental resources[32] and seeks to defend the government's view tooth and nail, and to neutralize civil organizations that truly represent human rights.[33] In 2022 it hosted the world conference of the American Conservative Political Action Conference, a gathering of extreme-right political actors, where Viktor Orbán was the keynote speaker.[34] Miklós Szánthó, director of the Centre for Fundamental Rights, is at the same time CEO of KESMA, the giant pro-Fidesz media holding.

Another strategy of the ruling party was to provide already existing NGOs with handsome subsidies, and make them its megaphone. I was most dismayed to discover that the National Association for Large Families (NOE), which is one of the oldest community-building NGOs in Hungary, with hundreds of local branches, and of which my mother was a founding member around the time of the regime change, has a special place in propagating the regime's family policy. Fidesz politicians attend the association's events in droves, and the leaders of NOE have borrowed the regime's propagandistic idioms of speech. In addition to their original, voluntary activities of assistance and service, they have often carried out the government tasks assigned to them, and thus unwittingly contributed to the erosion of the civil ethos, while society as a whole has lost its resilience.

Civil Courage

Although the Fidesz government dealt a huge blow to Hungarian civil society and called into question the power and very existence of thousands of NGOs through the drastic restructuring of funding, citizens' protests against the authorities have still spread.

'Our aim is to involve people through action. The emphasis is primarily on activism. [...] Democracy experience, that's what's important to us, that's why we do the forums. Activism, solidarity,

A PASSIVE PEOPLE?

community action and solidarity', said a university student to researchers about why he and others formed the Student Network.[35] In 2011 the government passed an amendment to the act on higher education, restricting universities' autonomy, drastically reducing the number of state-paid university places, and imposing onerous requirements on students who took out student loans. Lecturers and secondary school pupils also joined the Student Network, and for more than a year there were demonstrations and 'occupy' events in universities all over the country, to force the government to back down. The pressure was so strong the government was forced to respond to the students' protests.

The tactic they chose was to involve the official Student Union (HÖOK) in the negotiations, an organization of which every student was a member. After the government managed to co-opt this group, the more radical and more independent Student Network was crowded out of the negotiations. Finally, the Student Network was disbanded, but its organizers gained good political experience, and later took part in setting up a series of new civil and political groups, such as Momentum. The result of this one-and-a-half-year struggle was that the government withdrew its plans for reducing the number of funded places, but protesters were unable to prevent a deep-reaching transformation of higher education.

At the time, several large demonstrations were held. The most significant of these was the series of protests against the internet tax in 2014, which forced the government to backtrack. As a one-off issue, internet tax was easy to grasp. But when more complex problems arose, the situation for protesters wasn't so simple. One spring morning in 2015, hospital nurse Mária Sándor wrote a dejected post on Facebook asking her colleagues to wear black to work, in protest at the shortage of nurses and low salaries. Soon the movement grew, and thousands of nurses and doctors took part. Health workers, all dressed in black, took to the streets with their sympathizers, and demonstrated for months, until the government summoned their representatives for negotiations.

Just as with the students, Fidesz resorted to cunning. In this case, however, it sat down for talks not with the professional trade unions, but with the protesting nurses, who were less skilled negotiators, and rejected all of their demands outright. At the same time, it exploited the fact that the movement had a face, and the Fidesz smear-machine was set in motion against Mária Sándor. Although the nurses simply wanted to move forward on questions of health policy, Fidesz regarded them as an anti-regime movement. These ruthless, cynical attacks and the government's exhausting strategies eroded all the energy of the protesting health workers. The nurse who started the protest had a nervous breakdown, and announced the end of the movement. As the story of someone who simply wanted better working conditions for hospital nurses, these events deterred many others from mobilization and action. People understood that if they criticized the government, the regime would destroy them. The problem became very real: engaging in protests was counterproductive. After all, it might do less harm if an organization went knocking on doors at the ministry. Only years later, during the Covid pandemic, were health service organizations able to stand up, uniformly and firmly, against the government.

As well as interest advocacy and general activism, another form of resistance appeared in the decade 2010–20, based on participation and experience, primarily in the actions of the Two-Tailed Dog Party. This joke party entered the scene in 2015 during the migration crisis, when it covered the country in posters financed by community donations. The Dog Party parodied Fidesz's anti-refugee posters to produce texts such as 'If you come to Hungary, could you bring a sensible prime minister

A PASSIVE PEOPLE?

with you!' or 'If you are the prime minister of Hungary, you have to obey our laws!'

The spread of citizen protests did not mean that huge swathes of society joined in. When I was a politician, I took part in organizing countless demonstrations, and was present at even more, but I frequently found that I knew too many of the marchers. Demonstration surveys also showed that people who typically participated in protests were NGO activists or members of political parties,[36] and only 2.2% of Hungarians had taken part in open protest demonstrations.[37] Civil society organizations and the opposition were only rarely able to mobilize big crowds beyond the most committed critics of the government.

The attacks by the Fidesz government didn't let up for a moment. Before the 2018 elections the CÖF organized a march during which Viktor Orbán made an explicitly menacing speech: 'We did not hate anybody, and we shall hate nobody [...] But we shall fight against what George Soros and his network want to do to this country. [...] After the election, naturally we shall take our vengeance, a moral, political and legal vengeance'.[38] Orbán's calls for vengeance applied to everyone who was not in favour of Fidesz because, as he explained in the same speech, every opposition supporter who was not pro-Fidesz was actually a pro-immigrant 'Soros agent'.

In 2020, the government announced a 'change of model' for nine Hungarian state universities, and without consulting with the leadership of these universities, it set up a new type of public foundation, and gave the boards of these foundations the authority for university decision-making. The boards of trustees were filled with people loyal to the government party. The position of president of the board of trustees of the University of Theatre and Film Arts (SZFE) was entrusted to a particularly contradictory person. Attila Vidnyánszky, a theatre director, became notorious after the Fidesz government appointed him director of the National Theatre in 2012, and he started a brutal culture war in the name of spreading national culture. Although he had a great reputation as a talented director, he deeply divided the Hungarian theatre scene within a few years.

When the SZFE was transformed into the new foundation model, the government ran into an unexpected obstacle: the faculty and students unanimously rejected the government's dictate, saying that it eliminated the autonomy of the university. The academic leadership and the senate of the university resigned. As a show of solidarity, the students wound red-and-white ribbons (the type used at roadworks) all around the building, and barricaded themselves in, demanding that the government reinstate the university's professional autonomy and leadership. Public solidarity with the SZFE was unusually widespread. A street demonstration in front of the SZFE building became a permanent feature, supporting the university occupation with the slogan 'Free country—free university'. Hundreds came every day with sandwiches and cakes to express their support for the students. Outstanding figures of the Hungarian theatre world and legendary directors stood guard at night on the terrace of the university, and tended the flame of freedom every evening for several weeks. Film director Kornél Mundruczó, an alumnus of the university, whose film *Pieces of a Woman* had just then won an award at the International Venice Film Festival, accepted the prize in a T-shirt with the slogan '#FreeSZFE'.[39] Even Vidnyánszky's son, an actor himself, spoke out and asked the government to back down from its radical plan.

But the government toughened its stance. It didn't negotiate with anyone—in fact, it appointed a military officer as the university's new chancellor. In the end, it was the second wave of the Covid pandemic that put an end to this extraordinary, nearly three-month campaign. The students stopped their demonstration because of the danger of infection. The next day, security guards took over the building, and the new directors immediately declared all studies that semester invalid.

Like so much else, the pandemic was good for the Orbán regime: the government was able to restrict freedoms to a disproportionate extent.[40] One motorcade organized to protest about anomalies in handling the pandemic, at which people did not meet but sounded their car horns, resulted in the police imposing a fine of millions on the organizers.[41] Health workers were forbidden to resign from their jobs, and also to give out any information to the public.

In spite of all this, civil activism has undergone enormous development over the twelve years of the Orbán regime. Organizations under pressure have formed networks of unity and mutual support, and encourage others as well to stand up to Fidesz's local rulers and agents.

It seemed as though by 2022 the atmosphere of fear around Fidesz had been dispersed. The unexpected crowds who participated in the opposition's primary election and the weeks-long teacher strike launched in January showed a more conscious and resistant public. But this was an illusion. The Orbán regime would do anything to maintain citizens' political passivity. The middle class has been pacified by ensuring its well-being, and threats are made that if Fidesz's power were to cease, everything would be lost. The dissatisfaction of lower-status social groups has been defused by consigning them to a state of utter dependency for their subsistence.[42] Conscious, autonomous action had not yet resulted in the critical mass that could have prevented the erosion of democracy.

PART III

HUNGARY IN EUROPE AND THE WORLD

10

WHO CONTROLS THE PAST CONTROLS THE FUTURE

HISTORICAL REVISIONISM AND COLLECTIVE MEMORY

The lift to the second floor of the House of Terror museum moves slowly.[1] From the window you can see the cramped inner courtyard of the building, where a T55 Soviet tank has been squeezed in. Around it, for several storeys, the walls are covered with images of victims of the fascist and communist terror, etched into metal. Leaving the lift, we arrive in the Hall of Double Occupation. One of its walls is painted red, the other black. On the black side are monitors showing film footage from the 1939–44 period until the takeover by the Hungarian Nazis, known as the Arrow Cross. On the red side of the structure the films start with footage of Soviet military operations in the Second World War, and images of the ransacked country. This hall presents Nazi and communist occupations together, and the powerful colours and sound effects give a striking impression of the dual occupation, which serves as the basic concept for the entire museum.

TAINTED DEMOCRACY

Proceeding from the vehicle that represents the double occupation, the visitor is subjected to increasingly disconcerting experiences. The rooms that exhibit the meeting rooms of the Arrow Cross Party and Nazi propaganda or the communist police's practice in the 1950s of raiding homes and dragging people away are filled with frightening, excruciating noises. The most appalling part of the museum is the basement, where visitors are grouped around spine-chillingly small, dark cells presenting a selection of twentieth-century instruments of torture, with the moans and rattles of the victims. At the end of the series of cells is a shrine-like space, the Hall of Tears, where there are candle-lit crosses, while the whole is bathed in mystical light and music. In the Farewell room, with a considerable historical leap, visitors find themselves in 1989, at the ceremony for the reburial of Imre Nagy, the martyr prime minister. A film shows Viktor Orbán giving a ceremonial speech, then in another scene we witness the last Soviet soldier leaving Hungary in 1991.

The exhibition is powerful and uses provocative theatrical means to affect the emotions and senses, triggering horror and loathing. Because of the forceful techniques adopted, it feels more like a film shoot than an exhibition. The theatricality and the sound effects depicting human suffering are used to induce in the visitor a sensory experience of terror. The message of the exhibition is blindingly simple and clear: the dictatorships are comparable, and they were continuous; it is not possible to condemn only Nazism and fascism: we must give equal weight to the crimes of communism.

The exhibition presents the victims and perpetrators in opposition to one another. However, as a Hungarian historian wrote in criticizing the concept: 'There is no family in Hungary that was not affected by the Nazi or communist dictatorships one way or another. The greater part of society experienced the

WHO CONTROLS THE PAST CONTROLS THE FUTURE

two as both victim and perpetrator'.[2] In his view, the museum externalizes totalitarianism to establish a victim identity for the nation.

Parallel Historical Memories

The founders of the House of Terror did not wish to present a nuanced picture of history: their aim was to give shape to an interpretation of history based on Orbán's victim trope. (The museum was opened in 2002 during Orbán's first government.) The cornerstone of this interpretation is that in the interwar period, the Horthy regime was largely democratic and Hungary lost her independence in 1944 under the German occupation. The country was robbed of her freedom and economic base, first by Nazi Germany, and then by the occupying Soviet communists. The country regained its de jure sovereignty and political autonomy only decades later, with the regime change in 1990.

Choosing the date 1944, and cementing it in stone as a dividing line, was perhaps significant because this absolves us of the need to deal with the failures of the right-wing political elite in power between the two world wars, which led Hungary into catastrophe and collapse during the Second World War. The museum deliberately glosses over the complicity of the Horthy regime in the Holocaust in Hungary. Orbán and those like him regard pre-Second World War authoritarian Hungary as an important historical prototype, and consider themselves the heirs of the right-wing government of that period. The exhibition's designers have shifted responsibility for the national failures of the twentieth century onto foreign occupiers, primarily the communists.

The time of the 1944 German occupation was even written into the Fundamental Law passed by the Fidesz government in 2011. The text begins with what is called a National Avowal, which includes the words: 'We date the restoration of our country's self-determination, lost on the nineteenth day of March 1944, from the second day of May 1990, when the first freely elected organ of popular representation was formed'.[3] This selective, simplified, Fidesz-compatible interpretation of historical memory provides a key underpinning for Orbán's national-populist regime—so much so, that it even decreed that the central space in Budapest, the wonderful, historical Kossuth Square surrounding the Parliament building, be restored to its pre-February 1944 condition. The buildings and statues erected there since that time have been demolished and removed.

The next stage in affirming 1944 as a historical cornerstone came in 2014, when on the seventieth anniversary of the German occupation, the government erected a memorial to the 'victims of the occupation'. The work aroused heated resistance in Budapest as soon as the plans became public. The bizarre construction depicts a struggle between the Archangel Gabriel and the German imperial eagle, the most obvious interpretation of which is that Hungary (the defenceless figure of the Archangel Gabriel) merely endured the crimes of war, which were carried out by the occupying Germans. Critics of the sculpture say that in its message the work denies the fact that the apparatus of the Hungarian state provided great assistance in the deportation of Hungarian Jews, a fact documented by much historical research. Without the readiness of the pro-German Hungarian political elite, in this last stage of the war several hundred thousand lives could have been saved.[4]

The aim of the House of Terror museum and the memorial to the 'victims of the occupation' was to establish a new historical narrative. The general opinion on the right wing was that in Hungarian historical memory, the Holocaust was disproportionally strong compared with the trauma of the Trianon Treaty and communism. The new narrative claimed to create a balance between the memory of these historical events. However,

WHO CONTROLS THE PAST CONTROLS THE FUTURE

the new memorials made no attempt to foster rapprochement between the different historical memories. Instead, their aim was to tell another history of twentieth-century Hungary. The simplicity of the symbolism and storytelling stirred up long-standing prejudices and led to polarization.[5]

In 2014 many historians voiced their misgivings about this distortion of history by the memorial, and considerable protests were made. Around the sculpture, civil organizations erected what they called a Stage of Freedom, where discussions were held in the evenings, which continued years later. Talks were given by historians and artists, and an entire oral history collection was compiled from the memoirs of Holocaust survivors and their descendants.

In a manner typical of the Orbán regime, the contested sculpture was neither officially unveiled nor dismantled. Contradictory as it is, the work still stands to this day. Next to it can be seen the protesters' counter-exhibition, which recounts in pictures and documents what actually happened in Hungary in spring 1944. For tourists who have some degree of familiarity with European history, few spots in Budapest show so clearly just how absurd the Orbán regime is.

Hungary the Hero

'Russians go home!' 'Down with the red star!' 'Free elections!' chanted the vast crowd in '48 Square, in front of the university in Pécs. People were waving flags from which the communist crest in the middle had been cut out. Almost all the student body and most of the lecturers were there. The town workers arrived in lorries. From there they marched to Széchenyi Square, the heart of the town.[6]

Thus wrote Karola Péterfia, my grandmother, in the diary she kept during the days of the 1956 revolution. Half of her family were at the demonstration; the smaller children stayed at home with her husband, Zoltán, and listened to Radio Free Europe to find out what was happening in Budapest. The excitement was palpable. In the main square the leaders of the demonstration gave speeches amid thunderous applause. 'They announced that a revolutionary committee had been formed in Pécs too, and they asked anyone in the crowd who spoke Russian to help, because they needed an interpreter'. Karola was a language teacher, and she had recently had to retrain from German to Russian. She didn't need asking twice, and at the end of the speeches she went to the organizers to offer her services. 'I had to be a go-between', she wrote in her diary, 'translating the statements and letters of the revolutionary council for the Soviet Military Council'. She thought the situation was dramatic and precarious. 'The members of the revolutionary council are very immature and disorganized. There's hardly an intelligent head between them'. Apart from a few hours of elation, she and my grandfather were extremely tense and hardly slept for weeks. Yet they still hoped the revolution would succeed when on 4 November Soviet troops entered Hungary and Imre Nagy's government fled to the Yugoslav Embassy. In spite of the obvious risks, in October 1956 my family thought it self-evident that they should take part in revolutionary activity. They were swept away by the hope that communist Hungary might change. One of my uncles took part in organizing the students' resistance; later he was detained for months. My grandmother's brother Alajos Patek was put in prison because as the chief engineer of the Ganz Mávag Machine Works in Budapest, he supported the Revolutionary Workers' Council during the revolution.

The 1956 revolution was that rare historical moment when different social classes—the intellectuals, the young people and workers—were able to unify their aims in the face of the oppressive Stalinist regime. The aims of the revolution, though they were slightly eclectic, clearly showed what the Hungarian nation wanted. The flag with a hole in the middle from where the Soviet crest had been cut out, which became the main emblem of the revolution, symbolized national independence from the alien Soviet oppressor. The demands for a multi-party system, free elections, a free press and freedom of association were aimed at restoring the institutions of democracy. To replace the detested Stalinism, the framework of a left-wing state began to take shape, with state ownership, wage rises, workers' councils and the right to strike. These were the foundations on which the people of Hungary could unite and accept the reform-communist Imre Nagy as leader of the revolution and his coalition government.

However, the international community did not support Hungary in its struggle for independence. Assisting Hungary's request for neutrality carried greater risk than rewards within the delicate balance of the Cold War. In December 1956 in Budapest resistance groups were still fighting, and my grandparents, like thousands of other Hungarians, were listening to the news about the Hungarian debate at the United Nations on Radio Free Europe, still hoping that the Western world would intervene, but by then the die had been cast. After 1918 and 1945, Hungary's democratic progress was once more let down by the West.

The idea of the 1956 revolution as the primary national myth for democratic Hungary was suggested in 1990 by József Antall, centre-right prime minister of the first freely elected government. 'I think that remembering 23 October implies the need to reformulate an era of our national mythology. [...] In the absence of mythology, there would be no spiritual fellowship, no spiritual community'.[7] Historical research into the revolution started immediately in the newly founded 1956 Institute.

Soon, however, various memory policy approaches took shape, as did struggles over who was 'the real heir of 1956'. The successor to the communist party was burdened by its own past, and many years of falsifying history meant that it was unable to present a credible story to interpret the twentieth century. Kádár's long stint in power had begun precisely by quashing the 1956 revolution and with bloody retaliation. The liberal-leaning Alliance of Free Democrats was the direct continuation of the democratic movement of the 1980s, and by illegally publishing the memoirs and analyses of the intellectual leaders of the revolution, it sustained the memory of the 1956 revolution. For right-wing groups, a point of contact was the Catholic circles that became active in 1956. For Fidesz too, the memory of 1956 was very important, because the revolution was triggered by university students and many young people took part in the battles. In the speech he gave at Imre Nagy's reburial in 1989, Viktor Orbán pointed to this historical legacy. Multiple readings of the complex reality of 1956 were thus possible.

Recycled Myths

'A people said, "enough is enough!"' proclaimed posters plastered over the sides of buildings in Budapest in autumn 2016. The posters depicted armed revolutionaries of 1956, the legendary 'lads of Pest': determined-looking youngsters in berets, holding machine guns or Molotov cocktails which they were ready to throw at Soviet tanks. The poster campaign was part of the year-long series of celebrations organized by the government for the sixtieth anniversary of 1956. Orbán asked Mária Schmidt, director of the House of Terror, to develop the concept of the anniversary. Her thinking was not for a commemoration that attempted to interpret the past, but the production of an image of 1956 that served Fidesz's political purposes. As well as powerful political will, she had at her disposal a budget of 13.5 billion HUF, her own workshop of scholars and intellectuals, and countless media and propaganda outlets controlled by the governing party.[8]

WHO CONTROLS THE PAST CONTROLS THE FUTURE

Mária Schmidt and Viktor Orbán both well knew that collective memory can be shaped and is thus an important political tool. They also knew that history is not the same thing as collective memory. Collective memory emerges out of history as a result of an arduous process in the public sphere. To understand history means that we are aware of the complexity of things, and that we are sufficiently objective to look from several points of view at the facts and the motivations and dilemmas of the actors. Collective historical memory, on the other hand, is biased, and sees the events of the past from one single standpoint, simplifying it as a battle between goodies and baddies, finding archetypal actors in it, as in a fairy tale.[9] For Orbán's people the narrative of the 1956 revolution created for the 2016 anniversary built on precisely this: it captured an easily digestible moment for posterity in the image of heroic youngsters throwing petrol bombs at Soviet tanks advancing against them. The 'lads of Pest' was one of the strong tropes that have become fixed about the 1956 revolution, both in Hungary and worldwide. Orbán had long identified himself and his party with them.

The other trope was that of the communist Imre Nagy who, at the demand of the revolution, became the nation's democratic prime minister and who, after the revolution fell, said in his famous speech in court: 'I do not ask for mercy!' But Nagy has been deleted from Orbán's pantheon of 1956. Quite simply, the reformer communist leader did not fit into Orbán's rewriting of history. Nagy, whose historic reburial in 1989 was the foundation for Viktor Orbán's own political career, has been spirited away.[10] By erasing reformist communists, Orbán has endeavoured to enhance his own personal role in politics and legitimize his anti-communism. He has used this myth also to reinforce the foundation of his regime: sovereignty, which is always under threat and must be protected at all costs. Orbán dealt with this issue in his commemorative speech in 2016: 'We Hungarians have a natural capacity for freedom. [...] Freedom is always, everywhere, a simple question: do we decide about our own lives, or does somebody else decide for us?'[11]

Orbán's 1956 campaign took an old memory pattern, which has been present for centuries in Hungarian collective thinking, and filled it with new contents. The model is as follows: 1. A country still mourning its former glory experiences a foreign threat. 2. Overcoming their mourning, Hungarians enthusiastically confront the foreign threat and take up arms against the oppressors. 3. They fight to the end, even when there is no longer hope, and their only consolation can be glorious failure. 4. Yet they are sustained by the illusory hope, projected into the future, that there will come another glorious moment to rise up.[12] The 1956 commemoration year was built on this populist fairy tale. This can clearly be seen in the 1956 ceremonial speech by László Kövér, chair of Parliament:

> The power of the Hungarian revolution brought it to victory, even though it was overcome by the enemy's superior force, and deserted by the outside world, and this power lay in the people, in the Hungarian populace. [...] The 1956 revolution was not one of elites, of reformist communist party staff members, of various groups of intellectuals, but a revolution of the people, of simple folk.[13]

Orbán's ceremonial speech reinforced this story even more: 'Nobody knows where Hungarians find the strength and skill; every hundred years, attacking out of nothing, like David with his sling, they are capable of miracles',[14] he proclaimed on 23 October 2016 to the ten thousand people celebrating in front of Parliament, which was decorated with the flag with the hole.

Orbán's new myth for 1956 is as false as it is transparent. Like all revolutions, 1956 was complex and in many respects contradictory. The truly splendid aspect of it is precisely what Orbán and his people are trying to erase. In the brief two weeks of the revolution, Hungarian society, ground down and in the grip of Stalinism, proved itself capable of rapid organization and exceptional cooperation; people were able to overcome their prejudices to work together and achieve a higher goal. However, the true story does not serve Orbán's power interests, which are built on a simplified myth of good versus evil. Moreover, civil organization and pluralistic diversity, all the things that came to the fore in 1956, are not valued in his world. With Orbán, there are only two levels: the level of the individual and that of the 'nation'. Between the two, there is nothing; neither society nor institutions: 'If our homeland is not free, neither can we be free', he said in the speech given at the sixtieth anniversary.

At the concluding conference of the commemorative year, Mária Schmidt didactically voiced an important lesson for the regime: 'Hopefully, we have all learned from the example of 1956, that we can count only on ourselves, and we have to fight for everything for ourselves; the safest thing is if we take control of our fate with our own hands'.[15] But against whom? Studying the posters of the commemoration year and listening to the speeches, we notice that the 'Russians' who oppressed the people in 1956 are nowhere to be seen. It seemed as though the Hungarian freedom fighters had fought against some generalized, gigantic 'empire' belonging to various eras. But the Fidesz government's propaganda programmes and the phrases drummed in ad infinitum made it clear against which 'foreign powers' we must conduct our freedom fight today: none other than multinational companies, banks, the International Monetary Fund, the powers behind the 'hordes' of foreign refugees, and, most of all, the European Union. In 2016 the 'lads of Pest', reinterpreted by Fidesz theorists, were fighting the twenty-first-century 'enemies' of Hungary. For them, the key issue was how to protect Europeans from a global conspiracy of liberals in Europe and in Hungary that sought to turn the European Union into a 'modern-era empire'.

After the transformation of 1956 only one historical event remained for Orbán's transformation of twentieth-century Hungarian history to be complete: 1989.

The Man Who Drove Out the Soviet Troops Himself

In 2019, on the thirtieth anniversary of the end of the Cold War, all over Europe there were commemorations of the fall of the Berlin Wall. Large events were held in Berlin, Prague, Warsaw, Leipzig and Timișoara to celebrate freedom and the reunification of Europe. But in Hungary hardly anything happened, even though large historical commemorations have a great tradition and significance in Orbán's regime. The silence was conspicuous because, as we have seen, today's leaders of Fidesz count the Hungarian change of regime not from 1989, but from 1990.

It may be difficult to grasp this in the light of how important the year 1989 was in Hungary and in Fidesz's own history. In January 1989, Fidesz was an unknown opposition youth group; by December it had grown into a nationwide party and was well enough known to stand in the first free parliamentary elections as an independent force in 1990. During this extraordinary year, I too was one of the leaders of Fidesz.

Years later, after Viktor Orbán's liberal party targeted the now vacant space on the political right, it became important for Fidesz, in attempting to gain right-wing votes, to reinforce the historical narratives about the Christian middle classes being oppressed by socialism, including narratives that were initially embraced only by the extreme right.[16] Years later, in the mid-1990s, when Fidesz moved to the right, it was the rehabilitation of the interwar period, the reinterpretation of Hungary's role in the Second World War and the anti-communism that legitimized Fidesz for the traditional right-wing public. In this historical memory, 1989 could not be celebrated as the greatest moment of the regime change, because, as we have seen, in 1989 the 'communists', who were still in power, participated in the negotiated transition. In 1989 the last communist government conducted negotiations with Mikhail Gorbachev, Soviet general secretary of the party, on the withdrawal of Soviet troops. It was they who made possible the reburial of the heroes of 1956, and they who cut the wires of the Iron Curtain on the Hungarian–Austrian border. When the Berlin Wall fell in autumn 1989, the institutional regime change in Hungary and Poland was well under way. Naturally, the leaders of the communist state-party were acting under pressure from the increasingly strong local opposition, in which Fidesz too played a part with its smart 'actionist' politics. But whether we like it or not, the last reformist government in power, that of the Hungarian Socialist Workers' Party, had a part in implementing the democratic transition. By the end of the 1990s this was incompatible with Fidesz's primitive anti-communism as it shifted to the right. The Hungarian story of 1989 is a fly in the ointment of Orbán's historical memory.

Accordingly, the Orbán government held an extremely restrained commemoration of the thirtieth anniversary of 1989. The main attraction was a short film called *Annus Mirabilis* (Year of Miracles), for presentation at summer music festivals to remind the young generation of the historical era that had made their current freedom possible. But even though the footage of the most historical moments of 1989 was accompanied by the song 'Wind of Change' by the Scorpions,[17] young people didn't fall for the propaganda. For in this advertising film there is only one single Hungarian political actor from 1989: the young Viktor Orbán, demanding the withdrawal of Soviet troops. The film was immediately pilloried in the press, since the year 1989 was not about Orbán. Of course, he was there too, and his speech of 16 June was really very good. But the reburial of the heroes of 1956 was not organized by Fidesz. The wire of the Iron Curtain was not cut by Orbán. He was not the key protagonist of the round table negotiations but was one of the several dozen who participated in them. Thousands of people were active in the opposition organizations and hundreds of thousands took part in the anti-regime demonstrations. Most of the actors of the democratic transition live, write, make films and tell stories to their children. This is why Fidesz did not, and could not, manage to rewrite the story of 1989. Because of the protest, the *Annus Mirabilis* film was removed from the programme after the first summer festival, and no longer screened.

But Orbán did not give up rewriting the history of the 1989 democratic regime change, because he needed to present himself as the sole guardian of the Hungarian tradition of independence. According to him, 'true Hungarians' (his followers) are lovers of freedom *sui generis*. On 23 October 2019 he said:

> Hungarians are forever a freedom-loving people. [...] In the Western world we seem to appear as the land of dictatorships, and somehow we need to explain, to ourselves and to the world, that this is a misunderstanding. [...] In Hungary, no anti-freedom political force has ever gained a majority without external military help.[18]

The Special Nation

My children grew to love history very early on. I remember once my twelve-year-old boy came home from school most despondently. 'Mum, this is awful. Are we really such a bunch of losers?' he exclaimed after learning at school about the umpteenth occupation, failed revolution and still-born freedom fight. And his class hadn't even got to the twentieth century. We spent the entire evening chatting about it. We talked about how Hungarians indeed had many heroic revolutions, but the ruling elites at the time committed many serious errors. We pored over a map to see how in Central Europe, sandwiched between great powers, not just the Hungarians but other peoples suffered greatly down the centuries. We are not the only ones with this experience. We spoke about how good it was that today we are in a more fortunate part of the world and live in freedom and peace. We reminded ourselves that my children's grandparents had to grow up between wars and revolutions, but for their parents, my generation, their lot was peace and indeed, after 1989, freedom. As for them, they were born into the European Union. A few years later, my children threw themselves with great gusto into drawing up the family history for a school project. They made long interviews with their grandparents, who were born in the 1930s and 1940s, and were amazed at what difficult dilemmas they were confronted with during the twentieth century as a result of historical events. Orbán and his team simplify these human dilemmas and this complicated historical legacy or, if necessary, they even erase it.

With the myth of the 'special Hungarian people' Orbán has merely formed his current political community, while he endeavours to present a positive narrative of Hungarian history in place of 'whining'—that is, facing up to reality. In 2020, on the centenary of the Trianon Treaty, he actually said:

> For Hungarians, the horizon of history lies at a millennial height. From this height you can look around, from this height you can see far. [...] Back, to the beginning of time. We see hundreds of wandering tribes of the great steppe disappear and perish in the dust of history. We see that we Hungarians have neither disappeared nor perished, but have established our homeland in the ring of Latin, Germanic and Slavic peoples, preserving our unique quality. [...] There is not a single nation in the world that could have endured such a century. [...] Only one who walks his own Calvary can become a great nation. [...] Hungarians can never afford the luxury of weakness again. We can only have what we can protect. This is the law and this is our destiny. Therefore, for us, every match goes on until we win.[19]

This speech, Orbán's political credo, is a perfect populist fairy-tale speech. For him, the nation becomes a kind of mystical community, to which he ascribes not only historical greatness, exceptionality and superiority, but also strength, a lack of pity, and victory. The projection of the origin of the people as far back as possible into a past as glorious as possible is a central idea in all ethno-nationalisms. Leaders of small Eastern European nations which during the course of history repeatedly lost their independence, where the borders of the country moved back and forth over their heads, and which still today are in the thrall of the nation-state ideal, are particularly partial to rekindling mythical historical precedents to legitimize themselves. Orbán scorns the defeated. Ultimately, a great prime minister cannot lead a defeated people. In order to appear a victor, even in peacetime he has to rise up against forces embodying greater 'powers' than he: first and foremost, the European Union. Through the Pyrrhic victories, as well as failures communicated as victories, of his provocative anti-Europe campaigns, he shows his believers that he is capable of leading the Hungarians from the losers' side to the victors'. He builds the belief that we are greater than we truly are, that in spite of being a 'small country', we are born to accomplish great deeds, that we are a people created for leadership.

In Fidesz's memory policy, Hungary was always a victim, and though the crimes were committed by others, we suffered on account of them. This, as we have seen, does not contradict to the self-image that we are heroic. The consequence, however, is that we see our history as a series of traumas, and we have no reason to have a guilty conscience and have nothing to face up to.[20]

To canonize the new historical narratives, Fidesz not only founded its own research centres, but also incapacitated several institutions that might spawn different explanations of reality. In twelve years of Orbán's rule a whole series of academic institutions

WHO CONTROLS THE PAST CONTROLS THE FUTURE

were closed or integrated into a new system of government-controlled organizations, for example most of the universities and the entire research institution network of the Hungarian Academy of Sciences. In opposition to the independent academic research institutions, which study history, the mission of Orbán's history research workshops[21] is to work out an alternative historical memory and drum it into the Hungarian public.

Is a people that falsifies its own complex history, whose unprocessed legacy is present in our culture, our reflexes and our everyday dilemmas, suited to create a successful vision for the future? Orbán's memory politics, which, compared with previous decades, are more intensively built on mythical tales, primitive enemies and suppression, called this very much into question. Orbán had the historical opportunity, after one hundred years of division, to help create a consensual historical memory among Hungarians. Rather than a practical ideal of a possible and desirable future, he created unity around a false interpretation of the past. Without a shared vision of past and future, Hungarians will face great difficulties in navigating their way in Europe and the world.

11

A POLITICAL TAP DANCE
VIKTOR ORBÁN AT LARGE

'There is no agreement on anything until there is an agreement on everything', wrote Viktor Orbán to Ursula von der Leyen on 16 November 2020, when he announced that the Hungarian government was prepared to veto the European Union (EU) budget for 2021–7 and the historic financial stimulus package to counter the economic recession caused by the Covid pandemic.[1] Orbán threatened to do so because EU countries linked the fund to the norms of the rule of law, which he found unacceptable. Because this decision had to be made unanimously by the leaders of the twenty-seven member states, legally Orbán had an opportunity to obstruct the creation of the new fund, citing the Hungarian national interest.

The threat of a veto was a particularly unfriendly political tool, as most countries were suffering from the economic consequences of the Covid pandemic. Orbán's action outraged even the German Christian Democratic party, and led to Angela Merkel's party finally withdrawing support for Orbán, after ten years. This was the point at which, in the conservative family of parties in the EU and in the political elite of Europe, Orbán's politics became indefensible, because they eroded the unity of the EU and its power in the world.

For many years, Hungary's Western partners had looked on Orbán's construction of an authoritarian system as an isolated phenomenon, and watched on somewhat helplessly. Only by the end of the 2010s did allies realize that Orbán's politics were part of a broader international trend, and eroded the liberal democratic system, making it a security risk even for European countries.

Exploiting his political dominance at home, Orbán demanded more and more influence in the international arena too. In this chapter I shall show how Orbán managed to become an inescapable political player in Europe and what this meant for Hungary.

Freedom Always Comes from the West

For centuries, the smaller peoples in Central Europe, including Hungarians, have lived under the influence of the great powers of the European continent: Russia, the Austro–Germans, and the Ottoman Empire. They tried to navigate between these forces but were never able to create a truly broad alliance that would have enabled them to resist the influence of the great powers. Over the twentieth century, Hungary's fate was determined by the hegemonic endeavours first of Germany, then of the Soviet Union.

The collapse of the Soviet Union created a power vacuum in the Central European region, and the countries in the area decided unanimously and of their own volition to join the economic, political and defence cooperation organizations of the more developed, democratic Western countries. This clear orientation to the West was based on hundreds of years of historical experience.

When Fidesz was young, the foreign policy team was one of the strongest groups, and in 1991 we were the first to put forward a foreign policy concept, entitled 'Towards a new type of sovereignty'. The programme was organized around European unification. Optimistically, we believed that within ten years we too would be able to use the joint European currency. With topics ranging from transatlantic relations to policy towards minorities, this rigorous and rational document gave us a foundation to participate with conviction at international meetings we attended in our twenties.

In 1991, the heads of state of Hungary, Poland and Czechoslovakia created a pro-Europe alliance, the Visegrád Group, and one year later the three countries asked to be admitted to the European Community and NATO. From the mid-1990s the West treated the region from the Baltic states to the Balkans as a unit, and only slowly, after a long process of negotiation, did it allow Central European countries into its network of partners and allies. Hungary joined NATO in 1999, and in 2004, along with nine other states, it became a member of the EU. Joining the union, however, did not bring a noticeable immediate boom. In many respects, the Eastern European countries found themselves in competition with the Western ones. The political and economic elites had to learn to operate in a new framework, which required them to be adaptive.

At the time when Hungary joined the EU in 2004, the country started to slide into debt, a state made even graver by the 2008 financial crisis. Because of the decaying economy, Hungary's international influence began to wane, and its ambitions of being a regional power were dashed. Orbán, who was in the opposition, worried not only because of the growing indebtedness of the economy, but also because he believed the socialist-led government was bound too tightly to Russia. In 2007, in a speech given on the anniversary of the founding of Fidesz, he said:

> Hold out for a Western Hungary; don't let them divert Hungary from this path. Love the fact that Hungary is a Western country, which

means we believe in the freedom of human will, and we believe in taking mutual responsibility for one another, which is an indispensable part of Western culture. Oil might come from the East, but freedom always comes from the West.[2]

In the Hungarian political elite, there was still complete consensus on the three-pronged aims of integration into the Euro-Atlantic alliance system, a friendly policy towards neighbouring states, and reinforcing the rights of Hungarian ethnic minorities.

Dare to Be Great!

Compared with this, it seemed a radical change in 2010 when Orbán, now prime minister, started to speak of how Western-style capitalism was in crisis, and how he believed the countries that would survive economically were those that held true to their values, such as India and China. He stated that the countries of Central and Eastern Europe, in addition to taking into account their own interests, must learn how to engage in dialogue with Russia.[3] This idea was completely new from a leader of Fidesz who had previously been militantly anti-Russian.

In the international uncertainty that followed the financial crisis, Orbán saw an opportunity to reinforce the country's position in the international arena once more. After the economic and political decay of the first decade of the 2000s, I personally understood his desire for a more ambitious foreign policy. I also thought it logical that international trade relations should be better aligned with the country's diplomatic endeavours. However, I was most surprised by the marked opening to the East (see Chapter 5), and particularly by its ideological overtones. In his maiden speech as Prime Minister Orbán stated: 'We will overcome the "let's dare to be small" approach', to which he believed his socialist–liberal predecessors subscribed, and which was characterized by a constant need to adapt to the West.[4]

A POLITICAL TAP DANCE

Orbán first appointed János Martonyi, a very experienced diplomat, as foreign minister. In 2011 Martonyi drew up a new foreign policy strategy, which focused on reinforcing the country's role in Euro-Atlantic relationships, increasing Hungary's commitments in global health programmes, food provision and climate change, and aiming at energy diversification. He recommended more varied trade relationships with partners in the Middle East and Asia.[5] However, this strategy, which was deeply anchored in Western organizations and looked to the world from that position, was never realized. Within the framework of the Prime Minister's Office, Orbán appointed a parallel chief of foreign relations in the person of Péter Szijjártó, who later replaced Martonyi as minister of foreign affairs, with the added portfolio of foreign trade.

In 2014, at the annual meeting of ambassadors, Orbán gave a speech in which he proclaimed the policy of opening to the East. He stated that it was time to break with an ideologically led foreign policy, and the point of reference was no longer to be the system of organizations of which Hungary was a member (such as the EU or NATO) but the national interest. According to the head of government, the ideological approach had been 'invented by clever countries for halfwit countries'.[6] He pointed out that the United States, Germany and the Netherlands traded without qualms with China and Russia, and nobody had a moral right to call out Hungary for doing the same thing.

The apparently pragmatic, economically targeted 'opening to the East' programme coincided with his declaration about the 'illiberal state'. After Orbán's capture of democratic institutions and his second two-thirds majority win, he set the aim of building a state-dominated capitalist system similar to that of Eastern powers, and counted on the support of Eastern powers in doing so. The task of the new minister was to implement the 'opening to the East', and Péter Szijjártó radically transformed the structure of the foreign ministry to serve this aim. Within one or two years the majority of the members of the diplomatic corps were changed. Priority was given to the pragmatic realization of economic interests, to which classical diplomacy become a subsidiary tool.[7] The number of diplomats working on European and American partners fell significantly, especially those dealing with multilateral institutions.

The unfriendly treatment of the country's traditional partners, the neglect of international organizations, and the anti-democratic moves in Hungarian politics led to an increasing number of controversies between the government and its Western partners. But Orbán believed that conflict was a basic condition in a time of change and crisis. He spoke disdainfully of the conflict-averse diplomatic culture, and gave ambassadors the task of taking on confrontations with host countries and withstanding all pressures that threatened Hungary's sovereignty.[8]

Orbán strove to forge a greater advantage than others from the transformation of the world order, and to secure a better position for himself than before. He was of the conviction that diplomacy is nothing other than competition between the nations, and the one who moves fastest gains the advantage. According to this logic, the multilateral or bloc mentality was slow, and seemed less advantageous than building bilateral relations.[9]

The policy of 'opening to the East' was a key element of this rapid-reaction foreign policy and foreign trade strategy. When the rate of growth in the eurozone fell after the 2008 crisis, he thought that Hungary's trade relations could be stimulated by opening up to emerging Asian countries with their rapid economic growth.

The first striking result of the 'opening to the East' was the visit by Recep Tayyip Erdoğan, president of Turkey, to Budapest in 2013, accompanied by 125 business people and several hundred journalists. In the meetings, the parties set themselves ambitious goals. They planned to double the volume of trade in three years, and signed agreements on energy, military and cultural matters. Over the next few years, meetings between Orbán and Erdoğan became regular, full of symbolic and celebratory events, in both Ankara and Budapest. Orbán spoke more about historical Turkish–Hungarian ties of friendship, and to the astonishment of Hungarians in 2018 he asked for Hungary to be admitted to the Turkic Council, in order to bond even closer to these countries of the Caucasus and Asia.[10]

But as the years went by, Turkish–Hungarian cooperation had only modest results to show. In 2019, at the height of Orbán's economic success, trade between the region and Hungary accounted for only US$4 billion, which was a mere 2% of Hungary's trade with EU countries.[11] The otherwise pugnacious Orbán tried to counterbalance the small achievements by saying: 'Business is important [...] but Hungarians think that the most important thing in the world isn't business, or money, but that people should have friends'.[12] In the spirit of this strange friendship, the Hungarian government made political gestures to Erdoğan, for example by supporting Turkey in establishing a security zone on the Turkish–Syrian border in 2019.

One person who did very well out of the great Turkish–Hungarian friendship was Turkish businessman Adnan Polat. The Hungarian prime minister had for years been good friends with Polat, former owner of the Turkish football team Galatasaray, and had met him at a football match of the Champions League in 2005. Polat was a billionaire businessman who nursed close relationships with the Turkish political elite and supported Orbán in his endeavour to build links with Erdoğan's government. He became president of the Turkish–Hungarian Business Forum, and from 2015 his company operated the Hungarian National Trading House in Turkey, for small and medium-sized enterprises to find a market in Turkey. Through a complex web of companies, and through the Middle Eastern trading houses of the Hungarian state, the Polat family were linked to companies of Viktor Orbán's son-in-law István Tiborcz.[13] By the end of the 2010s Adnan Polat had become one of the most important investors in the Hungarian wind energy sector and luxury property market.

Getting Friendly with Russia

Orbán's secret agreements with Vladimir Putin on the construction of two new nuclear energy reactors in 2014 and on non-transparent gas prices drew attention to his complete change of attitude to Russia. In 2008, when Putin stormed Georgia, Orbán had said: 'Nothing like this has happened since the end of the Cold War. The enforcement of brute imperial power politics that Russia has now undertaken has been unknown in the last twenty years'.[14]

One year later in 2009, before the elections, Orbán met Putin, and a new chapter in their relationship began, in contrast to the cool reserve that had previously marked their interaction. Like most Central European countries, Hungary gains most of its energy sources from Russia,[15] and so at this meeting they spoke about the oil and gas supply. Later, it transpired that even then there was talk of plans to expand the nuclear power station in Paks, an idea Orbán had previously condemned. One of the prime minister's old acquaintances explained this change of heart towards Russia to a journalist by saying that 'Viktor realized that this had potential to give him leverage over the EU'.[16]

However, it was not easy for the Orbán government to build a new and pragmatic relationship with Russia, because the latter too was well aware of Fidesz's traditional anti-Russian sentiment. To create a basis for good relations it was necessary for Orbán to commit to the construction of new nuclear reactors in Paks, based on a Russian system and using a Russian loan, although the country was not at the time in need of them, because the existing power station was sure to provide electricity until 2032. From conversations in the corridors of Parliament, I learned that since only an extremely small circle of people knew of the secret Paks agreement, it took even Fidesz politicians by surprise, and caused them grave concern. Many in the party looked disapprovingly on this attempt to curry favour with Russia. They persuaded themselves, with Orbánist logic, that if a good relationship with Russia was unavoidable for pragmatic reasons, they should at least try to get the most out of it.

The cordial relationship between the Hungarian and Russian governments became a sensitive topic after 2014, when Russia annexed the Crimean Peninsula in Ukraine, and Russian troops entered eastern Ukraine. This territorial aggression was sternly condemned by the EU and the United States, which introduced economic sanctions and suspended bilateral diplomatic relations with Russia. Orbán tried to strike a balance in this increasingly conflicted situation. As a gesture to the Russians, he protested noisily against the sanctions, but in the European Council he voted for them repeatedly.

In February 2015 Putin came to Budapest with unprecedented security measures in place. Airspace over half the country was closed, and the fleet of the Russian president's planes was accompanied by military fighter jets from the borders to the capital. Strict security measures blocked Budapest's transport for an entire day. But opposition politicians found the event outrageous primarily because Orbán was receiving the Russian president in contravention of the European Council recommendation to suspend diplomatic relations with that country.[17] We were curious to know what unusual matter justified Orbán's receiving the Russian president personally, but we never found out.

Our frustration became even greater when Putin used the Budapest press conference to call on Ukrainian forces to give up their own city, Debaltseve.[18] The visit could not be interpreted as other than a demonstration of Russian strength to Western powers, showing that Putin could still manage to be received in pomp in Europe when the leaders of the continent were punishing his country with sanctions.

There was another surprise when in 2014 the Hungarian government joined the Russian-led International Investment Bank (IIB). In 2019 the Orbán government allowed the IIB to relocate its headquarters to Budapest, and gave it diplomatic immunity customary for international organizations. Serious misgivings were raised in the Hungarian Parliament's national security committee about whether a bank with diplomatic immunity might be used as a cover for espionage and might threaten Hungary's national interests.[19] The presence of the IIB in Budapest was objected to by Hungary's NATO allies as well, but Orbán brushed these objections aside.

In every public utterance, members of the government said that the only aim of the Russian relationship was to gain economic advantages for Hungary, and it was purely a matter of business. But the political nature of the relationship was all too apparent. Orbán had taken quite a few leaves out of the book of Putin's 'illiberal' system. The systematic bolstering of a 'national' business elite linked to himself, to the detriment of other players in the economy, was clearly modelled on Putin. Many laws curtailing democracy, such as the 'foreign-funded organization' law serving to denigrate and intimidate NGOs (see Chapter 9), or the so-called anti-paedophile law (which is actually homophobic), are similar in their language to Russian legislation.[20] The huge media empire linked to Fidesz systematically used fake news disseminated by Russian government media.[21]

Orbán's belief in his own exceptional abilities, that he could keep Russian policy in check, could not be relied on, because Putin's politics were shot through with imperialist logic. Ever since 2005 Putin had been of the opinion that the collapse of the Soviet Union was the greatest geopolitical catastrophe of the twentieth century.[22] From then on, he pursued expansionist politics. Since Putin always considered NATO as the greatest threat to Russia's security, Hungary, as a NATO member, could hardly play any other role for him than as a channel through which to influence Western organizations. This did not preclude Russia from making deals to its advantage with various European countries.

It was convenient for Putin to trigger conflicts between Western allies through Hungary. As well as Orbán's open shift to 'illiberalism', his anti-immigration stance served the same end. After 2014 Hungary pursued contradictory politics with its neighbours, especially Ukraine. On the one hand, like other Western countries, it stood in solidarity when Russia invaded Crimea and the Donbas. At the same time, within NATO the Orbán government made it impossible to set up a joint commission between the organization and Ukraine, claiming that the Ukrainian language law infringed the rights of the Hungarian minority in that country.[23] But blocking dialogue between Ukraine and NATO was a disproportionately harsh response to the problems of the language law.

Moreover, the Orbán government signed a new fifteen-year natural gas supply deal with Russia's state-controlled energy giant Gazprom in September 2021. Gas started to flow to Hungary through the south-eastern TurkStream gas pipeline, which opened at almost the same time. These events enabled Russia to transport gas to the EU by completely avoiding Ukraine, which was detrimental to Ukraine's national interest. All these activities of Orbán's government meant that over several years Hungary was actually speaking for Moscow's interests on various platforms. Moreover, long-term gas deals made Hungary's energy supply almost completely dependent on Russian gas for more than a decade. Orbán's decade-long special relationship with Putin put the Hungarian government inevitably in conflict with the EU when Russia finally attacked Ukraine in 2022.

Courting China

Trade relations with China were launched by the socialist-led government in 2003 with a journey to Beijing by Péter Medgyessy, then head of government. By the time Orbán came to power in 2010, a good few Chinese companies had set up in Hungary, but these accounted only for 2%–3% of total investments.[24]

As with Russia, Fidesz had previously been extremely critical of China. As an opposition party, it had in 2008 condemned the Chinese communist regime for violently crushing Tibetan protesters. In 2009, leading politicians in the party took part in demonstrations by the Tibet Assistance Society, and to show their commitment they invited the Dalai Lama to Budapest, to which he came in 2010. Meanwhile, Orbán had entered government, and members of the party leadership then failed to receive the very visitor they had invited. In preparation for leading the country, Orbán travelled to Beijing in 2009, and a new chapter started in Fidesz's China policy too. By then he had decided that he would open up to Eastern powers, and hoped that China would supply resources to finance the crisis-stricken Hungarian economy. The first Chinese leader to visit Hungary in twenty-four years was the prime minister Wen Jiabao, who came in 2011. One of the previously pro-Tibet ministers, Deputy Prime Minister Zsolt Semjén, received the Chinese leader personally at the airport, though another minister, Zoltán Balog, asked Orbán 'not to have to spit in his own eye'.[25] Fidesz politicians found this sudden change too difficult to stomach.

As we have seen in Chapter 5, Orbán set ambitious goals to increase trade with China, but, unsurprisingly, it was not easy for Hungarian companies to enter the Chinese market. Hungary had no special products or resources of interest to China; indeed it had no large companies that would have been able to build factories in China. The government thus focused rather on stimulating investments. This ambition aligned with the plan of the Chinese to invest in the Eastern European region. In 2013 China created the cooperative group 17+1 with small countries in Central and Eastern Europe, thereby treating the area as a single market. This cooperation, as part of the global 'Belt and Road' initiative, focused primarily on railway development and logistics and telecommunications investments. Hungary joined the initiative first in 2015, and in 2017 Budapest hosted the annual meeting of the 17+1 countries. At the gathering, Orbán claimed that the most competitive investment environment in Europe was Central Eastern Europe, and this region was the driving force behind the economic growth of Europe. Regarding the prospects for the world economy, he said: 'Now the star of the East shines brightly'.[26]

The first success in Orbán's plan to have China create grand long-term projects in the region came when his government made an agreement on the construction of a super-rapid railway link between Budapest and Belgrade in Serbia. This railway link was part of the Chinese programme 'Belt and Road' and, according to plans, would deliver goods from the Greek port of Piraeus to Budapest, in other words the EU. A huge scandal broke out when it was revealed that the Hungarian government had agreed to the project on extremely poor conditions. Merely 160 kilometres long, the planned railway had a draft budget of 750 billion HUF, two thirds of which the Orbán government would pay for with Chinese credit. Even the preliminary calculations showed that, based on the most optimistic estimate, the investment would only become profitable for Hungary after 130 years.[27] Never before had such an expensive railway been built in Hungary; moreover, it followed a route that touched no Hungarian towns, so it was useless for transport within the country. Shying away from fierce criticism, the government classified the feasibility study and the credit contract with the Chinese as confidential for ten years. In a radio interview, Orbán shamelessly explained that the railway was good 'because this is what will carry the goods. Whether it becomes profitable in forints, I consider secondary'.[28] The outrage only grew when in 2019 it was learned that the work for this huge investment had been awarded to a consortium made up equally of companies of the Chinese state railways and Lőrinc Mészáros's construction concerns. As with the Paks nuclear power station, here too Mészáros's companies were the Hungarian beneficiaries of the investment.

Huawei, the most significant Chinese company in Hungary, became the focus of attention when in 2018 the American administration accused it of espionage.[29] The Orbán government had made a strategic agreement with Huawei well before the introduction of 5G technology, and in 2019 the Chinese company opened a regional logistics centre in Hungary, creating 3,000 jobs, and participated in several state telecommunications developments. When rivalry between the US and China began to sharpen during the Trump administration, Huawei became a sore point: analysis of cyber-attacks against America showed that the 5G technology constructed by Huawei caused serious information vulnerability.[30] Although the Trump administration maintained a friendlier relationship with Orbán's government than the previous US leadership, during a visit to Budapest in 2019 Mike Pompeo, US secretary of state, reminded foreign minister Péter Szijjártó that Beijing's handshake sometimes involved obligations that made a country liable both economically and politically.[31] Szijjártó dismissed this; indeed, on another occasion he claimed that Huawei's presence in Hungary was a strategic and national security interest, because by constructing the 5G system Hungary wanted to surpass its rivals. This attitude was markedly divergent from the considerations of other Central European countries.

A POLITICAL TAP DANCE

In these years, the European Union's reservations about Orbán's regime grew stronger. European partners found it difficult to stomach Orbán's forging his own policy with Russia and China. In the European Council, he vetoed several joint statements that expressed harsh criticism of the oppression of human rights by the Chinese leadership, the oppression of Hong Kong, or threatening Chinese military manoeuvres carried out in the South China Sea. These gestures served to reinforce mistrust in Orbán, but the Hungarian government's actions related to Huawei were not criticized by Europe. The EU was rather slow to issue a common 'toolbox' on IT security, and several European countries had given the company the green light to take part in the development of the 5G network. According to one diplomat, the Hungarian government's approach to China was that if NATO asked for something explicitly, it fell into line, but where there was no shared stance, the government followed the lead of the Germans.[32] In the Huawei case, however, this changed after Germany made a restrictive law on IT security in 2021, but Hungary did not.[33]

Until another scandal broke out in April 2021, the Hungarian public was not particularly aware of or interested in Chinese affairs. An article by investigative journalists revealed that the Orbán government was planning the construction of a Chinese private university in Budapest, financed by another gigantic Chinese state loan of 540 billion HUF.[34] According to the government decree, issued confidentially, Shanghai-based Fudan, one of the largest private universities in China, was to open a campus for six thousand students in Budapest.

This news triggered public outrage. Adding fuel to the fire, the area on the bank of the Danube offered to the university had been earmarked, in a cooperation deal between Budapest and the Hungarian government, for a 'Student City' for ten thousand students, with apartments, student residences, service institutions and sports facilities. With the Fudan project, this plan was made completely impossible. Orbán's government offered everything the Chinese asked for in order to bring the university to Budapest, even agreeing that the campus would be built by Chinese workers with Chinese raw materials.

This event mobilized the entire opposition. Led by the mayor of Budapest, a grand ceremony was held to rename streets in the area, for example, Free Hong Kong Street, Dalai Lama Street, Uyghur Martyrs Street. An enormous demonstration was organized against the plan for Fudan University, and the opposition once more marched together. The project, given its sheer scale, endangered the national strategic aim of raising Hungarian universities to the standards of the best Western universities. The outrage was so great that the government resolved not to decide about the details of the project until after the 2022 elections, thereby taking the wind out of the sails of the opposition movement.

* * *

Although at the beginning of his term in government Orbán had agitated against Western financial institutions, saying that they were colonizing Hungary, later he himself saddled the population of Hungary with larger, less transparent loans—ones, moreover, which benefited the economic interests of a narrow group of people. Rather than serving the development of the economy, these enormous and risky investment projects helped to lubricate political relations. But during his twelve years in power, Russia and China also became more aggressive powers, and represented an even greater challenge to the EU. In this time of escalating tensions, Orbán's pro-East politics raised issues of security not only for Hungary, but for Europe too.

For Hungary this attitude was catastrophic, because the trust of the country's allies began evaporating. Orbán's opening to the East could take place only to the detriment of the Western alliance.

A POLITICAL TAP DANCE

Political Tap Dance with Allies

Orbán knew from the outset that his 'opening to the East' policy would cause conflict, yet his purpose was not to break with Western allies. In fact, it was the very membership of NATO and the EU, notably the veto power in critical policy areas, that enabled him to fly in the face of American or German political ambitions. The institutions in the Western alliances guaranteed a say in decisions even to the smallest member countries, which would have remained voiceless outside these systems.

In 2012, in a private conference Orbán explained the essence of balance to his supporters:

> The ballroom etiquette of diplomacy requires that we reject proposals giving the impression we want to make friends. These are manoeuvres related to the art of politics. Out of seven proposals we give the okay to two or three (which we'd already done, though they didn't notice) and the other two which we don't want, we refuse while actually accepting the majority. This tricky manoeuvre is a kind of political tap dance.[35]

Orbán taught his colleagues how to worm their way between opportunities and outdo less well-informed partners.

We Are of No Interest to America

In summer 2016, as a member of Parliament, I travelled with a small delegation to the United States. This was Barack Obama's last year in office. By then Orbán had mired himself in conflict with the American administration. During her visit to Budapest, Hillary Clinton levelled severe criticism at the Orbán government for its moves to erode democracy.[36] The American administration did not look favourably on Orbán's cosying up to Russia. Corruption too seemed to be a problem: in 2014 several Hungarian state officials were banned from entering the United Sates, including the president of the National Tax

Office. Relations between the US and Hungary were at a low. And yet, during our visit to Washington, it became clear that on the whole the Americans found the policies of the Orbán government satisfactory. The Hungarian government fulfilled all its NATO obligations; indeed, when the US asked its allies to join it in the war against the Islamic State in Iraq and Syria, the size of the contingent the Hungarian government sent to the war zone was large relative to the size of the country. For the Americans, Hungary was of interest in terms of defence and the economy, and Orbán was well aware of this. He did everything necessary to keep the relationship alive: he was cooperative in defence issues, and through strategic collaboration he supported the more important American companies investing in Hungary. In other issues, however, he was not interested in the American viewpoint.

Our visit to America coincided with the Brexit referendum in the UK. In America, the presidential campaign between Hillary Clinton and Donald Trump was under way. As a Hungarian who had already learned that previously unthinkable things can happen in politics, I saw that even Trump's victory was possible. Regardless of this, I was very surprised when Orbán stated that he thought Trump's election as president would be more advantageous for Hungary and Europe. Orbán was most impressed by Trump's anti-refugee policy, his proposal to reinforce the secret services, and his promise to stop exporting democracy.[37]

In this matter, Orbán didn't have much to lose. Fidesz's relationship with the Democratic Party had deteriorated so much that Orbán might have expected the political relationship to improve with a new Republican administration. The Hungarian government paid several million dollars to American lobbyists to smooth the way for the Orbán government to the top of the Trump administration outside official diplomatic relations, and to organize a meeting with the American president.[38]

A POLITICAL TAP DANCE

Although many on the American right had sympathy with Orbán's culture war against liberalism, it did not automatically follow that they would pander to the Hungarian prime minister's desire to enjoy special treatment. When Trump received Orbán in 2019, he expressed his appreciation that he was doing a good job and keeping the country safe.[39] But during the Trump era, the US saw Hungarian politics in terms of the Russian network of relationships, and foreign affairs experts did not look favourably on the investment of Russian capital, the strong energy dependency on Russia, or the appearance in Budapest of the International Investment Bank. Neither did the intensive cooperation with the Chinese help relations, as Mike Pompeo stated when he visited. Orbán's people continued to neutralize criticism by cooperating in defence matters. In addition to the high-level commitment to NATO, in summer 2020 the Hungarian government signed a $1 billion contract for the purchase of American–Norwegian anti-aircraft missiles.[40] It was particularly important to the American ambassador when the Orbán government made an agreement with Shell to buy liquefied gas from the LNG terminal to be built in the port of Krk in Croatia.[41] This created the possibility that Hungary would later purchase LNG from the United States, which could lessen Hungary's dependence on Russian gas. In 2021 Hungary also agreed to the 15% global minimum tax rate on multinational corporations, which was highly important to the US administration. Through these small gestures the Hungarian government was able to improve dialogue with the US during the Trump and even the Biden presidencies.

'Small Power' Politics

Orbán's outlier policies became clear to the public at large during the 2015 refugee crisis (see Chapter 8). The Hungarian prime minister was belligerent in portraying the crisis as a purely security issue: he built a fence and firmly condemned the EU's plan to distribute the refugees over the continent according to country quotas. In summer 2015 Orbán managed to persuade the Visegrád countries in Central Europe (Poland, Czechia and Slovakia as well as Hungary) to jointly reject Angela Merkel's *Willkommenskultur* policy.[42]

Before this event the Visegrád Group's only achievement in Europe was lobbying jointly for more money from the EU's Cohesion Fund. The joint rejection of EU policy on the refugee crisis helped to characterize the cooperation between the four countries. The harsh measures taken against immigration and the sealing of the border, which the international press and Western politicians roundly condemned, actually met with sympathy in some countries, as the EU had no settled measures to stem the crisis. It was a great victory for Orbán to succeed in aligning the policies of the Visegrád countries. In addition, he also managed to put forward this Central European viewpoint in opposition to Brussels, 'in defence of national sovereignty'. In doing so, he raised his 'policy of sovereignty' to an ideological level, and put it on Europe's political agenda.

The 2015 refugee crisis once more drew attention to the need to reform the EU in order to make decision-making more efficient. Exploiting this, Orbán framed the mission of the Visegrád countries as an authentic representation of Judaeo-Christian culture (unlike that of Western European countries). 'For us, Europe is at stake, the way of life of the European citizen, whether European values and nations survive, disappear, or change until they are unrecognizable', he declared in a speech.[43] Orbán fundamentally changed the profile of the Visegrád Group. From a previously committed pro-Europe cluster, he created an explicitly Eurosceptic group working to strengthen the influence of nation-states, which became able to influence European decision-making processes more forcefully than before, albeit often by means of delaying or blocking them.

A POLITICAL TAP DANCE

The strengthening of the Visegrád countries was motivated by their desire to acquire a greater influence over matters in the EU, of which they had been members for ten years. This could be taken as an entirely justified position. The problem for the Hungarian opposition and ultimately for neighbouring countries was that this community was dominated by Orbán's hard-line Eurosceptic politics.

Slovakia and Czechia looked on with antipathy at the Hungarian and Polish governments' stand on matters of the rule of law. Slovakia, as a member of the eurozone, adopted a strict pro-Europe policy in every matter. Poland and Hungary had traditionally close ties, but these were always tinged by Orbán's over-friendly relationship with Vladimir Putin.[44] An expansionist Russia and the possibility of Russian–Chinese rapprochement presented a fundamental security risk for Poland, and the relationship was damaged after Russia annexed Crimea in 2014. Still, regardless of the differences, the Visegrád Group helped Orbán to put forward his ideas in the international arena for a few years.

The Visegrád Group was not the only way Orbán tried to increase his influence in the region. By expanding dual citizenship to 1 million Hungarians living in neighbouring countries, by multiplying tenfold financial aid to them, and through enormous state investments, he spread his power base in the region. Neighbouring countries disapproved of these moves but tolerated them, albeit often with gnashing of teeth. No scandal broke out until in 2021 the Orbán government decided it would purchase several thousand hectares of arable land in the territory of neighbouring countries, using money from the Hungarian national budget. Then the Slovak government took a firm stand, and the Orbán government withdrew from the purchase.[45] Though formally the purpose was to support Hungarian entrepreneurs in agriculture, it was difficult not to see this as an attempt by the

Orbán government to buy back some of the land it lost a hundred years previously. The Hungarian government subsidized media in these countries; it bought registered historical buildings for non-diplomatic purposes; it renovated churches and kindergartens; and Hungarian state leaders came and went in neighbouring countries without prior announcement, breaking international conventions.[46] Orbán's government, which in the case of his own country was hypersensitive to national sovereignty, acted in the most undiplomatic manner in the territory of other countries.

One striking example of this occurred when diplomats of the Hungarian government helped Macedonian Prime Minister Nikola Gruevski, who had been convicted on corruption charges, flee Macedonia and took him without a valid passport to Hungary, where he was given political asylum.[47] Russophile Gruevski and Orbán had long been allies. This case prompted the EU to challenge Orbán, but on the one occasion he did speak in public, he merely said: 'One deals decently with one's allies'.[48]

Another contradictory example of attempts to gain influence in western Balkan countries happened in autumn 2021 when Orbán unexpectedly travelled to Bosnia-Herzegovina and met Milorad Dodik, the leader of the country's Serbian entity, and offered a significant sum of subsidy to the Serbian leader.[49] In these months Dodik was pursuing an ethnically based secession campaign in the extremely fragile Bosnian–Croatian–Serbian state, endangering the Dayton Accords which had put an end to the Bosnian War in 1995. I found Orbán's meddling in the highly sensitive western Balkan politics unjustified, risky and distressing.

As Hungarian diplomacy became involved in more and more murky affairs, the other Visegrád countries became more cautious. Then in 2020 when Orbán and Polish president Lech Kaczyński threated to veto the EU crisis package, the Czech and Slovak politicians clearly kept their distance. Some felt that the Hungarian government was abusing the brand of the Visegrád Four, with the

Slovak head of state going so far as to say that the Hungarian and Polish position might damage Slovakia's national interests.[50] Finally, Orbán's Putin-friendly politics during the war in Ukraine damaged Hungary's long-standing friendship with Poland.

Manoeuvring with Germany

Beginning with the refugee crisis in 2015, Orbán's activities became increasingly awkward for his European partners. As Hungarian diplomats were often put in a tight corner, Fidesz began a vigorous diplomatic offensive whose like had not been seen before. During the refugee crisis, Hungarian ambassadors all over Europe engaged in private conversations and wrote articles for host country newspapers to explain their government's position. A considerable part of this 'pacification' of Europe involved the persuasion of the German political elite.

In autumn 2015 I took part in the annual conference of the German–Hungarian Forum in Berlin, which was almost exclusively about the refugee crisis in Europe. At that time, the policies of the governments of the two countries were at loggerheads. Apart from me, the only people representing Hungary were Fidesz politicians, while from the German contingent there were representatives of every party in the Bundestag. I was invited because the foreign policy institute that was organizing the conference insisted that I too speak, as an opposition politician. The forum had been dominated by Fidesz for years. The Hungarian government politicians Zsolt Németh and József Szájer, both my former colleagues with whom I am still on speaking terms, were the most experienced diplomats in the party. At the meeting they explained the essence of Fidesz's refugee policy in a refined, persuasive manner, catering to the expectations of the German audience. I remember thinking how good it would be if such intelligent debate were conducted in the Hungarian Parliament too.

In those same weeks, Orbán was also in Germany: he spoke at the opening session of the Bavarian Christian Socialist Union (CSU), and had talks with Horst Seehofer, president of the party, the minister president of Bavaria and, crucially, the federal minister of the interior. In a joint press conference, Orbán said, 'I want to bring reality back into politics', and he thanked the CSU for helping him to get the question of defending the borders taken seriously in Europe.[51] Seehofer spoke appreciatively of Orbán's efforts to keep order. Orbán took every opportunity to win over the German conservatives, because he knew that if the Germans accepted what he was doing, then things would be easy for him in Europe.

This intensive liaising was necessary because relations between the Hungarian and German governments were continually beset by controversies. When German chancellor Angela Merkel was in Budapest in February 2015, she and Orbán publicly disagreed with each other at a press conference on the freedom of NGOs and the media in Hungary, the necessity of sanctions against Russia, and whether an 'illiberal state' could actually exist.[52]

Orbán's reputation in Germany was poor. Regardless of political leaning, the German press wrote extremely critically of developments in Hungary, from the time of the 2010 media law and the rewriting of the Fundamental Law. German social democratic, liberal and green parties all levelled strong criticisms at the Orbán government. For the Christian Democratic Union (CDU), however, which was in the same alliance as Fidesz, Orbán presented a challenge. Typically, German politicians raised problems with Hungarian democracy and human rights not in bilateral relations but in EU institutions. For Germany, the unity and integrity of the EU was always a national strategic interest— not just because the European free market served the interests of the German economy, but also because, since the war, the EU had ensured ideological stability beyond nationalism, and a broad

A POLITICAL TAP DANCE

framework for democratic development. After German unification in 1990, since Germany was by far the largest European country, the EU framework became even more important if its increased economic and political power was not to be viewed by smaller European countries as a challenge to their security.

In spite of the conflicts, the governing German conservative party stood by Fidesz for a very long time. Merkel consistently held the traditional German view that progress could be made even with the most problematic of partners by maintaining dialogue, rather than forcing them off the pitch. In 2020 one of Merkel's advisers told me that the CDU strategy regarding Fidesz was to involve the Hungarian party when it was absolutely necessary, but to isolate it in situations where its presence might cause difficulties. Seen from Berlin, Hungary was not nearly as important a player on the European stage, and the German government made much greater diplomatic efforts to maintain collaboration with the Polish party Law and Justice than to win over Orbán.

At the same time Orbán's government was extremely good for those German manufacturing companies with plants in Hungary, as mentioned in Chapter 5. Although German companies seemed to manage matters independently of political links, several cases show that they accepted the rules of play that Fidesz dictated. For instance, it came to light that, counter to earlier practice, German automobile manufacturers had ceased advertising in independent media because they did not want to risk losing subsidies from the Hungarian government.[53] The collaboration between the Orbán government and German industrialists operated smoothly and was beneficial to both parties.

And yet German politics were made up of far more complex players and interests. In order to maintain satisfactory political relations, Orbán needed to have stable supporters. Crucial laws were thus translated into German in advance, and the most civilized figures of Fidesz conducted regular talks with conservative politicians in the German government, the most important business leaders, and editors of the leading papers. Aiding in this effort was Frank Spengler, the influential director of the Konrad Adenauer Foundation office in Budapest. Spengler, whom I spoke to from time to time, once told me that he helped the moderate, good people inside Fidesz. He believed there was nothing to fear from Orbán, because Fidesz, like German parties, would eventually replace him if he did not bring results for the party. Whether this was extraordinarily opportunistic, or whether he had seriously misjudged Fidesz as a party, was difficult for me to tell.

Fidesz provided the German elite with what was most important for them: political stability, a favourable economic environment, and cheap skilled labour. Orbán struck a delicate balance between the expectations of the German political and economic elite, who compromised, and the protesters.

The European Arena

After Fidesz's third election victory, Orbán become extremely self-confident on the European stage and launched into the 2019 European Parliament campaign sizzling with energy. Orbán was so certain of himself that an anti-Europe campaign was designed and linked to the never-ending anti-refugee campaign (as we have seen in Chapter 8). When a photo of Jean-Claude Juncker, president of the European Commission and a member of the EPP, appeared on billboards, with the suggestive slogan 'You too have a right to know what Brussels is planning!', Fidesz's temporary peace with its European party (see Chapter 4) was upset once more.

'Viktor Orbán has caused serious damage to the European People's Party with the new Hungarian government campaign', said Manfred Weber, the group leader, to the German news magazine

Der Spiegel.⁵⁴ Orbán's use of his own fellow party members for a negative campaign sparked a heated debate, and finally the EPP decided to temporarily suspend Fidesz's membership. This, however, did not mean that Fidesz would be excluded from the EPP group in the European Parliament assembling after the 2019 elections. The party group very much needed Fidesz's votes for German member Ursula von der Leyen to receive the necessary majority to be elected president of the European Commission. Nevertheless, the customary expectations of political loyalty were slowly eroded by Orbán's open feud with Brussels, the Eastern opening, the Russian and Chinese spheres of interests, and his opaque meddling in Central Asia and the Balkans.⁵⁵

Orbán's aggressive and opportunistic behaviour in Europe made it difficult even for us, the opposition, to conduct an effective foreign policy. On many occasions, I faced the dilemma of deciding how far, and on what topics, I could agree with the Hungarian government when the problem it raised was justified, though the manner in which it did so was unacceptable. One such question concerned the Visegrád Group, which I considered very important, though I was convinced the Orbán government tried to exploit its neighbours for its own ideological ends. In Europe, the Visegrád Four were seen as troublemakers, an alliance harmful for Europe. Management of the refugee problem was another serious issue which, as I knew from personal experience, had placed a great burden on the Hungarian refugee and immigration authorities in 2015. At the same time, it was impossible to agree with the often inhumane policies, the utter rejection of the quota system, and the sickening anti-migrant campaign. The Hungarian government was justified in raising the issue that Western European countries systematically drained highly trained young people out of Hungary, creating an untenable situation in some professions, such as the health service. On many occasions the European Commission proved indeed to be applying double standards: for instance, fifteen years after EU accession, in most European research consortiums Eastern European academic institutions could still only participate as subcontractors. But Orbán's people declared that double standards were being applied every time the EU criticized Hungary, and this made it impossible to talk about genuine problems.

The Orbán government's cowboy politics in the European Union were, for most of the Hungarian opposition, shameful and seriously flawed. When I was an MP, I put considerable efforts into drafting proposals in the name of the Visegrád countries with Polish, Czech and Slovak politicians who were forward-looking and aimed at a more unified European Union. We held the view that Central European countries should join the eurozone as soon as possible, and also the European Public Prosecutor's Office, in which neither Hungary nor Poland participated. We urged the EU to create institutions to protect the rule of law, and shape a common foreign policy, and for money transfers within Europe to be tied to stricter conditions.[56] While publicizing our 'Visegrad 4 Europe' programme, we sometimes ran into unexpected obstacles. One of the leaders of the region's most important security policy conference, with whom I had an excellent working relationship, told me apologetically that although he supported our programme fully, he could not offer a place for it to be presented at the conference, because the Hungarian foreign minister had made it clear that if a Hungarian opposition politician was allowed to speak at the conference, he would not appear. The public debate between the region's foreign ministers was one of the key events of this forum, and the organizers did not want to jeopardize a good relationship with the Hungarian government. The hand of Orbán's people reached far beyond the border.

The geopolitical changes in the world prompted by China and Russia going on the offensive, by the Trump administration's withdrawal from transatlantic cooperation, and by Brexit caused European leaders to rethink the future of the continent. The deeper union of the EU essentially came to a halt when the Eastern European countries joined in the mid-2000s, because the integration of twelve states was an enormous burden for the bloc. A good decade later, though, it was obvious that they had to move forward.

In 2017 Emmanuel Macron was the first to proclaim far-reaching European reforms reflecting global changes. In order to reinforce European sovereignty, he made proposals to shape a common defence policy, joint safeguarding of the borders, the introduction of joint migration, climate and economic policies, and more efficient monitoring of democracy.[57] Angela Merkel put forward her ideas for reform a year later, which included a common euro budget and banking union. She also proposed that consensus-based decision-making in foreign policy be replaced by a majority decision, which would eliminate the problem of single countries exercising an unjustified veto. The two leaders announced their intentions for change at an important summit at Schloss Meseberg in Germany. 'We are, broadly speaking, opening a new chapter. Our goal is to keep Europe from becoming more divided', they stated.[58]

Orbán's and Kaczyński's rule-breaking governments strained the very basis of EU decision-making in this decisive period. Joseph Daul, president of the European People's Party (EPP), and Manfred Weber, leader of the EPP parliamentary group, indicated to Orbán at the time that his policies carried the risk of Fidesz being barred from the EPP. According to witnesses, Orbán then threatened the two leaders, saying, 'If you try to kick me out, I'll destroy you'.[59]

Macron's and Merkel's European reform plans posed a considerable risk for Orbán's regime, and Orbán wanted to prevent a deepening of the EU at all costs. In 2019, he openly proclaimed a year of rebellion (see Chapter 2), and tried to unite the extreme forces in Europe that were striving to prevent the further strengthening of the EU. An intensification of confrontation with the EPP was obvious.

Europe's Retort

Ten years after Fidesz's so-called constitutional revolution, in autumn 2020 the EU released its first report on the rule of law. This was an overview of the state of democracy across the Union, based on identical principles and criteria. The section on Hungary, albeit couched in guarded language, painted a bleak picture of the government's democratic performance.[60]

'Absurd and untrue', reacted the minister of justice with her usual vehemence. Orbán went further: he demanded that the European commissioner responsible for the report, Věra Jourová, resign from her post.[61]

When EU member states decided that the budget beginning in 2021 and the disbursement of the reconstruction fund would be tied to conditions of the rule of law, as I wrote at the beginning of the chapter, Orbán's government fought tooth and nail to prevent this. For Orbán, even the most trifling of investigations seemed to be a question of life or death, because it restricted his access to the enormous EU funds on which his system was built.

In this dispute, finally, relations between Fidesz and the European People's Party became utterly poisoned. Parliamentary group leader Manfred Weber stated that those who had nothing to hide would have nothing to fear from budget payments being linked to the rule of law.[62] Following this, in a TV interview Tamás Deutsch, a veteran Fidesz politician and MEP, likened Weber's statement to Gestapo methods.[63] Orbán, for his part, gave an interview to the German conservative weekly *Welt*, in which he compared the EU's procedure with the Soviet Union.[64]

A POLITICAL TAP DANCE

After its veto, the time was ripe for the EPP to break its ties with Orbán's party. In March 2021, just before the critical vote on Fidesz's membership of the EPP, Orbán decided not to hang around to be humiliated, and immediately had Fidesz MEPs leave the EPP.

Fidesz had been a member of the EPP for twenty years. Originally, the leaders of large European conservative parties had hailed Orbán. 'For Europe, the fresh breeze blowing from the east still comes from the generation of Fidesz, from Viktor Orbán, and his friends, who have defeated communism', Wilfried Martens, president of the EPP, had said in 2006.[65] Even in 2014, Western politicians in the party were still actively campaigning for Fidesz in Budapest, when the party was already seriously eroding the institutional system of democracy in Hungary. As the most powerful party grouping in Europe, the EPP shoulders great responsibility for Hungary's departure from European norms. After being forced out of the EPP, Orbán and his party drifted to the political periphery.

Yet Orbán's constant criticism of EU leaders and his harping on sovereigntist policies were aimed at hampering EU reform processes and, in the name of 'a Europe of the nations', at preserving the financial and political conditions that served the Hungarian prime minister's autocratic rule. Based on victimhood and denial and by constantly reiterating that Western countries cannot tell the Eastern ones what to do, he built up a successful narrative which resonated all over in Europe's periphery and made European institutions more cautious in pushing for reform. Orbán gained enormous influence by exploiting the hypocrisy of his Western partners, and, despite being the leader of a small country, he became the symbolic head of the anti-European forces.

The striking growth in the influence of Orbán's regime in the 2010s was due to the special system of the EU that gives the smallest countries a say in decisions, which they exploited to the utmost with aggressive politics. For Eastern powers, a small Hungary is of interest only as long as it sits at the same table as the most important decision-makers. These regimes made the most of Orbán's double-dealing politics: they took advantage of the greedy, corrupt Orbán government, while in political terms they divided the EU. Ultimately, Orbán's autocracy represented a threat to European social harmony. Hungary as a partner became unreliable.

Vladimir Putin's bloody war against Ukraine clearly showed how restricted Hungary's room for manoeuvre is in the world. Seeing Orbán's hesitant politics standing by Ukraine, his Central European allies fell quickly away and Hungary was crowded out of the Visegrád Group. Hungary's dependence on Russian energy gave Orbán little room for manoeuvre within the quickly converging NATO and EU. In 2022 Hungary arrived at a crossroads and the stakes become Hungary's membership in the EU.

* * *

There is a long history of criticizing the West in Hungary. Lajos Fülep, a religious minister and art historian of the early twentieth century, wrote in 1934 that he believed that turning away from the West was self-centred, and that the whole West–East dilemma was merely a 'hopeless stamping of feet', because the East was 'a trance shrouded in mist, dissolving in the air, or an inferior state of both attack and defence with a national-oriental slogan'.[66]

Viktor Orbán was intoxicated by the astounding rise of the East, and staked everything on it. He saw the opportunity for revolutionary changes during the Western economic crisis, and appeared as a visionary leader. 'If we dare to say that there is no sense in copying Western Europe, but in the spirit of freedom we must build our own economic systems, if we dare to say that, then we have made a huge step towards success', he declared.[67]

A POLITICAL TAP DANCE

Orbán persuaded many Hungarians that through him Hungary would become special, and he would make the country greater than it actually was. This filled his believers with pride, but at the same time he reawakened grievances against the West, saying that it did not recognize or respect Hungary's qualities. In fact, the situation in the 2020s was exactly the same as the one described by Lajos Fülep in 1934, that Hungary lagged slightly behind the West, and this was not so easy to change. The country may have developed continuously, but during the Orbán regime the dynamism with which this took place fell short compared with that of other countries in the region. Although integrating Eastern Europe into the EU was useful for the Western partners, it is not Europe but we Hungarians who determine Hungary's economic and social development. The task of the Hungarian political elite is, through astute governance, to get the best out of the country's circumstances and the capabilities of its people. The anti-West stance is nothing other than a cover for one's own failure, a mere 'trance dissolving in the air'.

Orbán's fortune-hunting politics have made Hungary neither greater nor stronger, but merely more dangerous and isolated. This may have serious consequences for Fidesz's politics and for the entire country. Going against the centre of gravity of the West is a risk that led to failure for Hungary three times during the twentieth century.

Over the last one hundred years, my grandparents, parents and ancestors tried to live free and autonomous lives in the shadow of oppressive regimes. All their lives, they hoped that Hungary would one day be free and take her place where she belonged: in Europe. They strove to pass on to us, their children and grandchildren, knowledge of Hungary's true history and special culture, but also wanted us to learn foreign languages, travel the world, live meaningful lives, and not mope in provincial self-pity. When Fidesz formed, this was the project it took on, and that is why I felt the party was for me, and I joined. When Hungary opened to the West, we in the young Fidesz did not want to defeat the developed regions of the world, but to reach out to them and live with them. To hope to compete with Western Europe would have been delusional.

During the twentieth century there were many European nations which, having lost territory or ceded colonies, were able to make the transformation from world powers to normal European countries, and reassess their ambitions in the world. It seems that we Hungarians have not yet managed to learn who we are, and accept what we are capable of. My generation, the Fidesz generation, who earned freedom in our youth, and for whom the sky was the limit, have failed. Our children must begin the difficult task of extricating themselves from the illusion of lost greatness.

AFTERWORD

The twelve years of Viktor Orbán's government have left a deep impression on my company of friends. Some of them left Hungary and found work at the European institutions in Brussels and Luxembourg or international NGOs in Berlin. One of them sold his successful tech company before any of Orbán's oligarchs could buy him out. Another of them, the head of a research institute, lost all state commissions but managed to save his company by supplying research for European consortia. All of my journalist friends lost their jobs and had to look for work in other media outlets, but some became so disillusioned that they eventually gave up journalism altogether. There were a few who stayed in the public administration. As for me, I spent a good few years in politics again. The Orbán regime upended all of our lives. Over these years, we have engaged in countless political discussions. The incredible pressure of the regime, and our professional and sometimes financial vulnerability, were a strain on our friendship. Meanwhile, our children grew up and went to university. Hardly any of them stayed in Hungary. We don't know whether they see any prospects in bringing the knowledge they have gained in the best universities in Europe back to Hungary.

When on 3 April 2022 Fidesz won two thirds of the seats in Parliament for the fourth time and the opposition performed disastrously, it was clear that the illiberal Hungary experiment would continue. However, as the 'years of abundance' had ended, Hungary faced a serious economic recession. This situation threatened more repressive government politics and growing conflicts with Hungary's Western partners.

The Hungarian opposition, which over twelve years has tested various strategies for better or worse, was facing a challenge, more than ever before. Would it continue the petty rivalry and fall into the position of Orbán's most loyal opposition? Or would it rise to the responsibility of leading the country and making Hungarians understand that departing from European democracy risks Hungary's eventual expulsion from the EU?

Orbán's hard-line regime will remain a serious challenge for Hungary's European partners as well, which will meet a more emboldened and hostile Orbán. Although some steps have been taken by European institutions to sanction the autocratic Hungarian government, the EU still lacks coherent and strategic policies to push back against autocracy in the bloc. While Russia's war in Ukraine is a warning sign for Europe's complacent political elite that history is not linear, the turbulent geopolitical changes now taking place can inhibit visionary thinking.

* * *

After the financial crisis in 2008 political entrepreneurs appeared all over the world, who exploited the dissatisfaction of people by promising a strong state and security. Viktor Orbán came to power at this exceptional juncture. By undermining political fairness, Orbán's twelve-year rule has hijacked Hungary's democratic development and the long-term civilizing process of the growth of the middle class. Hungarian society too has lost its moral compass under Orbán, because the coherent rules of democratic politics have disappeared. The long-term effects

AFTERWORD

of the spread of a political culture based on hate and mental manipulation are unpredictable.

There will be no easy revival of democracy in Hungary. The years-long entrenchment of illiberalism will pose a serious challenge for any future Hungarian government. As Hungary has been fairly unique in its path, we do not know if a restoration of democracy is possible or whether, instead, we face an alternation of democratic and autocratic governments that will pull the country into further decline.

Despite this, the renewal of Hungarian democracy is not inconceivable. A desire for autonomy and a self-regulating society goes back centuries. In spite of the efforts of the political elite, society is far from being too divided to reunite, as most people reject the culture wars which are being foisted upon them. Hungarians agree that with a legacy of political culture woven around the idea of liberty, we Hungarians are inseparably bound to the West.

Democracy is held together by an ethos of autonomy, the principle of political fairness, and the efforts of the community. My historically privileged generation, who believed that history always moves forward, have squandered this chance. All we can do now is, with all our strength, help the next generation, so that they can carry on pushing Hungarian democracy forward and manage to overcome the forces of autocracy, which are always ready to pounce.

EPILOGUE
TURNING THE TIDE?

Orbán's Charismatic Challenger: Péter Magyar

On 2 February 2024, a year and a half after Viktor Orbán's fourth election victory, it became public knowledge that President Katalin Novák had pardoned a man convicted of helping the head of a children's home cover up acts of paedophilia.[1] Within hours, the news snowballed into an enormous scandal, which would strike Fidesz to its core. How was it possible for a governing administration that had expended so much energy advocating the merits of pro-family Christian policies to be covering up cases of child abuse at the highest political level? The scandal forced Orbán to distance himself from two key women politicians of his party. Katalin Novák, who granted the pardon, and Judit Varga, the former minister of justice, who countersigned the request for pardon and was at the top of the Fidesz list for the European elections, were compelled to resign. But the matter continued to linger and a few days later, Varga's ex-husband, Péter Magyar, who until then had been an unknown cadre of the Fidesz system, gave an interview to the news portal Partizán. He accused several prominent politicians of abuse of power and corruption, and, in a bombshell revelation, stated that the issuance of the pardon in this case was such a sensitive matter that could not have happened without the prime minister's consent.² The interview reached a huge audience, and within days, the name Péter Magyar was on everybody's lips.

In the space of a month, Magyar's political capital skyrocketed. By March 2024, he was setting out his programme for opposition, embarking on a tour of the country, and had founded his own political party. Everywhere he went, people thronged to hear him. Who was this brave man, who left Fidesz and dared to oppose Viktor Orbán? His new party, Tisza (named after a river that passes through Hungary), took advantage of the momentum to run for the European parliamentary elections in June 2024, where, despite its infancy, it scored 29.7% of the vote—and saw Magyar and six other Tisza candidates secure election to the European Parliament.³

After many years of weakened opposition, the impression Magyar made as a man of action, a charismatic figure, sparked hope that Viktor Orbán could be defeated. Almost immediately, a vigorous smear campaign was launched against him, but he remained impervious to it. After the European elections, he encouraged his supporters to self-organize as 'Tisza islands,' so that the new movement would take root in every part of the country. A couple of months later, his party had caught up with Fidesz in public opinion polls.⁴

Magyar's energy, combative outspokenness, and resilience won over Orbán's critics on both the right and left, and absorbed practically the entire voter base of the previous opposition parties. He presented Hungarians with a viable alternative to the status quo. Magyar's harnessing of the populist behaviour and communication know-how of Orbán's Fidesz, and his use of the symbolic language and tactics hitherto utilized by the government, helped Tisza stir up the ambitions of those who were previously disillusioned. When in the summer of 2025

EPILOGUE

Magyar again set out on a village tour, he took with him an Orbán cardboard cutout to underline the fact that while he was here among the people, Orbán was inaccessible. The nationwide tour was a huge success.

Orbán's Failures Become Visible

Magyar's success has also, in large part, come from the visible failings of Orbán's most recent premiership—problems that were well, or more easily, concealed in previous terms.

The Hungarian economy had been in decline since the Covid-19 pandemic, and weighed down still further by the burden of the welfare measures introduced for the 2022 election, the energy crisis caused by the war in Ukraine, and other illiberal policies imposed on the economy. In 2023, Hungarian inflation was the highest in the European Union, with prices rising consistently between 2020 and 2025. This was particularly true of foodstuffs, which skyrocketed in value by 81.6% over this period.[5] The government introduced price caps and special taxes to control the price of basic foods, and forced companies to raise wages.[6] However, the cost-of-living crisis continued to hit ordinary Hungarians hard, while companies also came under increasing pressure due to the higher costs they were forced to bear. In order to balance the budget, the government was forced to borrow,[7] which in turn increased the national debt to 75.2% of GDP,[8] 10% higher than in 2020, and grew the state's interest payment obligations to 5% of projected GDP for 2025, the highest in Europe.[9]

The Orbán government's industrialization plan, financed to the tune of billions of euros,[10] also failed. State-controlled investments were funnelled into expensive infrastructure developments, and inward foreign investment was overwhelmingly directed towards the electric battery industry. By replacing economic rationality with frequently arbitrary interventions, wasteful resource management, failed reindustrialization, unreasonable and politicized welfare services, systemic corruption and, lastly, a confrontational foreign policy, Hungary slipped further and further down the European Union's development list.[11]

Taken together, this has made issues relating to the cost-of-living fertile ground for Péter Magyar. Throughout his roving trips across Hungary, he has highlighted the country's serious problems with attention-grabbing stunts. During the summer months, with temperatures hitting forty degrees Celsius, he visited hospitals with a thermometer. In the winter, he travelled by train to draw attention to serious delays and unheated coaches. During his eighty-day tour of the country, he visited 185 settlements, where he talked to people about their everyday problems: housing shortages, agricultural problems and poverty. Magyar's canoe tour along the Tisza River, which crosses eastern Hungary, was also a marked contrast to the luxurious lifestyles of local Fidesz figures and the yachting holidays of the party elite in the Adriatic—and brought the grandiose existence of some of Viktor Orbán's closest allies into sharper view.

More and more questions were directed at Lőrinc Mészáros, whose group of companies increased in value by €1 billion between 2024 and 2025.[12] Having built a luxury real estate empire consisting of 136 companies and having doubled their wealth in a year, Ráhel Orbán, the prime minister's eldest daughter, and her husband, István Tiborcz, moved to New York City with their family in September 2025 in order to become invisible during the election campaign.[13] But the best illustration of the Orbán family's wealth was its redevelopment of Hatvanpuszta, a former Habsburg estate near Budapest, as its private retreat.[14] Persistent investigative work uncovered a network of buildings, including a luxury garden and a safari park, constructed under the name of Viktor Orbán's elderly father, which exposed Orbán's hitherto

EPILOGUE

successful pretence that he was a man of the people, living like anyone else. This tore down the moral façade that Fidesz had erected over many years, and showed, contrary to smear campaigns—which branded Orbán's political rivals as thieves,[15] diabolical profiteers,[16] traitors,[17] bugs[18] and evil forces—that parasitic behaviour was now rampant between state leaders and the political-economic elite.

Hungary's behaviour on the world stage also undermined Orbán's pitch to voters. For a while, the Hungarian premier was able to persuade people that he was open to authoritarian powers for purely pragmatic reasons. However, being constantly at loggerheads with European allies, and vetoing the NATO membership of Finland and Sweden for a year and a half, has proved hard to justify. For many, the Orbán government's policy towards Ukraine was also jarring. Since Russia's invasion of Ukraine in 2022 the Hungarian government has constantly obstructed the European Union's policy in support of Ukraine[19] and continues to stand as an outlier in opposing Ukraine's integration into the European bloc.[20] The position, of straddling both sides of the conflict, was initially pitched as benefitting the Hungarian economy, given the country's energy dependencies. However, in 2025, after years of anti-Ukrainian sentiment in government messaging, the true Fidesz position came into view, with the launch of a nationwide propaganda campaign against Ukraine, which labelled Ukrainian president Volodymyr Zelenskyy as an enemy of the Hungarian people.[21]

Viktor Orbán's personal doctrine, of opening up in every direction, being everywhere, and thus constantly creating new opportunities, reflected his zealous ambitions to become a mover and shaker in world politics. In 2024, when Hungary held the presidency of the European Union, Orbán embarked on unilateral 'peace missions' to Kyiv and Moscow to meet Zelenskyy and Russian president Vladimir Putin; flew to Beijing for talks with

Chinese president Xi Jinping; and visited the then-presidential candidate, Donald Trump, on his private estate at Mar-a-Lago. It was an attempt to project influence and elevate Hungary's standing on the world stage.

However, this quickly unravelled when, upon reclaiming the presidency, Trump undertook his own unilateral approach to the conflict, and imposed considerable tariffs on European countries, including Hungary, as means of rebalancing US trade deficits. Far from being a close ally of the US president, Orbán, like other EU leaders, was pressured to stop buying Russian oil for good, with only limited concessions granted after high-level talks. The prime minister's direct engagement with global powers ultimately yielded no meaningful economic benefit for Hungary, and instead increased its indebtedness and alienation among European allies.

The Carrot and Stick

For Viktor Orbán and Fidesz, a defeat in the 2026 elections threatens to do more than just put the party in opposition. Orbán's greatest strength derived from the fact that others in the party, his supporters and even his rivals considered him unbeatable. An electoral defeat would destroy this belief, turn off the money taps and bring a reckoning for the party and its political and economic abuses. A vanquished Orbán could well be abandoned by his opportunistic supporters and companions-in-arms.

To mitigate this eventuality, the Fidesz government is increasingly trying to strengthen the repressive apparatus of the regime. In 2023, Orbán's governing coalition established the Sovereign Protection Office, which has the supposed purpose of protecting the independence of the Hungarian state against malicious intervention from abroad.[22] In reality, it has served as

EPILOGUE

a vehicle of intimidation, having unlimited authority to conduct investigations against independent Hungarian media, NGOs and individual citizens on the basis of its own suspicions. A few months later, Fidesz MPs submitted a bill to the National Assembly on the transparency of public life, which sought to blacklist foreign-funded media and NGOs, and place financial constraints upon their operations—effectively laying the groundwork for their shuttering.[23] However, this legislation, nicknamed the 'Ruination Bill', was ultimately postponed by Parliament due to the threat of civil unrest.

All the same, the amendment to the Assembly Act allowed arbitrary restrictions to be placed on the organization of demonstrations, and a fifteenth amendment to the Fundamental Law (the constitution) permitted citizenship to be revoked under certain circumstances. Together, these laws resulted in the outlawing of LGBTQ Pride parades in Hungary—a move Fidesz MPs championed and claimed was necessary for the physical, mental and moral development of children.

Previously, amendments to the Fundamental Law had rarely provoked opposition. However, by 2025, Hungarian society had become so discontented that, in June, a quarter of a million people took to the streets of Budapest to participate in an unofficial Pride parade. Everyday Hungarians were also increasingly willing to engage in acts of civil disobedience to protest the trajectory of the Orbán government.

For fifteen years, Orbán had successfully manipulated rules on the conduct of public figures in order to open up opportunities for his own political action and to intimidate, restrict and coerce others to adapt.[24] But, by 2025, he found himself running out of road. This has made the 2026 election campaign unusually volatile. Despite structural problems in the Hungarian economy, exacerbated by years of failed intervention, Orbán has again sought to game the election through a range of government handouts.

Cheap housing loans, salary increases for teachers, waivers on personal income tax for women with multiple children, increases in pensions, and 'arms money' for the law enforcement forces have all been introduced, targeted at groups of voters the government believes could swing its way come election day.[25] The government has also extended the state of emergency, originally introduced in response to the Covid-19 pandemic and maintained since the outbreak of the Ukraine War. This has allowed the ruling Fidesz-KDNP coalition to adopt hundreds of decrees, most of which fall outside of the broad definition of an 'emergency', and serve the government's political ends—including decrees restricting teachers' ability to protest, and permitting the Minister of Justice access to secret investigative material.

The digital campaign is also fierce. The rise of Magyar has prompted Fidesz to expend significant resources in the creation of its own activist 'Fight Club' and 'Digital Civic Circle'. In the summer of 2025, 'training camps' for these fighters were organized with no expense spared, and many thousands of Fidesz members responded to the party's 'call to arms'. Orbán himself addressed some of the problems Fidesz was facing in a pep talk to attending 'fighters', stating: 'Things aren't going well [...] Every day has to be won, in the digital arena as well. To do this, you need to devote at least half an hour every day to digital struggle [...] The core of the congregation of our opponents is the congregation of bad people [...] We must grind them down, weaken them, and on the day of the election bring in the fatal blow.'[26] And he had good reason to be concerned, since almost every independent opinion poll at the time suggested Fidesz was heading for defeat in 2026.

The digital attack space, in alignment with the wider campaign, centred—and continues to centre—on conspiracy theory. Activists online propagate content about war and violence, claiming that Hungary is being dragged into the conflict in Ukraine by Europe's liberal forces and by the Ukrainian president, Volodymyr Zelenskyy. Péter Magyar is portrayed as an evil puppet of Brussels and Ukraine, and a figure who will plunge Hungary into war and ruin. Government-allied news channels and billboards are flooded with anti-Ukrainian ads, with AI-created videos depicting an apocalyptic world of Ukrainian mobsters, empty bank accounts and Hungarian soldiers in coffins. Using 'war versus peace' rhetoric has worked for Fidesz previously, but given the sheer number of concerns that Hungarian citizens have, there is no guarantee such a campaign will keep the party in power in 2026.

Rebuilding Hungary

It is widely believed that authoritarian cycles follow the course of the sun, in that they rise, peak and decline.[27] In many cases, too, they crumble into dust upon defeat. However, in the case of Viktor Orbán, it is likely that some level of influence and legacy will live on, and inhibit the freedom of its successor administration. If it transpires that this is a government led by Péter Magyar, it seems almost inevitable that it will face immediate pressure in navigating public expectation, an unenviable economic backdrop, and an opposition Fidesz party that controls a huge shadow state and key levers of economic power.

Orbán will fight with all his might to survive. However, the time is up for his regime. Yet a renewed attempt at democratization, which might begin in Hungary after Viktor Orbán, must not only overcome a decade and a half of destruction and the fear that contaminates the thinking of the general public: it must also face the crisis of Western liberal democracy.

NOTES

PREFACE

1. János Széky, *'Day blindness – How Hungarians become like this'* (Hungarian), Pesti Kalligram, 2015.
2. Hungary emerged from the First World War as a defeated power as part of the Austro-Hungarian Empire and was forced to sign a humiliating peace treaty in the Grand Trianon palace at Versailles.

INTRODUCTION

1. Since 1989 the Hungarian electoral system has rested on two pillars: a 'winner-takes-all' majority system, and a proportional list system to complement it. In the 176 single-member constituencies there were two rounds of voting, and the candidate who got the most votes in the second round won the parliamentary mandate. A further 152 seats in Parliament were awarded on the basis of the votes given to the county lists, and fifty-eight seats were awarded from the so-called compensational list deriving from the votes cast for losing candidates in the single-member constituencies. In this way, a National Assembly of 386 MPs was formed.
2. Viktor Orbán's speech in Vörösmarty Square on 25 April 2010, Hungarian Prime Minister's Office, April 2010, https://2010-2014.kormany.hu/hu/miniszterelnokseg/miniszterelnok/beszedek-

publikaciok-interjuk/orban-viktor-beszede-a-vorosmarty-teren-2010-aprilis-25 (last accessed 7 June 2022).
3. Speech by Viktor Orbán at the Bálványos (Baile Tusnad) Summer School on 21 July 2007, Index, 21 July 2007, https://index.hu/belfold/ovibal0721/ (last accessed 7 June 2022).
4. Speech by Viktor Orbán in the Buda Castle District, 8 May 2002, http://archiv.fidesz.hu/index.php?CikkID=1922 (last accessed 7 June 2022).
5. MSZP won 43.21% of the votes; Fidesz 42.03%.
6. Prime Minister Ferenc Gyurcsány's speech on 26 May 2006 at a private session of the MSZP (Hungarian Socialist Party) parliamentary group, http://nol.hu/archivum/archiv-417593-228304 (last accessed 7 June 2022).
7. József Debreczeni, 'The autumn of 2006' (Hungarian), Budapest, DEHU, 2012.
8. 'The Programme of National Cooperation' (Hungarian), National Assembly, 22 May 2010, https://www.parlament.hu/irom39/00047/00047_e.pdf (last accessed 7 June 2022).
9. 'I want to be a man of the people' (Hungarian), Népszabadság, 25 June 2010.
10. 'Tölgyessy found two hundred problematic points in the Fundamental Law' (Hungarian), Origo, 18 April 2011, https://www.origo.hu/itthon/20110418-tolgyessy-peter-eloadasa-az-uj-alaptorvenyrol.html (last accessed 7 June 2022).
11. The new cardinal laws referred to fiscal and public education policy, introduced changes to the tax and pension systems, and stipulated that Hungary's currency would be the forint.
12. 'Orbán says the Fundamental Law is as solid as granite' (Hungarian), Mandiner, 3 January 2012, https://mandiner.hu/cikk/20120102_orban_granitszilardsagu_az_alaptorveny (last accessed 7 June 2022).
13. Andrew Arató, Gábor Halmai and János Kis, eds., 'Opinion on the Fundamental Law of Hungary', Amicus Brief to the Venice Commission, June 2011, http://lapa.princeton.edu/hosteddocs/amicus-to-vc-english-final.pdf; Gábor Attila Tóth, ed., *Constitution for a Disunited Nation: On Hungary's 2011 Fundamental Law*, Budapest, Central European University Press, 2012.

14. András Jakab, 'Informal institutional elements as both preconditions and consequences of effective formal legal rules: The failure of constitutional institution building in Hungary', *American Journal of Comparative Law*, vol. 68, 2020, pp. 760–800.
15. Viktor Orbán's speech on 15 March 2011, Prime Minister's Office, 15 March 2011, https://2010-2014.kormany.hu/hu/miniszterelnokseg/miniszterelnok/beszedek-publikaciok-interjuk/1848-es-2010-is-megujulast-hozott (last accessed 7 June 2022).
16. Sándor Petőfi, 'The whole sea has revolted' (transl. George Szirtes), 27 March 1848.
17. Ákos Szilágyi, 'The populist: The morphology of the political fairy tale' (Hungarian), Budapest, Irodalom, 2010.
18. Cas Mudde and Cristobal Rovira Kaltwasser, *Populism: A Very Short Introduction*, Oxford University Press, 2017.
19. Viktor Orbán's ceremonial speech on 15 March 2012, https://2010-2014.kormany.hu/hu/miniszterelnokseg/miniszterelnok/beszedek-publikaciok-interjuk/orban-viktor-miniszterelnok-unnepi-beszede-a-kossuth-lajos-teren (last accessed 7 June 2022).
20. Márton Békés, 'We ourselves' (Hungarian), *Kommentár*, vol. 1, 2020.
21. An expression from Gábor G. Fodor, 'I defend the truths of the system: Interview with Gábor G. Fodor' (Hungarian), *Magyar Narancs*, 8 March 2015.
22. This list showed the situation in 2010–18.
23. Péter Krekó and Zsolt Enyedi, 'Orbán's laboratory of illiberalism', *Journal of Democracy*, vol. 29, no. 3, July 2018.
24. Viktor Orbán's speech in Kossuth Square on 29 May 2010, https://2010-2014.kormany.hu/hu/miniszterelnokseg/miniszterelnok/beszedek-publikaciok-interjuk/orban-viktor-beszede-a-kossuth-teren-2010-majus-29 (last accessed 7 June 2022).
25. Balázs Böcskei, 'Orbán the creative rule' (Hungarian), *Népszava*, 15 May 2018.

1. WITHOUT ORBÁN, THERE'S NOTHING

1. Gábor G. Fodor, *The Orbán rule* (Hungarian), Budapest, Közép-és kelet Európai Történelem és Társadalom Kutatásáért Public Foundation, 2021, p. 26.

2. Online book launch at the XXI Század Intézet (Twenty-First Century Institute), 5 May 2021.
3. András Körösényi, Gábor Illés and Attila Gyulai, *The Orbán regime: The theory and practice of plebiscite leader democracy* (Hungarian), Budapest, Osiris Press, 2021, p. 139.
4. His father, Győző Orbán, had managed to become an agricultural engineer, and his mother is a speech therapist.
5. 'What will you be when you grow up?' (Hungarian), Interview with Viktor Orbán, 1989, https://film.indavideo.hu/video/f_mi_leszel_ ha_nagy_leszel (last accessed 7 June 2022).
6. Ibid.
7. Ibid.
8. Ákos Róna-Tas, 'Fidesz: Generations and parties' (Hungarian), in András Bozóki, ed., *Carte blanche: Fidesz in Hungarian politics* (Hungarian), Budapest, Fidesz Press, 1992, pp. 608–10.
9. István Hegedűs, *Brutal party strife: Parties and changes; Fidesz's political shift* (Hungarian), PhD thesis, Corvinus University, Budapest, 2001, http://phd.lib.uni-corvinus.hu/80/1/hegedus_istvan.pdf (last accessed 7 June 2022).
10. 'Fidesz, 1988 statement of the political programme' (Hungarian), in Bozóki, *Carte blanche*, pp. 110–13.
11. György Petőcz, ed., *This was just the orange* (Hungarian), Budapest, Irodalom Publishers, 2001, p. 121.
12. András Bozóki, *Political pluralism in Hungary* (Hungarian), Budapest, Osiris Press, 2003, p. 312.
13. In the parliamentary group of twenty-two, besides me there was one other woman: Klára Ungár, an economist.
14. Speech by Viktor Orbán in Mosonmagyaróvár, 26 October 1990, in László Kéri, *Viktor Orbán* (Hungarian) Budapest, Századvég Kiadó, 1994, p. 156.
15. 'Fidesz's economic philosophy', in Bozóki, *Carte blanche*, p. 608.
16. Tibor Závecz, 'How the parties were judged between the two elections' (Hungarian), in Rudolf Andorka, Tamás Kolosi and György Vukovich, eds., *Social report 1994* (Hungarian), Budapest, Tárki, 1994, pp. 447–59.

17. 'Viktor Orbán on the need for a liberal government', 1992, YouTube, https://www.youtube.com/watch?v=ARxL56UnIF4 (last accessed 7 June 2022).
18. 'Interview with László Kövér' (Hungarian), *Magyar Narancs*, 15 June 1994.
19. Interview with István Hegedűs, in Petőcz, *This was just the orange* (Hungarian), p. 275.
20. 'The country doesn't necessarily know what's good for it, says Orbán' (Hungarian), *Magyar Narancs*, 29 November 2019, https://magyarnarancs.hu/narancs30/hat-ezt-elhokiztuk-124927 (last accessed 7 June 2022).
21. 'Interview with László Kövér' (Hungarian), *Magyar Narancs*, 15 June 1994.
22. Quotations from Viktor Orbán taken from Pál Dániel Rényi, *Force to win* (Hungarian), Budapest, Magyar Jeti, 2021, p. 136.
23. Speech by Viktor Orbán on 12 June 1997 on Civic Opposition Day, in Viktor Orbán, *Speeches, writings, interviews 1986–2006* (Hungarian), Budapest, Heti Válasz Press, 2006.
24. József Debreczeni, *Portrait* (Hungarian), Budapest, Noran Libro Publishers, 2009, p. 388.
25. In Fidesz's usage, the word *polgári* (here translated as 'civic') is somewhat enigmatic; this is its very purpose. To some people, it means middle-class and respectable, to others it means right-wing, to yet others it means anti-communist. The expression also has connotations of communitarianism.
26. Gyula Tellér, 'The elite does not disappear ...' (Hungarian), *Beszélő*, vol. 3, no. 5, 1991.
27. Speech by Viktor Orbán on 12 June 1997 on Civic Opposition Day, in Viktor Orbán, *Speeches, writings, interviews 1986–2006* (Hungarian), Budapest, Heti Válasz Press, 2006.
28. 'Gábor G. Fodor's atom bomb, Fidesz's Balatonőszöd speech' (Hungarian), *Magyar Narancs*, 21 February 2015.
29. Peter Mair, *Ruling the Void: The Hollowing of Western Democracy*, London, Verso, 2013.
30. Pál Dániel Rényi, *Force to win*, (Hungarian), 444 Press, 2021, p. 34.
31. G. Fodor, *The Orbán rule*.

32. 'I think it will be like this: Interview with Viktor Orbán' (Hungarian), *Magyar Narancs*, 19 February 1998.
33. Debreczeni, *Portrait*, p. 141.
34. '"Now they are dogmatic too": Philosopher György Bence on Fidesz then and now' (Hungarian), *Magyar Narancs*, 20 March 2003.
35. Debreczeni, *Portrait*, p. 135.
36. Ildikó Szabó, 'The conceptual construction of the nation in Fidesz's discourse between 1998 and 2006' (Hungarian), *Politikatudományi Szemle*, vol. 16, no. 3, 2019, p. 131.
37. Speech by Viktor Orbán on 12 June 1997 on Civic Opposition Day, in Viktor Orbán, *Speeches, writings, interviews 1986–2006* (Hungarian), Budapest, Heti Válasz Press, 2006.
38. 'Clean-up in Fidesz: Almost everyone goes at every level' (Hungarian), *Magyar Narancs*, 25 March 2004.
39. Speech by Viktor Orbán in the Buda Castle District, 8 May 2002, in Orbán, *Speeches, writings, interviews 1986–2006*.
40. Béla Greskovits, 'Rebuilding the Hungarian right through civil organization and contention: The civic circles movement', *EUI Working Papers*, Robert Schuman Centre for Advanced Studies, RSCAS 2017/37.
41. Ibid.
42. Speech by Viktor Orbán at the 2003 Fidesz congress, in Orbán, *Speeches, writings, interviews 1986–2006*.
43. Ibid.
44. 'The transformation of Fidesz: The end of a chapter' (Hungarian), *Magyar Narancs*, 1 May 2003.
45. Ibid.
46. 'Clean-up in Fidesz: Almost everyone goes at every level' (Hungarian), *Magyar Narancs*, 25 March 2004.
47. Zsolt Enyedi, 'The role of agency in cleavage formation', *European Journal of Political Research*, 27 July 2005.
48. Debreczeni, *Portrait*, p. 203.
49. 'Fidesz's road to victory: From the cellar to the attic' (Hungarian), *Magyar Narancs*, 11 June 2009.
50. András Pethő, 'When Viktor Orbán floundered: The story of Fidesz's last crisis, Part 1' (Hungarian), Origo, 31 March 2010, https://www.

origo.hu/itthon/valasztas2010/kampanynaplo/20100331-a-fidesz-2006os-valasztasi-veresege-hattertortenet.html (last accessed 7 June 2022).
51. Ibid.
52. 'Battle within Fidesz: A new message' (Hungarian), *Magyar Narancs*, 25 January 2007.
53. Speech by Viktor Orbán at the Bálványos (Baile Tusnad) Summer School on 21 July 2006, in Orbán, *Speeches, writings, interviews 1986–2006*.
54. Pethő, 'When Viktor Orbán floundered: The story of Fidesz's last crisis, Part 1'.
55. Speech by Viktor Orbán in the Hungarian National Assembly on 6 October 2006, in Orbán, *Speeches, writings, interviews 1986–2006*.
56. 'The "intellectual power of the right wing" arrives in Kötcse—gallery' (Hungarian), HVG, 7 September 2019, https://hvg.hu/itthon/20190907_Igy_erkezett_meg_Kotcsere_a_jobboldal_teljes_szellemi_ereje (last accessed 7 June 2022).
57. 'Retaining the Hungarian quality of life' (Hungarian), Prime Minister's webpage, 17 February 2010, http://2010-2015.miniszterelnok.hu/cikk/megorizni_a_letezes_magyar_minoseget (last accessed 7 June 2022).
58. András Körösényi, Gábor Illés and Attila Gyulai, *The Orbán Regime: Plebiscitary Leader Democracy in the Making*, London, Routledge, 2020, p. 57.
59. Pethő, 'When Viktor Orbán floundered: The story of Fidesz's last crisis, Part 1'.
60. Körösényi et al., *The Orbán Regime*, p. 153.
61. 'János Lázár: Viktor Orbán takes and deals out blows, but if folk treat him properly, he becomes more compliant' (Hungarian), 24.hu, 26 January 2021, https://24.hu/belfold/2021/01/26/lazar-janos-godollo-fidesz-hodmezovasarhely-agrarium-nagyinterju/ (last accessed 7 June 2022).

2. 'MY WORLDVIEW IS HUNGARIAN'

1. 'Campus in Hungary is flagship of Orbán's bid to create a conservative elite', *New York Times*, 28 June 2021.

2. 'Tucker: Why can't we have this in America?', YouTube, https://www.youtube.com/watch?v=VXujFNBV63I (last accessed 7 June 2022).
3. Fox News, 'Hungarian prime minister hits back at Biden calling him a "thug" on "Tucker"', YouTube, https://www.youtube.com/watch?v=s01ZL5TnBNY (last accessed 7 June 2022).
4. 'Viktor Orbán is fighting for democracy' (Hungarian), Mandiner, https://mandiner.hu/cikk/20210804_orban_viktor_a_demokraciaert_harcol_tucker_carlson_a_mandinernek?utm_source=mandiner&utm_medium=link&utm_campaign=mandiner_202109 (last accessed 7 June 2022).
5. Fox News, 'Hungarian prime minister hits back at Biden calling him a "thug" on "Tucker"'.
6. 'Tucker: The mainstream media's job is to defend the ruling class', Fox News, 3 August 2021, https://video.foxnews.com/v/6266295237001?playlist_id=5198073478001#sp=show-clips (last accessed 7 June 2022).
7. István Csurka, 'Thoughts on the two years since the regime change and the MDF new programme' (Hungarian), *Magyar Fórum*, 20 August 1992. The Allied Control Commissions were set up by the victors after the Second World War to guarantee a ceasefire in the occupied countries and to check the work of the governments. As its first chairman, the Hungarian ACC had the Soviet Marshal Kliment Voroshilov, who played a key role in organizing the transfer of power to the communists.
8. Speech by László Kövér in the Hungarian National Assembly, 8 August 1992, https://www.parlament.hu/naplo34/219/2190012.html (last accessed 7 June 2022).
9. Fidesz political programme statement, 1988, in András Bozóki, ed., *Carte blanche: Fidesz in Hungarian politics* (Hungarian), Budapest, Fidesz Press, 1992, p. 110.
10. György Csepeli and Antal Örkény, 'The changing face of Hungarian nationalism' (Hungarian), in Rudolf Andorka, Tamás Kolosi and György Vukovich, eds., *Tárki social report* (Hungarian), Budapest, Tárki, 1996, pp. 272–95.
11. Viktor Orbán, Kossuth Rádió, *Vasárnapi újság* radio programme, 27 January 2002.

NOTES

12. 'Viktor Orbán: You can't restrict dreams' (Hungarian), Index, 20 August 2000, https://index.hu/belfold/alomhatar/ (last accessed 7 June 2022).
13. Lívia Blázsovics and Zoltán Pásztor, 'There will not be a wave of guest workers' (Hungarian), Magyar Nemzet, 29 December 2001.
14. Viktor Orbán's speech at the College for Physical Education, 9 April 2002, Origo, 10 April 2002, https://www.origo.hu/itthon/20020410orban.html (last accessed 7 June 2022).
15. 'Ribbon until the elections!' (Hungarian), Magyar Nemzet, 13 March 2002.
16. Ferenc Gyurcsány, Népszava, 30 November 2004.
17. Interview with Nándor Bárdi, historian, researcher at the Institute for Minority Studies, Centre for Social Sciences, Hungarian Academy of Sciences, 30 April 2020.
18. Viktor Orbán, 7 November 2004, Hír TV.
19. Gyula Tellér, 'The elite does not disappear...' (Hungarian), Beszélő, vol. 3, no. 5, 1991.
20. Mátyás Szűrös and Imre Pozsgay had been part of the top leadership of the MSZMP; János Martonyi, Imre Boros and Sándor Pintér worked in the upper echelons of the socialist apparatus of state; Imre Boros, state secretary László Tasnádi and mayor Károly Szita were secret service officers and informers; Béla Gyuricza was a military officer and Csaba Sümeghy was a businessman. They all became a part of the Fidesz political elite.
21. András Lánczi, Conservative manifesto (Hungarian), Budapest, Attraktor Press, 2002. After the manifesto was published, a prolonged debate started between new conservative thinkers, and many books and treatises were published.
22. László Sturm and András Lánczi, 'Conservative manifesto' (Hungarian), Szépirodalmi figyelő, vol. 2, no. 4, 2003, p. 102.
23. Tibor Mándi, 'Political thinking' (Hungarian), in András Körösényi, ed., Political system after 25 years (Hungarian), Budapest, Osiris Press, 2015, p. 25.
24. Zoltán Balázs, 'Political theory in Hungary after the regime change', International Political Anthropology, vol. 1, 2014.
25. Péter Techet, 'Carl Schmitt and National Socialism' (Hungarian), Politikatudományi Szemle, vol. 1, 2012.

26. Carl Schmitt, *A politika fogalma*, Budapest, Osiris, Pallas Stúdió and Attraktor Press, 2002 (originally published in 1932 as *Der Begriff des Politischen*).
27. Ákos Szilágyi, *The blues and the greens: Civil cold war in Hungary* (Hungarian), Budapest, Palatinus, 2010.
28. Rod Dreher, *Crunchy Cons: The New Conservative Counterculture and Its Return to Roots*, New York, Three Rivers Press, 2006.
29. Such institutions were Századvég, the XXI Század Intézet, the weekly magazine *Demokrata* (from 2006), the journals *Kommentár* and *Nemzeti Érdek*, and (from 2009) the online portals Mandiner and 888.
30. Anne Applebaum, *Twilight of Democracy*, New York, Doubleday, 2020.
31. Ivan Krastev, 'The strange death of the liberal consensus', *Journal of Democracy*, vol. 4, 2007.
32. Speech by Viktor Orbán at the Bálványos (Baile Tusnad) Summer School on 26 July 2014.
33. Ibid.
34. Fareed Zakaria, 'The rise of illiberal democracy', *Foreign Affairs*, November/December 1997.
35. Partick J. Deneen, *Why Liberalism Failed*, New Haven, Yale University Press, 2018.
36. Roger Scruton, *The Meaning of Conservatism*, London, Palgrave, 1980.
37. 'Orbán meets conservative US political scientist Deneen', *Hungary Today*, 15 November 2019, https://hungarytoday.hu/orban-meets-conservative-us-political-scientist-deneen/ (last accessed 26 March 2022).
38. 'Orbán lauds Sir Roger Scruton, "loyal friend of freedom-loving Hungarians"', *Hungary Today*, 4 December 2019, https://hungarytoday.hu/orban-lauds-sir-roger-scruton-loyal-friend-of-freedom-loving-hungarians/ (last accessed 7 June 2022).
39. 'PM Viktor Orbán: Political correctness no longer offers protection', *Hungary Today*, 12 January 2015, https://hungarytoday.hu/pm-viktor-orban-political-correctness-longer-offers-protection-24888/ (last accessed 7 June 2022).

40. 'The West is complacent; the East has awakened: Mária Schmidt and Imre Kozma on migration' (Hungarian), Mandiner, 28 November 2015, https://mandiner.hu/cikk/20151128_a_nyugat_ontelt_a_kelet_felebredt_schmidt_maria_kozma_imre_migracio (last accessed 7 June 2022).
41. 'Security policy aspects of migration in Sweden' (Hungarian), Institute of Migration Research, 1 July 2015, https://www.migraciokutato.hu/press/a-svedorszagi-bevandorlas-biztonsagpolitikai-vetuletei/ (last accessed 7 June 2022).
42. 'Migration and terror threat' (Hungarian), Institute of Migration Research, 2 October 2015, https://www.migraciokutato.hu/press/migracio-es-terrorveszely-helyzet-tenyezok-kilatasok/ (last accessed 7 June 2022).
43. *Limen*, journal of the Hungarian Institute of Migration Research: https://www.migraciokutato.hu/wp-content/uploads/2020/06/Limen-online_v_20200608_mki_hl.pdf (last accessed 7 June 2022).
44. 'The left wing does not like Hungarians because they are Hungarian' (Hungarian), Mandiner, 27 July 2015, http://man-diner.hu/cikk/20150727_orban_viktor_a_baloldal_azert_nem_szereti_a_magyarokat_mert_magyarok (last accessed 7 June 2022).
45. Csurka István, 'Memento' (Hungarian), *Magyar Fórum*, 8 February 1988.
46. Attila Juhász, Csaba Molnár and Edit Zgut, 'Refugees and migration in Hungary' (Hungarian), Heinrich Böll Foundation, 2017.
47. These parties included Norway's Progress Party, the United Kingdom Independence Party, France's National Front, the Danish People's Party, Hungary's Jobbik, the Freedom Party of Austria, and the Swiss People's Party. See http://www.results-elections2014.eu/en/election-results-2014.html; and Norwegian Social Science Data Services (NSD), http://www.nsd.uib.no/european_election_database/ (last accessed on 8 July 2014).
48. 'From liberal hero to right-wing icon, Orbán's appeal trumps rivals', Reuters, 8 April 2018, https://www.reuters.com/article/us-hungary-election-orban-idUSKBN1HF0YO (last accessed 7 June 2022).
49. Viktor Orbán interview in *Der Stern*, 'What would happen if one of your children came out as homosexual, Mr Orbán?' (German), *Der*

Stern, 4 February 2021, https://www.stern.de/p/plus/politik/viktor-orbán-im-interview-mit-dem-stern-30360300.html (last accessed 7 June 2022).

50. A *turul* bird is a mythical bird resembling an eagle, a falcon or a griffin, and a figure in pre-Christian ancient Hungarian legends. It is a characteristic figure of Eurasian shamanism and was believed to have protective powers. The *turul* and similar birds became symbols of belligerence during the nineteenth century.

51. After 1920 there was a paramilitary anti-Semitic group of university students called Turul. From the mid-1930s the *turul* became part of the fascist Arrow Cross Party's shield, and thus use of the symbol provokes harsh controversy to this day.

52. Speech by Viktor Orbán at the Bálványos (Baile Tusnad) Summer School, 28 July 2018, https://miniszterelnok.hu/prime-minister-viktor-orbans-speech-at-the-29th-balvanyos-summer-open-university-and-student-camp/.

53. Speech by József Antall, 'The legacy of national liberalism' (Hungarian), https://antalljozsef25.hu/politikai-beszedek/politikai-beszedek-interjuk/156-a-nemzeti-liberalizmus-oroksege (last accessed 7 June 2022).

54. Speech by Viktor Orbán at the Bálványos (Baile Tusnad) Summer School on 28 July 2018.

55. 'Are religious people happier, healthier? Our new global study explores this question', Pew Research, 31 January 2019, https://www.pewresearch.org/fact-tank/2019/01/31/are-religious-people-happier-healthier-our-new-global-study-explores-this-question/ (last accessed 7 June 2022).

56. According to the Pew Research Center (2018), 56% of the Hungarian population is Catholic, 20% Protestant, 3% belongs to another denomination, and 21% says they are not religious. Nuancing the picture somewhat, only 56% of the population said they believe in God, and only 14% claimed that religion plays an important part in their lives. See https://www.pewforum.org/2018/10/29/eastern-and-western-europeans-differ-on-importance-of-religion-views-of-minorities-and-key-social-issues/ (last accessed 7 June 2022).

57. Speech by Viktor Orbán before the National Assembly, Budapest, on 16 November 2015.
58. Viktor Orbán's interview with the German magazine *Bild*, 25 February 2016.
59. Zsolt Bayer, 'The Pope's mind' (Hungarian), Bádog, https://badog.blogstar.hu/2016/08/01/a-papa-esze/29105/ (last accessed 7 June 2022).
60. Tamás Fabiny (Evangelical Lutheran bishop) and Miklós Beer (Catholic bishop) in 2017. 'We support refugees. We call on you to join us!'—UNHCR advertisement.
61. 'I'm concerned about this country's moral decay: Tamás Fabiny on the bishops' video' (Hungarian), https://kotoszo.blog.hu/2017/07/07/fabiny_tamas_puspok (last accessed 7 June 2022).
62. Speech by Viktor Orbán at the Bálványos (Baile Tusnad) Summer School on 28 July 2018.
63. 'Together we will manage' (Hungarian), *Magyar Nemzet*, 9 August 2002, https://magyarnemzet.hu/belfold/2020/09/egyutt-ujra-sikerulni-fog (last accessed 7 June 2022).
64. 'Interview with Cardinal Péter Erdő about fasting, politics, and Christian Europe' (Hungarian), Válasz Online, 19 April 2019, https://www.valaszonline.hu/2019/04/19/erdo-peter-kereszteny-europa-nagypentek-interju/ (last accessed 7 June 2022).
65. 'Istanbul Convention: Action against violence against women and domestic violence', Council of Europe, https://www.coe.int/en/web/istanbul-convention/home? (last accessed 7 June 2022).
66. László Kövér's speech at the Fidesz congress on 13 December 2015, https://www.youtube.com/watch?v=NHWG-6QWkX4 (last accessed 7 June 2022).
67. Ibid.
68. Katalin Novák, 'How can a woman be successful?' (Hungarian), Axióma, https://www.youtube.com/watch?v=IANg9226Aro (last accessed 7 June 2022).
69. Inger Skjelsbæk, Eviane Leidig, Iris Beau Segers and Cathrine Thorleifsson, 'What role does gender play in the far right?', Center for Research on Extremism, University of Oslo, 7 September 2020, https://www.sv.uio.no/c-rex/english/groups/compendium/what-

role-does-gender-play-in-the-far-right.html#_ftn5 (last accessed 7 June 2022).
70. 'Poland and Hungary battle to eradicate "gender" in EU policies', EU Observer, 16 December 2020, https://euobserver.com/political/150395 (last accessed 7 June 2022).
71. Eszter Kováts, *Gender frenzies in Germany and Hungary* (Hungarian), Budapest, Napvilág Kiadó, forthcoming 2022.
72. For example, a so-called research paper of the Centre for Fundamental Rights, 'Two-third of Hungarians reject "gender theory"', Centre for Fundamental Rights, 20 April 2021, https://alapjogokert.hu/2021/04/20/a-magyarok-ketharmada-elutasitja-a-genderelmeletet/ (last accessed 7 June 2022).
73. 'Németh demonizes the convention protecting women' (Hungarian), Hír TV, 21 May 2017, https://hirtv.hu/ahirtvhirei_adattar/demonizalja-a-noket-vedo-egyezmenyt-nemeth-szilard-1395549 (last accessed 7 June 2022).
74. 'Hungary's pivotal role in the global network against sexual and reproductive rights', Institute for Strategic Dialogue, 17 December 2021.
75. Viktor Orbán's speech at the Second Budapest Demographic Forum on 25 May 2017.
76. Viktor Orbán's speech at the Budapest Demographic Summit on 23 September 2021.
77. Weronika Grzebalska, Eszter Kováts and Andrea Pető, 'Gender as symbolic glue: How gender became an umbrella term for the rejection of the (neo)liberal order', ResearchGate, https://www.researchgate.net/publication/350500293_Gender_as_symbolic_glue_how_'gender'_became_an_umbrella_term_for_the_rejection_of_the_neoliberal_order_In_Political_Critique_13012017 (last accessed 7 June 2022).
78. Interview with Eszter Kováts on gender issues, *Ellensúly*, vol. 3, 2021, pp. 3–17.
79. 'EU founding values: Commission starts legal action against Hungary and Poland for violations of fundamental rights of LGBTIQ people', European Commission, press release, 15 July 2021, https://ec.europa.eu/commission/presscorner/detail/en/ip_21_3668 (last accessed 7 June 2022).

80. '2017 will be a year of rebellion' (Hungarian), prime minister's webpage, https://miniszterelnok.hu/2017-a-lazadas-eve-lesz/ (last accessed 26 March 2022).
81. Viktor Orbán's speech on the anniversary of the 1848–9 revolution and War of Independence on 15 March 2016, in Orbán, *Speeches, writings, interviews 1986–2006*.
82. Project Europe, Századvég Foundation, https://szazadveg.hu/en/project-europe (last accessed 7 June 2022).
83. Milo Yiannopoulos, 'Dangers and chances in the twenty-first century' (Hungarian, video in English), https://www.youtube.com/watch?v=MfFj3Qy7Hvo&t=665s (last accessed 7 June 2022).
84. 'PM Orbán receives speakers from V4 conference "The Future of Europe" in Parliament', About Hungary, 25 May 2018, https://abouthungary.hu/prime-minister/pm-orban-receives-speakers-from-v4-conference-the-future-of-europe-in-parliament (last accessed 7 June 2022).
85. 'Ex-Trump strategist Bannon says to work with Hungary PM Orbán: media', Reuters, 17 November 2018, https://www.reuters.com/article/us-hungary-orban-bannon-idUSKCN1NM07X (last accessed 7 June 2022).
86. Karl Rove, https://www.rove.com/ (last accessed 26 March 2022).
87. Viktor Orbán, 'Preface', in Viktor Orbán, *20 years, speeches, writings, interviews* (Hungarian), Budapest, Heti Válasz Press, 2006.

3. 'ALONE WE WOULD FAIL, BUT TOGETHER WE WILL WIN!'

1. Gordon Bajnai's speech on 23 October 2012, Mandiner, 24 October 2012, https://mandiner.hu/cikk/20121024_bajnai_gordon_egyutt_2014_a_2012_oktober_23_an_elmondott_beszed (last accessed 7 June 2022).
2. Bajnai's own association Homeland and Progress made an alliance with the civil groups Milla and Szolidaritás.
3. Csaba Tóth and Gábor Török, 'The new party system' (Hungarian), in Tamás Kolosi and István György Tóth, eds., *Social report 2014* (Hungarian), Budapest, Tárki, 2014, p. 516.

4. 'Bajnai's party would be the strongest opposition' (Hungarian), Index, 7 November 2012, https://index.hu/belfold/2012/11/07/bajnaiek_lennenek_a_legerosebb_ellenzeki_part/ (last accessed 7 June 2022).
5. 'Never has Viktor Orbán been so unpopular' (Hungarian), Origo 28 May 2012, https://www.origo.hu/itthon/20120528-partok-es-politikusok-nepszerusege-felidoben.html (last accessed 7 June 2022).
6. Viktor Orbán called Fidesz, which was in the middle of the political scene as the new status quo formed after 2006, the 'central field of force'.
7. National Election Office: https://static.valasztas.hu/dyn/pv10/outroot/vdin1/hu/l403.htm, (last accessed 7 June 2022)
8. 'Orbán is the most popular politician, Gyurcsány is bottom of the list' (Hungarian), HVG, 17 May 2011, https://hvg.hu/itthon/20110517_orban_nepszeru_politikus_gyurcsany_vege (last accessed 7 June 2022).
9. 'Ipsos: Bajnai & co. can mobilize 300 thousand undecided voters' (Hungarian), HVG, 15 November 2011, https://hvg.hu/itthon/20121115_Ipsos_Bajnaiek_300_ezer_bizonytalan_szava (last accessed 7 June 2022).
10. 'Bajnai's party would be the strongest opposition' (Hungarian), Index, 7 November 2012, https://index.hu/belfold/2012/11/07/bajnaiek_lennenek_a_legerosebb_ellenzeki_part/ (last accessed 7 June 2022).
11. 'Bajnai can break the MSZP's resistance by persuading the members' (Hungarian), HVG, 15 November 2012, https://hvg.hu/itthon/20121115_Bajnai_Mesterhazy_MSZP (last accessed 7 June 2022).
12. 'Benedek Jávor's resignation' (Hungarian), HVG, 18 November 2012, https://hvg.hu/itthon/20121118_javor_benedek_lemondasa_video (last accessed 7 June 2022).
13. This included eight MPs (half of the parliamentary group), and a quarter of the membership.
14. 'Post-congress: "Orbán can't be shifted from the centre". Will Bajnai & co. be alone?' (Hungarian), HVG, 18 November 2012, https://hvg.hu/itthon/20121118_Orban_LMP_Bajnai_MSZP (last accessed 7 June 2022).

15. This expression was coined by András Keszthelyi, 'A union with a sneer' (Hungarian), *Magyar Narancs*, 30 December 2017.
16. Socialist politicians György Hunvald and Gyula Molnár were facing legal proceedings at that time on charges of corruption.
17. The core of my team consisted of campaign director Attila Solti, Márton Lennert, Tibor Zsitva and Péter Hunya.
18. According to Medián Polling and Market Research Institute, on 25 March the government party had support from 36% of the general public, and 47% of those who would 'certainly' vote.
19. Viktor Szigetvári, Péter Juhász, Levente Pápa and I.
20. Speech by Viktor Orbán on 28 February 2008 in Rákosmente, 'In 2008 Orbán had very different ideas about the Russians' (Hungarian), Origo, 12 February 2014, https://www.origo.hu/itthon/20140212-orban-2008-ban-meg-egeszen-mast-gondolt-az-oroszokrol.html (last accessed 7 June 2022).
21. Speech by Zsuzsanna Szelényi in the Hungarian National Assembly on 14 September 2014, Arcanum, 26 September 2014, www.arcanum.com.
22. 'Együtt: The government is pro-family in words only' (Hungarian), Mandiner, 5 November 2015, https://mandiner.hu/cikk/20151105_egyutt_csak_szavakban_csaladbarat_a_kormany (last accessed 7 June 2022).
23. Bálint Magyar, *Post-Communist Mafia State: The Case of Hungary*, CEU Press, 2016.
24. 'Downtown cronyism: After the Rogán scandal the Fidesz district can sell its real eastate even faster' (Hungarian), *Magyar Narancs*, 3 June 2019, https://magyarnarancs.hu/belpol/szemrebbenes-nelkul-119186 (last accessed 26 March 2022).
25. Magyar, *Post-Communist Mafia State*.
26. Steven Levitsky and Lucan A. Way, *Competitive Authoritariansim: Hybrid Regimes after the Cold War*, Cambridge University Press, 2010.
27. Fidesz eventually amended the act on conserving the appearance of settlements, saying that discounts cannot be given to advertisers whose annual state subsidies amount to half of their total subsidies.

This ruled out discounts for political parties, party foundations, and any organization connected with politics.

28. 'Government on the 'slave labour' law: Those who want to earn more should work more' (Hungarian), HVG, 28 November 2018, https://hvg.hu/itthon/20181128_A_kormany_a_rabszolgatorvenyrol_aki_tobbet_akar_keresni_dolgozzon_tobbet (last accessed 7 June 2022).
29. Karácsony won 50.86% of the votes, while his Fidesz-supported rival István Tarlós got 44%. In Budapest's twenty-three districts, opposition candidates won fourteen mayoral seats, Fidesz candidates seven, and two were won by independent mayors.
30. 'Fidesz's communication strategy in the 2018 municipal elections: Brief analysis' (Hungarian), Átlátszó, 13 November 2019, https://mertek.atlatszo.hu/a-fidesz-kommunikacios-strategiaja-a-2019-es-onkormanyzati-valasztasokon-gyorselemzes (last accessed 7 June 2022).
31. 'Second round of opposition primaries' (Hungarian), Átlátszó, n.d., https://atlo.team/ellenzekielovalasztas/ (last accessed 7 June 2022).
32. 'János Lázár "2022 will see the crudest campaign of the last 30 years"' (Hungarian), HVG, 20 December 2019, https://hvg.hu/itthon/20191220_Lazar_Janos_2022ben_az_elmult_30_ev_legdurvabb_kampanya_jon (last accessed 7 June 2022).

4. THE ILLUSION OF DEMOCRACY

1. 'A Fidesz lead, chances for the opposition' (Hungarian), Kozvelemeny kutatok, 13 February 2014, https://kozvelemenykutatok.hu/fidesz-vezetes-ellenzeki-eselyek-ipsos/ (last accessed 7 June 2022).
2. According to calculations by Transparency International, Jobbik spent 1.2 billion HUF, and the left-wing parties nearly 1.6 billion HUF. 'Elections in 2014–15' (Hungarian), Transparency International Hungary, June 2015, https://transparency.hu/kozszektor/valasztasok-part-es-kampanyfinanszirozas/2014-2015-evi-orszaggyulesi-onkormanyzati-es-idokozi-valasztasok-kampankoltesei/ (last accessed 7 June 2022).
3. In Fidesz's new election system the stable left-wing constituencies became more populous than others and isolated in cities; there were

more right-leaning constituencies formed, while swing constituencies became distinctly right-wing.

4. Róbert László, 'The new Hungarian election system's beneficiaries' (Hungarian), paper, 2014, https://cens.ceu.edu/sites/cens.ceu.edu/files/attachment/article/579/laszlo-thenewhungarianelectionsystems beneficiaries.pdf (last accessed 7 June 2022).

5. Róbert László, 'Between two election reforms?' (Hungarian), conference paper, Policy Research and Consulting Institute, 15 October 2015, http://www.valasztasirendszer.hu/wp-content/uploads/FES_PC_tanulmany_20151015_interactive.pdf (last accessed 7 June 2022).

6. Bernát Török, 'On Hungarian regulation of political advertising' (Hungarian), in *Election dilemmas* (Hungarian), Budapest, National University of Public Service, 2015, pp. 151–74.

7. Resolution Kvk.III.37.328/2014/6 of the Curia, 18 March 2014, https://kuria-birosag.hu/hu/valhat/kvkiii3732820146-szamuhatarozat (last accessed 7 June 2022).

8. Róbert László, 'Election facelift based on Fidesz interests' (Hungarian), *Fundamentum*, nos. 2–3, 2018.

9. 'Changes in the "highway code": Parliament prepares to make a surprising decision' (Hungarian), Napi, 2 June 2015, https://www.napi.hu/ado/valtoznak_a_kozlekedesi_szabalyok_meglepo_dontesre_keszul_a_parlament.598584.html (last accessed 7 June 2022).

10. 'Hungary parliamentary elections 8 April 2018', OSCE Report, 27 June 2018, https://www.osce.org/files/f/documents/0/9/385959.pdf (last accessed 7 June 2022).

11. 'The opposition in Nyiregyház reports the disappearance of their posters to the police' (Hungarian), *Népszava*, 20 September 2019, https://nepszava.hu/3050862_feljelentest-tett-a-nyiregyhazi-ellenzek-a-plakatjai-eltuntetese-miatt (last accessed 7 June 2022).

12. András Bozóki, ed., *Carte blanche: Fidesz in Hungarian politics* (Hungarian), Budapest, Fidesz, 1992, p. 315.

13. Viktor Orbán's speech in the Hungarian Parliament on 9 August 1991, https://www.parlament.hu/naplo34/125/1250010.html (last accessed 7 June 2022).

14. 'The National Election Commission will censure me, lawyers will defend me, and that's that' (Hungarian), Index, 21 April 2006, https://index.hu/belfold/orban4945/ (last accessed 7 June 2022).
15. On 17 May 2016 the European Court of Human Rights declared that the fining of Hungarian MPs for their conduct in Parliament constituted a violation of freedom of expression.
16. 'Orbán get away question with a perfect answer' (Hungarian), 11 December 2017, 444, https://444.hu/2017/12/11/pharaon-tiborcz-orban-tokeletes-valasszal-uszta-meg-a-felkerdezest
17. 'Comparative data on the activity of the National Assembly in the cycles 2006–10, 2010–14, and 2014–18' (Hungarian), Legislative Directorate of the Hungarian National Assembly, 9 May 2018, https://www.parlament.hu/documents/10181/56582/Összehasonl%C3%ADtó+a datok+a+2014-18%2C+2010-14%2C+2006-10.+ciklusról/532418f3-5a26-464c-64d5-160c9b560070 (last accessed 7 June 2022).
18. Tamás Bod, 'The career of László Domokos, president elect of the State Audit Office: "He likes money"' (Hungarian), *Magyar Narancs*, 24 June 2010.
19. 'According to the state secretary universities were not always good keepers' (Hungarian), Eduline, 2 Aug 2014, https://eduline.hu/felsooktatas/Palkovics_indokolt_a_kancellari_rendszer_be_QR1Y4H, (last accessed 7 June 2022)
20. 'Barroso concerned about rule of law in Hungary' (Hungarian), Index, 8 March 2013, https://index.hu/belfold/2013/03/08/barroso_felhivta_orbant/ (last accessed 7 June 2022).
21. 'USA concerned by the latest amendment to the Fundamental Law' (Hungarian), Index, 8 March 2013, https://index.hu/belfold/2013/03/08/az_egyesult_allamokat_is_aggasztja_az_alaptorveny_legujabb_modositasa/ (last accessed 7 June 2022).
22. Opinion on the Fourth Amendment to the Fundamental Law of Hungary, Venice Commission, June 2013, https://www.venice.coe.int/webforms/documents/?pdf=CDL-AD(2013)012-e (last accessed 7 June 2022). As a result of the fourth amendment of the Fundamental Law, the constitutional system of Hungary underwent a deep structural change. The power of the government grew significantly, and the parliamentary majority could bolster it at any time.

23. Later the government was forced to backtrack slightly, but it was prepared to make concessions only in the matter of the independence of the judiciary and the National Office for the Judiciary.
24. László Sólyom, 'The end of the division of power' (Hungarian), *Népszabadság*, 11 March 2013.
25. László Sólyom, 'A symbolic blow to the new democracy' (German), *Die Presse*, 30 May 2013.
26. Sixth (later, Seventh) Amendment to the Fundamental Law, https://www.parlament.hu/irom41/00332/00332.pdf (last accessed 7 June 2022).
27. Pál Sonnevend, András Jakab and Lóránt Csink, 'The constitution as an instrument of everyday party politics: The Basic Law of Hungary', in Armin von Bogdandy and Pál Sonnevend, eds., *Constitutional Crisis in the European Constitutional Ares*, Oxford, Hart/Beck, 2015, pp. 33–110.
28. 'One thousand years of the Hungarian state, 150 years of the independent judiciary' (Hungarian), *National Office for the Judiciary*, 24 April 2019, https://birosag.hu/hirek/kategoria/birosagokrol/ezer-eves-magyar-jogallam-szazotven-eves-fuggetlen-biraskodas (last accessed 7 June 2022).
29. 'Judicial independence and rule of law in Hungary still under threat', International Bar Association, Human Rights Institute, 2015, https://www.fidh.org/IMG/pdf/hungary_admin_court_system_brief_latest_version.docx.pdf (last accessed 7 June 2022).
30. Although the filling of the positions of judges is the result of internal competition, the president repeatedly disqualified the leading applications, and to these positions she temporarily nominated persons who in some cases had not even applied for the post. 'Fourteen judges spoke of how the independence of the judiciary is being eliminated in Hungary' (Hungarian), 444, 6 April 2020, https://444.hu/2020/04/06/14-biro-beszelt-arrol-hogy-szamoljak-fel-az-igazsagszolgaltatas-fuggetlenseget-magyarorszagon?utm_source=projectagora&utm_medium=contentdiscovery (last accessed 7 June 2022).
31. Report of the National Judicial Council for the National Assembly, 8 May 2019, https://orszagosbiroitanacs.hu/az-orszaggyuleshez-fordul-az-orszagos-biroi-tanacs (last accessed 7 June 2022).

32. Tünde Handó's interview on 10 June 2018 on the programme *Vasárnapi Újság* on Kossuth Radio.
33. Eighth Amendment to the Fundamental Law, 12 December 2019.
34. Countless court decisions unfavourable to the regime have been brought in matters including data of public interest, electoral procedure (e.g. decisions condemning ruling party municipalities for party propaganda), and the right to privacy.
35. 'Hungary: Fearing the unknown; How rising control is undermining judicial independence in Hungary', Amnesty International, 6 April 2020, https://www.amnesty.org/download/Documents/EUR2720512020ENGLISH.PDF (last accessed 7 June 2022).
36. 'Orbán says it is unjust that Roma children segregated for years at school get compensation' (Hungarian), 444, 9 January 2020, https://444.hu/2020/01/09/orban-szerint-igazsagtalan-hogy-karteritest-kaptak-a-roma-gyerekek-akiket-eveken-at-elkulonitettek-az-iskolaban (last accessed 7 June 2022).
37. 'One thousand years of the Hungarian state, 150 years of the independent judiciary' (Hungarian), *National office for the Judiciary*, 24 April 2019, https://birosag.hu/hirek/kategoria/birosagokrol/ezer-eves-magyar-jogallam-szazotven-eves-fuggetlen-biraskodas (last accessed 7 June 2022).
38. Szilárd Teczár, 'Overtaking on the right' (Hungarian), *Magyar Narancs*, 22 October 2020.
39. As constitutional justice, András Zs. Varga was the rapporteur for the decisions that found the criminalization of fake news and the Stop Soros laws punishing NGOs to be constitutional. See https://curia.europa.eu/jcms/upload/docs/application/pdf/2021-11/cp210203en.pdf (last accessed 7 June 2022).
40. 'Truly the least dangerous power? Does a natural limit exist to judicial independence?' (Hungarian), in Zoltán J. Tóth, *The various layers of the law* (Hungarian), Budapest, Károli Gáspár Református Egyetem Állam- és Jogtudományi Kar, 2020, p. 79.
41. 'A few years ago Szájer thought very differently about the system of checks and balances to Orbán now' (Hungarian), 444, 15 December 2014, https://444.hu/2014/12/15/szajer-meg-egeszen-mast-gondolt-a-fekek-es-ellensulyok-rendszererol-mint-orban (last accessed 7 June 2022).

42. 'Viktor Orbán's response in the European Parliament' (Hungarian), 19 January 2011, https://www.youtube.com/watch?v=RKnyvex6EnE (last accessed 7 June 2022).
43. *Report on the Situation of Fundamental Rights: Standards and Practices in Hungary* (Tavares Report), European Parliament, 16 February 2012.
44. Speech by Viktor Orbán before the Hungarian National Assembly on 4 July 2013, https://2010-2014.kormany.hu/hu/miniszterelnokseg/miniszterelnok/beszedek-publikaciok-interjuk/a-tavares-jelentes-csorbitana-magyarorszag-szuverenitasat (last accessed 7 June 2022).
45. Resolution on equal treatment for Hungary, National Assembly, https://www.parlament.hu/irom39/11729/11729.pdf (last accessed 7 June 2022).
46. 'Daul: "Orbán is the 'enfant terrible' of the EPP family, but I like him"', Euractiv, 3 July 2015, https://www.euractiv.com/section/uk-europe/interview/daul-orban-is-the-enfant-terrible-of-the-epp-family-but-i-like-him/ (last accessed 7 June 2022).
47. 'Double standards in the Sargentini report' (Hungarian), Nézőpont Institute, 6 September 2018, https://nezopont.hu/kettos-merce-a-sargentini-jelentesben-liberalisok-a-keresztenydemokratak-ellen/ (last accessed 7 June 2022).
48. OSCE Office for Democratic Institutions and Human Rights, 'Final report on Hungary's parliamentary elections', 27 June 2018, https://www.osce.org/files/f/documents/0/9/385959.pdf (last accessed 7 June 2022).
49. 'What is the problem with the Hungarian law on foreign funded NGOs?', Hungarian Helsinki Committee, 9 October 2017, https://helsinki.hu/wp-content/uploads/What-is-the-Problem-with-the-Law-on-Foreign-Funded-NGOs.pdf (last accessed 7 June 2022).
50. 'Hungary passes bill targeting Soros-funded university', Politico, 4 April 2017, https://www.politico.eu/article/hungary-ceu-story/ (last accessed 7 June 2022).
51. 'Hungary launches fraud probe into EU-funded projects', Politico, 8 February 2018, https://www.politico.eu/article/hungary-launches-fraud-probe-into-eu-funded-projects-viktor-orban-olaf/ (last accessed 7 June 2022).

52. Sargentini Report (by Judith Sargentini, Dutch MEP for the Green Party), European Parliament, 4 July 2018, https://www.europarl.europa.eu/doceo/document/A-8-2018-0250_EN.html (last accessed 7 June 2022).
53. Viktor Orbán's speech at a sitting of the European Parliament on 11 September 2018.
54. According to identical reports by several persons present.
55. The Article 7 procedure was initiated against Poland in December 2017, and after 2019 the two states were able to mutually veto the procedure against the other being taken to the next stage.
56. 'The judgment of the Federal Constitutional Court cannot stand as it is' (German), *Der Spiegel*, 25 September 2020.
57. 'Commission Vice President Věra Jourová insulted Hungary, therefore must resign', Prime Minister's Office, 29 September 2020, https://miniszterelnok.hu/commission-vice-president-vera-jourova-insulted-hungary-therefore-must-resign/ (last accessed 7 June 2022).
58. Speech by László Kövér at the opening of the conference held on the occasion of the 150th anniversary of the independence of the judiciary, 24 April 2019, https://birosag.hu/sites/default/files/2019-05/az_orszaggyules_elnokenek_nyitobeszede.pdf (last accessed 7 June 2022).
59. Balázs Orbán and Attila Palkó, 'The expansion of the universe of the rule of law and its dangers' (Hungarian), *Kommentár*, February 2019.
60. 'Strengthening the rule of law within the European Union: Diagnoses, recommendations, and what to avoid', policy brief, June 2019, https://reconnect-europe.eu/wp-content/uploads/2019/07/RECONNECT-policy-brief-Pech-Kochenov-2019June-publish.pdf (last accessed 7 June 2022).

5. 'NEITHER THE IMF NOR THE EU IS MY BOSS'

1. 'Viktor Orbán: Hungary, the victorious state' (Hungarian), Hungarian government official website, https://2010-2014.kormany.hu/hu/miniszterelnokseg/hirek/orban-viktor-a-magyar-gyoztes-nemzet (last accessed 7 June 2022).
2. Gábor G. Fodor, 'Economy/policy' (Hungarian), *Nemzeti Érdek*, vol. 1, nos. 11–12, 2015.

3. Fiscal alcoholism refers to fiscal policies where the government deliberately and significantly overspends its revenues.
4. Unlike the black economy, consisting of illegal transactions, the grey economy covers activities that are engaged in to avoid paying tax. Actors in the grey economy gain an unfair advantage over their legally operating rivals and cause a significant shortfall in the state's revenue.
5. In November 2008, the IMF, the European Union and the World Bank provided Hungary with stand-by loans totalling €20 billion, initially for seventeen months, later extended.
6. 'Orbán promises a tax declaration no bigger than a beermat' (Hungarian), Adó Online, 26 April 2010, https://ado.hu/ado/soralatet-nagysagu-adobevallast-iger-orban/ (last accessed 7 June 2022).
7. Before 2011 income tax for income below 1,900,000 HUF per month (€5,400) was 18%, tax for income above this level was 35%. People on the minimum wage or with unemployment benefit did not pay income tax.
8. This tax was later repealed by Fidesz when the party would have had to apply it to its own staff.
9. Ákos Keller Alánt, 'On the trail of private pension funds: Divide, levy, take' (Hungarian), *Magyar Narancs*, 18 November 2015.
10. 'This is how pension fund assets disappeared' (Hungarian), Origo, 11 March 2014, https://www.origo.hu/gazdasag/20140306-a-magan-nyugdijpenztari-rendszer-tortenete.html (last accessed 7 June 2022).
11. 'We are drowning in special taxes' (Hungarian), HVG, 16 March 2016, https://hvg.hu/gazdasag/20160316_kulonadok_leitnerleitner_adiztatas_allami_bevetelek (last accessed 7 June 2022).
12. Viktor Orbán's state of the nation speech in Budapest, 6 March 2009, http://2010-2015.miniszterelnok.hu/beszed/uj_irany_magyarorszag_uj_irany_magyarok (last accessed 7 June 2022).
13. The state-owned MVM got an opportunity to trade with the state's security gas reserves.
14. Viktor Orbán's speech at the twenty-fifth congress of the Fidesz—Hungarian Civic Alliance, 28 September 2013, http://2010-2015.miniszterelnok.hu/beszed/2014_a_rezsiharc_eve_lesz (last accessed 7 June 2022).

15. 'It wasn't Orbán's frown that gave them cold feet' (Hungarian), HVG, 19 June 2015, https://hvg.hu/gazdasag/20150619_nem_orban_osszevont_szemoldoketol_gaz_ar (last accessed 7 June 2022).
16. According to calculations by the Regional Energy Economy Research Centre (REKK), between early 2014 and the 2018 elections the Hungarian public paid 100–200 billion HUF more for gas than it actually cost. 'The state earns enough on consumer gas to provide it for free for six months before the next election' (Hungarian), G7, 10 August 2020, https://g7.hu/kozelet/20200810/olyan-sokat-keres-az-allam-a-lakossagi-gazon-hogy-a-kovetkezo-valasztas-elott-akar-ingyen-is-adhatja-fel-evig/ (last accessed 7 June 2022).
17. 'Forbes: Almost half of the gas service provision for Hungary may pass to Mészáros et al.' (Hungarian), 24.hu, https://24.hu/fn/gazdasag/2020/12/15/tigaz-meszaros-lorinc-felcsut-foldgaz-opusmet (last accessed 7 June 2022).
18. 'MKB with enormous losses, a burden on the parent bank' (Hungarian), HVG, 31 August 2010, https://hvg.hu/gazdasag/20100831_mkb_bank_veszteseg (last accessed 7 June 2022).
19. 'The state's new bank may break even this year' (Hungarian), Index, 19 May 2015, https://index.hu/gazdasag/bankesbiztositas/2015/05/19/nullara_johet_ki_iden_az_allam_uj_bankja/ (last accessed 7 June 2022).
20. 'MKB bank to be nationalized!' (Hungarian), Index, 24 July 2014, https://index.hu/gazdasag/2014/07/24/allamositjak_az_mkb_bankot/ (last accessed 7 June 2022).
21. 'The story of a murky bank deal' (Hungarian), Index, 9 May 2017, https://index.hu/gazdasag/2017/05/09/mkb_bankmentes_szanalas_eladas_matolcsy_szemerey_balog_adam/ (last accessed 7 June 2022).
22. 'Magyar Bankholding Zrt. formed with the participation of three banks' (Hungarian), Index, 29 June 2020, https://index.hu/gazdasag/2020/06/29/magyar_bankholding_zrt_mtb_magyar_takarekszovetkezeti_bank_mkb_budapest_bank/ (last accessed 7 June 2022).
23. Because of higher productivity, employees in multinational companies produce on average two and a half times as much tax revenue as workers in a small Hungarian company. Balázs Muraközy and Balázs Reizer,

'The heterogeneity of Hungarian corporation taxation' (Hungarian), *Közgazdasági Szemle*, December 2017.

24. László Vértesy, 'The role of multinational companies in the economy and the labor market', 2018, Munich Personal Re Pec Archive, https://mpra.ub.uni-muenchen.de/90262/1/MPRA_paper_90262.pdf.

25. Péter Mihályi, 'Renationalization in the second and third Orbán governments' (Hungarian), MTA KTI, https://www.mtakti.hu/wp-content/uploads/2018/04/10_Visszaallamositas_KTRK_eloadashoz.pdf (last accessed 7 June 2022).

26. List of strategic partnership agreements, Ministry for Foreign Affairs, https://kormany.hu/kulgazdasagi-es-kulugyminiszterium/strategiai-partnersegi-megallapodasok (last accessed 7 June 2022).

27. 'Lifting the lid on lobbying: National report on Hungary', Transparency International, https://transparency.hu/wp-content/uploads/2016/03/Lifting-The-Lid-On-Lobbying-National-Report-of-Hungary.pdf (last accessed 7 June 2022).

28. 'Ideology is not a factor in investments' (German), *WirtschaftsWoche*, 7 April 2018, https://www.wiwo.de/politik/europa/ungarn-ideologie-ist-kein-investitionsfaktor/21149368.html (last accessed 7 June 2022).

29. 'Multinationals got three times more money from Fidesz governments than before 2010' (Hungarian), *Szabad Európa*, 4 February 2021, https://www.szabadeuropa.hu/a/haromszor-tobb-penzt-kaptak-a-multik-a-fidesz-kormanytol-mint-2010-elott/31086092.html (last accessed 7 June 2022).

30. Andrea Nestor and András Kaszap, 'Who do we subsidize out of EU money? It matters' (Hungarian), research paper, KPMG, 30 April 2016.

31. 'Added value per capita by branch of the economy and headquarters of end owner (2008–)' (Hungarian), Central Statistics Office, last updated 6 April 2021, http://www.ksh.hu/docs/hun/xstadat/xstadat_eves/i_qtd014f.html (last accessed 7 June 2022).

32. These serious corruption allegations were brought forward based on the Foreign Corrupt Practices Act, and only avoided court because the parent company, Microsoft, settled out of court with the US

Department of Justice. See https://www.wsj.com/articles/microsoft-to-pay-25-million-to-settle-foreign-bribery-probe-11563811097, (last accessed 7 June 2022).

33. In 2013 it was equal to 2.8% of the central government revenues. On its profit in 2015 and 2018, it paid 50 billion HUF in dividends into the central budget, and in 2019 it paid 250 billion HUF.

34. Amendment to Act CXXXIX of 2013 on the Hungarian National Bank, National Assembly, 1 March 2016, https://www.parlament.hu/irom40/09380/09380.pdf (last accessed 7 June 2022).

35. 'We're making 200 billion HUF confidential tomorrow? First I've heard of it!' (Hungarian), Index, 29 February 2016, https://index.hu/video/2016/02/29/mnb_alapitvanyok_infotorveny_parlament/ (last accessed 7 June 2022).

36. 'Index journalists banned from parliament' (Hungarian), Index, 26 April 2016, https://index.hu/belfold/2016/04/26/kitiltottak_az_index_ujsagiroit_a_parlamentbol/ (last accessed 7 June 2022).

37. 'Assets of the Hungarian National Bank foundations passed into the weird state of quasi-public money' (Hungarian), HVG, 5 November 2020, https://hvg.hu/360/202045_baratnok_kozt (last accessed 7 June 2022).

38. 'Orbán gives a new task to ambassadors' (Hungarian), Origo, 25 August 2014, https://www.origo.hu/itthon/20140825-orban-uj-feladatot-szabott-a-nagykoveteknek.html (last accessed 7 June 2022).

39. 'The Foreign Ministry company and a corporation close to Orbán's relations keep mum about last year' (Hungarian), 24.hu, 7 June 2017, https://24.hu/fn/gazdasag/2017/06/07/a-kulugy-cege-es-az-orban-rokonaihoz-kotodo-vallalat-is-titkolozik-a-tavalyi-everol/ (last accessed 7 June 2022).

40. 'Trading house's 3 billion apple claim can be traced to Orbán's relatives' (Hungarian), Index, 2 September 2016, https://index.hu/gazdasag/2016/09/02/orban_rokonaiig_er_a_kereskedhohaz_3_milliarods_almazasa_mnkh_cider/ (last accessed 7 June 2022).

41. 'Closing in the south, 15 of the government's trading houses are closing' (Hungarian), 444, 28 November 2017, https://444.hu/2017/11/28/deli-csukas-bezar-a-kormany-15-kereskedohazat (last accessed 7 June 2022).

42. Hungary's export ratio to China grew from 1.6% to 1.7%, imports decreased from 9.9% to 7.7% of total trade between 2010 and 2020. Hungarian Central Statistics Office, 2020, https://www.ksh.hu/docs/hun/xftp/idoszaki/kulker/2020/index.html (last accessed 7 June 2022).
43. 'Hungary's success is that nothing has changed' (Hungarian), Telex, 7 May 2021, https://telex.hu/gazdasag/2021/05/07/keleti-nyitas-szijjarto-orban-kina-gazdasag-vilaggazdasag-befektetes-kifektetes-agyrem (last accessed 7 June 2022).
44. 'The government's great plan, the opening to the East, breaks a negative record' (Hungarian), HVG, 4 April 2019, https://hvg.hu/gazdasag/20190404_keleti_nyitas_kulkereskedelem_eurostat (last accessed 7 June 2022).
45. 'In 2019 the government bought nearly seven thousand jobs, at 16 million forints each' (Hungarian), HVG, 23 January 2020, https://hvg.hu/gazdasag/20200123_A_kormany_kozel_hetezer_munkahelyet_vett_2019ben_darabjat_16_millio_forintert (last accessed 7 June 2022). This sum includes subsidies for all the investors, not just the Eastern ones.
46. 'The 20,000 holders of residency bonds came to Hungary from fifty-nine countries' (Hungarian), G7, 16 January 2019, https://g7.hu/kozelet/20190116/59-orszagbol-jott-magyarorszagra-a-huszezer-letelepedesi-kotvenyes/ (last accessed 7 June 2022).
47. Tamás Wiedermann, 'Dealing in fictive bonds in the residency bond programme, which brought 162 billion HUF to offshore companies close to Fidesz' (Hungarian), G7, 21 December 2018, https://g7.hu/kozelet/20181221/fiktiv-kotvenyekkel-is-uzleteltek-a-letelepedesi-programban-amely-162-milliardot-hozott-a-fidesz-kozeli-offshore-cegeknek/ (last accessed 7 June 2022).
48. 'Együtt files a complaint about the residency bonds' (Hungarian), Népszava, 10 October 2015, https://nepszava.hu/1072808_letelepedesi-kotveny-feljelentest-tesz-az-egyutt (last accessed 7 June 2022).
49. 'Rogan's people did not break the rules on the residency programme because there were no rules' (Hungarian), G7, 5 April 2018, https://g7.hu/kozelet/20180405/roganek-nem-vetettek-a-a-letelepedesi-

program-szabalyai-ellen-mert-nem-voltak-szabalyok/ (last accessed 7 June 2022).
50. 'The role of residency bonds in financing the Hungarian state: Corruption and loss of public funds in the practice of the state between 2013 and 2017' (Hungarian), Transparency International Hungary, Budapest, 2018.
51. 'Members of Putin's apparatus have acquired Hungarian papers in Orbán's bond programme' (Hungarian), 444, 10 September 2018, https://tldr.444.hu/2018/09/10/putyin-gepezetenek-tagjai-kaptak-magyar-papirokat-orbanek-kotvenyprogramjaban (last accessed 7 June 2022).
52. 'Lázár says those who have nothing are worth as much' (Hungarian), Index, 19 March 2011, https://index.hu/belfold/2011/03/19/lazar_szerint_akinek_nincs_semmije_az_annyit_is_er (last accessed 7 June 2022).
53. 'The money we spend on workfare would be enough to set up a Scandinavian-quality system' (Hungarian), G7, 20 October 2018, https://g7.hu/podcast/20181020/abbol-a-penzbol-amit-kozmunkara-koltunk-egy-skandinav-szinvonalu-rendszert-lehetne-kiepiteni/ (last accessed 7 June 2022).
54. Dorottya Szikra, 'Welfare for the wealthy: Social policy of the Orbán regime, 2010–2017', Friedrich Ebert Foundation, Budapest, March 2018, https://library.fes.de/pdf-files/bueros/budapest/14209.pdf.
55. While in other countries in the region inequality lessened overall in the decade from 2010, in Hungary the difference in income between the rich and the poor increased dramatically: the Gini coefficient increased from 24.1 (in 2010) to 28.7 (in 2018), though it is still under the average in the EU.
56. 'Hungarian economy in transition', CNN Business, 9 June 2012, https://edition.cnn.com/videos/business/2012/06/07/marketplace-europe-matolcsy-hungary-economy.cnn (last accessed 7 June 2022).
57. 'Report on balance and debt of the governmental sector' (Hungarian), Central Statistics Office, 2020, https://www.ksh.hu/docs/hun/xftp/stattukor/edp/edp20200422/index.html (last accessed 7 June 2022).
58. 'Level of economic development in Hungary relative to Europe, 2019' (Hungarian), Central Statistics Office, 2019, https://www.ksh.hu/

docs/hun/xftp/stattukor/gdp_eu/2019/index.html (last accessed 7 June 2022).

59. 'Budget Report 2019' (Hungarian), Hungarian National Bank, https://www.mnb.hu/letoltes/ko-ltse-gvete-si-jelente-s-2019-szeptember.pdf (last accessed 7 June 2022).

60. 'Growing together: The EU support to Hungary since 2004', fact sheet, European Commission, https://ec.europa.eu/regional_policy/sources/docgener/factsheet/eu10_2004/factsheet_growing-together_hu_en.pdf (last accessed 7 June 2022).

61. 'Analysis of the use and impact of EU funds in Hungary' (Hungarian), KPMG, March 2017, https://www.palyazat.gov.hu/magyarorszagi_europai_unios_forrasok_elemzese (last accessed 7 June 2022).

62. István Magas, 'Ten years after the world economic crisis' (Hungarian), *Pénzügyi Szemle*, http://real.mtak.hu/112296/1/magas-2019-1-mpdf_20190413133317_25.pdf (last accessed 7 June 2022).

63. Taking GDP in 2008 as 100%, then by 2018 Hungary had achieved GDP growth of 115%, Czechia 116%, Slovakia 125%, and Poland 140%. 'Has the Hungarian economy never been better?' (Hungarian), Index, 29 April 2019, https://index.hu/gazdasag/2019/04/29/gazdasagpolitika_makrogazdasag_gdp_100_ev (last accessed 7 June 2022).

64. 'The Orbán government has never done this before—extreme last-minute spending' (Hungarian), Portfolio, 25 December 2020, https://www.portfolio.hu/gazdasag/20201225/ilyet-meg-soha-sem-csinalt-az-orban-kormany-rendkivuli-koltekezes-meg-az-utolso-pillanatban-is-463078 (last accessed 7 June 2022).

65. 'Room with privilege, Transparency and corruption exposure around the tourism subsidies during the Covid-19 pandemic' (Hungarian), Transparency International Hungary, 2021, https://transparency.hu/wp-content/uploads/2021/12/TIHu_szoba_kivaltsaggal.pdf (last accessed 7 June 2022).

66. 'Corruption in Hungary in the shadow of the Covid pandemic: Findings of the Corruption Perceptions Index in 2020' (Hungarian), Transparency International Hungary, n.d., https://transparency.hu/wp-content/uploads/2021/01/TI-Magyarorszag_CPI-2020_jelentes.pdf (last accessed 7 June 2022).

67. 'Another 100 billlion to the MCC' (Hungarian), Telex.hu, 25 December 2020, https://telex.hu/belfold/2020/12/25/ujabb-100-milliardot-kap-az-mcc (last accessed 7 June 2022).
68. 'András Tombor: Businessman, lobbyist, and alleged Fidesz money launderer, bagman', Budapest Beacon, 22 December 2016, https://budapestbeacon.com/andras-tombor-businessman-lobbyist-and-alleged-fidesz-money-launderer-bagman/ (last accessed 7 June 2022).
69. 'The government is stuffing MCC with a huge stock of shares of MOL and Richter', (Hungarian), 444, 10 Apr 2020, https://444.hu/2020/04/10/a-mol-es-a-richter-hatalmas-reszvenycsomagjaval-tomi-ki-a-kormany-a-mathias-corvinus-collegiumot (last accessed 7 June 2022)
70. Ninth Amendment to the Fundamental Law, https://www.parlament.hu/irom41/13647/13647.pdf (last accessed 7 June 2022).
71. 'Balázs Orbán: I have two hats' (Hungarian), 444, 19 October 2020, https://444.hu/2020/10/19/orban-balazs-ket-sapkam-van (last accessed 7 June 2022).
72. 'Privatization by stealth: In recent years several billion forints worth of assets has passed from the state to foundations controlled by the ruling party' (Hungarian), Átlátszó, 29 December 2021, https://atlatszo.hu/kozpenz/2021/12/27/rejtett-privatizacio-az-elmult-evben-tobb-ezermilliardos-vagyon-kerult-az-allamtol-a-kormanypart-altal-uralt-alapitvanyokhoz/ (last accessed 7 June 2022).
73. 'Only dead fish swims with the tide' (German), Kronen Zeitung, 6 October 2011, https://www.krone.at/267398 (last accessed 7 June 2022).
74. 'András Lánczi: The opposition is at the level of loony parties' (Hungarian), Magyar Idők, 21 December 2015, https://www.magyaridok.hu/belfold/lanczi-andras-viccpartok-szinvonalan-all-az-ellenzek-243952/ (last accessed 7 June 2022).

6. 'I DON'T DEAL WITH BUSINESS MATTERS'

1. 'Fidesz and MDF shared several billion forints?' (Hungarian), Népszabadság, 25 May 1993.
2. László Kéri, Viktor Orbán (Hungarian), Budapest, Századvég Publishers, 1994.

3. Attila Ószabó and Éva Vajda, 'The lucky and the geniuses: Boys in the mine' (Hungarian), *Élet és Irodalom*, vol. XLIII, no. 44, 5 November 1999.
4. Personal statement of a former colleague of Orbán and Simicska.
5. 'Campaign mist: Monitoring campaign expenses for the parliamentary and local elections in 2014' (Hungarian), Transparency International Hungary, 2015, https://transparency.hu/wp-content/uploads/2016/02/Kampanykod.pdf (last accessed 7 June 2022).
6. András Pethő, 'Building the financial background for Fidesz' (Hungarian), Origo, 5 March 2012, https://www.origo.hu/itthon/20120305-a-fidesz-gazdasagi-hatorszaganak-epulese-i-resz.html (last accessed 7 June 2022).
7. 'Peaks of white-collar crime' (Hungarian), HVG, 31 August 2008, https://hvg.hu/itthon/20080831_fehergalleros_bunozes_iteletek/2 (last accessed 7 June 2022).
8. 'The Orbán government's aces of trumps have swept the board' (Hungarian), *Magyar Narancs*, 11 July 2002.
9. 'Orbán gets less from Fidesz: Declarations of assets, 2008' (Hungarian), Origo, 2 February 2009, https://www.origo.hu/itthon/20090202-2008as-vagyonnyilatkozatok-minden-aktiv-kepviselo-leadta-nyilatkozatat.html (last accessed 7 June 2022).
10. 'Business people close to members of government: Family businesses' (Hungarian), *Magyar Narancs*, 28 March 2002.
11. 'We are seeking for the most corrupt Hungarian case' (Hungarian), Index, 9 December 2010, https://index.hu/gazdasag/magyar/2010/12/09/botranyok/?token=08617f7ad7994eee3df6e2c74fd90903.
12. Attila Mong and Bence György, *Magicians of billions: Secrets of the broker scandal*, (Hungarian), Budapest, Vízkapu Press, 2003, pp. 110–11.
13. Corruption Perceptions Index, 2008, Transparency International Hungary, 23 September 2008, https://transparency.hu/adatok-a-korrupciorol/korrupcio-erzekelesi-index/cpi-2008 (last accessed 7 June 2022).
14. Statement by Noémi Alexa in 'Corruption in Hungary. Loss due to friction' (Hungarian), *Magyar Narancs*, 4 October 2007.
15. 'Corruption risks in the business sector: National integration study, Part 2' (Hungarian), Transparency International Hungary, 2008, https://transparency.hu/wp-content/uploads/2016/05/Korrupciós-

kockázatok-az-üzleti-szektorban-Nemzeti-integritás-tanulmány-teljes-jelentés.pdf (last accessed 7 June 2022).
16. This included the 2010 arrest of socialist mayor Miklós Hagyó (who was found guilty six years later of abuse of office); the allegations of corruption against György Hunvald (who was later convicted of misappropriation of public funds); and various corruption allegations in relation to the Budapest Transport Company.
17. András Pethő, 'The Orbán government is haunted by the old suspicion' (Hungarian), Origo, 7 June 2012, https://www.origo.hu/itthon/20120528-a-keteves-orbankormany-es-a-korrupcio.html (last accessed 7 June 2022).
18. Pál Dániel Rényi, 'Viktor Orbán vs. Lajos Simicska: Only one of them can stay' (Hungarian), *Magyar Narancs*, 21 September 2014.
19. 'Mysterious forces at work in the government's first internal war' (Hungarian), Origo, 6 March 2012, https://www.origo.hu/itthon/20120306-fellegi-tamas-fejlesztesi-miniszter-tavozasa-kapcsolata-simicska-lajos-es-nyerges.html (last accessed 7 June 2022).
20. '"This is a well-organized sharing-out system": An insider on the construction industry' (Hungarian), Átlátszó, 20 March 2012, https://atlatszo.hu/2012/03/20/ez-egy-jol-szervezett-leosztasi-rendszer-egy-bennfentes-az-epitoiparrol (last accessed 7 June 2022).
21. 'Conquerors in the shadow of power: The rise of Közgép is linked to politics' (Hungarian), Origo, 6 December 2010, https://www.origo.hu/itthon/20101206-a-kozgep-es-a-fidesz-kapcsolata-a-ceg-tortenete.html (last accessed 7 June 2022).
22. 'Over 300 billion' (Hungarian), *Magyar Narancs*, 13 January 2013.
23. 'Simicska is the true owner of Közgép according to a company statement' (Hungarian), Origo, 16 April 2012, https://www.origo.hu/itthon/20120416-simicska-a-kozgep-tenyleges-tulajdonosa-a-ceg-nyilatkozata-szerint.html (last accessed 7 June 2022).
24. 'So, what is the government's favourite company?' (Hungarian), Index, 8 January 2014, https://index.hu/gazdasag/2014/01/08/395_milliard_a_kozgep_2013-as_teljesitmenye/ (last accessed 7 June 2022).
25. 'Here is the list! They are the richest and most influential people in Hungary' (Hungarian), Napi, https://www.napi.hu/magyar-

gazdasag/itt-a-lista-ok-a-leggazdagabbak-es-a-legbefolyasosabbak-magyarorszagon.580954.html (last accessed 7 June 2022).

26. 'Underground corruption' (Hungarian), Transparency International Hungary, 17 January 2014, https://transparency.hu/hirek/underground-korrupcio/ (last accessed 7 June 2022).

27. 'Corruption risk in Hungary 2011, National Integrity Study' (Hungarian), Transparency International Hungary, https://transparency.hu/wp-content/uploads/2016/05/Korrupcios-kockazatok-Magyarorszagon-2011-Nemzeti-Integritas-Tanulmany.pdf (last accessed 7 June 2022).

28. 'For some company directors, their name is enough to ensure there will be no tax inspection' (Hungarian), 444, 10 November 2013, https://444.hu/2013/11/10/vannak-cegvezetok-akiknek-a-neve-elegahhoz-hogy-ne-legyen-adoellenorzes (last accessed 7 June 2022).

29. 'Drastic drop in initiation of criminal proceedings in corruption matters since Péter Polt was appointed' (Hungarian), Átlátszó, 6 February 2015, https://atlatszo.hu/2015/02/06/polt-peter-kinevezese-ota-meredeken-zuhan-a-politikai-korrupcios-ugyekben-inditott-buntetoeljarasok-szama/ (last accessed 7 June 2022).

30. 'Polt's result: 119 complaints, zero charges' (Hungarian), 24.hu, 28 October 2020, https://24.hu/belfold/2020/10/28/polt-peter-feljelentes-vademeles/ (last accessed 7 June 2022).

31. 'Fidesz MP unveils cronies deal' (Hungarian), HVG, https://hvg.hu/itthon/20130430_trafikmutyi_Szekszard_fideszes_kepviselo.

32. József Péter Martin, 'Does it lubricate the gears or make them squeak? How the system of National Cooperation performs in corruption and business in an international comparison' (Hungarian), in Tamás Kolosi, Iván Szelényi and György Tóth István, eds., *Social report 2020* (Hungarian), Budapest, Tárki, p. 60.

33. 'Sándor Csányi: There are no oligarchs in Hungary' (Hungarian), HVG, 18 December 2019, https://hvg.hu/kkv/20191218_Csanyi_Sandor_Magyarorszagon_nincsenek_oligarchak (last accessed 7 June 2022).

34. State capture occurs when certain players on the market write (or have written) the regulations governing their own operation. In functioning market economies, it is generally lobbyists who play the intermediary role between corporations and the state; but in the

current Hungarian situation, people linked to the affected companies or interest groups actually occupy the most important regulatory, decision-making, and inspecting positions.
35. 'Simicska: I'll fire every Orbánite' (Hungarian), Index, 6 February 2015, https://index.hu/belfold/2015/02/06/simicska_lajos_orban_egy_geci/ (last accessed 7 June 2022).
36. Rényi, 'Viktor Orbán vs. Lajos Simicska: Only one of them can stay'.
37. András Pethő, András Szabó, 'The secret story of Simicska's fall is revealed' (Hungarian), 444, 13 January 2019, https://444.hu/2019/01/13/feltarul-simicska-bukasanak-titkos-tortenete (last accessed 7 June 2022).
38. Ibid.
39. Officially this was due to the European Commission's assertion that the subcontractors had formed a cartel agreement; the commission later denied this.
40. 'So ends Közgép's golden age on the public procurement scene' (Hungarian), Átlátszó, 12 April 2016, https://atlatszo.hu/2016/04/12/igy-lett-vege-a-kozgep-aranykoranak-az-epitoipari-kozbeszerzesek-piacan/ (last accessed 7 June 2022).
41. 'What lies behind the current de-Simicskaization' (Hungarian), Népszabadság, 1 October 2015.
42. 'One year after 'scumbag': Orbán attacks Simicska on ten fronts' (Hungarian), Index, 6 February 2016, https://index.hu/belfold/2016/02/06/orban_tiz_fronton_szivatja_simicskat (last accessed 7 June 2022).
43. Gábor Hamza, 'Secrets of the Simicska–Orbán compromise: The price of a free retreat' (Hungarian), Magyar Narancs, 5 August 2018.
44. 'The good Lord above, good fortune, and Viktor Orbán: That's how Lőrinc Mészáros got rich' (Hungarian), Átlátszó, 3 June 2014, https://atlatszo.hu/2014/06/03/a-joisten-a-szerencse-es-orban-viktor-szemelye-igy-vagyonosodott-meszaros-lorinc/ (last accessed 7 June 2022).
45. 'He's a real business miracle'(Hungarian), Index, 20 February 2017, https://index.hu/gazdasag/2017/02/20/meszaros_lorinc_vagyona/ (last accessed 7 June 2022).

46. 'Changes in the assets of the richest people in Hungary since 2014' (Hungarian), *Forbes*, 9 January 2020, https://forbes.hu/uzlet/megmutatjuk-hogyan-valtozott-magyarorszag-leggazdagabb-embereinek-vagyona-2014-ota/ (last accessed 7 June 2022).
47. 'Lorinc Meszaros', *Forbes*, n.d., https://www.forbes.com/profile/lorinc-meszaros/ (last accessed 7 June 2022).
48. 'The gas fitter who is perhaps cleverer than Zuckerberg' (Hungarian), HVG (video), 27. February 2017, https://www.youtube.com/watch?v=U_mTA1Sd_v8 (last accessed 7 June 2022).
49. 'Lőrinc Mészáros's hotels filled with state loans in secret' (Hungarian), 24.hu, 13 October 2016, https://24.hu/fn/penzugy/2016/10/13/titokban-kitomik-allami-hitellel-meszaros-lorinc-szallodait/ (last accessed 7 June 2022).
50. Gergely Brückner, 'The bearable lightness of being a straw man' (Hungarian), Index, 27 November 2018, https://index.hu/gazdasag/2018/11/27/a_stromanlet_elviselheto_konnyusege_-_viszont_csalas_hazugsag_es_nagy_riziko/ (last accessed 7 June 2022).
51. András Bódis, 'The results of five years of the Mészáros era: Now the country supports four Simicskas' (Hungarian), Válasz Online, 10 June 2020, https://www.valaszonline.hu/2020/06/10/meszaros-szijj-garancsi-2019-nyereseg-merleg (last accessed 7 June 2022).
52. Györgyi Balla, '"Where Antal Rogán appears, it's wise to be cautious": The NER may take the rest of the Balaton' (Hungarian), HVG, 14 February 2019, https://hvg.hu/kkv/20190214_balatoni_hajozas_meszaros_oligarcha_ner_kikoto_allamositas_lenyulas_bahart (last accessed 7 June 2022).
53. András Bódis, 'The NER took over Balaton, here are the 42 giga projects' (Hungarian), valaszonline.hu, 29 May 2020, https://www.valaszonline.hu/2020/05/29/balaton-szalloda-molo-fejlesztes-tiborcz-garancsi-csanyi/ (last accessed 7 June 2022).
54. 'NER has occupied Balaton', 24.hu, https://24.hu/fn/gazdasag/2020/05/29/turizmus-szallodafejlesztes-mtu-tamogatas/ (last accessed on 7 June 2022).
55. 'Szigliget's former mayor: "We are defenceless against certain investors"' (Hungarian), *Magyar Narancs*, 2 August 2020.

56. 'Damage done to the state by Mátrai Erőmű four times that were previously known' (Hungarian), 444, 28 July 2020, https://444. hu/2020/07/28/az-eddig-ismertnel-negyszer-tobbe-fajhatott-a-matrai-eromu-a-magyar-allamnak (last accessed 7 June 2022).
57. 'The avalanche Mészáros started on the stock market goes on' (Hungarian), *Privát Bankár*, 23 January 2019, https://privatbankar. hu/cikkek/reszveny/nem-all-meg-a-lavina-amit-meszaros-lorinc-inditott-a-tozsden-324142.html (last accessed 7 June 2022).
58. '4iG continued to grow in spite of Covid' (Hungarian), Porfolio, 27 November 2020, https://www.portfolio.hu/uzlet/20201127/a-koronavirus-ellenere-tovabb-nott-a-4ig-459344 (last accessed 7 June 2022).
59. '4iG may become a global service provider', 4ig, n.d., https://www.4ig.hu/4ig-may-become-a-global-service-provider-in-space-telecommunications (last accessed 7 June 2022).
60. 'NER awash in money: 14 infographics on what a good deal it is to be related to or friends with Viktor Orbán' (Hungarian), HVG, 12 June 2019, https://hvg.hu/gazdasag/20190612_14_infografika_NER_vallalkozasok (last accessed 7 June 2022).
61. 'Tokaji company assemble in the prime minister's residence' (Hungarian), Index, 17 March 2005, https://index.hu/belfold/orbankft0317/?token=0d2dec4f6bb58a0731cb5fe0eea5db59 (last accessed 7 June 2022).
62. András Pethő and Anita Vorák, 'Orbán has been fighting the EU for 5 years, while those closest to him have been getting rich from it' (Hungarian), Direkt36, 26 February 2015, https://www.direkt36.hu/orban-ot-eve-harcol-az-eu-val-legszukebb-kore-addig-gazdagodott-belole/ (last accessed 7 June 2022).
63. 'EU pursues Orbán son-in-law case despite Hungary ending probe', Politico, 8 November 2018, https://www.politico.eu/article/istvan-tiborcz-viktor-orban-olaf-eu-pursues-orban-son-in-law-case-despite-hungary-ending-probe/ (last accessed 30 June 2022).
64. 'Orbán on Elios: EU money is not a subsidy, it is our money' (Hungarian), Index, 9 January 2020, https://index.hu/gazdasag/2020/01/09/orban_viktor_elios_tiborcz_istvan_rtl_kerdes/ (last accessed 7 June 2022).

65. 'Orbán's son-in-law and partners bought a yacht harbour for Christmas in Keszthely' (Hungarian), Átlátszó, 21 January 2015, https://atlatszo.hu/2015/01/21/orban-veje-es-uzlettarsai-vitorlaskikotot-vettek-karacsonyra-keszthelyen/ (last accessed 7 June 2022).
66. 'István Tiborcz owns 17 companies, he has the dream project in the Danube Bend' (Hungarian), Index, 3 January 2018, https://index.hu/gazdasag/2018/01/03/tiborcz_istvan_bdpst_longoria_holding/ (last accessed 7 June 2022).
67. It was unclear what resources Tiborcz used to acquire the asset management company Appeninn because the income of BDPST would certainly not have allowed for such a purchase. One answer to this anomaly may be that the deal was clinched at a figure much lower than the listed share price.
68. 'Ráhel Orbán has a say in directing tourism' (Hungarian), Index, 6 March 2018, https://index.hu/gazdasag/2018/03/06/orban_rahel_is_beleszol_a_turizmus_iranyitasaba/ (last accessed 7 June 2022).
69. 'The most influential Hungarian women: Katalin Novák and Ráhel Orbán lead' (Hungarian), Forbes, 3 March 2020, https://forbes.hu/uzlet/forbes-legbefolyasosabb-magyar-nok-novak-katalin-elre-ugrik-orban-rahel-elott-2020/ (last accessed 7 June 2022).
70. 'Ráhel Orbán has a message for the Hungarian people' (Hungarian), Index, 18 December 2014, https://index.hu/belfold/2014/12/18/orban_rahel_uzent_a_magyar_nepnek/ (last accessed 7 June 2022).
71. To name a few key Fidesz politicians: Antal Rogán with his links to residency bonds, control of tourism, and the real estate market in downtown Budapest; János Lázár with his connections to the tobacco concession, agricultural corporations, and provincial castles and real estate; and László Palkovics with his links to the Hungarian 'Silicon Valley' and the automotive manufacturing and testing centre.
72. Eurobarometer Report on Corruption, European Union, June 2020, https://ec.europa.eu/commfrontoffice/publicopinion/index.cfm/survey/getsurveydetail/instruments/special/surveyky/2247 (last accessed 7 June 2022).
73. 'Global corruption barometer 2020: Public attitudes to corruption in Hungary' (Hungarian), Transparency International Hungary, 2021,

https://transparency.hu/wp-content/uploads/2021/06/GCB_2021_ elemzes.pdf (last accessed 7 June 2022).

74. 'Public perception of corruption in Hungary' (Hungarian), Transparency International Hungary, n.d., https://transparency.hu/wp-content/uploads/2020/06/CEU-TI-magyar-nyelvű-összefoglaló_final.pdf (last accessed 7 June 2022).

75. Mengyi, who had reportedly demanded that local business people address him as Lord Voldemort, the antagonist in the Harry Potter series, was convicted of budgetary fraud in 2019 and sentenced to time in prison.

76. 'Zsolt Borkai sex scandal goes on, interesting sound recordings have come to light' (Hungarian), HVG, 23 November 2019, https://hvg.hu/itthon/20191123_borkai_zsolt_szexbotrany_rakosfalvy_zoltan_hangfelvetel_poczik_jozsef (last accessed 7 June 2022).

77. 'New Hungarian national costume: Barbara Rogán and Ráhel Orbán's watch, the Audemars Piguet Royal Oak' (Hungarian), Qubit, 6 February 2021, https://qubit.hu/2021/02/06/ime-az-uj-magyar-nepviselet-rogan-barbara-es-orban-rahel-oraja-az-audemars-piguet-royal-oak (last accessed 7 June 2022).

78. 'Two sides to perception of corruption: The most important factors in perception of everyday and state-level corruption' (Hungarian), Transparency International Hungary, 21 May 2020, https://transparency.hu/wp-content/uploads/2020/05/Gerő-Mikola-2020-A-korrupcióérzékelés-két-arca.pdf (last accessed 7 June 2022).

7. PRESS-GANGED INTO SERVICE

1. 'Index journalists going to resign' (Hungarian), 24.hu, https://www.youtube.com/watch?v=Ti-Qj6ufN6k (last accessed 7 June 2022).

2. 'List of the most read news portals and webpages in 2020' (Hungarian), The Pitch, 6 May 2019, https://thepitch.hu/legolvasottabb-hirportalok-hazai-weboldalak-listaja/ (last accessed 7 June 2022).

3. 'Zsuzsa Szelényi: Orbán & co. knew from the beginning what politics and power are all about' (Hungarian), Index, 11 August 2020, https://index.hu/belfold/2020/08/11/kibeszelo_rendszervaltas__podcast_fidesz_szelenyi_zsuzsa_politika_hatalom_orban_viktor/ (last accessed 7 June 2022).

4. 'Media freedom in Hungary ahead of the 2022 election', International Press Institute, March 2022, https://ipi.media/wp-content/uploads/2022/03/HU_PressFreedomMission_Report_IPI_2022.pdf (last accessed 7 June 2022).
5. 'Orbán: The Hungarian media are freer than the German' (Hungarian), *Szabad Európa*, 30 November 2020, https://www.szabadeuropa.hu/a/orban-viktor-demeter-szilard-soros-gyorgy-martin-schultz-antiszemita-megnyilatkozas/30976302.html (last accessed 7 June 2022).
6. 'Until now Orbán said something different about the media' (Hungarian), Index, 24 September 2019, https://index.hu/belfold/2019/09/24/orban_media_foleny/ (last accessed 7 June 2022).
7. 'Centralized media system: Soft censorship, 2018' (Hungarian), report, Mérték Media Analysis Workshop, 30 November 2019, https://mertek.eu/wp-content/uploads/2020/01/MertekFuzetek17.pdf (last accessed 7 June 2022).
8. Veszprém is a city of 60,000 in western Hungary and my electoral district in 1990.
9. István Csurka, vice-president of the MDF, quoted by Zoltán Farkas, 'The "successful sector" of the Antall government: media policy' (Hungarian), in Csaba Gombár, Elemér Hankiss and László Lengyel, eds., *Government assessed 1990–1994* (Hungarian), Budapest, Korridor Kiadó, 1994.
10. This involved the privatization of *Új Magyarország*, *Új Hírek*, and *Magyar Nemzet*, and pressures placed on journalists at *Heti Magyarország*. See Péter Bajomi-Lázár, 'Between authoritarianism and liberalism' (Hungarian), *Politikatudományi Szemle*, vol. 26, no. 1, 2019, pp. 79–104.
11. Duna Television broadcast its programmes via satellite, so this could be viewed far beyond the borders of the country. The mission of Duna TV was a legitimate aim and it was supported by all parties.
12. The National Radio and Television Body (ORTT) created independent supervisory boards for Hungarian Radio, Hungarian Television, Duna Television, and the Hungarian News Agency (MTI). The boards consisted of members delegated by all parliamentary parties and NGOs. The president of the media authority was appointed by the prime minister and the president of the republic, by mutual agreement.

13. József Debreczeni, *Viktor Orbán* (Hungarian), Budapest, Osiris Press, 2002.
14. 'Ervin Tamás: I drafted newspaper banners, that' s all' (Hungarian), 24.hu, 3 January 2022, https://24.hu/belfold/2022/01/03/tamas-ervin-nepszabadsag-interju/ (last accessed 7 June 2022).
15. István Elek, 'Television—press—politics' (Hungarian), in *Political yearbook of Hungary*, 1999 (Hungarian), Budapest, Demokrácia Kutatások Magyar Központja Alapítvány, 1999, pp. 250–6.
16. *Magyar Nemzet* and *Magyar Hírlap*.
17. The allocation of two radio frequencies to Class FM (linked to Fidesz) and the socialist-linked Neo FM was a result of one of the most scandalous political pacts, and was later found in court to be unlawful.
18. György Petőcz, 'The Milla feeling' (Hungarian), *Magyar Narancs*, 19 October 2012.
19. Dorottya Karsay, 'I don't like the system' (Hungarian), song, https://www.youtube.com/watch?v=R6zrs0r7JIc.
20. The National Media and Infocommunications Authority was set up in August 2010. The December act consolidated the system of media administration and the mandates of the officials, and sealed it in the Constitution.
21. Hungarian Radio, Hungarian Television, Duna Television and the Hungarian News Agency (MTI).
22. 'The lawnmower sets off in the public media' (Hungarian), Index, 6 July 2011, https://index.hu/kultur/media/2011/07/06/beindult_a_funyiro_a_kozmediaban/ (last accessed 7 June 2022).
23. This was proved by an international report in 2019, 'The independence of media regulatory authorities in Europe', European Audiovisual Observatory, Council of Europe, 2019, https://rm.coe.int/the-independence-of-media-regulatory-authorities-in-europe/168097e504 (last accessed 7 June 2022).
24. 'Study of the implementation of the new provisions in the revised Audiovisual Media Services Directive (AVMSD)', European Commission, 1 February 2021, https://digital-strategy.ec.europa.eu/en/library/study-implementation-new-provisions-revised-audiovisual-media-services-directive-avmsd (last accessed 7 June 2022).

25. 'Retaining the Hungarian quality of existence' (Hungarian), Viktor Orbán's speech at the Kötcse forum, https://2010-2015.miniszterelnok.hu/cikk/megorizni_a_letezes_magyar_minoseget (last accessed 7 June 2022).
26. Accusations of paedophilia surfaced in the 1990s in regard to a book Daniel Cohn-Bendit had written in the 1970s. The accusations proved untrue.
27. 'What is the Hírcentrum's problem with Cohn-Bendit?' (Hungarian), Index, 8 April 2011, https://index.hu/kultur/media/2011/04/08/a_hircentrum_meghamisitja_a_hireket/ (last accessed 7 June 2022).
28. Ibid.
29. Survey by the Republikon Institute, 5 January 2011, http://index.hu/kultur/media/2011/01/05/jobbra_tolodott_az_mtv/ (last accessed 13 January 2011).
30. '"I suppose the mafia might be like this": What it's like in state TV' (Hungarian), *Szabad Európa*, 10 November 2020, https://www.szabadeuropa.hu/a/a-maffiaban-lehet-hasonlo-gondolom-ilyen-a-kozteve-belulrol-mtva-m1/30938814.html (last accessed 7 June 2022).
31. 'State media say it infringes their freedom if they have to call in opposition politicians' (Hungarian), HVG, https://hvg.hu/itthon/20180330_A_kozmedia_szerint_az_o_szabadsagukat_serti_ha_ellenzekieket_is_be_kell_hivniuk (last accessed 7 June 2022).
32. 'New Hungarian media regulation' (Hungarian), National Media and Infocommunications Authority, November 2011, https://nmhh.hu/dokumentum/191862/az_uj_magyar_mediaszabalyozas_hun_web.pdf (last accessed 7 June 2022).
33. News items about Fidesz were 90% positive, and those about opposition parties were 86% negative and mostly ridiculous. Political parties got a total of five minutes campaigning time on Hungarian Television, while Fidesz was a constant presence. 'Preliminary report on Hungary: Parliamentary elections 2018', OSCE ODIHR, n.d., https://www.osce.org/files/f/documents/0/0/377410.pdf (last accessed 7 June 2022).
34. 'Editors' instructions in state TV: "In this institution we do not support the opposition alliance"' (Hungarian), *Szabad Európa*,

12 November 2020, https://www.szabadeuropa.hu/a/szerkesztoi-utasitas-a-koztevenel-ebben-az-intezmenyben-nem-az-ellenzeki-osszefogast-tamogatjak-mtva-fidesz/30940923.html (last accessed 7 June 2022).
35. 'Demonstrators received 14 million HUF fine' (Hungarian), HVG, 17 June 2020, https://hvg.hu/itthon/20200617_szel_bernadett_dudalos_tuntetes (last accessed 7 June 2022).
36. 'The Media Council has no competence over public media audio recordings', MNHH, 8 December 2020, https://english.nmhh.hu/article/216512/The_Media_Council_has_no_competence_over_public_media_audio_recordings.
37. Euro Publicity and Publimont.
38. The newspaper *Metropol* was purchased from the Swedish Modern Times Group.
39. For example, Ringier and Axel Springer.
40. Right-wing online media include MNO, PestiSrácok, and Tutiblog.
41. Communications agencies falling under Fidesz's business interests from 2010 to 2014 were IMG, VivaKi, Bell & Partners, Initiative Media, Hung-Ister, Y&P, HG360 and the Mahir Group. The majority of these agencies were small companies in 2010; thanks to winning public procurement tenders, they grew into the biggest players in the Hungarian communications sector.
42. Attila Bátorfy presented the operation of this empire in his article 'How did Orbán and Simicka's media empire operate?' (Hungarian), Kreatív, 18 February 2015, http://kreativ.hu/cikk/hogyan_mukodott_orban_es_simicska_mediabirodalma (last accessed 7 June 2022).
43. Ibid.
44. The highest profit rates were achieved by Publimont (39%), Class FM (35%), Hung-Ister (28%), EuroAWK (27.7%), and *Magyar Nemzet* (23%).
45. Amendment to various tax Acts, other related Acts, and Act CXXII of 2010 on the Hungarian Tax and Customs Authority, National Assembly, October 2014, https://www.parlament.hu/irom40/01705/01705.pdf (last accessed 7 June 2022).
46. Balázs Weyer and Péter Nádori were both founders of Origo.

47. Interview with András Pethő and Péter Uj (https://www.youtube.com/watch?v=6RMcVicfVWE (last accessed 7 June 2022), originally broadcast on 11 October 2016, *Alinda*, Hír TV.
48. András Pethő in conversation with Szabolcs Panyi and Róbert Pálinkás Szűcs on a Direkt36 podcast, https://open.spotify.com/episode/2uqOGwwjNu8IdtqIZAQCy2 (last accessed 7 June 2022).
49. 'The veil over János Lázár's secret missions begins to flutter' (Hungarian), Origo, 8 May 2014, https://www.origo.hu/itthon/20140508-lazar-janos-titkos-kulfoldi-kikuldetesei-es-szallaskoltsege.html (last accessed 7 June 2022).
50. 'Telekom sold Origo to New Wave media' (Hungarian), 444, 17 December 2015, https://444.hu/2015/12/17/a-telekom-eladta-az-origot-a-vs-t-kiado-new-wave-medianak (last accessed 7 June 2022).
51. 'Origo passes to Matolcsy's son' (Hungarian), 24.hu, 28 June 2017, https://24.hu/media/2017/06/28/matolcsy-fianak-cegehez-kerult-az-origo/ (last accessed 7 June 2022).
52. 'Origo journalist leaves because of senseless servility' (Hungarian), Index, 27 March 2017, https://index.hu/kultur/media/2017/03/27/birkas_peter_origo_techrovat/ (last accessed 7 June 2022).
53. 'Dismissed Origo journalist says they've turned the magazine into a worthless factory of lies' (Hungarian), Index, 10 March 2017, https://index.hu/kultur/media/2017/03/10/origo_elbocsatas_bucsulevel/ (last accessed 7 June 2022).
54. 'Government-friendly media lose 109 correction cases in 2018' (Hungarian), Átlátszó, 7 February 2019, https://atlatszo.hu/2019/02/07/109-helyreigazitasi-pert-vesztett-2018-ban-a-kormanykozeli-media/ (last accessed 7 June 2022).
55. 'TV2 may be the jewel of the Simicska–Nyerges empire' (Hungarian), HVG, 17 May 2013, https://hvg.hu/gazdasag/20130517_Nyerges_Tv2_Infoncenter_vasarlas (last accessed 7 June 2022).
56. 'Andy Vajna gets 672 billion from the state for TV2' (Hungarian), 444, 15 December 2015, https://444.hu/2015/12/15/heti-valasz-andy-vajna-672-milliardos-hitelt-kap-az-allamtol-a-tv2-re.
57. 'Deutsch admitted that the advertising tax is a political weapon' (Hungarian), HVG, 18 September 2014, https://hvg.hu/

itthon/20140918_Deutsch_elismerte_hogy_a_reklamado_politi (last accessed 7 June 2022).
58. 'Not Balkan, more like Ukraine: War breaks out in the TV market' (Hungarian), HVG, 10 March 2014, https://m.hvg.hu/itthon/20140310_RTL_TV2_mediapiac_harc (last accessed 7 June 2022).
59. 'We'll show you who is behind TV2 but the owner may soon hide' (Hungarian), G7, 25 September 2019, https://g7.hu/vallalat/20190925/megmutatjuk-ki-all-most-a-tv2-mogott-de-hamarosan-elrejtozhet-a-tulajdonos/ (last accessed 7 June 2022).
60. 'Lajos Simicska: The media war isn't about money' (Hungarian), Origo, 6 February 2015, https://www.origo.hu/gazdasag/20150206-simicska-lajos-szerint-a-mediahaboru-nem-a-penzrol-szol.html (last accessed 7 June 2022).
61. 'EU and Hungarian public money in the service of the government party takeover of the media' (Hungarian), Kmonitor, 22 December 2016, https://adatbazis.k-monitor.hu/hirek/magyar-hirek/unios-es-magyar-kozpenzek-a-kormanyparti-mediafoglalas-szolgalataban-2014-2016 (last accessed 7 June 2022).
62. Elena Vartanova, 'The Russian media model in the context of post-Soviet dynamics', in Daniel C. Hallin and Paolo Mancini, eds., *Comparing Media Systems Beyond the Western World*, Cambridge University Press, 2011, pp. 119–42.
63. Act CXXIX of 2015 on the right of informational self-determination and on freedom of information.
64. Section 17 of Act XLIII of 2010 on the legal status of members of the government and state secretaries.
65. Pál Dániel Rényi, 'Orbán's people build a gigantic central media holding' (Hungarian), 444, 27 August 2018, https://444.hu/2018/08/27/gigantikus-kozponti-mediaholdingot-epitenek-orban-emberei (last accessed 7 June 2022).
66. 'KESMA trial: Questions and Answers' (Hungarian), Tasz, n.d., https://tasz.hu/kesma (last accessed 7 June 2022).
67. Ibid
68. 'Jourová: Commission unable to act on Orbán-allied Hungarian media giant', Euractiv, 4 May 2021, https://www.euractiv.com/

section/politics/short_news/jourova-commission-unable-to-act-on-orban-ally-hungarian-media-giant/ (last accessed 7 June 2022).
69. 'Judit Varga: "We are the hard core in Europe who say: Hey guys, this is madness"' (Hungarian), 444, 26 July 2019, https://444.hu/2019/07/26/varga-judit-mi-vagyunk-a-kemenymag-akik-vaganyan-elmondjak-europaban-hogy-gyerekek-ez-hulyeseg (last accessed 7 June 2022).
70. 'Infected media system: Resources for information on politics in Hungary, 2020' (Hungarian), Mérték Media Analysis Workshop, November 2020, Friedrich Ebert Foundation, https://mertek.eu/wp-content/uploads/2020/12/Megfertozott_mediarendszer.pdf (last accessed 7 June 2022).
71. 'Strawmen and oligarchs' (Hungarian), RTL Klub, programme entitled *Házon kívül*, 9 March 2021.
72. András Pethő and András Szabó, 'The secret story of Simicska's downfall revealed' (Hungarian), Direkt36, 14 January 2019, https://www.direkt36.hu/feltarul-simicska-bukasanak-titkos-tortenete/ (last accessed 7 June 2022).
73. Ibid.
74. A series of financial investigations was launched against Spéder, with a house search and a press campaign, and he had to cede many of his more important companies to Orbán's new people.
75. 'The expansion of the pro-government media empire from 2010' (Hungarian), Átlátszó, n.d., https://atlo.team/wp-content/uploads/2020/08/mediaeng.png (last accessed 7 June 2022).
76. Péter Bajomi-Lázár, 'The patron–client media system and the Maslow pyramid of journalists' needs' (Hungarian), *Médiakutató*, vol. 20, no. 1, 2019.
77. 'Ripost staff member quits' (Hungarian), 24.hu, 18 April 2017, https://24.hu/media/2017/04/18/felmondott-a-ripost-egyik-munkatarsa/ (last accessed 7 June 2022).
78. 'Media freedom in Hungary ahead of the 2022 election', International Press Institute, 23 March 2022, https://vsquare.org/ipi-mission-report-media-freedom-in-hungary-ahead-of-2022-election/ (last accessed 7 June 2022).
79. Fanni Tóth, Sabina Mihelj and Václav Štětka, 'A media repertoires approach to selective exposure: News consumption and political

polarization in Eastern Europe', *International Journal of Press*, 12 January 2022.

8. FROM COMMUNICATION TO PROPAGANDA

1. Roxette, 'Listen to your heart', https://www.youtube.com/watch?v=yCC_b5WHLX0 (last accessed 7 June 2022).
2. Péter Kóczián, Attila Ószabó and Éva Vajda, 'Face the camera: Two-faced people in the media' (Hungarian), *Élet és Irodalom*, 5 February 1999.
3. Pál Dániel Rényi, 'The shadow president' (Hungarian), *Magyar Narancs*, 1 September 2011.
4. Arthur Finkelstein presentation at the CERVO Institute Forum, 'Political campaigns in the 21st century: Challenges and perspectives', 2011, https://www.youtube.com/watch?v=IfCBpCBOECU (last accessed 7 June 2022).
5. Pál Dániel Rényi, 'The brains of the castle: The career of Arthur J. Finkelstein' (Hungarian), *Magyar Narancs*, 7 March 2013.
6. 'Jobbik's image of minorities and the media representation of it in the 2010 parliamentary election campaign' (Hungarian), *Médiakutató*, Spring 2011, https://www.mediakutato.hu/cikk/2011_01_tavasz/05_jobbik_kissebsegkepe (last accessed 7 June 2022).
7. The official numbers of those seeking asylum in Hungary were in 2014: 42,777, in 2015: 177,135, in 2016: 29,432, in 2017: 3,397, in 2018: 617. See National Statistical Office, https://www.ksh.hu/docs/hun/xstadat/xstadat_eves/i_wnvn003.html.
8. Viktor Orbán's speech on 15 March 2016, https://miniszterelnok.hu/speech-by-prime-minister-viktor-orban-on-15-march/.
9. Pro-government media were reportedly given instructions to select mostly pictures of young men and not women and children in their publications in order to underline the government's message of an impending threat.
10. In 2016–17 only a few thousand refugees were admitted to Hungary, and they immediately went to Western Europe.
11. 'Woman who spoke on M1 about returning to Hungary because of safety concerns in Sweden convicted on several counts' (Hungarian),

HVG, 12 March 2018, https://hvg.hu/itthon/20180312_Tobbszor_is_eliteltek_a_not_aki_az_M1en_arrol_beszelt_a_rossz_sved_kozbiztonsag_miatt_tert_haza (last accessed 7 June 2022).
12. 'One hundred lies of the Fidesz media empire' (Hungarian), 444, 24 October 2018, https://444.hu/2018/10/24/a-fideszes-mediabirodalom-100-hazugsaga (last accessed 7 June 2022).
13. 'Origo whipping up panic' (Hungarian), Index, 28 April 2018, https://index.hu/kultur/media/2018/04/28/migransfrasz_az_origon/ (last accessed 7 June 2022).
14. 'On the anti-migration quota referendum campaign' (Hungarian), Transparency International Hungary, 14 December 2014, https://transparency.hu/hirek/a-kvotaellenes-nepszavazasi-kampanyrol/ (last accessed 7 June 2022).
15. 'Campaign on Hungarian quota referendum costs more than the British spent altogether in the Brexit campaign' (Hungarian), Átlátszó, 28 September 2016, https://igyirnankmi.atlatszo.hu/2016/09/28/tobbe-kerul-a-kvotakampany-mint-amennyit-a-britek-osszesen-koltottek-a-brexit-kampanyban/ (last accessed 7 June 2022).
16. According to current Hungarian law, for a referendum to be valid the number of votes has to be 50% of those entitled to vote +1.
17. Sixth Amendment to the Fundamental Law, National Assembly, May 2018.
18. Between July 2015 and October 2017, support for Fidesz–KDNP increased by 17 percentage points in the entire population, and by 20 percentage points among those who expressed a party preference. 'Tárki: Ruling parties continue to gain sway' (Hungarian), Tárki, 26 October 2017, https://www.tarki.hu/hu/news/2017/kitekint/20171026_valasztas.html (last accessed 7 June 2022).
19. Anikó Bernát, Endre Sik and Blanka Szeitl, 'Fluctuation of xenophobia and fears related to migration in Hungary and the Visegrád countries' (Hungarian), *Regio*, vol. 24, no. 2, 2016, pp. 81–108.
20. 'Easter interview with the prime minister in *Magyar Idők*' (Hungarian), Prime Minister's Office, 15 April 2017, https://miniszterelnok.hu/orban-viktor-interjuja-a-magyar-idokben/ (last accessed 7 June 2022).

NOTES pp. [277–281]

21. 'The complete national consultation questionnaire' (Hungarian), 444, 28 September 2017, https://444.hu/2017/09/28/itt-a-teljesen-nemzeti-konzultacios-kerdoiv (last accessed 7 June 2022).
22. 'We sued the secret service for the confidential Soros study: Orbán's crowd are playing Finkelstein's tune again' (Hungarian), Átlátszó, 2 February 2017, https://atlatszo.hu/kozpenz/2017/01/11/bepereltuk-a-titkosszolgalatot-az-eltitkolt-soros-tanulmanyert-orbanek-megint-finkelstein-kottajabol-jatszanak/ (last accessed 7 June 2022).
23. 'The Finkelstein formula' (German), *Das Magazin*, 12 January 2019.
24. Ibid.
25. 'The Soros phenomenon in public opinion' (Hungarian), *Századvég*, n.d., https://regi.szazadveg.hu/hu/kutatasok/az-alapitvany-kutatasai/piackutatas-kozvelemeny-kutatas/a-soros-jelenseg-a-kozvelemenyben (last accessed 7 June 2022).
26. 'Rogán's mega-office can spend 25 billion HUF' (Hungarian), *Népszabadság*, 30 September 2015, http://nol.hu/belfold/roganteriti-a-penzt-1566209 (last accessed 7 June 2022).
27. Most of the government's polls are carried out by the Code, Market, Opinion and Media Research Institute.
28. Pál Dániel Rényi, 'This isn't journalism, this is political heavy weaponry' (Hungarian), 444, 18 May 2017, https://tldr.444.hu/2017/05/18/fideszmedia (last accessed 7 June 2022).
29. Ibid.
30. The best-known media in this category are Ripost, PestiSracok, Karc FM, 888, and the *Bayer* Show on Echo TV.
31. *Bayer Show*, Echo TV, 13 January 2019, https://echotv.hu/videok/2019/01/13/bayer-show/7402 (last accessed 7 June 2022).
32. József Spirk, 'Measuring everything: Rogán's cabinet office commissioned 400 opinion polls in two and a half years' (Hungarian), 24.hu, 15 January 2020, https://24.hu/belfold/2020/01/15/orban-kormany-kozvelemeny-kutatas-rogan-antal-kabinetiroda-szazadveg/ (last accessed 7 June 2022).
33. 'The state may spend a stadium's worth on propaganda' (Hungarian), G7, 20 February 2020, https://g7.hu/kozelet/20200220/egy-puskas-stadionnyi-penzt-kolthet-propagandara-az-allam/ (last accessed 7 June 2022).

34. These include *Magyar Idők, Lokál, Figyelő*, and the online versions of the county papers owned by Mediaworks, then in Mészáros's ownership. 'The past ten years of Hungarian media' (Hungarian), Atlo, n.d., https://atlo.team/media2020/ (last accessed 7 June 2022).
35. 'PM Orbán buys gov't-critical news to prove freedom of Hungarian press' (Hungarian), *Hungary Today*, 7 July 2021, https://hungarytoday.hu/hungary-press-freedom-viktor-orban-news/ (last accessed 7 June 2022).

9. A PASSIVE PEOPLE?

1. 'You have the right to say no to the Olympics' (Hungarian), Index, 19 January 2017, https://index.hu/sport/futball/2017/01/19/joga_van_nemet_mondani_az_olimpiar/ (last accessed 7 June 2022).
2. István György Tóth, 'Lack of confidence, disturbing the norm, sense of justice, and paternalism in the value structure of Hungarian society' (Hungarian), Tárki Social Research Institute, 2009, https://www.tarki.hu/hu/research/gazdkult/gazdkult_elemzeszaro_toth.pdf.
3. György Csepeli and Gergely Prazsák, 'Feudalism that won't go away' (Hungarian), *Társadalomkutatás*, vol. 29, no. 1, 2011, pp. 63–79.
4. Annamária Gáti, 'Active citizenship in Hungary: An international comparison' (Hungarian), *Tárki-Tudok*, 10 January 2010.
5. Ibid.
6. Gábor G. Fodor, 'Good and bad governance in Hungary, or the problem of measuring democratic quality' (Hungarian), *Politikatudományi Szemle*, vol. 17, no. 1, 2008, pp. 131–44.
7. Gábor G. Fodor and István Stumpf, 'Neo-Weberian state and good governance' (Hungarian), *Nemzeti Érdek*, Autumn 2008, pp. 5–6.
8. Hungarian Central Statistics Office, 'Labour survey 2015, Q2 supplementary survey' (Hungarian), Budapest, 2015.
9. Between 1989 and 2011 there were on average five–six strikes a year among those required to provide 'a sufficient service', but since 2014 there has been only one. Sára Hungler, 'Effective opportunities for and limitations of interest advocacy in the light of the current labour regulations' (Hungarian), Friedrich Ebert Foundation, 16 November 2016.

10. 'PISA 2015: Results in focus', OECD, 2016, https://www.oecd.org/pisa/pisa-2015-results-in-focus.pdf (last accessed 7 June 2022).
11. 'On the track of workfare in Borsod County' (Hungarian), *Szabad Európa*, 9 February 2021, https://www.szabadeuropa.hu/a/a-kozmunka-nyomaban-borsodban/31090537.html (last accessed 7 June 2022).
12. 'The Fidesz secret: Economic voting in Hungary' (Hungarian), 21 Kutatóközpont, n.d., https://21kutatokozpont.hu/wp-content/uploads/2020/06/Fidesz_titok_21_Kutat%C3%B3k%C3%B6zpont_tanulm%C3%A1ny.pdf (last accessed 7 June 2022).
13. Márton Gerő, 'Turned away, and a choking embrace: The changing relationship between NGOs and the state in a phase of growing control' (Hungarian), in Anna Fejős and Dorottya Szikra, eds., *Support and attack* (Hungarian), Budapest, Centre for Social Sciences, 2020.
14. Thomas Carothers and Saskia Brechenmacher, *Closing Space: Democracy and Human Rights Support under Fire*, Washington DC, Carnegie Endowment for International Peace, 2014.
15. 'Lázár wants to suspend the Norway Grants' (Hungarian), Index, 9 May 2014, https://index.hu/belfold/2014/05/09/lazar_felfuggesztene_a_norveg_civil_alap_tamogatasait/ (last accessed 7 June 2022).
16. 'Timeline of governmental attacks against Hungarian NGO sphere', Helsinki Commission, 18 November 2014, https://helsinki.hu/wp-content/uploads/Timeline_of_gov_attacks_against_HU_NGOs_18112014.pdf (last accessed 7 June 2022).
17. Speech by Viktor Orbán at the Bálványos (Baile Tusnad) Summer School on 26 July 2014.
18. 'We found out that Viktor Orbán personally ordered the attacks on NGOs' (Hungarian), Tasz, 6 October 2016, https://tasz.hu/cikkek/kideritettuk-hogy-orban-viktor-szemelyesen-rendelte-el-a-civilek-vegzalasat (last accessed 7 June 2022).
19. 'Interview with Viktor Orbán: "We don't want a multicultural society"' (German), *Frankfurter Allgemeine*, 5 February 2015.
20. '"Norway owes us," says Hungary, after Oslo suspends aid in NGO row', Euronews, 23 July 2021, https://www.euronews.com/2021/07/23/norway-suspends-aid-to-hungary-over-who-should-control-funds-for-ngos (last accessed 7 June 2022).

21. 'Orbán personally ordered the attacks on NGOs' (Hungarian), 444, 6 October 2016, https://444.hu/2016/10/06/orban-szemelyesen-rendelte-el-a-civilek-elleni-hadjaratot (last accessed 7 June 2022).
22. 'Here's the new enemy: Another attack launched against NGOs' (Hungarian), *Magyar Nemzet*, https://magyarnemzet.hu/archivum/belfold-archivum/megvan-az-uj-ellenseg-ujabb-tamadas-indul-a-civilek-ellen-3894465/ (last accessed 7 June 2022).
23. Act LXXVI of 2017 on the transparency of organizations funded from abroad.
24. 'Russia: Four years of Putin's "foreign agents" law to shackle and silence NGOs', Amnesty International, 18 November 2016.
25. 'Orbán claims there are sixty-three organizations in Hungary financed by Soros' (Hungarian), 24.hu, 10 January 2019, https://24.hu/belfold/2019/01/10/a-nap-amikor-orban-viktor-szoba-all-az-ujsagirokkal/#63-olyan-szervezet-van-magyarorszagon-amelyeket-soros-gyorgy-finansziroz-allitja-orban (last accessed 7 June 2022).
26. For the timeline of events of the CEU attack, see https://www.ceu.edu/istandwithceu/timeline-events (last accessed 7 June 2022).
27. Karc FM radio station, programme entitled *Paláver*, 25 April 2017, 16:00.
28. https://curia.europa.eu/jcms/upload/docs/application/pdf/2020-06/cp200073en.pdf; https://curia.europa.eu/jcms/upload/docs/application/pdf/2020-10/cp200125en.pdf.
29. 'Mesterházy wins case against CÖF' (Hungarian), HVG, 4 June 2014, https://hvg.hu/itthon/20140604_Mesterhazy_pert_nyert_a_COF_ellen_a_bohoc (last accessed 7 June 2022).
30. '20 million HUF party money, 290 million HUF private donations to the government's NGOs' (Hungarian), Átlátszó, 20 June 2014, https://atlatszo.hu/2014/06/06/20-millio-forint-partpenz-290-millio-forint-maganadomany-a-kormany-civiljeinek (last accessed 7 June 2022).
31. 'It's cool to demonstrate pro-government' (Hungarian), Átlátszó, 22 October 2012, https://atlatszo.hu/2012/10/22/itt-a-civil-tamogatasok-listaja-a-kormany-mellett-demonstralni-meno/ (last accessed 7 June 2022).
32. 'The Centre of Fundamental Rights receives public funding through another foundation' (Hungarian), Átlátszó, 4 March 2021, https://

atlatszo.hu/kozpenz/2021/03/04/egy-alapitvanyon-keresztul-onti-a-penzt-a-kabinetiroda-az-alapjogokert-kozpontba/ (last accessed 7 June 2022).
33. 'A super state or an alliance of sovereign states?', Centre for Fundamental Rights, https://alapjogokert.hu/en/2019/08/27/a-super-state-or-an-alliance-of-sovereign-states/.
34. 'US conservative conference with Hungary's hardline leader reflects Republican divide', Reuters, 5 April 2022, https://www.reuters.com/world/us/us-conservative-conference-with-hungarys-hardline-leader-reflects-republican-2022-04-05/.
35. Dániel Oross and Andrea Szabó, 'Is the national student representation a social movement?' (Hungarian), *Educatio*, vol. 26, no. 1, 2017, pp. 15–25.
36. Dániel Mikecz, 'Nothing about us without us: Demonstrations, political activism under the Orbán regime' (Hungarian), TK Institute for Political Science and Napvilág Kiadó, 2021, p. 241.
37. Dataset from the European Social Survey, 2019.
38. Viktor Orbán's ceremonial speech on 15 March 2018, About Hungary, https://abouthungary.hu/speeches-and-remarks/orban-viktors-ceremonial-speech-on-the-170th-anniversary-of-the-hungarian-revolution-of-1848.
39. 'Mundruczó et al. take to the red carpet in Venice in a FreeSZFE T-shirt' (Hungarian), 444, 5 September 2020, https://444.hu/2020/09/05/mundruczoek-freeszfe-s-poloban-nyomulgatnak-a-velencei-voros-szonyegen (last accessed 7 June 2022).
40. 'EU2020: Demanding on democracy; Country and trend reports on democratic records by civil liberties organisations across the European Union', Civil Liberties Union for Europe, https://dq4n3btxmr8c9.cloudfront.net/files/AuYJXv/Report_Liberties_EU2020.pdf p. 89 (last accessed 7 June 2022).
41. The police lost all subsequent court cases.
42. Imre Kovách, ed., *Mobility and integration in Hungarian society* (Hungarian), Budapest, Centre for Social Sciences, Argumentum Publishers, 2020.

10. WHO CONTROLS THE PAST CONTROLS THE FUTURE

1. The title of this chapter quotes George Orwell's bon mot from *Nineteen Eighty-Four*.
2. Krisztián Ungváry, 'The House of Chaos' (Hungarian), *Magyar Narancs*, 7 March 2002.
3. Fundamental Law of Hungary, National Avowal, in English: https://2015-2019.kormany.hu/en/doc/the-hungarian-state/the-fundamental-law (last accessed 7 June 2022).
4. Zsolt Sarkadi, 'The man who took the whole country in the dock with him' (Hungarian), 444, 20 November 2021, https://444.hu/tldr/2021/11/20/aki-az-egesz-orszagot-maga-melle-ultette-a-vadlottak-padjara (last accessed 7 June 2022).
5. 'In Hungary everyone wants to be victim' (Hungarian), Telex, 11 March 2021, https://telex.hu/tudomany/2021/03/11/magyarorszagon-is-mindenki-aldozat-akar-lenni (last accessed 7 June 2022).
6. György Majtényi, Zsuzsanna Mikó and Csaba Szabó, eds., *Revolution! Twenty-four found stories*, Budapest, Libri Publishers, Hungarian Historical Archives, 2016, p. 84.
7. Speech by Prime Minister József Antall on 23 October 1990 in the Hungarian Parliament, József Antall Foundation, https://antalljozsef.igytortent.hu/8-beszedek/orszaggyulesi-beszedek/11-az-orszaggyules-1990-evi-oszi-ulesszakanak-10-45-unnepi-ulesnapja-1990-oktober-23 (last accessed 30 June 2022).
8. 'This is how the budget of the memorial year was spent', (Hungarian), 444, 2 Aug 2016, https://444.hu/2016/08/02/eddig-erre-ment-a-56-os-emlekev-135-milliardja (last accessed 7 June 2022).
9. James V. Wertsch, *Voices of Collective Remembering*, Cambridge University Press, 2002.
10. In 2019 Imre Nagy's statue was removed from near the Parliament to a less prominent site in Budapest.
11. Viktor Orbán's speech on 23 October 2016, Prime Minister's Office, https://miniszterelnok.hu/orban-viktor-unnepi-beszede-az-1956-os-forradalom-60-evfordulojan/ (last accessed 7 June 2022).
12. Ferenc Pataki, 'Collective memory and memory policy' (Hungarian), *Magyar Tudomány*, vol. 171, no. 7, 2010.

13. László Kövér's speech at the ceremonial session of the Parliament on 23 October 2016, https://www.parlament.hu/-/az-orszaggyules-unnepi-ule-1 (last accessed 7 June 2022).
14. Orbán's speech on 23 October 2016, 'Today the task of Europe's freedom-loving peoples is to save Brussels from Sovietization', About Hungary, 23 October 2016, https://miniszterelnok.hu/orban-viktor-unnepi-beszede-az-1956-os-forradalom-60-evfordulojan/ (last accessed 30 June 2022).
15. Mária Schmidt's speech at the closing conference of the 1956–2016 commemorative year, given on 16 June 2017, https://www.magyarforradalom1956.hu/v/schmidt-maria-ma-is-ossze-kell-fognia-szabadsagert/, (last accessed 7 June 2022).
16. In the traditional right-wing discourse in the 1920s, Christian often meant simply 'not Jewish'; the 'Christian middle classes' were differentiated from the Jewish bourgeoisie.
17. Scorpions, 'Wind of change', https://www.youtube.com/watch?v=XjFsZj1aHow.
18. 'This homeland is not a free gift to us' (Hungarian), Infostart, 23 October 2019, https://infostart.hu/belfold/2019/10/23/orban-viktor-ezt-a-hazat-nem-ajandekba-kaptuk (last accessed 7 June 2022).
19. Viktor Orbán's commemorative speech, 6 June 2020, https://www.kormany.hu/en/the-prime-minister/the-prime-minister-s-speeches/prime-minister-viktor-orban-s-commemoration-speech.
20. Máté Zombori, *Trauma society*, Budapest, Kijárat Press, 2019.
21. These are the Terror House Museum, the Twentieth Century Institute, and the Twenty-First Century Institute, which are all directed by the same public foundation headed by Mária Schmidt.

11. A POLITICAL TAP DANCE

1. 'Poland, Hungary veto EU budget over new rules linking funding to rule of law', France24, 17 November 2020, https://www.france24.com/en/europe/20201117-poland-hungary-veto-eu-budget-over-new-rules-linking-funding-to-rule-of-law (last accessed 7 June 2022).
2. 'Viktor Orbán's message to young people on the anniversary of the foundation of Fidesz in 2007' (Hungarian), speech by Viktor Orbán,

https://www.youtube.com/watch?v=NtKwEovr5Wo (last accessed 7 June 2022).
3. Speech by Viktor Orbán at the Bálványos (Baile Tusnad) Summer School, 24 July 2010, https://2010-2014.kormany.hu/hu/miniszterelnokseg/miniszterelnok/beszedek-publikaciok-interjuk/orban-viktor-beszede-a-balvanyosi-nyari-szabadegyetemen-es-diaktaborban-2010-julius-24 (last accessed 7 June 2022).
4. 'Speech by Viktor Orbán in Vörösmarty Square', Hungarian Prime Minister's Office, 25 April 2010, https://2010-2014.kormany.hu/hu/miniszterelnokseg/miniszterelnok/beszedek-publikaciok-interjuk/orban-viktor-beszede-a-vorosmarty-teren-2010-aprilis-25 (last accessed 7 June 2022).
5. 'Hungarian foreign policy after the EU presidency' (Hungarian), Hungarian Ministry of Foreign Affairs, 2011, pp. 36–7, https://2010-2014.kormany.hu/download/a/cb/60000/kulpolitikai_strategia_20111219.pdf (last accessed 7 June 2022).
6. 'There is nobody in the world who can call us to account' (Hungarian), Origo, 25 August 2014, https://www.origo.hu/itthon/20140825-orban-uj-feladatot-szabott-a-nagykoveteknek.html (last accessed 7 June 2022).
7. 'Szijjártó: Transformation of foreign policy is at the midpoint' (Hungarian), Infostart, 30 December 2014, https://infostart.hu/kulfold/2014/12/30/szijjarto-a-felenel-tart-a-kulpolitika-atalakitasa-692199/amp (last accessed 30 March 2022).
8. Speech by Viktor Orbán at the meeting of leaders of diplomatic missions, 29 February 2016, https://miniszterelnok.hu/orban-viktor-beszede-a-missziovezetoi-munkaertekezleten (last accessed 7 June 2022).
9. Erin Kristin Jenne and Péter Visnovitz, 'Populist argumentation in foreign policy: The case of Hungary under Viktor Orbán, 2010–2020', *Comparative European Politics*, 14 September 2021, pp. 683–702.
10. Hungarian is one of the Uralic languages, more specifically a Finno-Ugric language. Related languages are those of the Khanty and Mansi peoples who live along the Urals, and also Finnish and Estonian. The Turkic Council was founded by Azerbaijan, Kazakhstan, Kyrgyzstan, Turkey and Uzbekistan in 1992.

11. 'Hungarian foreign policy's Turkic-Kipchak move is not about the economy' (Hungarian), G7, 17 October 2019, https://g7.hu/kozelet/20191017/nem-a-gazdasagrol-szol-a-magyar-kulpolitika-turk-kipcsak-fordulata/ (last accessed 7 June 2022).
12. 'Not much explanation why the Orbán–Erdoğan friendship is good for Hungary' (Hungarian), 444, 22 October 2019, https://444.hu/2019/10/22/nem-nagyon-van-ra-magyarazat-hogy-magyarorszagnak-miert-eri-meg-az-orban-erdogan-baratsag (last accessed 7 June 2022).
13. 'Turkish work: Business deals between the Orbán family and Adnan Polat' (Hungarian), *Magyar Narancs*, 8 July 2016.
14. 'Russian military action reminds Orbán of 1956' (Hungarian), Index, 14 August 2008, https://index.hu/belfold/ovgruzorsz08/ (last accessed 7 June 2022).
15. In 2022 64% of oil and 80% of gas were imported from Russia, and the Paks nuclear plant which provided 45% of Hungary's energy is supplied from Russian sources.
16. András Pethő and András Szabó, 'Orbán's game: The secret story of the relationship he built with Putin comes to light' (Hungarian), 444, 11 March 2018, https://444.hu/2018/03/11/orban-jatszmaja-feltarul-a-putyinnal-kiepitett-kapcsolat-titkos-tortenete (last accessed 7 June 2022).
17. 'EU restrictive measures in response to the crisis in Ukraine', European Council, 19 January 2022, https://www.consilium.europa.eu/en/policies/sanctions/ukraine-crisis/ (last accessed 7 June 2022).
18. 'This is what Orbán and Putin held talks on' (Hungarian), Index, 17 February 2015, https://index.hu/belfold/2015/02/17/ebben_allapodott_meg_orban_es_putyin/ (last accessed 7 June 2022).
19. 'Why is what the government claims about the Russian-linked bank not true?' (Hungarian), Index, 17 June 2019, https://index.hu/velemeny/2019/06/17/nemzetkozi_beruhazasi_bank_orosz_befolyas_racz_andras_velemeny/ (last accessed 7 June 2022).
20. 'Hungary: The Russian-style propaganda law violates human rights and threatens LGBTI people', Amnesty International, 22 July 2021, https://www.amnesty.org/en/documents/eur27/4492/2021/en/ (last accessed 7 June 2022).

21. 'Breaking Europe: Revealing Russian disinformation networks and active measures fuelling secessionism and border revisionism in Central and Eastern Europe', Political Capital, 2020, https://www.politicalcapital.hu/pc-admin/source/documents/zinc_revisionism_comparative.pdf (last accessed 7 June 2022).
22. 'Annual address to the Federal Assembly of the Russian Federation', Kremlin, 25 April 2005, http://en.kremlin.ru/events/president/transcripts/22931 (last accessed 7 June 2022).
23. In 2017 Ukrainian legislators amended the act on education, which restricted the rights of national minorities in Ukraine (primarily the Russian minority) to use their own language. This amendment also had an adverse effect on the 150,000-strong Hungarian community in Ukraine. The law was later declared unconstitutional by the Ukrainian Constitutional Court.
24. 'Sino-Hungarian trade relations', Hungarian Central Statistics Office, 11 March 2014, https://www.ksh.hu/docs/hun/xftp/stattukor/magyarkinaigkapcs.pdf (last accessed 7 June 2022).
25. 'The government "found it difficult to accept" the deepening friendship with China' (Hungarian), Origo, 28 June 2011, https://www.origo.hu/itthon/20110628-a-fidesz-es-a-kdnp-vezetoi-kinaellenes-kijelenteseirol.html (last accessed 7 June 2022).
26. 'Orbán says "Right now, the star in the East shines bright"' (Hungarian), *Magyar Narancs*, 27 November 2017.
27. 'The exorbitantly priced Chinese railway might become profitable after 130 years' (Hungarian), Index, 1 December 2017, https://index.hu/gazdasag/2017/12/01/budapest_belgrad_megterules_vam_kereskedelem_pireusz_kina_131_ev/ (last accessed 7 June 2022).
28. 'Who wins the 500 billion HUF public procurement may become public by Christmas' (Hungarian), G7, 17 October 2018, https://g7.hu/kozelet/20181017/karacsonyra-dolhet-el-ki-nyeri-az-500-milliard-forintos-kozbeszerzest/ (last accessed 7 June 2022).
29. 'Canada arrests Huawei CFO: She faces US extradition for allegedly violating Iran sanctions', CNBC, 5 December 2018, https://www.cnbc.com/2018/12/05/canada-reportedly-arrests-huawei-cfo-facing-us-extradition-for-violating-iran-sanctions.html (last accessed 7 June 2022).

30. 'Assessing Huawei risk', RWR Advisory Group, May 2019, https://www.rwradvisory.com/wp-content/uploads/2019/05/Assessing-Huawei-Risk.pdf (last accessed 7 June 2022).
31. Szabolcs Panyi, 'Hungary's government is quietly neck-deep in the US–Huawei war' (Hungarian), Direkt36, 1 November 2019, https://www.direkt36.hu/en/csendben-csinalja-de-mar-nyakig-benne-van-a-magyar-kormany-a-huawei-haboruban/ (last accessed 7 June 2022).
32. Szabolcs Panyi, 'How Orbán's Eastern opening brought Chinese spy games to Budapest' (Hungarian), Direkt36, 15 March 2021, https://www.direkt36.hu/kemjatszmakat-hozott-budapestre-orban-kinai-nyitasa/ (last accessed 7 June 2022).
33. In 2022 Hungary was the only EU member country that had not restricted any 5G vendors and declined to join a US-led initiative to freeze out Chinese components. See European Court of Auditors, 2022, https://www.eca.europa.eu/Lists/ECADocuments/SR22_03/SR_Security-5G-networks_EN.pdf (last accessed 7 June 2022).
34. Szabolcs Panyi, 'Hungary's mega-investment in higher education to be made from a Chinese loan' (Hungarian), Direkt36, 6 April 2021, https://www.direkt36.hu/en/kinai-hitelbol-keszul-a-magyar-felsooktatas-oriasberuhazasa-a-kormany-mar-oda-is-igerte-egy-kinai-cegnek/ (last accessed 7 June 2022).
35. Speech by Viktor Orbán at the Századvég conference on 30 April 2012, https://www.youtube.com/watch?v=k6QeO1zTLg8 (posted 12 August 2016, last accessed 7 June 2022).
36. 'Hillary Clinton spoke to Orbán about checks and balances' (Hungarian), Index, 30 June 2011, https://index.hu/belfold/2011/06/30/hillary_clinton_szerint_tovabb_kell_epiteni_a_demokraciat/ (last accessed 7 June 2022).
37. 'Orbán is the first in the world to stand behind Trump', Index, 23 July 2016, https://index.hu/belfold/2016/07/23/orban_a_vilagon_elsokent_allt_be_trump_moge/ (last accessed 7 June 2022).
38. 'Hungary's leader fights criticism in U.S. via vast influence campaign', *New York Times*, 4 October 2021.
39. 'Trump lauds Hungary's nationalist PM Orbán for "tremendous job"', *The Guardian*, 13 May 2019.

40. 'Trump requested it, Orbán's people provided it: The "historic" gas deal and what lies behind it' (Hungarian), HVG, 9 September 2020, https://hvg.hu/360/20200909_USA_Orban_Shell_gaz_lng_raketarendszer_jogallam_lebontasa (last accessed 7 June 2022).
41. 'Szijjártó announces a historic gas deal' (Hungarian), HVG, 4 September 2020, https://hvg.hu/kkv/20200904_szijjarto_peter_shell_gaz (last accessed 7 June 2022).
42. 'Joint statement of the heads of government of the Visegrad Group countries (19 June 2015)', Bratislava. See www.visegradgroup.eu/calendar/2015/joint-statement-of-the (last accessed 7 June 2022).
43. 'According to Viktor Orbán, the survival of Europe is at stake' (Hungarian), speech by Viktor Orbán at Bálványos 2015, Hirado, 25 July 2015, https://hirado.hu/2015/07/25/hallgassa-eloben-orban-viktor-tusnadfurdoi-beszedet (last accessed 7 June 2022).
44. 'Diverging voices, converging policies: The Visegrad states' reactions to the Russia–Ukraine conflict', Heinrich Böll Foundation, 2015, https://www.ivo.sk/buxus/docs/publikacie/subory/Diverging_voices_converging_policies.pdf (last accessed 7 June 2022).
45. 'Tension between Slovakia and Hungary: Orbán's people sound a 100 billion forint retreat' (Hungarian), *Szabad Európa*, 21 October 2021, https://www.szabadeuropa.hu/a/szlovakia-es-magyarorszag-egymasnak-feszul-orbanek-100-milliardos-visszavonulot-fujtak/31518929.html (last accessed 7 June 2022).
46. György Kerényi, 'Jealous of Orbán and silently angry: The relationship between neighbouring countries and the Hungarian government' (Hungarian), *Szabad Európa*, 29 March 2021, https://www.szabadeuropa.hu/a/orban-irigyseg-es-nema-duh-a-szomszedos-orszagok-es-a-magyar-kormany-viszonya/31162938.html (last accessed 7 June 2022).
47. 'How the Hungarian government smuggled the Macedonian ex-head of government into the country' (Hungarian), *Deutsche Welle*, 14 November 2018.
48. 'Orbán on Gruevski: "One treats one's allies decently"' (Hungarian), 444, 23 November 2018, https://444.hu/2018/11/23/orban-gruevszkirol-az-ember-tisztessegesen-banik-a-szovetsegeseivel (last accessed: 7 June 2022).

49. 'Why is it good for Hungary to line up behind Bosnian Serb extremists?' (Hungarian), *Szabad Európa*, 20 December 2021, https://www.szabadeuropa.hu/a/orban-viktor-bosznia-szerb--dodik-tamogatas/31603157.html (last accessed 7 June 2022).
50. 'The Polish and Hungarian stance might be against Slovakia's interest, says Čaputová' (Hungarian), Ma7, 27 November 2020, https://ma7.sk/aktualis/caputova-a-magyar-es-a-lengyel-allaspont-sertheti-szlovakia-erdekeit (last accessed 7 June 2022).
51. 'Orbán's circuit to Bavaria before EU summit' (Hungarian), Euronews, 23 September 2015, https://hu.euronews.com/2015/09/23/orban-bajororszagi-kiteroje-az-eu-csucs-elott (last accessed 7 June 2022).
52. 'Merkel took on a conflict with Orbán' (Hungarian), Index, 2 February 2015, https://index.hu/belfold/2015/02/02/merkel_orban_talalkozo_konfliktus/ (last accessed 7 June 2022).
53. Szabolcs Panyi, 'How Orbán played Germany, Europe's great power' (Hungarian), 444, 18 September 2020, https://www.direkt36.hu/en/a-magyar-nemet-kapcsolatok-rejtett-tortenete/ (last accessed 7 June 2020).
54. 'Viktor Orbán is following the wrong political path' (German), *Der Spiegel*, 1 March 2019.
55. In 2011 Orbán extradited to Azerbaijan an Azeri soldier who had been convicted of murder, and who on his return home was immediately set free and feted as a hero.
56. 'A pro-European vision for the European Union: The perspective of the Visegrad countries', V4 Europe Project, 26 July 2018, https://europatarsasag.hu/sites/default/files/open-space/documents/magyarorszagi-summarydiscussionpaperv4europefinal20180816.pdf (last accessed 7 June 2022).
57. 'President Macron's speech on new initiative for Europe', 26 September 2017, https://www.elysee.fr/en/emmanuel-macron/2017/09/26/president-macron-gives-speech-on-new-initiative-for-europe (last accessed 7 June 2022).
58. 'Merkel, Macron bridge differences on EU reform', Politico, 19 June 2018, https://www.politico.eu/article/angela-merkel-emmanuel-macron-bridge-differences-on-eu-reform-france-germany/ (last accessed 7 June 2022).

59. 'How the E.U. allowed Hungary to become an illiberal model', *New York Times*, 3 January 2022.
60. 'Rule of law report: Country chapter on the rule of law situation in Hungary', European Commission, 30 September 2020.
61. 'Hungary calls Vera Jourová to quit over "sick democracy" comment', Euronews, 29 September 2020, https://www.euronews.com/my-europe/2020/09/29/hungary-calls-for-eu-commissioner-jourova-to-resign-over-derogatory-comments (last accessed 7 June 2022).
62. '"This is not the time for vetos": Stalemate in the EU' (Hungarian), *Szabad Európa*, 17 November 2020, https://www.szabadeuropa.hu/a/ez-nem-a-vetok-ideje-patthelyzet-az-eu-ban/30954946.html (last accessed 7 June 2022).
63. 'Tamás Deutsch suspended from EPP group, 18 December 2020', *Parliament Magazine*, https://www.theparliamentmagazine.eu/news/article/tamas-deutsch-suspended-from-epp-group-following-gestapo-remarks (last accessed 7 June 2022).
64. 'Manfred Weber has insulted the Hungarian people' (Hungarian), *Die Welt*, 21 December 2020, https://www.welt.de/politik/ausland/plus222862768/Viktor-Orban-Manfred-Weber-hat-unser-ganzes-Volk-beleidigt.html?cid=onsite.onsitesearch (last accessed 7 June 2022).
65. 'With Hungarian eyes, head, and heart' (Hungarian), *Magyar Nemzet*, 20 March 2006.
66. Lajos Fülep, 'National self-centredness' (Hungarian), *Válasz*, vol. 1, no. 1, May 1934.
67. Speech by Viktor Orbán at the Bálványos (Baile Tusnad) Summer School on 28 July 2012, http://2010-2015.miniszterelnok.hu/beszed/a_jo_romaniai_dontes_tavolmaradni_az_urnaktol (last accessed 7 June 2022).

EPILOGUE

1 'Supreme Court rulings: Court decisions' (Hungarian), Supreme Court, vol. 72, January 2024, pp. 31–6, https://kuria-birosag.hu/sites/default/files/kuriai_dontesek/72_evfolyam_1_szam.pdf
2 'Péter Magyar, Judit Varga's ex-husband, speaks out' (Hungarian),

Partizán, 10 February 2024, https://www.youtube.com/watch?v=8cJulnczg2E

3. 'The results of the European Parliament election', National Election Office (Hungary), 20 June 2024, https://vtr.valasztas.hu/ep2024

4. 'Hungary—National parliament voting intention', Politico, 27 November 2024, https://www.politico.eu/europe-poll-of-polls/hungary/ (last accessed 5 January 2026).

5. 'Hungarian food prices exploded so much the echo can still be heard' (Hungarian), Portfolio, 14 October 2025, https://www.portfolio.hu/gazdasag/20251014/akkorat-szolt-a-magyar-elelmiszerarak-robbanasa-hogy-meg-most-is-visszhangzik-792896 (last accessed 28 November 2025).

6. 'Data on average earnings, net and gross' (Hungarian), Net Jogtár, 2 October 2025, https://net.jogtar.hu/jogszabaly?docid=00000003.min&txtreferer=A0300080.TV (last accessed 28 November 2025).

7. 'It turns out that the Hungarian government quietly took out a huge foreign currency loan from China' (Hungarian), Portfolio, 25 July 2024, https://www.portfolio.hu/gazdasag/20240725/kiderult-szep-csendben-gigaosszegu-devizahitelt-vett-fel-kinatol-a-magyar-allam-700357 (last accessed 28 November 2025).

8. 'Financial accounts of the national economy, Q III 2025' (Hungarian), Hungarian National Bank, 31 December 2025, https://sta.mnb.hu/Reports/powerbi/STA/NemzetgPenzugyiSZLA_HU?rs:embed=true (last accessed 5 January 2026).

9. 'State debt repayments cost so much that Hungary is bound to slump' (Hungarian), G7, 13 April 2025, https://telex.hu/g7/penz/2025/04/13/olyan-sokba-kerul-az-allamadossag-torlesztes-hogy-kodolva-van-magyarorszag-lemaradasa (last accessed 28 November 2025).

10. 'Each job in a battery factory costs the Hungarian state 64 million forints' (Hungarian), G7, 20 March 2023, https://telex.hu/g7/adat/2023/03/20/64-millio-forintba-kerul-egy-akkumulatorgyari-munkahely-a-magyar-allam-szamara (last accessed 28 November 2025).

11. Gábor Gulácsi and Ádám Kerényi, 'The Hungarian economy in the European Union: Catching up, losing the way, on a different

track at the edge of the EU' (Hungarian), in Tóth István György, Gábos András and Medgyesi Márton (eds), Társadalmi Riport: 2024. Budapest: TÁRKI, 2025.
12. 'The largest Hungarian family company with over one and a half trillion forints: here is Forbes' new list' (Hungarian), Forbes, 4 September 2025, https://forbes.hu/uzlet/csaladi-lista-2025-meszaros-felcsuti-csanyi/ (last accessed 28 November 2025).
13. 'The 100 richest Hungarians, Lőrinc Mészáros, Sándor Csányi, István Tiborcz, Gellért Jászai' (Hungarian), HVG, 22 May 2025, https://hvg.hu/gazdasag/20250522_100-leggazdagabb-magyar-meszaros-lorinc-csanyi-sandor-tiborcz-istvan-jaszai-gellert-ebx (last accessed 28 November 2025).
14. 'All the secrets of Hatvanpuszta in one place' (Hungarian), Válasz Online, 11 September 2025, https://www.valaszonline.hu/2025/09/11/hatvanpuszta-majorsag-hadhazy-akos-alaprajzok-fenykepek-epitkezes (last accessed 28 November 2025).
15. 'Viktor Orbán's speech at the event "Fight Club is the beginning"' (Hungarian), miniszterelnok.hu, 18 May 2025, https://miniszterelnok.hu/orban-viktor-beszede-a-harcosok-klubja-a-kezdet-cimu-rendezvenyen/?!? (last accessed 28 November 2025).
16. 'Viktor Orbán: "This war has no winners"' (Hungarian), Magyar Nemzet, 22 February 2023, https://magyarnemzet.hu/belfold/2023/02/orban-viktor-ennek-a-haborunak-nem-lehet-gyoztese (last accessed 28 November 2025).
17. 'Kocsis: "We are submitting bills on protecting sovereignty against foreign-financed journalists, fake NGOs and dollar-financed politicians"' (Hungarian), Telex, 21 September 2023, https://telex.hu/belfold/2023/09/21/fidesz-kdnp-kocsis-mate-simicsko-istvan-kihelyezett-frakcioules-esztergom-sajtotajekoztato (last accessed 28 November 2025).
18. 'Orbán spoke about bugs and promised a major clean-up on March 15' (Hungarian), YouTube, 15 March 2025, https://www.youtube.com/watch?v=ZZhVspo_fm8 (last accessed 28 November 2025).
19. 'Hungary blocks €50bn of EU funding for Ukraine', BBC, 15 December 2023, https://www.bbc.com/news/world-europe-67724357 (last accessed 28 November 2025); 'EU accession negotiations for Ukraine

delayed. Hungary remains an obstacle', Eunews, 29 May 2024, https://www.eunews.it/en/2024/05/29/eu-accession-negotiations-for-ukraine-delayed-hungary-remains-an-obstacle/ (last accessed 28 November 2025).
20. 'Orbán's real reasons against Ukraine's EU accession exposed', VSquare, 2 February 2024, https://vsquare.org/viktor-orban-ukraine-eu-accession-hungary/ (last accessed 28 November 2025).
21. '"It seems stupid, boring, and lacking credibility"—reaction of the Ukrainian Foreign Ministry to the government's anti-Zelenskyy poster campaign' (Hungarian), 24.hu, 3 July 2025, https://24.hu/belfold/2025/07/03/zelenszkij-magyar-peter-plakatkampany-ukrajna-reakcio/ (last accessed 28 November 2025).
22. 'Office for the Protection of National Sovereignty: Questions and Answers' (Hungarian), Amnesty International, Magyar Helsinki Bizottság and Tasz, May 2024, https://helsinki.hu/wp-content/uploads/2024/05/Szuverenitasvedelmi-Hivatal-Kerdesek-Valaszok.pdf (last accessed 28 November 2025).
23. 'Hungary: Foreign funding bill poses most serious threat to independent media in years', International Press Institute, 16 May 2025, https://ipi.media/hungary-foreign-funding-bill-poses-most-serious-threat-to-independent-media-in-years/ (last accessed 28 November 2025).
24. 'Thirty-nine steps to the restriction of political freedoms in Hungary: Part II' (Hungarian), Szabad Európa, 2 April 2025, https://www.szabadeuropa.hu/a/a-politikai-szabadsagjogok-korlatozasanak-39-lepese-magyarorszagon-2010-ota-ii-resz/33365501.html (last accessed 28 November 2025).
25. 'Welfare measures are coming one after another, the minister announced good news' (Hungarian), Világgazdaság, 29 July 2025, https://www.vg.hu/vilaggazdasag-magyar-gazdasag/2025/07/nagy-marton-joleti-intezkedesek-szeptembertol (last accessed 28 November 2025).
26. 'We are not doing well. We are not doing well, Viktor Orbán told his supporters, then detailed what he expects from them in the campaign' (Hungarian), Telex, 20 October 2025, https://telex.hu/belfold/2025/10/20/orban-viktor-beszede-a-harcosok-klubja-edzotaborban (last accessed 28 November 2025).

27. 'Tölgyessy: Tisza can win if the election becomes a referendum on Orbán' (Hungarian), Partizán, 1 September 2025, https://www.youtube.com/watch?v=Lqk7NHrGbqk (last accessed 5 January 2026).

INDEX

Note: Page numbers followed by '*n*' refer to notes

'Active Citizens Fund', (see Norway Grants' Active Citizens' Fund)
Áder, János, 20, 53
Africa, 180
Alliance of Christian Intellectuals, 41
Alliance of Free Democrats (SZDSZ), 5–6, 36–7, 200, 312 went into government with the Socialist Party 40
American administration, 336, 339
American Conservative Political Action Conference, (see Conservative Political Action Conference)
Americans, 62, 340
Ankara, 329
Annus Mirabilis (short film), 317, 318
Antall, József, 38, 65, 84–5, 311
anti-CEU laws, 293
anti-communism, 65, 73, 313, 316
anti-Enlightenment, 81
anti-Europe campaign, 320, 348
anti-European forces, 353
anti-feminism, 90
anti-gender ideas, 91
anti-gender movement, 90–1
anti-liberal policies, 76
anti-migration campaign (2015), 89, 210, 274
anti-NGO (laws), 293
anti-Orbánism, 116
anti-paedophile law, 332
anti-pluralism, 75
anti-Semitism, 63, 67
anti-Soros campaign, 278
anti-Westernism, 67, 81
Arrow Cross Party, 306
Article (7) (Treaty on European Union), 148, 153, 384*n*55
Asia, 327, 329
Átlátszó (Transparent) team, 260

INDEX

Austria, (border was opened) 5
Austro–Germans, 324
Austro-Hungarian Empire, 63
Axel Springer (German), 251
Az Orbán szabály (G. Fodor), 25

Baji, Csaba, 205
Bajnai, Gordon, 10, 97–8, 100–1, 104, 268–9, 375n2
Balaton, (see Lake Balaton)
Balaton Shipping (Bahart), 214
Balatonalmádi, 213, 215
Balatonőszöd, 52
Balkan immigration route, 266
Balkans, 349
Baló, György, 231
Balog, Zoltán, 334
Bálványosfürdő, 51-2, 66
Bannon, Steve, 94
Bayer, Zsolt, 25, 280
Bayerische Landesbank, 170
BDPST, 222
Beijing, 334
'Belgian ideology', 30
Belgrade, 335
'Belt and Road' initiative, 335
Bence, György, 45
Bende, Balázs, 241–2
Berlin Wall, 32, 316, 317
Berlin, 316, 345, 347
Berlusconi, Silvio, 43
Birnbaum, George, 277–8
Bodolai, László, 258
Bosnia-Herzegovina, 344
Bosnian War (1992–95), 344
bourgeois revolution (1848), 15
Brexit, 19, 274, 351

Brezhnev, Leonid, 267
Brussels, 93, 147, 349
Buda Castle, 47, 61, 188–9
Budapest Bank, 171
Budapest Sziget Festival, 285
Budapest, 17, 83, 289, 329, 335
  Putin Budapest visit, 331–2
Budapest–Belgrade railway, 188
Bundestag, 345
Bush, George W., 95

cardinal laws, 13, 140
Carlson, Tucker, 61–2, 94
Catholic Church (Hungary), 41
Caucasian countries, 180, 329
CDU. *See* Christian Democratic Union (CDU)
CEMP (Central European Media and Publishing), 257, 259
Central Asia, 349
Central Eastern Europe, 335
Central Europe, 213, 318–19
Central European Press and Media Foundation (KESMA), 254–6, 280
Central European University (CEU), 152, 279, 292–3
Centre for Fundamental Rights, 295–6
Charlie Hebdo (magazine), 265
China, 188, 326, 334, 336, 337, 350–1
Christian democracy, 84–5
Christian Democratic People's Party (KDNP), 41
Christian Democratic Union (CDU), 149, 346–7

INDEX

Christian democrats, 87–8
Christian Hungary, 84, 85, 87
Christian Socialist Union (CSU), 149, 346
Christianity, 14, 85–6, 88, 95
CitizenGO, 92
civic circles movement, 48
'civic Hungary', 42, 44
Civil Information Portal, 292
Civil Public Education Platform, 287
civil society, 30, 288, 296, 299
Civil Union, (see Civil Unity Forum)
Civil Unity Forum (CÖF), 104, 293, 295, 299
'civilizational crisis' theme, 82
Clinton, Hillary, 339, 340
Cohesion Fund, (EU) 342
Cohn-Bendit, Daniel, 239
Cold War, 311, 316
communism, 29, 78, 306, 308
'compensating the winner' (Election Law), 129–30
Competition Authority, 244, 255
'congealed structures', 73
Conservative Political Action Conference, 95, 296
Constitutional Court, 11, 130, 137–8
Corruption Perceptions Index, 201
Corvinus University, 25
Council of Europe, 88, 140
Court of Justice of the European Union, 12, 141, 293
Covid vaccination, 62
Covid-19 pandemic, 84, 87, 187–8, 214, 298, 300–1
Crimea, 331, 333, 343
'crisis taxes', 167
Croatia, 341
Csányi, Sándor, 206
Csizmadia, László, 295
CSU. *See* Christian Socialist Union (CSU)
Csurka, István, 65, 80, 233, 368*n*7
Curia, 131, 142–3, 178
Czechia, 343

Dalai Lama, 334
Danube, 16, 29, 61, 337–8
Daul, Joseph, 149, 351
Dayton Accords, 344
Debaltseve, 331
debt-to-GDP ratio, 161
Dederick, Yvonne, 248
'deep state' theory, 73
Democratic Coalition (DK), 100
Deneen, Patrick J., 78–9
Der Spiegel (magazine), 349
'de-Simicskaization', 209
Deutsch, Tamás, 352
Deutsche Telekom, 159, 246
Dialogue for Hungary (PM), 103, 105
Digital Government Agency, 217
Dodik, Milorad, 344
Domokos, László, 20, 139, 204–5
Donbas, 333
'Dreamers of dreams', 68
Dull, Szabolcs, 259

INDEX

E.ON (German company), 159, 168
East Asia, 180
Eastern Europe, 32, 64, 76, 326, 355
eastern Ukraine, 331
Echo TV, 236
economic nationalism, 67
Economic Protection Fund, 188
Együtt 2014 (Together 2014), 97–8, 99, 105, 268
   LMP and, 103
   popularity surge, 102
Együtt-PM, 105, 106–8, 182
Elections Act, 110, 115, 128, 133, 150
Eni (Italian company), 169
EPP. *See* European People's Party (EPP)
Erdő, Péter, 88
Erdoğan, Recep Tayyip, 328–9
ESMA, 131–2
ethical journalism, 263
ethnic Hungarians, 130
ethno-nationalisms, 320
EU development funds, 186
EU institutions, 93, 187, 346
EU. *See* European Union (EU)
Euro- Atlantic alliance system, 326
Europe, 67, 82, 84, 274
   refugee crisis (2015), 151–2
European alt-right movement, 94
European Commission, 12, 17–18, 147, 154–5, 188, 349–50, 396n39
European competition law, 256
European Council, 151, 275

European elections (2019), 94, 154
European Network of Councils for the Judiciary, 143
European Parliament (MEPs), 149, 150, 153–4
European Parliament, 93, 147, 148, 348
European People's Party (EPP), 149–50, 153–4, 349, 351, 353
European Union (EU), 47, 141, 315, 323, 342
   Hungary joined in, 325
   ideological stability, ensuring, 346–7
   rule of law report, 352
Evangelical Lutheran (church), 86
Excess Deficit Procedure, 163
Eximbank, 248

family policy campaign, 89–90
family subsidies, 68, 90
family tax system, 89, 183–4
fascism, 78, 306
fear-mongering campaign (2015), 266
Federation of Young Democrats. *See* Fidesz (political party)
Felcsút, 211
Fidesz (political party), 1, 10, 27, 137–8, 150, 193–4
   anti-Russian sentiment, 330
   changed Electoral Act, 128–9
   constitutional revolution, 352
   cooperation agreement with SZDSZ, 38
   election campaign (1998), 44, 267

INDEX

elections (2002), loss of, 200
Hungarian politics entry, 39
Fundamental Law, 12–13
landslide election victory
  (2010), 54
MPs, 55, 136, 137, 148, 182,
  237
negative campaign against
  Bajnai, 104
Orbán elected as party's first
  president, 6
regained supermajority in
  2018, 133
relationship with (US)
  Democratic Party, 340
relationship with Germany,
  294
'winner-takes-all' electoral
  system, 98–9
Fidesz government, 81, 130, 147,
  162, 190, 286
  clashes with stakeholder, 166
  national consultation, 254
Fidesz—Hungarian Civic Party
  (Fidesz-MPP), 49–50
Finkelstein, Arthur J., 268,
  269–70, 277–8
5G (network/technology), 336,
  337
flat-tax system, 184, 185
Fodor, Gábor G., 25, 37–8, 285
foreign investors, 159, 168
foreign trade strategy, 328
'foreign-funded organization', 279,
  292
Forza Italia, 43
444 (news site), 253, 257, 279

4iG, 217–18
Fox News, 61
France, 93
'Free country—free university', 300
freedom fighters, 315
#'FreeSZFE', 300
Fudan University, 338
Fülep, Lajos, 354–5
Fundamental Law, 12–14, 18, 138,
  139–40, 380n22
Funke-WAZ publishers, 251

Ganz Mávag Machine Works, 310
Gazprom, 333
'gender ideology', 90
Georgia, 330
German Christian Social Union,
  (see CSU)
German economy, 346–7
German politics, 347–8
German–Hungarian Forum, 345
Germans, 308, 337
Germany, 93, 186, 324, 327, 337,
  346
Gorbachev, Mikhail 4–5, 30, 317
'goulash communism', 29, 64
Grand Trianon, 63
Growth and Credit Programme,
  246
Gruevski, Nikola, 344
Györgyi, Kálmán, 45
Gyurcsány, Ferenc, 7, 8, 50, 70–1,
  100, 105

Habony, Árpád, 268
Handó, Tünde, 20, 143–4,
  382n32

INDEX

'headquarters corruption scandal',
  38
Hegedűs, István, 35, 39
Helms, Jesse, 268
Heroe's Square, speech, 31
Heti Válasz (newspaper/magazine),
  199, 211, 235
Hír TV, 236, 252
Hódmezővásárhely, 122
Hodosán, Róza, 26
home-building programme, 68
Homeland and Progress
  Foundation, 101–2, 122
homophobia, 92
homosexuality, 62, 92
Honecker, Erich, 267
Horthy regime, 307
hotel development programme
  (Kisfaludy programme), 189
House of Terror (museum), 305,
  307
Huawei, 336, 337
Human Rights Watch, 29
Hungarian Academy of Sciences,
  321
Hungarian Credit Bank (MKB),
  170–1
Hungarian Democratic Forum
  (MDF), 5, 29, 40–1, 44
Hungarian Development Bank
  (MFB), 199
Hungarian economy, 17, 161, 172,
  186
Hungarian Electricity (MVM),
  168, 204–5, 216, 244, 295
Hungarian Fashion and Design
  Agency, 223

Hungarian foreign policy, 289
Hungarian government, 12, 82–3,
  88, 91, 230, 277
  American–Norwegian anti-
    aircraft missiles, purchase
    of, 341
  approach to China, 337
  Brussels infringement
    procedure against, 147
  made political gestures to
    Erdoğan, 329
Hungarian Jews, 308
Hungarian Journalists' Association,
  242
Hungarian National Assembly, 88,
  92–3, 361n1 (ch.1)
  passed 4th amendment to
    Fundamental Law, 148
Hungarian National Bank (MNB),
  170–1, 176–7, 186–7, 246,
  388n34
Hungarian National Trading
  House, 180, 329
Hungarian Nazis, 305
Hungarian News Agency (MTI),
  238, 253, 401n12
'Hungarian philosophy', 69
Hungarian Post, 254
Hungarian Revolution (1848), 69
Hungarian Revolution (1956), 9,
  30–1, 309–10
Hungarian Socialist Party
  (MSZP), 5–6, 7, 38, 72, 98,
  100, 129
  elections (1998), loss of, 200
  negotiations between Együtt-
    PM and, 106

INDEX

Hungarian Socialist Workers' Party
   (MSZMP), 4, 30, 317
Hungarian sovereignty, 180
Hungarian State Railways, 216
Hungarian Television, 121, 231,
   242, 293
Hungarian Tourism Agency, 214,
   223
Hungary
   Catholic tradition, 85
   financial crisis (2008), 10, 100
   joined NATO, 7, 46
   joined the EU (2004), 325
   relationship with Poland, 343
   relationship with US, 340
   Ukraine and, 333
   under Excess Deficit
      Procedure, 163
   under the German occupation
      (1944), 307
Hunguest Hotel chain, 189
HVG (news site), 253

Ibrahim, Kaya, 198
'illiberal democracy', 77
IMF (International Monetary
   Fund), 10, 17, 315, 385n5
Immigration Office, 271
Independent Smallholders Party,
   6, 44
Index (online news portal), 229,
   236, 253
   history and growth, 257–61
India, 77, 326
individual strategic agreements, 173
International Investment Bank
   (IIB), 332, 341

International Monetary Fund. *See*
   IMF (International Monetary
   Fund)
International Press Institute, 230
International Venice Film Festival,
   300
Iranians, 181
Islamic State in Iraq and Syria, 340
Istanbul Convention, 88
Italy, 93, 253

Janis, Irving, 35
Jászai, Gellért, 218
Jávor, Benedek, 103
Jews, 65
Jobbik (party), 7, 71, 79, 98
Jourová, Věra, 154–5
Judaeo-Christian culture, 342
Juncker, Jean-Claude, 348

Kaczyński, Lech, 344
Kádárism, 63–4, 73
Karácsony, Gergely, 121, 378n29
KDNP. *See* Christian Democratic
   People's Party (KDNP)
KESMA. *See* Central European
   Press and Media Foundation
   (KESMA)
Kész, Zoltán, 117
Kibeszélő (Speak out), 230
Kisrabló restaurant, 26
Kocsis, Máté, 210
Konrad Adenauer Foundation, 348
Konzervatív Kiáltvány (Lánczi), 74
Kósa, Lajos, 35
Kossuth Square, 121, 308
Kötcse, 53–4

445

INDEX

Kovács, Zoltán, 256
Kövér, László, 20, 28, 36–7, 178, 314
 gender issues speech, 89
 views on polarization, 40
 See also Orbán, Viktor
Közgép, 203, 204, 208
Krastev, Ivan, 76
Krk (port), 341
Kronen Zeitung (Austrian paper), 191

Labour Code (2011), 286
'lads of Pest', 312, 313, 315
Lake Balaton, 213–14, 215, 222
Lambsdorff, Otto Graf, 34
Lánczi, András, 25, 74–5, 192, 369n21
Latin America, 180
Law and Justice (Polish party), 151, 347
Lázár, János, 123, 182, 246, 258, 290
Le Pen, Marine, 94
'leftish liberal elite', 19, 279
Leipzig, 316
Lesbos, 270
Lévai, Anikó, 219, 223
Levinsky, Steven, 116
Lex NGO, (see NGO Act)
liberalism, 30, 341
Liszkay, Gábor, 255
LMP. *See* Politics Can Be Different (LMP)
LNG terminal, 341
'lower utility bills' campaign, 168–9

Macedonia, 344
Macroeconomic indicators, 160
macroeconomic stability, 185
Macron, Emmanuel, 240, 351
Madzsar Alíz group, 144
Magyar Bankholding, 171
Magyar Hírlap (newspaper), 26–7
Magyar Narancs (newspaper), 232, 236
Magyar Nemzet (newspaper), 199
Magyar Telekom, 245, 246
Mahir Cityposter, 236
Maréchal, Marion, 94
Márki-Zay, Péter, 119, 122
Marshall Plan, 186
Martens, Wilfried, 353
Martonyi, János, 327, 369n20
masculinity, 90
Mathias Corvinus Collegium (MCC), 61, 189
Matolcsy, György, 20, 162, 184, 246
Mátra Erőmű, 215–16
MDF. *See* Hungarian Democratic Forum (MDF)
Medgyessy, Péter, 7, 334
Media Act, 147, 151, 241
Media Council, 238
Media Services Support and Asset Management Fund (MTVA), 238, 243
Mediaworks, 250–1
MEPs. *See* European Parliament (MEPs)
Merkel, Angela, 272, 342, 346, 347, 351

446

INDEX

Mérték Media Analysis Workshop, 230, 256
Mesterházy, Attila, 104, 108
Mészáros, Lőrinc, 21, 171, 189, 211, 249
   bought the Mátra Erőmű, 215–16
   rise of, 212–13
Meta (company), 212, 281
Metropol (newspaper), 252, 404n38
Mezort, 209
MFB. *See* Hungarian Development Bank (MFB)
Microsoft Hungary, 175–6
Middle East, 270, 327
Migration Research Institute, 80
Milla (movement), 100–1, 237
MKB. *See* Hungarian Credit Bank (MKB)
MNB. *See* Hungarian National Bank (MNB)
Modern Times Group (Swedish), 251
MOL (oil company), 169
Molotov cocktails, 312
Momentum Movement, 283
Móra, Veronika, 290
MSZMP. *See* Hungarian Socialist Workers' Party (MSZMP)
MSZP government, 201
MSZP. *See* Hungarian Socialist Party (MSZP)
MTI. *See* Hungarian News Agency (MTI)
multiculturalism, 92
Mundruczó, Kornél, 300
municipal elections (2019), 133–4
Murray, Douglas, 94
Muslim immigrants, 274
MVM. *See* Hungarian Electricity (MVM)

Nagy, Imre, 306, 311, 313, 415n10
Nagymaros, 29
National Assembly, 11, 13, 33
National Association for Large Families (NOE), 296
National Avowal, 307–8
National Bureau of Investigation, 216, 222
'national business people', 218
National Civil Fund Programme (2004), 288, 289
National Communications Office, 279, 281
National Cooperation Fund (NEA), 295
National Development Agency, 202
National Election Commission, 134, 241
National Judicial Council, 143, 146
National Lottery, 244
National Media and Infocommunications Authority (NMHH), 237–8, 242
National Museum, 15, 16–17
National Office for the Judiciary, 138, 144
National Police Headquarters, 176
'national ribbon movement', 69
National Tax and Customs Administration 176, 198, 205

447

INDEX

National Teachers' Chamber, 286
National Utility, 168–9
Nationalism, 65
NATO (North Atlantic Treaty Organization), 333, 337, 341, 354
Nazi Germany, 63, 307
Nazis, 75
 Hungarian, 305
Nazism, 306
NEA. *See* National Cooperation Fund (NEA)
Németh, Zsolt, (TV director) 241
Németh, Zsolt, (politician) 345
Népszabadság, 250–1
Netherlands, 93, 327
Network of Free Initiatives, 29
New Wave Media, 246
NGO Act, 152, 293
NGOs (Non-Governmental Organizations), 77, 277, 288–9, 291–2, 295
NMHH. *See* National Media and Infocommunications Authority (NMHH)
NOE. *See* National Association for Large Families (NOE)
Norway Grants' Active Citizens' Fund, 290, 291-2
Norwegian government, 290
Novák, Katalin, 90, 91
Nyerges, Zsolt, 203, 210, 247, 253
Nyíregyháza, 134

Ökotárs Foundation, 289–90
OLAF (European Anti-Fraud Office), 152–3, 221–2

'old elite', 106, 107
Oltyán, József, 259
One Million People for Press Freedom. *See* Milla (movement)
Open Society Foundations, 294
'opening to the East' programme, 327–8, 339
opinion journalism, 262
Opposition Round Table, 4
Optimus Press, 251
Orbán government, 93, 137, 140–1, 145, 301, 333, 344, 355
 German industrialists and, 347
 Hungarian judiciary, reshaping of, 142
 private pension funds, 165–6
'Orbán project', 46
Orbán, Balázs, 190
Orbán, Ráhel, 220, 223–4
Orbán, Viktor, 2–3, 15, 47–8, 95–6, 239, 376n6
 anti-communist campaign, 39
 Carlson and, 62
 centenary of the Trianon Treaty speech, 319–20
 hard-line Eurosceptic politics, 343
 patron–client media system, 263
 populist fairy tale, 16–17
 secret agreements with Putin, 330
 Simicska and, 196–7, 202
 and Trump, 341
 views on Christian democracy, 85
 See also Fidesz (political party)

INDEX

'Orbánism', 62, 116
Organization for Security and Cooperation in Europe (OSCE), 133
Origo (online news portal), 236, 245–7, 257
Ottoman Empire, 324

Paks (Nuclear Power Plant), 111–12, 330–1, 336
Pallas Athéné foundations, 177, 179, 190
Papp, Dániel, 121, 239–40
Paris, 265
Parliament, 9, 33, 138, 234, 380n15
   Fidesz-led coalition impact on, 45
   Fundamental Law adopted by, 12
   journalists banned from entering, 253
parliamentarianism, 75
Partizán (YouTube channel), 263
party financing, 197
Pataki, George, 157
Patek, Alajos, 310
patron–client (media) system, 261, 263
Patyi, András, 134
Pecina, Heinrich, 250
Pesti Srácok (online portal), 243, 404n40
Péterfia, Karola, 309–10
Pethő, András, 246
Petőfi, Sándor, 15
'phantom companies', 198

Piraeus (Greek port), 335
PM. *See* Dialogue for Hungary (PM)
Poland, 30, 317, 343
Polat, Adnan, 329–30
Polish Catholic Church, 85
Polish communist party (PZPR), 30
political Christianism, 63
'political correctness', 92
'political information campaign', 295
Politics Can Be Different (LMP), 98, 99–100, 102–3
Polt, Péter, 12, 20, 138, 198
Pompeo, Mike, 336, 341
Pope Francis, 86
post-communism, 74, 75
'post-communist Hungary', 44
Prague, 316
private pension funds, 165
privatization, 160
pro-government press, 256
Programme for International Student Assessment (PISA), 286–7
Prosecution Service, 138, 146, 182, 205, 227
ProSiebenSat.1 Media (P7S1), 247, 251
pseudo-NGOs, 91
Public Procurement Authority, 202, 244
public utility services, 169
Putin model, 263
Putin, Vladimir, 111, 281, 330, 331–2

449

INDEX

PZPR. *See* Polish communist party (PZPR)

Quest, Richard, 184

radical conservatism, 76
Radio Free Europe, 28, 310, 311
Ramada hotel, 213
Reformed Church, 41
Republican Party (US), 81, 268
Revolutionary Workers' Council, 310
Ringier (Swiss company), 251
Rogán, Antal, 214, 279
Roma, (people) 66
Romania, 66, 130
Rosatom (Russian company), 111
Rove, Karl, 95
Roxette (Swedish band), 267
RTL Klub, 249
Russia, 77, 111, 187, 253, 263, 331
   annexation of Crimea, 343
   attacked Ukraine, 281, 334
   invaded Crimea and Donbas, 333
Russian 'foreign agent' law (2012), 292
Russian empire, 31
Russian troops, 331
Russians, 181, 331
RWE, (German) 159

Saint Stephen, (Hungarian king) 83
Sáling, Gergő, 246
Sándor, Mária, 297–8
Sanoma (Finnish), 251

SAO. *See* State Audit Office (SAO)
Sargentini, Judith, 153–4
Savings and Mortgage Bank (Takarék Jelzálogbank), 171
Schloss Meseberg, 351
Schmidt, Mária, 26, 51, 80, 312–13, 416*n*21
Schmitt, Carl, 75
Schmitt, Pál, 11–12, 164
Schüssel, Wolfgang, 157
Scruton, Roger, 78–9
Second Demographic Congress, 91
Seehofer, Horst, 346
Semjén, Zsolt, 334
Serbia, 130, 335
Simicska era, 212, 216
Simicska, Lajos, 38, 45, 118, 194–5, 198–9
   downfall of, 207–10
   Orbán and, 196–7, 202
Simon, Zsolt, 248
Singapore, 77
'slavery law', 120
Slovakia, 343
Sólyom, László, 140, 164
Sopron, 34–5
'Soros agent', 299
Soros Foundation, 32
'Soros plan', 277
Soros, George, 58, 276–7, 278, 292–3
South America, 90
South China Sea, 337
Soviet communists, 307
Soviet empire, 32
Soviet tanks, 305, 312, 313
Soviet troops, 5, 31–2, 310, 317

450

INDEX

Soviet Union, 5, 324, 333, 352
Spengler, Frank, 348
'spirit of Trianon', 70
Stage of Freedom, 309
Stalinism, 310, 315
State Audit Office (SAO), 138–9
state workfare programme, 183
'Stop Soros' package, 294
Strabag, (Austrian) 213
Strasbourg, 153
'Student City', 337–8
Student Network, 297
Student Union (HÖOK), 297
Stumpf, István, 20, 26
Supreme Court, 142–3
Swietelsky, (Austrian) 213
Switzerland, 223
Syrian refugees, 265–6
'System of National Cooperation', 11, 21
Szabad sajtó útja (Free Press Road), 236
Szájer, József, 20, 93, 345
Szalai, Annamária, 20
Szánthó, Miklós, 296
Századvég Foundation, 268, 279
SZDSZ. *See* Alliance of Free Democrats (SZDSZ)
Szeklerland, 66, 130
SZFE. *See* University of Theatre and Film Arts (SZFE)
Szigliget, 215
Szijjártó, Péter, 57, 178, 327–8, 336

Talentis Group, 254
Tállai, András, 20

Tanítanék (teacher movement), 287
Tavares Report, 148–9
Telenor, 172
Tellér, Gyula, 73
Tények (Facts), 249
Tibet Assistance Society, 334
Tiborcz, István, 220, 221–2, 330, 399n67
Tihanyi Foundation, 189–90
Timișoara, 316
T-Mobile, 172
tobacco products, 173, 205
Tocsik, Marta, 200
Tölgyessy, Péter, 13
Tot, Josip, 198
totalitarianism, 307
traditional sexual roles, 90
traditionalist thinkers, 64
Transparency International Hungary, 128, 173, 182, 189, 204
Treaty of Trianon, 63
Treaty on European Union, 148, 293
'true Hungarians', 318
Trump administration, 336, 340–1
Trump, Donald, 82, 93, 340–1
Turkey, 77, 140
Turkic Council, 329
Turkish–Hungarian Business Forum, 329
TurkStream gas pipeline, 333
turul (bird), 83, 84, 370n50, 370n51
TV2 group, 247–9
Two-Tailed Dog Party, 298–9

INDEX

Uj, Péter, 257
Ukraine, 130, 187, 281, 331, 333, 354, 419n23
UN High Commissioner for Refugees, 86
United Nations (UN), 311
United States of Europe, 93
University of Theatre and Film Arts (SZFE), 299–300
'unorthodox economic policy', 163–4, 186
US (United States), 257, 270, 293, 327, 336, 340

Vajna, Andrew G., 248, 249
Varga, András Zs., 137, 146, 177, 382n39
Varga, Tamás, 194–5
Vaszily, Miklós, 245, 255, 259
Vatican, 90
Vegyépszer, 199
Venice Commission, 17–18, 140
Vida, József, 171
Vidnyánszky, Attila, 299–300
'Visegrad 4 Europe' programme, 350
Visegrád Group, 342-3, 343, 349
Vodafone, 172
von der Leyen, Ursula, 155, 323, 349

War of Independence (1848), 69
Warsaw, 316

Washington, 340
Weber, Manfred, 149, 154, 348–9, 351, 352
Weekly Terror (TV programme), 274
'welfare chauvinism', 71
Welt (news channel), 352
Wen Jiabao, 334
Wermer, András, 42, 267
western Balkan countries, 344
Western civilization, 25
Western Europe, 80, 82, 91, 186, 274, 408n10
Wilders, Geert, 82
Willkommenskultur (policy), 272, 342
'work-based society', 89, 121, 184
World Congress of Families, 91
World Federation of Hungarians, 70
World War I, 63, 361n1 (preface)
World War II, 63, 305

xenophobia, 67, 79, 275

Yiannopoulos, Milo, 94
Young Communist League, 27

Zakaria, Fareed, 77–8
Zemmour, Éric, 94
Ziegler, Zoltán, 259
Zoltán, Spéder, 258, 259, 407n74
Zuckerberg, Mark, 212